Managing Multimedia and Unstructured Data in the Oracle Database

A revolutionary approach to understanding, managing, and delivering digital objects, assets, and all types of data

Marcelle Kratochvil

[PACKT] enterprise 88
PUBLISHING
professional expertise distilled

BIRMINGHAM - MUMBAI

Managing Multimedia and Unstructured Data in the Oracle Database

Copyright © 2013 Packt Publishing

First published: March 2013

Production Reference: 1110313

Published by Packt Publishing Ltd.
Livery Place
35 Livery Street
Birmingham B3 2PB, UK.

ISBN 978-1-84968-692-1

www.packtpub.com

Cover Image by Artie Ng (artherng@yahoo.com.au)

Credits

Author

Marcelle Kratochvil

Reviewers

Gokhan Atil

Ben van Eyle

Satishbabu Gunukula

Tim Hall

Pete Sharman

Acquisition Editor

Rukhsana Khambatta

Lead Technical Editor

Arun Nadar

Technical Editors

Sharvari Baet

Kaustubh S. Mayekar

Ankita Meshram

Project Coordinator

Leena Purkait

Proofreaders

Ting Baker

Lindsey Thomas

Indexer

Monica Ajmera Mehta

Graphics

Aditi Gajjar

Sheetal Aute

Valentina D'silva

Production Coordinator

Aparna Bhagat

Cover Work

Aparna Bhagat

Nitesh Thakur

About the Author

Marcelle Kratochvil is an accomplished Oracle Database administrator and developer. She is CTO of Piction and has designed and developed industry-leading software for the management and selling of digital assets. She has also developed an award-winning shipping and freight management system, designed and built a booking system, a digital asset management system, a sport management system, an e-commerce system, a social network engine, a reporting engine, and numerous search engines. She has been an Oracle beta tester since the original introduction of Oracle Multimedia. She is also a well known presenter at Oracle Conferences and has produced numerous technical podcasts. In 2004 she was the Oracle PL/SQL Developer of the year. Born in Australia, she lives in Canberra. She is actively working as a database administrator supporting a large number of customer sites internationally. She is also campaigning with Oracle to promote the use of storing all data and any data in a database. In her spare time she plays field hockey and does core research in artificial intelligence in database systems. She has a Bachelor of Science Degree from the Australian National University and majored in computing and mathematics.

Acknowledgement

I would like to acknowledge my business partner and CEO of Piction, Erick Kendrick. I have been working with him for over twelve years and he has been instrumental in a lot of the designs as well as the implementation of the ideas presented in the book. Without his unconditional support in all the good and bad times, the ability to get to the stage of writing this book would not have been possible.

Special thanks go to all those in the Piction team: Jimmy Nguyen, Martin Channon, Serkan Harar, Lusana Ali, and Adam LaPorta, who have done the tough work and been able to embrace the vision and advance the concept of digital asset management systems, bringing forth leadership in this new technology.

Thanks also go to Chris Muir, Richard Foote, and Tim Hall who have sparred with me on a lot of the controversial issues that dealing with multimedia can raise. By debating with them honestly, I have been pushed outside the box and into new territory. In addition Steven Feuerstein has always expressed his support and helped where he could regarding multimedia in the database. Also, I would like to thank Victoria Lira and Lillian Buziak of the Oracle ACE Director program who over the last five years have work tirelessly to help me promote the usage of multimedia inside the Oracle Database.

Special mention goes to my mother, my sister, her husband, Andrew and children, Jeremiah, Elisha, and Abigail, who have accepted me unconditionally, which also gave me the strength and motivation to do the hard, long yards and put this book together. I would like to recognize my brother Mark Kratochvil who worked with Piction in the early days and is a keen and talented photographer. It is my hope that his family will get to see this book.

I would like to acknowledge the reviewers who have been challenged by the unique and varying content within the book. They are Ben Van Eyle, April Chin, Tim Hall, Pete Sharman, and Tony Quinn.

And finally I would like to thank Liza Sherd who was there for me during the hard times and who I know will be there for me when I need it the most.

About the Reviewers

Gokhan Atil is an independent consultant who has been working in IT since 2000. He worked as a Development and Production DBA, Trainer and Software Developer. He has a strong background in Linux and Solaris systems. He's an Oracle Certified Professional (OCP) for Oracle Database 10*g* and 11*g*, and has hands-on experience with Oracle 11*g*/10*g*/9*i*/8*i*. He is an active member of the Oracle community and has written and presented papers at various conferences. He's also a founding member of the Turkish Oracle User Group (TROUG).

He was honored with the Oracle ACE Award in 2011. He has a blog in which he has shared his experience with Oracle since 2008:

```
http://www.gokhanatil.com
```

Ben van Eyle is an independent consultant with 26 years of experience in the IT industry with most of that time dealing with databases and database systems, including Oracle, SQL Server and Ingres.

He has designed and built distributed database systems and high availability systems, as well as worked on SAP systems and Oracle data warehouses, mostly for government department.

Ben currently resides in Canberra.

Satishbabu Gunukula has over 13 years of experience in the IT industry. He has extensive experience in Oracle and SQLServer Database Technologies, and is specialized in high availability solutions such as Oracle RAC, Data Guard, Grid Control, and SQL Server Cluster. He has a master's degree in Computer Applications.

He has been honored with the prestigious Oracle ACE Award. He has experience with a wide range of products, such as Essbase, Hyperion, Agile, SAP Basis, MySQL, Linux, Windows, and Business Apps admin and he has implemented many business critical systems for Fortune 500, 1000 companies.

He review articles for SELECT Journal – the publication of IOUG – and reviews books for Packt Publishing. He is an active member in IOUG, Oracle RAC SIG, UKOUG, and OOW and has published many articles and presentations. He shares his knowledge on his websites:

http://www.oracleracexpert.com and http://www.sqlserver-expert.com.

Tim Hall is an Oracle Certified Professional (OCP) DBA/Developer, Oracle ACE Director, OakTable Network member and was chosen as Oracle ACE of the Year 2006 by Oracle Magazine Editor's Choice Awards. He has been involved in DBA, design, and development work with Oracle Databases since 1994.

Although focusing on database administration and PL/SQL development, he has gained a wide knowledge of the Oracle software stack and has worked as a consultant for several multinational companies on projects ranging from real-time control systems to OLTP web applications.

Since the year 2000, he has published over 400 articles on his website (www.oracle-base.com) covering a wide range of Oracle features.

Pete Sharman is a Principal Product Manager in the Enterprise Manager team at Oracle. He has worked at Oracle for 18 years in a variety of roles both in Australia and the USA, and has presented at a number of conferences, including Oracle Open World, the Hotsos Symposium and RMOUG Training Days. He is also a member of the OakTable Network.

www.PacktPub.com

Support files, eBooks, discount offers and more

You might want to visit www.PacktPub.com for support files and downloads related to your book.

Did you know that Packt offers eBook versions of every book published, with PDF and ePub files available? You can upgrade to the eBook version at www.PacktPub.com and as a print book customer, you are entitled to a discount on the eBook copy. Get in touch with us at service@packtpub.com for more details.

At www.PacktPub.com, you can also read a collection of free technical articles, sign up for a range of free newsletters and receive exclusive discounts and offers on Packt books and eBooks.

![PACKTLIB logo]

http://PacktLib.PacktPub.com

Do you need instant solutions to your IT questions? PacktLib is Packt's online digital book library. Here, you can access, read and search across Packt's entire library of books.

Why Subscribe?

- Fully searchable across every book published by Packt
- Copy and paste, print and bookmark content
- On demand and accessible via web browser

Free Access for Packt account holders

If you have an account with Packt at www.PacktPub.com, you can use this to access PacktLib today and view nine entirely free books. Simply use your login credentials for immediate access.

Instant Updates on New Packt Books

Get notified! Find out when new books are published by following @PacktEnterprise on Twitter, or the *Packt Enterprise* Facebook page.

Table of Contents

Preface

Digital data can be broken down into structured and unstructured data. Unstructured data outweighs structured by 10 to 1. The most well known unstructured data type is multimedia, which comprises digital images, audio, video, and documents.

For a very long time the topic of unstructured data and managing it has been pushed to the side lines and given the label of being just too hard to deal with. More time and attention has been given to relational data, which has been analyzed, conceptualized, and understood since it was first mathematically defined in the 1970s. Since then the market has changed. New technologies have introduced new rules and requirements for dealing with unstructured data. Structured data, which has been leading the market as a subset called relational data, shows to have limitations. It cannot encompass, correctly describe, and manage the large variety of multimedia types appearing in the market. The move to adapt to new technologies that interface more directly with people has shown that smart media is friendlier and easier to understand.

With the iPhone, iPad, Android, and equivalent smart devices now proliferating in the market, the whole world has been given access to computers. Sidelined are the complex, virus-prone PCs that a large number of people could never comprehend or correctly use. The multimedia centric iPad is a device that most people can learn in minutes and master in under an hour. The keyboard is nearly gone and digital images, video, and audio give a richer, entertaining, and a more productive environment to work in.

Structured data isn't gone. Its importance cannot be overlooked. It is just not the dominant data structure anymore that we have been taught to believe. What is yet to be realized when it comes to the future of computer human interfaces, is that its existence is really there to support unstructured data. To give it extra meaning and to enhance its use. The key factor to realize and what this book will show, is that structured data is not the pinnacle of data management. It has an important role, but its role is to provide a solid foundation and core base for which unstructured data can work on.

The aim of this book is to try and give a basic understanding to a lot of concepts involving unstructured data. Particular focus is given to multimedia (smart media or rich media). This is the most popular and well understood subtype of unstructured data in the market place today. The book will cover key concepts from first principles. Later chapters are designed for database administrators though developers and storage architects can gain a good understanding on the key concepts covered. An attempt has been made to future proof some chapters so that as technology changes, the core concepts can be remolded and adapted to meet those changes. Where areas are deemed immutable, they are highlighted so the reader can be aware that these ideas can become dated or need to be reviewed to assess their validity as technology changes.

This is the first of two books in the series. The first book is designed for technology architects, managers, and database administrators. The second book will focus on developers and storage architects. It will cover methods for building multimedia databases and techniques for working with very large databases.

This book uses the Oracle 11*g* R2 database as the core database. Special sections are devoted to adapting the concepts covered for the Oracle 11 XE release.

Some of the chapters draw citations from Wikipedia. These citations are additional to the ones provided and are there for those who make extensive use of Wikipedia. In a number of cases the citations given are to highlight that useful information is found at the site rather than justifying a particular claim. As the topics covering multimedia are very new and in some cases have only been released in the last one to two years, the most accurate and up to date information on them can be found at the Wiki site.

The exercises found at the end of each chapter are purposely designed so that the answers to them are not found in the book or on the Internet. The lessons and techniques gained from reading the chapter will provide the necessary solution to each exercise, but the reader will need to use their skill and experience to correctly determine the answer. All exercises have valid answers but they are deliberately not included. Answers will be provided in the second book. This book will cover developer and programming topics, disk storage and techniques for integration of multimedia using a variety of programming tools, including Java, PHP, C, C++, Perl, Python, Ruby, PL/SQL and Visual Basic.

What this book covers

Chapter 1, What is Unstructured Data?, covers what a digital object is from first principles. This chapter will provide the reader with new insights into the basics of unstructured data.

Chapter 2, Understanding Digital Objects, answers all the questions generally raised about multimedia objects. This chapter takes the reader through all the different types of smart media currently being used and how they can work with them intelligently.

Chapter 3, The Multimedia Warehouse, discusses all the concepts behind a multimedia warehouse and how it differs from a relational data warehouse, using real life case scenarios.

Chapter 4, Searching the Multimedia Warehouse, continues from the previous chapter. This chapter takes the reader further into the multimedia warehouse architecture and explorers all the issues behind doing simple and complex searches and then how to best display the results.

Chapter 5, Loading Techniques, will help storage and database administrators learn about all the different techniques and database issues involved in loading large numbers of digital objects into a database.

Chapter 6, Delivery Techniques, covers all the concepts behind setting an e-commerce system and delivering digital objects. Learn about copyright management, protection from privacy, price books, business rules, and processing workflows.

Chapter 7, Techniques for Creating a Multimedia Database, will help the Oracle Database Administrators and Developers to learn how to configure an Oracle Database and web server for managing multimedia. They will discover which database parameter and storage configuration settings work and why they work.

Chapter 8, Tuning, will help the Oracle Database administrators learn new concepts, skills, and techniques that are required to manage very large multimedia databases.

Chapter 9, Understanding the Limitations of Oracle Products, gives an overview of all the Oracle products and key features and helps you learn how well each one works with multimedia. Readers will also begin to appreciate what is truly involved in the real configuration and setup of a multimedia based database.

Chapter 10, Working with the Operating System, will help database administrators and developers gain a better understanding of how to extend the Oracle database to work and integrate with open source code. This is generally required to perform additional and complex processing, which is currently beyond the normal bounds of the Oracle Database.

Appendix A, The Circa Data Type, describes the Circa datatype syntax.

Appendix B, Multimedia Case Studies, has eight case studies listed that are based on real-life sites in countries around the world. The details have been generalized and simplified to make the underlying architecture simpler to understand.

Appendix C, Proactive Database Tuning, explains the relation between the environment and the DBA. It covers various topics that revolve around proactive database tuning, such as Ensuring optimal performance, Cyclic maintenance, Database review, Forecasting, Securing the database, and Data recovery.

Appendix D, Chapter References, has the list of references that are marked in the individual chapters.

Appendix E, Loading and Reading, is not present in the book but is available for download at the following link: `http://www.packtpub.com/sites/default/files/downloads/AppendixE_loading_and_reading.pdf`

Who this book is for

If you are an Oracle database administrator, museum curator, IT manager, developer, photographer, Intelligence team member, warehouse or software architect then this book is for you. It covers the basics and then moves to advanced concepts. This will challenge and increase your knowledge enabling all those who read it to gain a greater understanding of multimedia and how all unstructured data is managed.

Conventions

In this book, you will find a number of styles of text that distinguish between different kinds of information. Here are some examples of these styles, and an explanation of their meaning.

Code words in text are shown as follows: "We can include other contexts through the use of the `include` directive."

A block of code is set as follows:

```
myimage ORDSYS.ORDIMAGE
...
begin
myimage := NULL;
```

When we wish to draw your attention to a particular part of a code block, the relevant lines or items are set in bold:

```
myimage ORDSYS.ORDIMAGE
...
begin
myimage := NULL;
```

New terms and **important words** are shown in bold. Words that you see on the screen, in menus or dialog boxes for example, appear in the text like this: "Clicking the **Next** button moves you to the next screen".

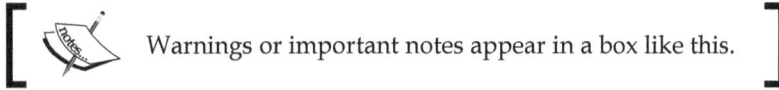

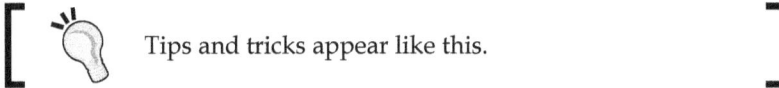

> Warnings or important notes appear in a box like this.

> Tips and tricks appear like this.

Chapter References

There are few words/phrases marked with numbers in superscript. For example, (commonly referred to as being photoshopped)[1], color space[2], and so on. You can find more information on these concepts at the links given in *Appendix D, Chapter References*.

Reader feedback

Feedback from our readers is always welcome. Let us know what you think about this book—what you liked or may have disliked. Reader feedback is important for us to develop titles that you really get the most out of.

To send us general feedback, simply send an e-mail to `feedback@packtpub.com`, and mention the book title via the subject of your message.

If there is a topic that you have expertise in and you are interested in either writing or contributing to a book, see our author guide on `www.packtpub.com/authors`.

Customer support

Now that you are the proud owner of a Packt book, we have a number of things to help you to get the most from your purchase.

Errata

Although we have taken every care to ensure the accuracy of our content, mistakes do happen. If you find a mistake in one of our books—maybe a mistake in the text or the code—we would be grateful if you would report this to us. By doing so, you can save other readers from frustration and help us improve subsequent versions of this book. If you find any errata, please report them by visiting http://www.packtpub.com/support, selecting your book, clicking on the **errata submission form** link, and entering the details of your errata. Once your errata are verified, your submission will be accepted and the errata will be uploaded on our website, or added to any list of existing errata, under the Errata section of that title. Any existing errata can be viewed by selecting your title from http://www.packtpub.com/support.

Piracy

Piracy of copyright material on the Internet is an ongoing problem across all media. At Packt, we take the protection of our copyright and licenses very seriously. If you come across any illegal copies of our works, in any form, on the Internet, please provide us with the location address or website name immediately so that we can pursue a remedy.

Please contact us at copyright@packtpub.com with a link to the suspected pirated material.

We appreciate your help in protecting our authors, and our ability to bring you valuable content.

Questions

You can contact us at questions@packtpub.com If you are having a problem with any aspect of the book, and we will do our best to address it.

1
What is Unstructured Data?

There has been a noticeably slow uptake in the use of databases to manage unstructured data, in particular multimedia data. The technology at both the hardware and software levels for the management of multimedia is both mature and stable. What is preventing sites from the move to storing multimedia in the database is attributed to a lack of expertize, understanding, and a conservative view fostered by a number of factors including historical issues with performance and integration software.

Initially it is important to define what multimedia is in relation to structured and unstructured data. Unstructured data is any data that is not stored in a structured format. Structured data is anything that has an enforced composition to the atomic data types[1].

A relational database stores data in a structured format. Other non-relational databases also store their data in a structured format, so relational data can be considered a subset of structured data. XML is also considered structured, as well as data stored inside object-oriented databases. Because the structure of XML is fluid, one can consider XML as semi-structured.

There is a large amount of unstructured data in the real world that needs managing. In the last ten years most organizations have begun to recognize that there is a great need to manage it and to understand it. As unstructured data refers to anything that is not structured; it can become very difficult to understand what is out there and how to deal with it. The traditional thinking has been to just treat it as a blob (binary large object), but with a greater understanding of the variety of unstructured data types that exist, the need to manage them has grown.

To help understand this point think of geometry and the rules (mathematics) associated with it. When mathematicians tried to come to grips with circles, triangles, and shapes it was seen to be so complex, they started on the basic concepts first. This was dealing with geometry in a two-dimensional world. In this world view, triangles had three sides with three angles that always added up to 180 degrees. Parallel lines never met. By just focusing on this world view a greater understanding of geometry was formed. Core principles were calculated along with a lot of formulas and mathematics. In this analogy, the two-dimensional world is equivalent to the structured data.

Once this two-dimensional world reached a stage of becoming well studied and understood, focus was moved to the real three-dimensional world to see how it would behave. The three-dimensional world proved to be very complex and so made us focus on key areas that could be understood. This included the study of knots, symmetry, surfaces with holes, and curves. Some of the two-dimensional rules flowed through to the three-dimensional world but fewer didn't. Parallel lines can meet and triangles can have more or less than 180 degrees.

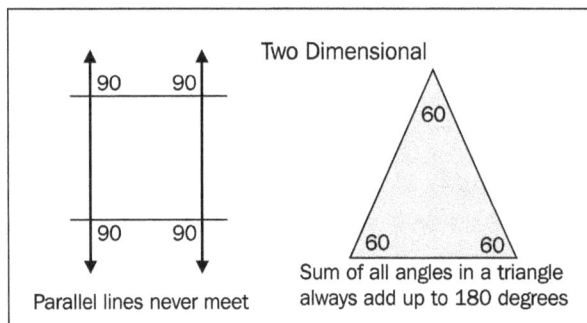

In this analogy the unstructured data is the three-dimensional world and there is a need to understand what is in it. Just like there exists no thorough understanding of three-dimensional geometry, so there is no full understanding of the unstructured data. It is an evolving and growing discipline as more information and experiences are gathered, tested, and learnt. So, like the notion of studying knots, holes, and curves, one can also focus on key areas of the unstructured data and learn from them. One key component is multimedia, which contains video, audio, photographs, and documents.

Multimedia is also referred to as rich media. It's not just limited to the four types identified and some even might debate whether documents are a component of multimedia. As will be shown, when breaking down multimedia into its fundamental components, one can classify these multimedia types and then develop new types from it. This includes three-dimensional objects, simulation data, and neural network data.

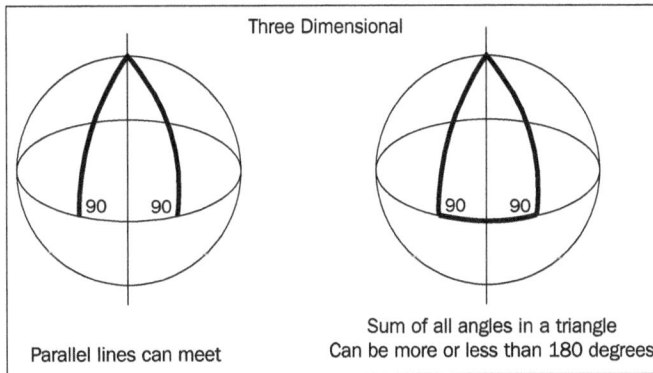

The analogy of comparing three-dimensional geometry to unstructured data works well and one has to also consider that mathematicians have gone beyond three-dimensional geometry into multi-dimensional geometry in an effort to help explain some key components of string theory, quantum theory, and astronomy. There are still a lot of unknowns with unstructured data. The recent introduction into the world of quantum computing using qubits to store information will undoubtedly push the field of unstructured data management into complete new areas[2].

Just like there is overlap between the two-dimensional world with the three-dimensional world, so there is between multimedia and structured data. The two are dependent on each other at the moment, but eventually with improvements in technology this might change. The rules formulated today might change tomorrow. It's important to realize that as technology changes the rules change. Working in multimedia is trying to hit a moving target. What is right today might be invalidated tomorrow.

Digital data

Digital data can be broken down into structured digital data and unstructured digital data. Structured data is best known as **relational data**, but is really any text-based data stored in such a way that enables it to be accessed and queried to an agreed standard.

For relational data, it is stored in a well defined mathematical structure with official rules and standards for accessing and manipulating it. In the market there are other types of databases that store text data that conform to other standards (for example, ADABAS, IMS/DB).

Any data that is not stored in a well-defined structured format can by default be seen as unstructured. The traditional view is that unstructured data is just any binary data.

There is a fuzzy area between structured and unstructured, more akin to saying there are degrees of structure and there is a lot of overlap.

It's possible to store unstructured data in a column in a relational table, which is structured. The physical database files containing structured data are binary and stored in a propriety format without well-defined rules and are considered unstructured. A propriety format is one where the vendor (the maker of the format) controls and decides its behavior. There is no agreed standard or peer review for its format. There are gray areas covering this as can be shown with the the Adobe PDF format. Though the format was controlled by Adobe and considered proprietary, in 2008 it was made open and released to the general community[3].

Data stored in NoSQL or XML can be considered to be stored in a semi-structured format. For XML there are rules for accessing and querying it, but the data itself and its structure can vary. It can conform to agreed standards or be stored in a raw format.

Just saying that text data is structured and binary data is unstructured is not sufficient, as a text file (notepad or vi) can contain a random set of characters without definition, rules, or conform to any standard.

The unstructured data can be broken down into different groups. A well-known group is multimedia or rich media. Here there are types such as digital image, audio, video, and document (though there are more in this list). Some of these types are well-defined and can contain embedded XML that conform to an agreed set of standards (this is covered further in *Chapter 2, Understanding Digital Objects*). The format of the binary data can also follow agreed rules. The digital image format JPEG is an open standard. For video, MPEG is also an open standard. Multimedia would be a category of unstructured data that is well defined. Its category is fluid and changing as technology changes and unlikely to conform to the mathematical and well-proven relational structure.

So we can now define all data as follows:

- **Structured**: The structured data is any data stored in a well-defined, non-propriety system. This data is primarily text based. It typically conforms to ACID[4].

  The structured data is anything that has an enforced composition to the atomic data types[5].

- **Semi-structured**: The semi-structured data is any data stored in a system that conforms to some rules and can be proprietary. This data is primarily text based. It does not have to conform to ACID.

- **Well-defined unstructured**: It is the binary data that is well defined and conforms mostly to an agreed standard.

- **Unstructured**: It is the binary data that is proprietary.

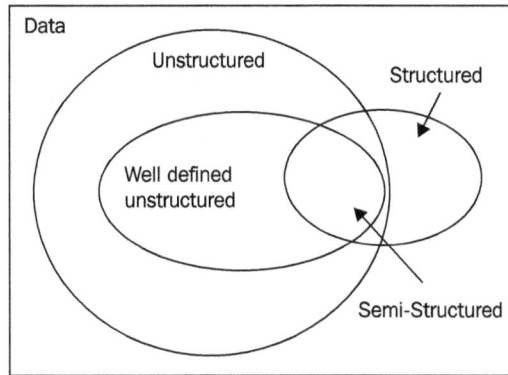

The challenge is that, even based on these definitions, some data falls across one or more definitions. This is typical of what one encounters when dealing with unstructured data. There is no concise and easy to use definition. The temptation is to say that unstructured data is just any data that is not structured. But with example data sets such as NoSQL, XML, and a multitude of other storage systems, there is a feeling that they should belong to structured. In that case, is HTML structured or unstructured? HTML in theory is a subset of XML, but errors are allowed in HTML and it's not case sensitive, whereas XML is. A raw text file can be labeled as HTML and be a valid HTML file, but you can't do the same with XML. An XML file with one syntax error in it is not XML because it doesn't conform to the XML rule set.

A well known joke is, what is the name of a boomerang that doesn't return? A stick! Except that when one looks at the true history of boomerangs, most were designed not to return. Yet we associate a boomerang as any object that when thrown returns. An object of any shape can be used as a boomerang. This has been shown by boomerang experts, who use letters of the alphabet as the shape of boomerangs just to show how versatile the ability of an object when thrown to return can be. The point to be made is that our traditional, innate sense of what something should be and belong to, is not always right.

One can also say that unstructured data is really structured data that hasn't been defined correctly yet. Because of the exceptions to the rule it might not even be valid to break data up into structured and unstructured. Yet by breaking it up and identifying each set, one can associate rules with it, understand its limitations, and formulate new concepts around it. So it is useful to be able to do this.

When we look at the situation of a digital image being stored in a relational database like Oracle, we actually see two different situations. We see the digital image, which is binary data conforming to a well-defined standard, but it's being stored in a structured system. We can see what the data represents and where it is stored as two different systems.

So let's look at this further. If we now separate the storage mechanism from the data itself, we can have unstructured data stored in a relational database. The unstructured data is a separate entity and even though it's handled using ACID that is not important as the data itself is unstructured. Of course, that raises some new issues. What about some of the text elements stored in a structured database, are they structured or unstructured? What if we store a date value that behaves as structured, is fixed in its definition and conforms to a mathematical standard? If the date is stored in a `varchar` field (which means variable character length) then it's not structured. This is because any value can be put into it. We could enter in `12th Jan 2005`, `30-Feb 2012`, or `01.02.03`. Any value without validation can be stored in it. If we store an address in a `varchar` field, is that structured or unstructured? If we store the values in an abstract data type, it can be classified as structured data as methods can be applied to it and the structure is well defined and controlled. If the address is stored in only a `varchar` field, then any value can be added in free-form and it is unstructured. A similar situation holds for names and a raft of other values (this is covered further in *Chapter 3, The Multimedia Warehouse*). So it appears that a lot of the individual data items in a structured database might actually be unstructured. This issue is well known in data warehouses, where a lot of time is spent cleaning the data into a structured format.

So again we come to a situation where trying to clearly define structured and unstructured data always brings up inconsistencies and exceptions to the rule. At this point we realize that this isn't an issue at all and come to a better understanding of how one has to rethink the whole strategy of working with the unstructured data. A document can contain only photos. Is it a document or a photo album? If a video only has an audio track but no picture, is it still a video? Is a GIF animated image a video? Even when looking at two images and comparing, how can we say they are the same? If one image differs from the other by one byte, is it still the same? If comparing two seemingly identical videos, but one is missing only the final frame, which has no audio or picture, is it the same or different? The world of unstructured data introduces us to a world where our traditional rules for dealing with commonly held concepts break down and don't make sense any more. The strict definitions we are used to and comfortable with for defining relational data fall apart when dealing with the unstructured data.

For a database management system to begin to correctly handle the unstructured data, it must initially have support for objects. An **object** can be seen to be a grouping of fields with associated rules. The grouping of fields can be referred to as an **Abstract Data Type** (or **ADT**). The associated rules are called **methods**. The data as stored can be linked directly to other data items, which is referred to as a reference. The data items themselves can repeat and can be stored hierarchically or in a nested structure. Object-oriented systems are known to conflict with the relational systems because they break a number of the rules involved in the data normalization[6]. In the late 1990s this caused the market to divide between using relational or object databases, as each offered strengths and weaknesses. Oracle managed to combine the two in its database allowing data architects to pick up the best method. With the embedding of **Online Analytical Processing** (**OLAP**) and XML into the database in later releases, the Oracle database grew from being relational to one supporting most structures.

With the recent rise in popularity of NoSQL, again the debate has been raised about which is better to use, a relational system or a NoSQL one? The experienced data architects, who remember the relational/object debate, will realize that it's not really one or the other, it's using the one that can satisfy a number of conditions that are business dependent, including the ability to do the following:

- Scale (support large numbers of users and/or large volumes of data)
- Be open (not proprietary) or be locked into a vendor
- To provide data integrity and prevent data corruption or loss

Most databases can enable unstructured data to be stored in them, but do not support the management, control, and manipulation of that data. Most provide the equivalent of lip service to unstructured data and encourage it to be stored externally. Even in the case of Oracle, which has built-in support of the unstructured data and provides a powerful database environment for handling it, it still has serious limitations with it (this is covered further in *Chapter 9, Understanding the Limitations of Oracle Products*). Even though it is a market leader in unstructured data management there are still a large number of major improvements the database needs.

Metadata

Throughout this book, most chapters will cover the usage of metadata. With unstructured data management, metadata is crucial. It is the data that describes the unstructured data and gives meaning to it. Each type of unstructured data object has its own metadata. It might be as simple as a filename, or as complex as a complete set of relational records. Without metadata the unstructured data loses meaning.

The metadata is primarily used for searching. Without it, it's not possible to construct a multimedia warehouse. It is also used for assigning a description. A person might see a photo of a plant. The metadata might have a description of what that photo is, giving meaning and context to the photo.

The metadata is also used to relate unstructured data objects, which in turn adds intelligence and structure to it. It is also used to store information about the object like its name, when it was created, who created it, and who modified it.

The metadata can be used to represent any knowledge about the unstructured object. It's typically stored in a structured format. Currently the trend is to use XML, but this has not always been the case. Additionally, metadata can be matched to data in relational databases or NoSQL databases.

As will be shown in the following chapters, the metadata usage can be rich, varied, and complex. At the moment because of limitations in computer technology, metadata is crucial for most systems that want to extensively use unstructured data. A computer if asked the question, find me the video with the picture of the person John in it, would have great difficulty answering it. Likewise, a question asking, find me all audio files with a lyre bird singing after sunset, would be equally hard to answer. By having a human operator attach metadata with this information in it, then while searching multimedia with that information, the questions raised can be answered.

Unfortunately, the need to manually attach metadata is a time consuming and costly exercise. A number of sites are investigating crowd sourcing to resolve it (see *Chapter 3, The Multimedia Warehouse*) or just bringing in a number of people to go through and identify the unstructured data.

As computer technology improves and new algorithms are discovered, the need to store metadata will disappear. Computers are already good at facial recognition and can convert speech to text. They do have major limitations and still struggle in complex situations that humans do easily. It is envisaged that in the next 20 years technology will improve to the point where algorithms will become commonplace that will be able to identify objects and people in a video or photo, and understand sounds and complex speech in audio files. When this point is reached, the need for metadata will be reduced and constrained to a smaller, more tightly controlled subset. The metadata will always exist and always be needed.

As the veil over the unstructured data is slowly removed, and as knowledge and understanding grows, so will the use of metadata. As covered in the previous point, the use will change and diminish over time, and the market for its use will grow. For example, if the current market represented 100 units, and if multimedia represented 30 percent that would be 30 units. If its usage over time dropped to 5 percent that would be 5 units. But if the growth of the market expanded to 10,000 units, 5% would be 500 units, which is five times bigger than the current market. So even though the need will be reduced, the market as it grows will demand an increasing usage for metadata.

The uses for metadata will start to strain relational databases, and object relational databases will be pushed to their limits to identify and handle the changing complexities of it. Time-based structures (effectively four-dimensional) will be needed. Oracle's flashback capabilities will need to be ramped up in data warehouses to handle large-scale, complex queries. The fuzzy data structures, which are needed to handle the vagaries of some multimedia types, struggle to be easily represented and queried against in most databases. Neural structures are another story altogether and most computer systems can't even cope with the basic handling of them. It's feasible in concept to attach a neural network as a metadata to an object type, which details how to recognize and handle components within it[7].

Defining unstructured data

A starting point is needed for defining exactly what is unstructured data. The goal of this section is to begin to describe and define the base components of unstructured data.

Terminology

In reviewing this book, an important question was raised. And that was, what is the best term to describe the concept of storing and delivering digital information? On investigation, a number of terms that closely fit the mark were discovered, though none truly described the concept that was trying to be expressed.

The following are a list of some of the terms discovered and reviewed, including definitions found on the Internet.

Image

An image is a collection of data logically grouped together.

Digital file

A digital file is a collection of binary data represented as bytes, contained and assigned a name to identify it. Digital files traditionally exist within a filesystem. They can also be captured and stored in a database.

Digital image

A digital image is a representation of a two-dimensional image as a finite set of digital values, called picture elements or pixels[8]. It is commonly known as a digital photo.

Digital object

In various current usages, a digital object or asset may comprise a single media file or group of files including or excluding some or all associated metadata. The framework's apparent usage of a digital object to denote a single media file excluding its associated metadata should be made explicit to avoid misreading in opposition to the term's other contemporary usages. This recommendation for explicit definition would apply equally to the term digital asset should that language be adopted instead[9].

Digital content

There are a number of definitions available. They are as follows:

- Any digital data traffic should be viewed as a digital content product
- Digital content products would seem logically to include those that have a digital representation
- Digital content products would include any products that are encoded in digital form
- Products that are in digital format and that form part of the content of a repository, collection, exhibition, or archive[10]
- The definition of digital content encompasses images, music, and videos[11]

Digital asset

A digital asset is a digital object that can be clearly identified as a singular item or component, which may be ascribed a value. Computer systems can be built to manage these assets also referred to as a **Digital Asset Management System (DAMS)**, which is a system for organizing and managing access to digital materials.

Digital material

This is a broad term encompassing digital surrogates created as a result of converting analogue materials to digital form (digitization), and born digital, for which there has never been and is never intended to be an analogue equivalent, and digital records[12].

Digital library

Digital libraries (DLs) are organized collections of digital information. They combine the structuring and gathering of information, which libraries and archives have always done, with the digital representation that computers have made possible[13].

A DL contains digital representations of the objects found in it. Most understanding of the DL probably also assumes that it will be accessible via the Internet, though not necessarily to everyone. But the idea of digitization is perhaps the only characteristic of a digital library on which there is a universal agreement[14].

Analyzing the digital object

Each of the preceding definitions are correct, but the issue is that none truly conveys the meaning behind what it is to manage the unstructured data and deliver it. Each definition is restrictive and not adaptive to the changing digital technology. Most assume a digital image is a photo or document, and all assume they are owned. As will be shown further, these assumptions do not stand up on a closer scrutiny.

What did stand out was that most definitions conveyed the idea of representation, that is the digital information is meant to symbolize something, be it a photo, document, or video.

So which term should be used? After reviewing all terms the one that seems to have the most potential is a digital object. This is the term that will be used throughout most of the book. It is far easier to use an existing term that people are familiar with than it is to create a new one or define an acronym.

It is then important to accurately define what a digital object actually is. With technology changing, any classic definition we give today is likely to be out of date within a couple of years. The standard perception that the general public has of a digital object is a photograph taken by a digital camera. As will be explained later, a digital photograph is just a subset of type `Picture`. In fact, when looking at digital objects we are looking at ways of representing data, which is ultimately used by one of our traditional five senses.

When looking at the types of digital objects available they can be broken up as shown in the following table:

Digital image type	Definition	Examples
Picture	It is a two-dimensional representation of anything	Photos, drawings, paintings, and icons
Document (text based)	It is a set of pictures with each picture optionally representing a character from one or more well-defined character sets	Microsoft Word, e-mails, Adobe PDF files
Audio	It is a time-based set of sounds	WAV files, CDs, and MP3s
Video	It is a combination of an optional set of time-based pictures and an optional set of time-based sounds	A video, DVD

These are the traditional object types used throughout the world, but one needs to address the need of what types of images will exist in 50 years time. It is nearly impossible to predict this, so to accurately define a digital object we need to look at how we as humans deal with digital objects and use this to future proof our definition. This involves looking at the senses humans use for viewing digital objects and then expand on this.

So let's redefine the definition of a digital object to the following:

A **digital object** is a representation of anything, stored in binary format, to be used by our senses.

Why to be used by our senses? If there is no intention of use for a digital object, it can be classified as a digital file. A Windows DLL, a Unix executable, or security attributes are all digital representations of something, but they are not digital objects because they are not used by our senses. They are used by computers for the management of data. By specifying that the binary representation has to be used by our senses, then the boundaries of use for that digital object are captured and can then be further defined.

The traditional view is that we have five senses: sight, sound, touch, taste, and smell. When looking in greater detail at these senses we can break them down as shown in the following table:

Human sense	Images	Core physical concept	Human physical concept
Sight	Picture, document, video	Photons of light	Light, sensitive cells within the eye tuned to certain wavelengths of light fire when hit by photons of light
Sound	Audio	Vibrations of air	Very fine hair follicles located within the ear fire when vibrated at certain frequencies
Touch	Braille, sculpture	Pressure and temperature	Nerve cells fire when pressure is applied to them or when subjected to a temperate variation
Taste	Food	Chemical	Cells on the tongue fire when they come into contact with certain chemical substances
Smell (Olfaction)	Scratch and sniff card	Chemical	Cell receptors within the nose fire when they come into contact with chemical substances

There is not much difference between taste and smell, as both involve chemical reactions. Interestingly, we can actually taste with our nose[15]. When it comes to sound we can actually feel certain low vibration sounds. For watching movies on DVDs, this is an important experience and part of the entertainment value. In this case the deep bass, which is emitted by certain speakers, is felt by the body through touch. So one digital object can be used by multiple senses.

By equating it to a sense we can resolve a number of real world problems associated with defining an image. For example, a document that can be viewed or read using sight, can be converted to Braille and then read by touch. For those familiar with the TV show Red Dwarf, in that series they even explored the concept of reading a book using smell.

Just because we currently are not using one of our senses for viewing a digital object, it does not mean it should be excluded. A good example is taste. Currently it is very hard to simulate taste in a digital sense, but this doesn't mean that in ten years' time the concept of artificial taste will not be invented.

Digital object types

A digital object can be broken down into image types. Each image type can be further broken into image subtypes. We can then apply conversion and transformation rules to each subtype to modify the digital object.

By breaking down the senses into their core concepts and then equating them to traditional image concepts, it now becomes possible to identify traditional object types and then define them.

A digital object does not need to have any meaning associated with it, nor does it have to represent a real world scene (which is the traditional view of a photograph). A picture of an abstract painting is a digital object and the white noise of an empty TV channel can be classified as a digital object.

For simplicity we will maintain a digital object as having to be stored in the binary format. Though there are audio and video formats that use analogue signals, these formats can be expressed in a binary digital format. Even when looking at artificial intelligence and the use of neural networks, this can be represented in a binary format.

Core types

Digital objects can be composed of two core types and the dimension of time. By combining these core types into different combinations, a variety of base types can be created.

The core types are as follows:

- Image
- Audio

The use of the dimension of time is very fluid and varies based on how it is used. Video uses a very strict definition of time. Animated GIFs use a very simple time-based sequence, whereas heraldry uses a very loose definition of time. The use of time is covered later in greater detail.

When expanding this definition to handle three-dimensional objects, the concept of an **artifact** is introduced. This is an object created from physical materials, but created digitally. An example is a model created from a three-dimensional printer using resins and glue.

Subtypes

For each object type we introduce object subtypes. For example, we can define a photograph as a real world representation of a picture. A line drawing is a hand drawing. The CGI is a computer-generated image.

Human sense	Example of image subtypes	Examples
Sight	Photo, drawing, DVD, font	A wedding photo, a line drawing of a plant
Sound	Music, sonar, radar	An MP3 file
Touch	Braille, sculpture	A pin-map converts an image into a surface, which can be felt, force feedback glove
Taste	Human taste, animal taste	A recipe
Smell	Chemical formula for smell	Perfume

Picture

A picture is a two-dimensional representation of anything. A picture can be viewed using all senses. A picture is defined as having a width and height assuming the picture is rectangular. For non-rectangular pictures the width and height describe the upper boundary lengths of the picture.

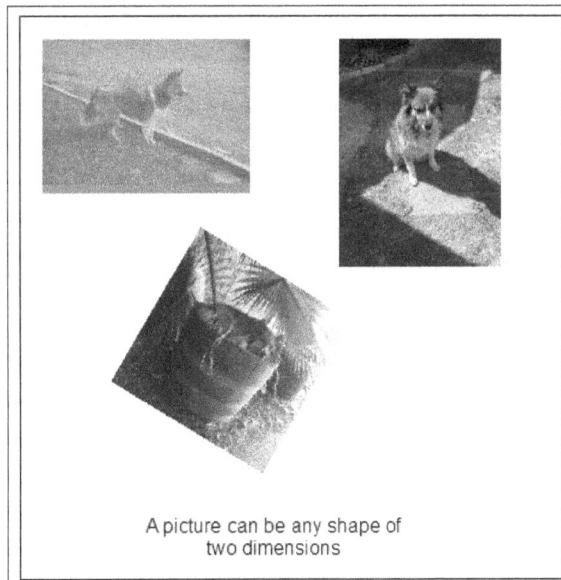

A picture can be any shape of two dimensions

The following are the examples of subtypes:

- Geo-raster
- Photo
- Art
- Line drawing
- Montage
- 3D view using a set of 2D (but still 2D)
- Stereoscopic image

Audio

Audio is a time-based set of sounds. If we investigated hard enough, we could eventually equate a sound to a picture. This is not required and to keep things simple this is not going to be done.

The following are the examples of audio subtypes:

- Music
- Audio book

Model

A model is a three-dimensional object that is a representation created using binary data. Three-dimensional printers are now available that can produce physical structures from three-dimensional drawings.

Creating new base types

When looking at these definitions it can be seen that the definition for a document and video can be expressed using the terms of a picture and an audio. By adding a rule set we can create new digital image types. The two new rule definitions as used previously are as follows:

1. Digital image types can be time based, a set of digital objects linked together using the dimension of time.

2. A well defined character set. It is a set of pictures or icons grouped together. UTF8 and US7ASCII are character sets. Egyptian hieroglyphs can be grouped together to form a character set.

Using new rules we can create new digital object types based on the core picture and audio image types.

The following are examples of non-traditional digital object types:

Document

The document is a set of pictures with each picture optionally representing a character from one or more well-defined character sets. Each picture can be classed as a font.

The example subtypes are as follows:

- Ephemera
- Structured documents (used for signaling)
- Forms

Video

A video is a combination of an optional set of time-based pictures and an optional set of time-based sounds. A DVD is an example of a video subtype. A photo montage is not an example of a video subtype. In this case we have a set of pictures but because they are not time based, they can only be classified as type picture.

The example subtypes are as follows:

- Film
- TV
- Documentary
- Surveillance

Multimedia (Rich Media)

Multimedia is a combination of one or more object types that is optionally time based. Usually, they are created to be interactive, such as an educational program or game.

The example subtypes are as follows:

- VRML
- SVG
- SMIL

- Macromedia Flash
- Java Applet

Data

Data is a document that is perceived by its users as a collection of tables (and nothing but tables). This is a slight expansion on the original definition of relational. Relational data is treated as image data, as it can be transformed into a picture (creating a graph) or a document (creating a report) or even a video (creating a view using data mining analysis).

The example subtypes are as follows:

- Relational
- XML
- Object
- Metadata

Simulation

This is where we take the data, convert parts of it into well-defined objects, and then extend it over a well-defined period of time. A simulation can be converted into video. A simulation, which is given a set of tightly enforced rules, can be extended into a self-evolving artificial neural network with the resulting output being an enhanced pattern-matching algorithm. Such an algorithm can be subsequently used for transforming digital object subtypes.

Genealogy

The genealogy is a record of the descent of a person, family, or group from an ancestor or ancestors[17]. It involves taking data, documents, photos, video, and audio and extending it over time.

The subtypes include the following:

- **Heraldry**: It is the study and classification of armorial bearings and the tracing of genealogies[18]
- **Private record**: It is a privately defined record hierarchy position[19]

Virtual digital object

It is possible for a digital object to be categorized into multiple object types. This is because the line on what actually constitutes a digital object can change depending on how it is delivered. For example, an MP3 file is classified as an audio type. If it is delivered using the Real Player server and streamed to a client, it is treated as a video type. Another example is an animated GIF, which is a time-related set of images enclosed within a repeating cycle. An animated GIF is by definition a video, yet for ease of delivery, it is delivered as a specialized GIF (that is, a type of static picture).

This means it is important to separate the storage of the digital object from the delivery mechanism. The delivery mechanism might involve a virtual change of the digital object. The digital object exists in two (or possibly more) states and it isn't until the object is delivered that its true state is determined. When this happens it is called a **virtual digital object**.

In a perfect world there is no difference between a digital object and its delivery mechanism. But because of Internet standards that limit what can be seen (for example, browsers by default only view JPEG and GIF images and not TIFF ones) and due to limitations in network bandwidth and cost of delivery, virtual digital objects have had to be created to address these issues. These issues are subject to current environmental constraints and will change over time. HTML5 is attempting to define a set of supported video standards. This is covered further in *Chapter 3, The Multimedia Warehouse*.

Digital object delivery

One goal in this book is to describe how to deliver a digital object. This is covered in great detail in *Chapter 6, Delivery Techniques*. At the moment we have classified what a digital object is, but have not defined what it is to actually deliver it.

We expand on the original definition and add the following:

Only when that digital object has been successfully consumed by one of our senses can it be considered to be delivered.

This means a photograph viewed on the computer screen has been delivered. A DVD streamed to a computer terminal has been delivered and a document viewed and read has been delivered.

It is not important that money has been transacted when delivering a digital image. Buying a digital image is an optional part of the delivery process.

But what about the scenario where an audio file is cut to CD and then shipped to a customer? What if that customer does not listen to it? By the preceding definition it has not been consumed therefore it has not been delivered. Common sense indicates that the image has been delivered. From a traditional consumer viewpoint it is on actual receipt of the digital image that the image can be considered to be delivered. This view is now starting to conflict with new e-commerce concepts starting to appear on the Internet. That is, consumers are now only being charged for use of a digital image only when it has been consumed and not when they have received it.

So when defining consumption of an image and ensuring that definition is future proof, we have to be careful that our traditional viewpoint of commerce does not interfere with that definition. With e-commerce the rules are changing, consumer habits are changing, and new ideas for image delivery are being tried.

At this point we will leave the definition as it is. In *Chapter 6, Delivery Techniques*, we will explore this concept in greater detail. Here we will be looking at who the consumer is and who the producer is. With e-commerce our traditional perspectives need to be challenged.

Manipulating digital objects

This section is an introduction to the methods available for managing and manipulating a digital object. When working with digital objects it soon becomes apparent that techniques have to be utilized to view and understand what they actually are. The digital object itself can contain other digital objects and only by processing it can these other objects be discovered.

Conversion

Conversion is when we change an object subtype into another object subtype. Major conversions occur when we convert between types. For example, when we go from a picture to a document. Minor image conversions occur when we convert an image between subtypes, a common example is when converting a JPEG image to a GIF image.

In converting a digital image the process might be irreversible, meaning once converted it cannot be converted back again. For example, in converting a video to a photograph, we cannot convert that photograph back to the same video.

The process might also lose information in the conversion. In converting a JPEG image to a GIF image and back to a JPEG image, color information is lost. Though the image might look like the original image, it is not the original image. This is a lossy conversion and covered in greater detail in *Chapter 2, Understanding Digital Objects*. At the end of this chapter there is a chart detailing how it's possible to convert between all the major types.

Transformation

Transformation occurs when a digital object is modified. For example, we can rotate, watermark, or crop a photo. We can convert the bit rate of an audio file, change a Word document into an Adobe document, or add special effects to a video. Transforming does not change the object subtype.

Extraction

A digital object can be composed of multiple digital objects. The extraction process involves unpacking those digital objects. For example, a DICOM image can be composed of multiple photographs and documents that are in turn digital objects themselves.

Compression

We live in a world where storage is limited. The storage not only includes the volume of space a digital object uses, but the bandwidth required to deliver that image. As such with digital objects, compression becomes important. And for all digital objects we deal with lossless or lossy compression.

With lossless compression the digital object is compressed (reduced in size) and when uncompressed the original digital object is reconstructed without the loss of any original information.

With lossy compression, the obtained object is not the same on reconstruction as the original object. This is covered in greater detail in *Chapter 2, Understanding Digital Objects*.

Image comparison

After the compression or conversion of an object, we may lose some information in the process, therefore it now becomes important to be able to define whether that modified object is still the original object.

The technical definition is, two digital objects are classified as absolutely identical such that when they are compared in an uncompressed format each byte exactly matches the byte in the same corresponding position.

With a digital object, this definition does not match with real world expectations. For example, we can convert a WAV file to MP3 and then back to WAV. The technical definition says the two are different, but to the human ear listening to the original and the converted WAV file, there will be no difference.

In another example, it is possible to embed hidden watermarks in a JPEG image. To a person viewing the original image and the modified image, they will not be able to tell them apart. They will say they are the same digital image.

To address this we can then add a new definition: two digital objects are classified as observably identical when they are perceived to be identical.

Now that we have defined digital object comparison, we can apply this to our compression definition as follows.

On compressing a digital object, if the obtained compressed object matches with the original object, the compression is said to be lossless. If they do not match, that compression is lossy.

This in turns raises a new issue. If the resultant lossy image when viewed is not perceived to be identical to the original image, that image is termed as being **badly compressed**.

Badly compressed

The skill comes in balancing compression to reduce the size of the original digital object without it becoming noticeably badly compressed.

It should be understood that stating an object is identical just because it is perceived to be identical is highly dependent on the individual doing the comparison checking. It is this area that moves into a very gray area by going into image searching. It will be discussed in more detail in *Chapter 3, The Multimedia Warehouse,* and *Chapter 4, Searching the Multimedia Warehouse*. It is an imprecise area that is not suited for traditional binary logic but well suited for neural networks, pattern matching, and fuzzy logic.

Thumbnail

A thumbnail is a digital object that has been transformed and/or converted into a format which uses less storage. The goal in creating thumbnails is to improve the performance of object delivery. It is not fair to classify a thumbnail as an index, for the simple reason that it is not transparent. In a relational database the data is perceived by the user as tables (and nothing but tables)[20]. An **index** is an object designed to improve performance. It cannot be seen as a table, so the corollary is that it must be transparent. A thumbnail is seen and yet is designed to improve performance like an index, so it breaks the original relational rule. A thumbnail fits in the structure referred to as a **pyramid index**.

From an Oracle perspective the closest equivalent is to treat thumbnails as a form of materialized view. Multiple thumbnails can be created from an original image of varying size. Two types of thumbnails are the web quality thumbnail and the standard thumbnail. The standard thumbnail is the smallest size produced, whereas the web quality is the largest size thumbnail produced.

In the case of a Georaster Image (which is a very large digital photograph typically seen as a satellite image), hundreds of thumbnails can be created of varying sizes based on the original.

Thumbnails are optional and do not have to be produced.

As will be shown throughout this book, a lot of traditional relational concepts are broken when applied to the world of unstructured data. The thumbnail and indexing is just one good example. This can be unsettling for those who have been trained and skilled in the relational database world. Unstructured data is seen as either a threat or an anomaly that is best treated by placing it into a blob field or insisting that it be stored externally and not in the database. The psychology behind this resistance to adopt and use unstructured data in itself cannot be easily dismissed and must be factored in by the data designer, database administrator, and developer. The introduction to the market of multimedia centric devices, such as the iPad or Android are beginning to break down the notion of keeping all unstructured data outside the database, as users start to become better educated and fluent in the usage of multimedia and are insisting on greater use and access to it in their applications.

Transposition

This is the act of combining multiple object subtypes into a new object subtype while still keeping each subtype separate and distinct.

The traditional example of this is mapping spatial data over an image. The data is separate and can be searched. For example, we can search for a grid reference point on a map. Another example is seen when attaching metadata to an object. We can add EXIF data to a camera picture. The metadata is a specialized case and will be looked at in more detail in *Chapter 3, The Multimedia Warehouse*.

> A photo of a book is not a transposition, it is a photo. This is because the data within the book is not separate but part of the photo. To do a search on the book title involves running the photo through a transformation process to extract the book title (OCR) before searching on it.

Searching

Searching for a digital object is a complex topic and is covered in greater detail in *Chapter 3*, *The Multimedia Warehouse*, and *Chapter 4*, *Searching the Multimedia Warehouse*.

Due to the complexity in searching a digital object, the current method is to search within a transposed object, with data being transposed over the digital object. Searching against data is simpler than trying to search within the image. Searching using this technique is called **Data Transpose Searching**. For example, the standard search method for looking for images involves searching against metadata attached to the image.

One key goal when searching is to search on the actual digital object. For example, find me all photos with a tree in it, or find the audio file that contains a lyric, or find the video that has Elvis Presley singing the song "you were always on my mind" in it. Currently, computer technology has not progressed to a stage where this is easily possible. A search using this method is called **Actual Searching**.

Another form of searching involves expanding on the concept of badly compressed objects and finding related or similar digital objects. We might want to find all pictures that have a sunset in them and use an existing photo as a base for the search engine to use them. This type of searching is called **Similarity Searching**, and the technology is now available to search on a variety of digital objects.

Similarity searching has the potential to be used in a number of fields, especially in fraud and copyright protection. For example, software is now available for universities where they can find all essays that are similar to ones submitted by students. By adjusting the similarity parameters a teacher can then compare two essays and determine with a high degree of certainty whether one is a copy of the other and has been slightly modified.

Product group

A set of images linked together is referred to as a **product group**. This is not to be confused with the composite type discussed further in the chapter. A product group in an intelligence warehouse that might be a set of digital images of a crime scene. In an electronic commerce system it might be a set of songs, videos, and digital booklets relating to an album.

Location

It is an origin or destination point for a digital object. This can be related to where it was taken or where the digital object is being delivered to.

Defining multimedia in the Oracle database

It's important to exactly define what multimedia is. The common thinking is that multimedia is just a photo taken using a digital camera (or scanned in). Multimedia is much more than this.

To try and define what multimedia is, it's best to look at examples and see how they work with the Oracle database.

Photograph

The photograph is also referred to as a picture, but the proper usage is a digital image.

It can be taken by a digital camera or can be scanned in. A photograph can have the metadata embedded in it (common formats include EXIF, IPTC, Adobe XML, Dicom). A photo can be of type JPEG, TIFF, PNG. There are well over 300 other types. Some camera manufacturers use a raw option when storing their digital images (two of the most common formats being DNG and NEF).

The photo is stored in the Oracle multimedia `ORDSYS.ORDIMAGE` data type. More complex photos can be stored in the `ORDDICOM` data type along with other multimedia types.

A photo can also be of type Georaster, in which case it's best stored using the Oracle Spatial Georaster data type.

A photo can be defined as a two-dimensional object composed of binary data. The photo is typically stored in compressed format using compression software built for that image type.

Video

A video is a time-based set of two-dimensional photographs with optional audio. A video can contain metadata. It can also optionally contain an audio track (audio type) and a caption (document type). The video can be compressed and photographs can be extracted from the image. Common examples include MPEG, Divx, AVI, and QuickTime.

In Oracle multimedia, a video is stored using the `ORDSYS.ORDVIDEO` data type.

Audio

An audio image is a time-based collection of analog-based sounds. An audio image can be compressed. It can also optionally contain a caption (document type).

In Oracle multimedia, audio is stored using the `ORDSYS.ORDAUDIO` data type.

Document

It is a set of two-dimensional pictures that conform to a well-defined set. A document can also contain within it all image types. As a result, a document is stored as binary not character. Microsoft Word and Adobe PDF are two well known examples. There are over 3000 examples of documents found in the marketplace.

A document can be indexed using Oracle text.

In Oracle multimedia, a document is stored using the `ORDSYS.ORDDOC` data type.

Text

Text is a document that is not binary but composed of character data only. It can contain structured data (the two best known examples being relational and XML). Depending on the type, it is determined where to store the data. It can be stored in an XML type, an Oracle table, a CLOB, or a `varchar` field. It can be indexed using Oracle text.

Artifact

It is a three-dimensional representation of an object. Though still in its infancy, some cameras can create a 3D view of an object. It can also be referred to as a blueprint, equating to a three-dimensional drawing used by architects[16].

In Oracle multimedia, an artifact is stored using the `ORDSYS.ORDSOURCE` data type.

Additional multimedia types

The multimedia is not just limited to the types mentioned. It can include anything. In the next decade we will be seeing new types of multimedia containing very large amounts of data. Some of these will be based on life sciences and simulation. Individual multimedia files will be on an average over a 1 TB in size.

For those familiar with VMware, it is feasible (but not currently practical) to store whole VMware instances as a multimedia type. These can be of any size. As more sites move down the virtualization path, the ability to create many installs will be simplified and organizations will be creating more of them. In the next decade we will see computers with a large number of cores and very large amounts of memory being able to host one VMware instance per user. Thus going down the path of each user having their own client computer, which is centrally stored and managed. Once more we see the rules for tuning and management change. Smart use of virtualization will ensure that the CPU use is fairly distributed. But as the number of these virtualizations grow, they will need to be managed and archived. And the most logical place to put them is in a database.

Other smaller sized types can include e-mail messages, flash files, and executables.

Composite types

It is a set of one or more multimedia types stored in the one type. A ZIP, RAR, or TAR file can contain a mixture of multimedia. Further multimedia can then be extracted. A Dicom file can contain multiple multimedia types. Certain photographic file formats can contain multiple images within them. A GIF can be animated, a TIFF can contain multiple images, and a JPEG can contain other JPEGs within it. How the multimedia is going to be used best determines how it is stored.

A composite type is different to a product group or a container.

A composite type introduces the concept of multiple originals. Our traditional notion of an image needs to extend to deal with a multimedia type that is related to other multimedia. A good example is with a DICOM image. This is typically an image that contains information about a medical patient. It can contain patient history, x-rays, ultrasound, and scans. Each is a different image type, but together they all represent the one patient. If we view the patient as an object, then the object is a digital image composed of multiple original with each one being another multimedia type. Another example is a museum painting. The one painting can have multiple photographs taken of it. It might have an associated video showing how it was painted and an audio commentary of it by the artist. Each is a separate image but together they create one image with multiple originals in it. Another example is when a photographer takes a mosaic picture. This is a set of photographs of a scene that can be stitched together to create a new picture (like a jigsaw puzzle). Each image is still treated separately.

For a composite type, one digital image is chosen as the representative image and used as the thumbnail. Depending on the context in which the image is used or accessed, this representative image can dynamically change.

Composite types are best handled using the Oracle database's object/relational capabilities.

Container

It is used to describe the fact that a file type can have multiple encoding algorithms used within it. A video file of type AVI is a container because different compression formats can be used within it. This is covered in greater detail in *Chapter 2, Understanding Digital Objects.*

ZIP files

A ZIP file is a specialized composite type. The goal is compression. ZIP is now used in the vernacular, even though there are other products that can do the same task. Some of these include Winrar, Unix Tar, and Unix Gzip. With ZIP the idea is to create one or more large files containing all the other files and to compress them within it. This is useful for backups or delivery/transfer of large number of images between computer systems.

Within Oracle there are a number of methods for dealing with a ZIP file. The context or how it's designed to be used determines what the ZIP file actually is. The following highlights three different uses of a ZIP file:

- **Delivery**: It extracts all the multimedia within it. It treats each file extracted as a separate file and discards the original ZIP file. This is useful for loading up a set of images via the web browser to the database.

- **Index**: It extracts one image for display and indexing purposes and stores the original ZIP. It is useful when a large number of images need to be delivered. The original ZIP is delivered to the customer.

- **Composite**: It extracts all the files but treats the set of images as a composite type and discards the original ZIP. The one digital image is composed of multiple originals.

The Oracle PL/SQL Package `UTL_COMPRESS`, will not prove to be useful for handling zipped images. This package assumes the ZIP contains exactly one file. To unzip multiple files requires writing a Java program (which runs in the database and can unzip multiple files, even if they are in subdirectories). Another option is to use Java to shell out to the operating system. Dump the ZIP file to a temporary location then invoke the operating system unzip (now supported in Windows as well as Unix) and then load in the extracted files.

Metadata

The metadata is a text data associated with a digital object for the purpose of searching and providing structured or semi-structured information about the digital object. Metadata is covered in greater detail in *Chapter 3*, *The Multimedia Warehouse*. In Oracle metadata can be stored in tables.

The NULL case

For a multimedia type, the NULL equivalent should be discussed. It's possible for the digital images associated with metadata to exist, but the actual multimedia component to not yet exist. For example, a museum has information about an object that needs to be photographed and stored in the database. The object could be a painting, a vase, a person, or any general collection object. They first store the metadata about the object in the database. At a later time the object is scanned, photographed, or a video is taken of it. The digital image is then associated with the initial metadata.

Because the metadata for the object exists but its associated multimedia does not, this is considered the NULL case for the multimedia type. The definition of NULL is related to the potential of what the image could become and avoids confusing a NULL image with one that is empty or blank.

Why store unstructured data in a database?

As the business imperative grows for companies to start managing and then publishing their digital image assets, the issue about where those image assets are stored is raised. More recently, multiple analysts have estimated that data will grow 800 percent over the next five years. The unstructured information accounts for more than 70–80 percent of all data in organizations and is growing 10–50 times more than the structured data[21].

This then grows to include any type of data. The initial choice is to store it on a disk file system. This can be seen as the quickest and simplest approach. Another, better, alternative is to store the images in the database.

A database is not normally considered to be an ideal repository for multimedia or any form of unstructured data. Historically they are known to have had issues with performance with large volume data retrieval. There has also been a noticeable lack of support with third-party tools, leaving any data in the database well and truly locked in. With the Oracle database this was seen in the older Oracle7 release and the use of long fields.

Only recently the possibility of storing multimedia in a database has become realistic. Though the capability has been around for some time, with the increase in disk capacity, and introduction of low-cost, high volume SANs, there has been a greater push towards moving any multimedia from the filesystem into the database. In the past five years, with changes in database technology and improvements in disk performance and storage, the rules have changed and it now makes business sense to use the Oracle database to store and manage all of an organizations digital assets.

Most companies are also now recognizing that large amounts of corporate knowledge and assets are stored within their filesystems. Accessing them is difficult and most do not follow standards for managing and dealing with them. As such, most are now looking to acquire or build some sort of digital asset management system.

Currently the type of unstructured data is limited to those classified as digital assets, which includes multimedia and some other forms of data. The notion of storing a whole operating system inside the database is yet to be reached due to the logistics of adhoc retrieval versus any perceived performance issues. Given time the question will be raised, should the database be the operating system? Having the database as the operating system changes the mentality for its use. It already has security, auditing, extensible programming languages, schemas, backup and recovery, diagnostic management, and a built-in web server. Though such a scenario does not exist, it's plausible and would definitely appeal to a niche market that only uses the database on its server. It would not replace a Windows or Mac PC, it might replace a Unix or Windows server.

The following are the strengths an Oracle database can offer over traditional filesystem storage.

Manageability

Images stored in the database can be directly linked with metadata. In the one transaction an image can be manipulated, a thumbnail of that image created, and all associated metadata modified. Related information is kept in sync. If an image is stored in a file system, it is possible for external processes to delete or modify that image, causing the image itself to either become orphaned or lose synchronicity with its corresponding relational data. Another common issue is web quality images losing their associated thumbnails, meaning web page displays become broken.

Oracle multimedia, which extends control over images, allows images to be manipulated inside the database. They can be resized, copied, converted, and rotated. This simplifies management of them and allows for the one programming environment (PL/SQL or Java).

Moving multimedia is simplified as only one object is being moved. When deleting any multimedia all associated thumbnails and metadata is deleted. Management becomes simpler and less prone to error, especially on recovery and when doing general database maintenance.

Security

If all images are stored in a directory, fine grained control is not possible. That is, it is not possible to restrict access of the images to individual users. Once users can gain access to an image in the directory they can access all of them (this is based on the assumption of using Digest Authentication).

By storing an image in the database, fine grained security becomes possible. Access to an image can be restricted to individual users and it also becomes possible to achieve the following:

- Attach a timeout to access the image
- Include check in/check out capabilities
- Audit who accessed the image and when
- Offer image exclusivity (one user accesses an image for a set period of time during which no one else can access it)

Using Oracle security it becomes possible to attach roles to images and introduce fine grained access on them. Security can be configured so that a user can access a thumbnail but not the original. Full auditing of who accessed each image and how they accessed it can be tracked. Auditing can also be included to keep track of network capacity used per user, making it possible to track and then charge for network usage.

Backup/recovery

The one backup program that is used to backup the database will also backup the images. This simplifies the backup process. In the event of failure the whole database can be recovered to the last committed transaction.

The traditional behavior for backing up a filesystem is to back it up daily or weekly. This means in the event of failure the filesystem on recovery will be out of sync with the database by at least one day.

So by having the images in the database only one backup program is required and in the event of failure only one recovery procedure is needed.

Another advantage that can be seen comes when using some of the more advanced database features such as standby databases and replication. Images are automatically replicated if the advanced replication option is used, and for disaster recovery situations, image data is automatically transferred to a standby database.

The Oracle database is designed to handle backing up and recovering very large volumes of data. Using RMAN, incremental backups ensure only the changed blocks are backed up. Backup and recovery can be done in parallel. The database supports full rollback. Recovery is done until the last committed transaction, meaning no data is lost. This is important as it ensures that when the database is recovered all multimedia and associated metadata match. If a filesystem was used to store the multimedia and a database to store the metadata, when failure occurs it becomes possible for the metadata to become out of sync with the files recovered on the filesystem.

Though the latest generation of SANs can do high volume and high-speed backups of data, there is still no way to guarantee complete consistency between the database on the SAN. With changes in technology, a number of SANs now support real-time block level replication and can ensure consistency. This capability is vendor and database specific.

Integration

All the data is in one location. The digital image becomes an object and can be accessed using the one query. Client server and web applications can access the one image and retrieve its associated metadata using the one SQL statement. Image management is also subject to the same transactional rules as relational data. Using PLSQL and/or Java, the one query can access a variety of multimedia types in the one query. For example, a photo with its associated metadata and video can be retrieved in the one simple query. It's also possible to do a query that not only retrieves the metadata, but also performs a spatial query to do analysis of it.

The simplistic nature of these highly complex tasks makes it a powerful option to use.

Extensibility

An image stored in the database can be indexed. If an image is a document it can be thematically searched and gists (summaries) can be extracted from it.

An image can be converted from one format to another. Metadata can be extracted from it. It can be copied, re-sized, and the image quality controlled.

Flexibility

When it comes to managing and controlling the images in the database, the Oracle database offers the greatest in flexibility. Sets of images can be deleted, updated, or copied as easy as it is to write a query.

Images can be linked together and metadata can be easily attached to them. All data related to an image or set of images can logically co-exist.

This adds flexibility, which gives a DBA and developer greater control over managing and working with the images.

Features

The Oracle database has various built-in features, which when used makes it easier to manage and deliver multimedia:

- The Oracle database can extract metadata from a number of multimedia types. The metadata is stored in XML format making it easier to manipulate and control. For images, metadata can also be saved back into it. Using Oracle's built-in XML handling capabilities, accessing the XML data is easily done.
- **Transportable tablespaces**: Multimedia can be migrated en-masse by copying them to a transport tablespace and then moving this tablespace to the new location. This is useful when firewalls are involved. It also allows for the large scale copying of image databases.
- **Database links**: Multimedia can be copied between databases directly using a database link.
- Oracle supports streaming of videos directly from the database.
- Photos can be processed within the database. They can be rotated, re-sized, watermarked, or translated from one type to another.
- **Embedded gateway**: Web access, including multimedia loading and retrieval is simply done using the built-in HTTP gateway.

Why not store the multimedia in the filesystem?

When managing multimedia, the argument should now be, please justify why the files should be stored in the filesystem and not the database. There might be business cases for storing multimedia in the filesystem, especially if there are older applications and tools that need to access the files, but can only access a filesystem. As will be covered in *Chapter 9, Understanding the Limitations of Oracle Products*, there is a strong case for the use of the Oracle Database File System.

Only by using web services and integrating access into these tools to access the database can these restrictions be removed. It's possible to build programs that can be integrated into Windows File Explorer, Adobe Photoshop, Microsoft Word, and PowerPoint that can directly access the database and retrieve the files.

The following are some arguments why storing unstructured data in the filesystem might not be a good idea:

- **Security**: Different operating systems have different types of filesystem security. Some are quite powerful but most offer basic course grain which cannot easily integrate with database security. If using Apache and all your images are in one directory, how do you configure it so that a user can access only a set of files, while another user can only access others? It can be done with a lot of effort and using specialized plugins, but it doesn't easily integrate with the database security and it's very hard to monitor, audit, integrate, and control. There is more likelihood of holes in the security being opened by trying to implement a tight security policy. Applying security to unstructured data stored in the database is so much easier.

- **Backup/recovery**: Database backups are well known. The challenge is to try and ensure the filesystem backups are coordinated with the database.

- **Filesystem limitations**: Most filesystems can only store 65,536 per directory. For a multimedia warehouse it's feasible to want to store millions of digital objects in one directory.

- **Performance**: Filesystems are notoriously slow for accessing and managing. Put 10,000 digital objects in a Windows filesystem and try to use File Explorer to look at it. Try to mass rename or change the security on 20,000 digital objects. Try to do a search against a filesystem looking at all directories when the filesystem might contain a million or more digital objects. It's incredibly slow. In some cases it fails. Try highlighting 1,000 objects in File Explorer and moving them to another location. It's painfully slow and difficult to do. Digital objects stored in the database offer the ability to make changes to millions of objects in seconds. There is no real performance comparison. Searching for and manipulating objects in the database is much faster than trying to achieve the same in the operating system. Arguments might be made about load and retrieval times, but with the latest release of Oracle with Securefiles this argument doesn't hold much weight anymore.

Why use Oracle multimedia and not a blob?

Oracle multimedia is tightly integrated into the database. Application development can be greatly simplified when the images and all associated metadata is stored together in the database. Oracle multimedia uses blobs within its type definition, which can be accessed and used as required. In addition, it supports a variety of methods that simplify the act of loading and manipulating digital images. This is covered in greater detail in *Chapter 7, Techniques for Creating a Multimedia Database*.

Addressing the concerns

Even though the focus should always be to store the images in the database first, this experience is still to be accepted in the marketplace. The attitude is still to store it in the filesystem. Most management when confronted with the idea of putting images in the database invariably come up with the same set of fears that first appeared over ten years ago when database vendors first tried to push the idea of storing images in the database and failed. What's different now is that the rules have changed, the technology has changed and experience has shown that a lot of the previously raised issues are not valid anymore.

Performance

Isn't it slower to retrieve an image from the database compared to a filesystem?

This might have been true ten years ago on older disk systems, but with improvements in disk technology this issue has subsequently disappeared. Tests have shown that it is just as fast to retrieve an image from a database as it is from a disk filesystem.

In addition, by using optional caching technology, it is possible to cache frequently accessed images thus improving the time to retrieve them.

Fine grained control over where an image is stored and how it's accessed is possible. A thumbnail can be stored on a local disk and cached in the SGA to ensure the fastest possible speed for retrieval. The original can be stored on lower speed disks. The architecture of the Oracle database is one that inherently supports scalability. This makes it simpler to develop applications that load and deliver images.

Oracle's new Securefile Lobs offer speeds nearly twice as fast as previous versions, for loading and retrieval.

Database size

Doesn't it take more storage to put in an image in the database compared to a file system?

Yes it does. The storage format used in the database adds extra overheads to manage locking and to reserve storage for growth. In addition, Oracle puts indexes on images to improve the time it takes to retrieve and manipulate them.

Though there is extra storage required, it is not significant in the overall storage requirements. When tens of thousands of images are stored in the database, the extra required is dwarfed by the overall size of the images. It is also fair to say that disk is cheaper than it once was, and when it comes to database management, the strategy now is to sacrifice storage for performance. When dealing with relational data it is now common practice to add additional indexes and use locally managed tablespaces to improve performance. These extra features come at an additional storage cost. In some cases with data warehouses just for storing relational data, the rule of thumb is to factor in eight times the raw storage to handle all the additional overheads.

So increasing the storage requirements in the database by storing images in it, only ensures that the image data is retrieved optimally and consistently.

Complexity

Isn't it more complicated and time consuming having to put images into the database and retrieve them compared to a filesystem?

This was exactly the same argument used fifteen years ago when relational databases first appeared. But at that time the argument was concerned with storing data in what was known as flat files versus putting it into a relational database. Time has shown that the overheads of putting data into a relational database offer more benefits and ultimately greater control than when storing it in a flat file. The same argument can be applied to images. Yes there is some programming overhead to put them in, but the advantages gained from having them in the database (as explained previously) is greater than when not having them in the database.

So when it comes to storing and managing those digital assets, keep in mind that ultimately it is easier, safer, and better to keep them stored in a database.

Summary

Unstructured data is more than just any data which isn't structured. It's a complete set of different types of data that can be categorized into different groups, with rules that can be used to define and manage them.

The introduction of digital objects enables a large set of unstructured data to be classified using the human senses as a base for that classification. By describing multimedia, digital images, video, audio, and documents can be categorized and methods detailed for the handling and manipulation of those digital objects.

The use of a database that can support objects makes it a lot easier to manage large volumes of digital objects. Though these objects can be stored in a filesystem, there are now a lot of advantages to having them stored inside the database.

Chapter 2, Understanding Digital Objects, will go into detail on each of the different multimedia types and how they work in the real world.

Exercises

These questions are designed to have the reader go beyond the traditional method of answering questions. They involve using the concepts designed in the chapter and doing additional research on the Internet to come up with the best solution to address the questions raised.

1. Name a human sense not included above that can be digitized.

   Can these senses be digitized?

   - ° temperature
   - ° balance
   - ° pain

2. 3D printers can now be used to take CAD designs stored digitally and to print them out. How would a recipe for cooking be digitally stored?

3. How would one store a database in itself?

   What concepts would be required to achieve this?

   How does this relate to the concept of read consistency?

4. The table below shows how the different types of unstructured data can be converted between the different forms. Expand the table to include:

   Which types conversions are one way (information is lost on the conversion, so it's impossible to reverse it).

   Name three other unstructured data types that can be added to the table.

Unstructured data conversion table

From → / To	Photo	Document	Audio	Video	Blueprint	Relational	Neural Network
Photo		OCR. Read textual data from an image. Can be a fax or data on an existing image.	Audio commentary is attached to image.	Multiple photos are combined into a video or animation like a slideshow.	3D imaging such as VRML	Metadata is extracted about the photo (EXIF, IPTC).	Network visualizes and understands the photo.
Document	Pages are scanned in or converted to an image.		Text to speech conversion.	The closest equivalent is animation.	Pages are transformed into 3D virtual book	Metadata is extracted about the document (header).	Network reads and understands the document contents.
Audio	Waveforms of audio turned into an image.	Speech is converted to text.		Audio is streamed as per video.	3D visualization of the audio is created	Metadata is extracted about the audio (ID3).	Network listens and understands the audio file.
Video	A frame is extracted from the video.	Metadata about the video is extracted.	Audio stream is extracted from the video stream.		An animated 3D version of the video is created	Metadata is extracted about the video.	Network views and understands the video.
Blueprint	A scene, icon or screen shot is extracted from the program.	Instructions, manual, code is extracted.	Audio is extracted from the visual structure.	Animation is extracted from the visual structure.		Metadata is extracted.	Network looks at and can interpret the 3D view.
Relational	Data is converted into graphical (see Excel, Reports).	Report is generated.	Data is converted to speech as per document.	Data mining analysis converts to video.	Instructions (similar to SVG) is converted to visual		Network interprets and understands the data.
Neural network	A visual representation of the network is displayed.	Report / documentation about the simulation is produced.	Commentary is given on the simulation.	The simulation is animated.	A VRML representation of the network	Metadata is extracted.	

2
Understanding Digital Objects

This chapter will focus on the definitions and terminologies one frequently encounters when working with digital objects. Multimedia objects such as digital images, audio, and video will be covered, as these are currently the most widely used.

Definitions

All digital objects have a variety of formats and most are compressed or encrypted. This section defines some of the most common characteristics associated with a digital object.

Raw format

When a digital photo is taken, a video is recorded, and a document is scanned, the resulting data stored is referred to as the raw format. Some cameras immediately compress the raw format to save it on a storage. Most videos are immediately compressed, because the storage required – if the raw format was used – would exceed its storage limit. The raw format image is also referred to as the original image. The original should never be changed. If it is modified or transformed, then the resultant changed image should be saved as a derivative.

Compression

Is an algorithm used to encode digital information to reduce its storage size? With the introduction of high megapixel cameras, it's possible for a photo to be over 1 GB in size in its raw format. It's possible for a video to be over 100 GB uncompressed in size. For each media type, there are a large number of compression formats available. Each format aims to compress and saves maximum storage with minimal image quality loss.

Lossy data compression

Lossy compression is a term to indicate that information is lost on compression and decompression. Repeated compression and decompression may result in image degradation. Most algorithms employ data-loss algorithms that are typically found to be imperceptible to human senses. The most well-known lossy compression is the JPEG image compression used by most cameras and was the first popular compression format used in web browsers. The audio MP3 compression will remove data that is beyond the audio frequency range that most people can hear. JPEG and MPEG-4 both use lossy compression.

This compression sacrifices quality for storage. The formats enable a movie to be stored on a DVD. The compression also sacrifices quality for delivery speed. It enables sites, such as YouTube and Hulu to stream large amount of high-quality video over average speed network connections.

In the mid 1990s when Internet bandwidth was very low, lossy compression proved to be very popular for the delivery of images.

There are four main issues with this compression:

- **Long-term archival**: Museums always focus on the future, and they are aware of the variable and changing nature of technology. Even though it might not be cost-effective to store digital objects in their raw format, keeping a small lossy equivalent and destroying the original one will be a long-term issue as information in the image will have been lost. The goal is to not lose information, as in the future, the technology will improve making it easier to store large numbers of digital objects. 5 years ago, a low-cost 3 TB disk was unheard, unlike now, as they are being used commonly. 10 years ago, computer monitors had a resolution that was 800 x 600, now they are three times that resolution enabling high definition viewing. Back then, it took a lot of bandwidth to transfer a original image of 5 MB, and there was a delay in displaying it due to the limitations in the speed of a CPU. The focus was to reduce the size to make it quicker to deliver and faster to display. Now the same original image can be downloaded in seconds and displayed instantly. Today downloading a HD video can take an hour or longer and so has to be compressed to enable it to be downloaded and viewed quickly. In 10 years' time with anticipated improvements in broadband speed and CPU speed, mobile devices will be able to routinely download and play HD video in real time. This is why, it's important not to destroy the original and replace it with a compressed format.

- **Legal**: In a court case, if a digital object is used as evidence, then it's important that object has not been modified or tampered with. Software is now available to test if an image has been edited using Adobe Photoshop (commonly referred to as being photoshopped)[1]. Lossy compression effectively changes the image, and even though it looks like the original, it is not the original image. It cannot be trusted.

- **Medical**: Small sections on a digital image can be crucial for a diagnosis when looking at digital X-ray. If information is lost on compression, then the doctors analyzing the image will not be able to trust what they see. Is that blur or slight shadow on the image a result of a tumor or due to information lost when the image was compressed? The information shown in a medical image has to be accurate, and there should be no lost information.

- **Compression and decompression times**: It can take a lot of CPU time to compress a digital object. Most compression algorithms aim to have faster decompression times than compression times. In the case of a video, it's possible that a high-speed CPU is used for the compression, but the computer that plays it might have a low-speed CPU. Also, if a mobile device has a battery, then the less CPU involved in decompression, the less likelihood it will drain the battery, resulting in the mobile device being able to play the video. This is an important business directive, and the market has clearly shown that mobile devices that have a longer battery life and can play most video formats are more popular and easier to sell. The MPEG format can employ variable compression where an operator can choose which scenes have stronger compression compared to other scenes.

Lossless data compression

Is there a term to indicate that compressing and then decompressing results in no data loss? Compression algorithms that use lossless are typically not as efficient as a lossy one. Some TIF compression formats are lossless. The JPEG-2000 compression standards enable both lossy and lossless compression.

Lossless compression algorithms can be broken down into ones that are designed to look for repetitive patterns and ones that are designed to look for structures within a digital image. Additionally, some algorithms are designed to look for differences between images or frames (such as video), but generally these ones fall into the lossy category.

The traditional lossless compression algorithms used were initially designed for text. They could achieve very large compression on them, especially, if they contained a lot of blank space or similar-based character sets. When applied to icons with a small color range, they worked quite well and were adopted in them (GIF is a good example), but do not work well for digital photos or videos, as the characters are binary-based and generally appear random. When fractal geometry is applied, only then can patterns be seen. These initial compress algorithms include:

- ZIP
- Gzip
- RAR
- TAR

In most cases, when a digital image of JPEG format is zipped, it might become slightly bigger than the original. Zipping a set of JPEG images is only useful when compression is disabled, and all that is done is to group the files together into one larger file for easier distribution.

Codec

A codec is a device or computer program capable of encoding or decoding a digital data stream or signal. Audio and video files contain streams of data. They are encoded and decoded using a codec. For video, there is an audio codec and a video codec, which are two separate data streams.

A codec can be lossless or lossy. A codec can also be used to decrypt an encrypted format.

Containor

A container or wrapper format is a metafile format, whose specification describes how different data elements and metadata coexist in a computer file. Video formats, such as MPG (.mpg), Flash (.flv), and AVI (.avi) are containers, meaning that the compression formats they use can vary. It is possible for two files of MPG type to use completely different audio and video compression algorithms. TIF is also a container and uses a number of different compression algorithms.

The goal of a container is to simplify and hide the complexity of the codec from the user. An AVI video is a container, and it supports a large number of audio and video codecs within it. A TIF digital image is a container. It supports a variety of encoding algorithms within it. In both these cases, the user only has to deal with the the fact that the digital objects is a TIF or AVI. The Flash (.flv) is now a container, as it supports both the flash codec and the MPEG codec.

Most of these digital image and video formats were not designed to be containers. Most evolved this way to encompass new technology while providing backwards compatibility support for the older codecs. The file extension one sees for a digital image or video might not necessarily be indicative as to what codec was used to encode it.

The DCOM digital object format is not a container.

Understanding each image type

When looking at the different types of digital images, it becomes apparent that there is a lot more to understanding them. Each has different characteristics and capabilities, which when well understood can add a new depth to their usage. This section covers those features.

Photo

A photo is a two-dimensional representation of anything — also referred to as a digital image. A photo can be taken with a digital camera or it can be scanned in. It is composed of pixels, where each pixel represents information, typically a color. The more pixels that are able to be compacted together, the higher the resolution of the display. The iPhone 4 introduced a display format, where the pixel format is so tightly compacted that the human eye cannot discern the pixels, making it appear as true color (which represents all the colors the human eye can see). The goal is to produce displays that are true colors.

Displaying pixels on a computer screen is a completely different process to printing a photo on paper. Paper does not use the concept of a pixel, and combining different colors on a computer screen produces different results when printing (see *Color space* later).

Icon

An icon is also a two-dimensional representation of anything. It is created manually and not scanned in or photographed. Its format is simpler and can be stored uncompressed (bitmap) or compressed using an algorithm that is lossless. The two most common formats are GIF and PNG. An icon is generally used for screen display and is also used to help with navigation, to convey information, or represent a digital object. An icon can be used to visually represent an audio file.

Color space

A color space is used to define how a color is digitally represented.

Colors when printed to paper are represented as **CMYK (cyan, magenta, yellow, and black)**. Newspapers and photo labs use CMYK to combine the inks and print the image. Color printers include a three-tone color cartridge and black to cover the range of all visible colors.

Computer display screens cannot use CMYK for display. They use **RGB (red, green, blue)** to cover the range of colors. Cathode ray tube screens, LCD screens, or ones using LEDs all use the RGB format, as when they are combined in different amounts they can cover the whole visible light spectrum.

One key goal of a color space is to ensure consistency in picture display across devices. As different electronic devices use different methods for emitting color, the idea of the color space is to ensure when a color is displayed, it represents as closely as possible the true color.

Color calibration

Even though a color space[2] is used, there is no true way to calibrate the image with the color. There is no sure way to guarantee that the color you see on the electronic device is the correct color. When you have gone to an electronic store to buy a television, you can easily see all the different monitors. Each one displays the same picture with a different brightness or color hue. This shows how easy it is to separate colors that are similar to the light spectrum.

One method for addressing this is *Windows Color System*[3], which is a model that extends the color space and takes into account the characteristics of the display device and can adjust the color to better match it.

The simplest and traditional method is to embed a color chart into the image. The chart is a set of color boxes that are included in the picture. On viewing the picture, the photographer can then visually adjust the color balance to match what the expected colors are. Some photo management tools can automatically adjust the balance by detecting the color chart.

The disadvantage of a color chart is that it is visibly seen on the image. Most organizations will take two pictures. One with the color chart embedded in it, and one without the embed. The assumption being that by adjusting the colors using the photo with the color chart in it, this can also be applied to the photo taken without the color chart.

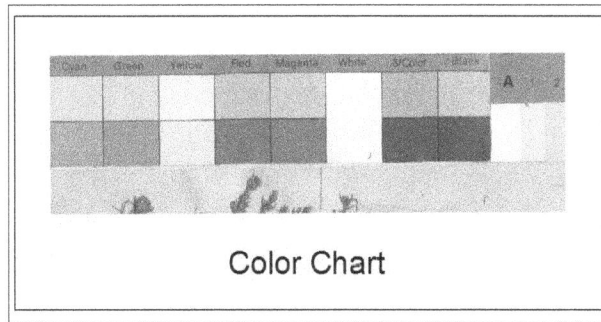

Color Chart

Different products use different color spaces when storing digital images. The color space is stored embedded in the image. With changes in technology, the color space itself can be updated to handle the new technology. The most common is the RGB color space. A variation called *sRGB*[4] is now being extensively used, as it is designed for home and office viewing.

The RGB color model family

With RGB, 3 bytes are typically used to store one pixel of information. Each byte represents a number. A byte equals 8 bits, which represents 256 values. Each of the RGB values are referred to as a channel or a triplet. The combination of these three values enables 16,777,216 colors to be displayed (256 x 256 x 256). In some color spaces, 2 bytes or 16 bits can be stored. This doubles the size of the image but enables a greater color range to be stored. A 16-bit number enables 65,535 different values.

- **RGB**[5]: All of the RGB color spaces are additive, meaning that by combining the light emanating from a color element, they can achieve the colors in the light spectrum.

- **sRGB**[6]: Is color space designed by companies including Microsoft and Hewlett Packard? The goal was to ensure the colors presented on a computer screen in most typical home and work environments matched correctly. It is now the most popular color space and used in the display of most JPEG images one finds on the Internet.

- **Adobe RGB**[7]: Is a color space that closely matches CMYK ensuring the color on the screen matches the one that is printed out on a color printer? This is important for photographers, who provide a visual and printed copy of photos. This includes photo laboratories, portrait, and wedding photographers. It is also referred to as Adobe RGB 98.

- **ProPhoto RGB**[8]: Is a color space designed to handle all possible color combinations occurring in the real world? It can even include colors that are not visible. The recommendation when using it is to use 16 bits rather than 8 bits to store the RGB values.

Viewing colors

It must be pointed out that with the improvements in technology for taking images and devices for displaying them, there is a drive to try and have a system that truly matches real-life colors. The problem is that this is an impossible goal to achieve. All that can be achieved is to match the colors at the exact time the photo was taken.

Cloud color, time of day, and shadows can change the color display of any real-world object. Also, people view colors differently. It is estimated that between 1 to 10 percent of the male population exhibits some form of color-blindness. With females, it less than 0.3 percent[9]. Color perception and sensitivity can also change overtime. It can be impacted by glasses or any eye wear.

Though being color-blind might be considered to be a deficiency, it is now realized that, in some cases, there is an advantage[10]. A person who exhibits some form of color-blindness will not be able to see or discern a difference between a photo using sRGB or ProPhoto RGB. The desire to match colors exactly to the real world is not a driving concern.

The strong desire to exactly match viewed colors to the real world can be seen as an impractical aspiration and one in which the rewards and time spent in trying to achieve that match, can only be appreciated by a tiny fraction of the world population, who have the color sensitivity to see it. A similar argument was and still is raised with listening to a digital CD versus listening to the same music being played on Vinyl. Those with a well-trained ear and not suffering from any form of hearing impairment can, when the music is played on a vinyl-playing system that is of high quality with exceptional speakers, be able to discern a difference to the one being played on a CD. The conclusion is that the Vinyl system is better, because no information is lost, whereas the CD in the digitization process has lost information.

The question is not whether one is better, but whether it's cost effective to attempt to achieve this level of accuracy when only a small percentage of the population, when focused, can truly tell there is a difference. The analogy of Don Quixote is tilting at windmills[11] seems apt for those intent on achieving a 100-percent color match of the image displayed to the one appearing in the real world.

As covered in *Chapter 3, The Multimedia Warehouse* the multimedia environment is not the one designed to be exact. It is fuzzy. It's full of scenarios where things do not match correctly or can be interpreted differently.

Though it is a worthwhile goal to achieve a view of the digital object that exactly matches the real world, the more realistic and cost-effective goal is to achieve the one that very closely matches it, the one in which the vast majority of the population viewing it will not be able to discern any difference.

Printing using the CMYK colorspace

CMYK[12] is referred to as a subtractive color model. Unlike RGB, in which colors are added together to achieve the color spectrum, with CMYK, the brightness is subtracted to achieve the desired color. By adding more colors together, the resultant color becomes darker. In RGB, the opposite happens. The more colors added, the greater the tendency there is to move to a white color. CMYK coloring occurs when real-world ink or dyes are added together. Black is added because when used it saves on ink. To achieve black, otherwise, would require adding the CMY colors together.

An image encoded using the RGB color space needs to be recoded into CMYK to enable it to be printed. As covered, the Adobe RGB color space is designed to make this translation with minimal errors.

Other color spaces

The are the color spaces:

- **YIQ**[13]: This color space is designed for NTSC TVs. These are the ones used in North and Central America.

- **YpbPr**[14]: This color space is also designed for TVs. The goal was to separate the colors out into separate cables. It only had a use for analog systems, as digital systems transfer the information using bits rather than waves.

- **YCbCr**[15]: This color space is the digital equivalent of YpbPr and is designed for taking an RGB signal, making it more efficient for transferring TV signals.

- **LAB**[16]: This color space is found in TIF images and is designed to approximate human vision. Its focus is more on the perception of lightness. It was originated before RGB and was used extensively in the 1990s, as there was no loss in quality in the color of the image, unlike RGB, which had an 8-bit limitation on the color range. With 16-bit RGB support, the requirement for using the LAB color space has diminished and is now typically found in archaic images.

Little endian and big endian

When digital images are stored, numbers are routinely used to represent values in those images. This can be a pixel color or the instructions for drawing a rectangle. In documents, we are used to storing numbers in their character format. How those numbers are read in, from left-hand side to right-hand side or right-hand side to left-hand side, is referred to as endian. A detailed description is covered in *Appendix E, Loading and Reading*, which can be downloaded from link given in the *Preface*.

The Intel CPU uses little endian, whereas the Motorola and SPARC CPU use big endian. This means that for some image formats, copying them between environments with different CPUs can effectively corrupt the format. Fortunately, this doesn't happen as the number stored in each image format is locked into little or big endian in its core specification, and the CPU used is taken out of the equation. The JPEG and PNG formats always use big endian. The TIF image format indicates within the header whether little or big endian is used, and the program used to decode it has to handle the byte conversion accordingly[17].

Digital image storage formats

Digital image formats can be broken down into the following:

- **Raster graphics**[18]: These graphics are also referred to as a bitmap. An image is represented as a set of pixels typically in a rectangular structure with a width and height. Each pixel represents a color and can be stored using multiple bytes.

- **Vector graphics**[19]: These graphics create an image using a set of instructions (mathematical expressions). These can include points, lines, curves, shapes, text, and polygons—the most well-known format is SVG. Creating shapes in Microsoft PowerPoint, Adobe Illustrator, or figures in OpenOffice Draw can be stored using vector graphics.

Raster graphics formats

The following is a simplified table containing commonly used digital image file formats. Over time, each format has grown to handle different characteristics and capabilities. The GIF format can handle animation. There are exceptions to the rules for each format. A GIF is typically limited to 256 colors but can support a transparent color enabling the image to blend in with the background

Format	Compression method/ encoding	Metadata	Max image size	Natively supported in browsers	Lossy	Lossless	Natively supported in Oracle Multimedia
JPEG[20]	JFIF	EXIF, XMP	65k x 65k	Y	Y	Limited	Y
GIF[21]	LZW	Free-form comments	65k x 65k	Y	N	Y	Y
PNG[22]	DEFLATE (zlib)	Key, value pairs	2G x 2G	Y	N	Y	Y
TIFF[23]	None, Huffman, PackBits	IPTC, EXIF, XMP	4G x 4G	N	Y	Y	Y

Format	Compression method/ encoding	Metadata	Max image size	Natively supported in browsers	Lossy	Lossless	Natively supported in Oracle Multimedia
BMP[24]	Huffman, RLE	none	2G x 2G	N	N	Y	Y
PSD[25]	RLE	IPTC, XMP, EXIF	30k x 30k (but can be larger)	N	N	Y	N
EPS	TIF, PICT	none	As for TIFF	N	N	Y	N
PPM[26]/ PGM/ PBM	None	none	Greater than 65k x 65k	N	N	Y	Y
TGA	None, RLE compression	Textual	32k x 32k	N	N	Y	Y
JP2[27]	Wavelet	EXIF, XMP	Greater than 65k x 65k	N	Y	Y	N
MrSID[28]	Wavelet	XML	Greater than 65k x 65k	N	N	Y	N
CALS	None, CCITT group 4	Proprietary structure called TextFileId.	Six numeric characters by six numeric characters	N	N	Y	Y
FPIX	Tiling	EXIF, XMP	65k x 65k	N	Y	N	Y
PCX	Run length encoding	None	65k x 65k	N	N	Y	Y

The following table includes information about the various formats:

Format	Details
JPEG	**Joint Photographic Experts Group (JPEG)** was formulated in 1986 and released in 1992. It uses lossy compression and was designed for photos achieving compression ratios of 20:1 or even higher (with visible image degradation). Over time, the standard has evolved enabling thumbnails to be stored inside the image, as well as a variety of metadata.
	As an open standard, it has been accepted by the Internet-driven camera manufacturers who natively support the format in their camera, enabling images to be easily transferred to the Internet. Simple cameras embedded in mobile devices usually only support JPEG. High-spec cameras enable the image to be stored in a proprietary format, TIF, and JPEG, giving users the choice for image delivery.
	The format is so well-known and supported that most photo display devices, ones found in TVs, PVRs, and even LCD keystrings, all use the JPEG image format.
GIF	**Graphics Interchange Format (GIF)** was first formulated in 1987 and has a built-in limit of 256 colors for the display. The compression used is very simple, and in the early days of the Internet, its popularity grew due to its ability to easily store icons. When a patent was raised and all companies using it required a license, its usage on the Internet was replaced with PNG, which had no patent issues. Though the patent has, since, expired its acceptance was questioned, and the user community adopted PNG, which was natively supported in the browser. The GIF format is not designed for photos.
PNG	**Portable Network Graphics (PNG)** is an image format that uses lossless compression and became more popular when the license issues with the GIF format appeared. With browser makers readily adopting PNG support and the ability for PNG to compress as good as or better than PNG, its usage increased rapidly. Though PNG can also display photos, its compression of approximately 10:1 is not as good as JPEG's compression of 20:1. The PNG format is mostly limited to icon and animation display.

Format	Details
TIFF	**Tagged Image File Format (TIF)** is currently owned by Adobe. Though a proprietary standard, its popularity came about with the massive increase in use and acceptance of the premium photo editing tool, Adobe Photoshop. The format enabled metadata to be embedded in the image, and over time, the format changed to become a container. This enabled it to support a variety of other formats and compression natively within it. As, over time, other manufacturers increased support for TIF as a storage format in their products, its usage become more popular as one for digital image transfer without data loss (whereas, JPEG is a lossy format). Though TIFF supports compression, its ability to compress never competed with JPEG. Even though plugins for viewing TIFF are available, most organizations prefer to store their originals in a TIFF for distribution and then create a JPEG for viewing. The TIFF format supports both, little endian and big endian, within it, which made it ideal as a cross platform digital image format. This again resulted in its popularity with photographers, as TIFF files could be created on any device including Windows, Macintosh, Linux, and Solaris.
BMP	**Bitmap Format (BMP)** is well-known as a storage format for Windows icons. It's used by Windows Paintbrush program and is not designed for digital photos; it is designed more for desktop icons. The format is simple and initially could only handle a small range of colors. Recent enhancements to the standard allow it to handle most colors (referred to as true color). The standard also supports compression.
PSD	**Photoshop Document (PSD)** is the format used by Adobe Photoshop. The format enables most color spaces to be stored within it, as well as additional information. Used extensively by most photographers, the format is widely used and treated as the master or original image, with JPEG or TIFF version being derived from it. The format is proprietary but is well-documented at the Adobe site.
EPS	**Encapsulated Postscript (EPS)** is an extension to Postscript, enabling it to handle graphics. Postscript is a language used extensively when printing, and it focuses on font control. When printing, most applications convert the output into Postscript before sending it to the printer. With EPS, digital images can be converted to TIF and then printed. EPS is used by Adobe Illustrator, and some applications enable the output from a printer to be saved in EPS format.
PPM / PGM / PBM	**Portable Pixel Map (PPM)** is a color image format that is considered to be a common or base format. It is used when converting between different formats. The image is converted to PPM and then converted from PPM to the other format. The format is used extensively by ImageMagick. The format is not efficient and stores a lot of redundant information.

Format	Details
TGA	It is a raster format that was developed in 1987. It was designed for standard TV screens and had the ability to represent true colors within it (up to 32 bits per pixel).
JP2	JPEG 2000 was designed as a future replacement for JPEG. In addition to its ability to compress better than JPEG, it also offered lossless compression, making it ideal for sites that did not want to lose information when storing their digital images. Due to a possible hidden patent in it, its acceptance was put on hold. Like GIF and other digital image formats, their acceptance and usage in browsers is limited if they are not open source and/or have any potential licensing/patent issues on them.
MrSID	This format which came out in the mid 1990s used a lossless wavelet compression. It offered compression ratios of 22:1, which is better than JPEG. By integrating with an image server, high-resolution images could be quickly retrieved with the ability to zoom in to greater detail on the image. The key strength of wavelet compression is that parts of the image can be decompressed without having to decompress the whole image. Though the technology is easily available, it is not open source, which limits its usage to specialized installation.
CALS	It is developed by Computer Aided Acquisition and Logistics Supports (US Defence)[29]. It is designed to be used with the exchange of documents across different platforms. As its been mandated to be supported by US Defence, its use has extended to many software developers to ensure compliance. Internally, there are two formats, with the header being in text to make it easy to understand when looking at the raw image.
FPIX	**FlashPix (FPIX)**[30] is a format that contains multiple resolutions of the same image. The goal is to overcome the requirement to pass down a large image when only a small one is needed. The calling program sends the screen resolution requirements and only the resolution that matches within the FPIX image is returned. So, the FPIX digital image might be quite large (containing a variety of resolutions), but only the smaller, correct size is sent to the web browser. It was developed by Kodak with assistance from Microsoft and Hewlett Packard.
PCX	It is an old format whose development originated in a product called PC Paintbrush from ZSoft[31]. It became popular on DOS and then was used in Windows. It uses a color palette similar to a GIF for mapping pixels to colors. It compresses images but is designed for low-resolution graphics or animation.
RPIX	**Raw Pixel (RPIX)**, is a format designed by Oracle for translation. Similar in concept to PPM, the goal is to store the digital image in a raw uncompressed format, which can then be easily referenced by other external applications.
RASF	Sun Raster[33] image format is designed by Sun for use on the Solaris platform. The format is still widely used on Oracle Sun[32].

Raw

The JPEG 2000 image compression was touted as being the standard that would replace JPEG. It could compress better, it offered lossless compression, error resilience, and progressive transmission. The format looked promising until it was pointed out that there is an undeclared and obscure submarine patent in it. This effectively killed its use, as companies would not utilize it if there was a legal risk or potential licensing and cost issue that might appear years down the track (exactly what happened with GIF). An open source standard would have resulted in the usage of JPEG 2000, and web browser builders would have included it in all the browsers. Unfortunately, this didn't happen and the result was that camera manufacturers started to work on their own image storage formats for their cameras. Each one was touted as being the next standard. The result were a sort of new proprietary formats that camera manufacturer started to use. Adobe pushed its own standard DNG, and this one seems to be leading the group as the most popular raw image format.

The idea behind having a raw format is to be able to have a format, where the original is not modified. The original is the exact picture that was taken. Additional smarts might be included in the raw format to enable easier changes in color spaces, fix blurry images, and correct for common issues such as red eye. The following are some of the more common raw formats available:

- **Adobe Digital Negative (DNG)**
- **Nikon Electronic Format (NEF)**
- **Kodak Digital Camera Format (DCR)**
- **Olympus Digital Camera Format (ORF)**

Vector graphics

Vector graphic formats do not use pixels for storage. Instead, they instructions for how to draw the image. This makes the image scalable and is used for drawing and designing, especially three-dimensional graphics. The following are some of the more popular formats:

- **Scalable Vector Graphics (SVG)**
- **Computer Aided Design (CAD)**
- **Drawing Exchange Format (DXF)** – CAD format used to enable interoperability between different products
- **DraWinG (DWG)** – CAD format used for three-dimensional design

Audio

Audio encompasses the capturing and storage of sound over a period of time. The following describes some of the key attributes one will come across when dealing with audio.

Bit rate

Bit rate is a number of bits of data conveyed in a unit of time, typically per second. Format is usually expressed as bits per second. Note that 8 bits make a byte, so the bit rate is usually a lot less than the interpreted value, which might be confused with bytes per second.

For MP3, the bit rate is expressed in kilobits per second. The lower the bit rate, the more noticeable the loss in quality of the audio file:

- 64 to 96 kbit/s is the quality of an FM radio signal
- 128 to 192 kbit/s is DVD quality
- 224 to 320 kbit/s is high-quality audio storage

Encoding

This is the codec used for compressing the audio stream. Common formats include MP3, 3GP, AIFF, ASF, and WAV.

Channels

This is a single track or audio stream. Multiple channels are combined to create stereo. The more channels, the greater the perceived depth of the audio track. A channel can also hold a separate audio track to the main one.

Video

Video encompasses the capturing and storage of visual information and optionally sound over a period of time. The following describes some of the key attributes one will come across when dealing with video.

Frame

A frame is a single digital image taken from within the video. A frame is a treated as the lowest common denominator in a video. Using the old film cell (that is equivalent to a frame) is exactly one cell.

Frame resolution

Frame resolution is the width by height in pixels of the video image. Different video standards have different resolutions. There can be a large variation in width by height supported for different mediums. TV quality is approximately 640 x 480 pixels, DVD is around 720 x 575 pixels, and HD can be either 1280 x 720 or 1920 x 1080.

Frame aspect ratio

Frame aspect ratio is the ratio of the width by height of the frame resolution. The two most common formats are 16:9 (wide screen) or 4:3 (TV screen). Converting a video from 4:3 to 16:9 will result in image distortion and might require cropping to remove the distortion.

Frame rate

Frame rate is the number of frames displayed per second. The more frames shown, the smoother the picture appears to the human eye. The higher the frame rate, the higher the storage requirement, as more information is required to display the video.

Progressive scan versus interlaced

Interlaced was designed for cathode ray tube screens. It breaks up the screen into horizontal lines and alternatively displays one line and then the other. This can result in a flickering effect. Progressive scan displays the horizontal lines in sequence offering a sharper picture. Progressive scan is used extensively in LCD monitors.

Codecs/containers

The following section covers some of the more popular video codecs used in the marketplace today:

- **Moving Picture Experts Group (MPEG)**: It's an open standard designed for the compression of video. The MPEG format can be considered to be a container, as it supports a variety of codecs. Each one has attributes well suited to compress different video sizes.

  - MPEG-1 was designed for compression of low-quality video on DVD.

  - MPEG-2 was designed for digital TV broadcast.

  - MPEG-3 was merged with MPEG-2 and is not the same as the audio MP3.

- ○ MPEG-4[34] is designed for video that uses high-quality graphics. The format is used by Blu-ray. It's an incredibly robust and adaptable format used in a variety of applications. MPEG-4 Part 10 matches the H.264 standard. MPEG-4 Part 12 and 14 is better known as MP4, which is a format suited for Internet streaming, especially streaming to small devices. An earlier version was used on mobile phones and had a .3gp extension.

- **Audio Video Interleave** (**AVI**): It is a container managed by Microsoft and was first crafted in 1992. The original codecs used within it are not supported any more. The format can now use MPEG and Real Video. As AVI is an old format, it suffers from limitations that have naturally restricted it as technology changes. Issues with aspect ratio, variable frame rate and bit rate means that even though codecs such as MPEG-4 can be used within the AVI container, their usage is restricted.

- **H.264**: It is a codec accepted for the use on Blu-ray discs. Its standard overlaps with MPEG-4 Part 10, and the two are kept in sync. Its popularity grew, because it was efficient in compression and flexible in what it could compress. With support from Google and Apple and now with native support of the format in Firefox and Chrome browsers, the acceptance of its usage is growing.

- **Real Player** :It is a format that dominated the market because of its capability to stream video. It's managed by the company Real Networks. The product used a streaming video server (which could integrate with Oracle) enabling real-time streaming capabilities of video. The format is a container but originally supported two codecs, one for audio and one for video. They were recognized by the .ra and .rv file extensions. Since then the container has been enhanced to support the MPEG, Flash, and Microsoft formats.

- **Flash Video**: This format became popular as the Adobe Flash Player gained popularity. The video format could be embedded in a Flash SWF enabling applications to easily create interfaces with embedded video. With the rise in popularity of YouTube, which natively supported Flash, it looked like its format would dominate the video market. With the gain in popularity of Apple and its refusal to use Flash, the container was enhanced to support H.264.

Issues when converting

When converting video between different formats, the following issues need to be addressed:

- **Frame resolution**: Most formats have limits in the width and height they support. It might not be possible to convert one format directly to the other if that other format doesn't support the frame resolution. In this case, the video might need to be converted to an intermediate format before being finally converted.

- **Frame rate**: It might not be possible to go from a video with a lower frame to one with a higher frame rate. There might not be enough information available. In some cases, frames can be repeated to increase the frame rate.

- **Audio**: For video with supporting audio, the codec used with the audio might not be supported in the video format its being converted to. In this case, the audio codec will need to be converted.

Documents

A document is primarily a set of text based on a character set optionally grouped into pages. A document can contain audio, video, and digital images. There are a large number of document formats in existence. Oracle has an indexing feature called Oracle Text, which can index and enable sophisticated searches to be performed against the documents using a structure embedded in a SQL statement.

Terminology

Though there over 3,000 document formats available in the market, the predominate number of document types fall into the following products.

PDF

Is a format supported by Adobe that was originally designed to be an open standard for document exchange. The goal being that when organizations and individuals pass a document around, they will convert it to PDF first. It became an open standard in 2008 and has been accepted and used extensively in the market place. Most browsers support PDF for display. PDF is also now considered secure and unlikely to contain a virus or Trojan within it.

In most cases, the PDF document when converted is read-only, but it is possible to create a PDF document that enables data to be entered into it; this is like a form. PDF supports images to be embedded in it and can be used primarily as a method for transferring digital images between sites.

A PDF document can be encrypted and digitally signed to ensure it's authentic. The number of pages within a PDF can be easily extracted. Metadata can also be stored in either a name, value pair, or using XMP.

The Oracle Database does not internally support the conversion of an existing document or image to PDF. The database can extract an HTML version of the document, as well as a summary using the Oracle Text index. There are third-party PL/SQL tools available that can create a PDF file using a combination of routines to build up the base PDF document.

DOC/DOCX

This is the Microsoft format for document storage. DOCX is the later XML version designed to be open and conform to the ISO/IEC 29500 Strict standard. The two formats together are dominant in the market place and used in a large number of sites.

ODT

Open Document (ODT)[35] is originally developed by Sun and used in the OpenOffice product set. It is XML-based and conforms to the ISO/IEC 26300:2006 standard.

TXT

This is any digital file containing just characters. There is no structure in the text file unless defined by the author. There is an ambiguity concerning when a text file ends and a structured document begins. A text file can contain XML. A text file can contain multi-part mime attachments. A text file can contain CSV data as well as HTML characters.

The common feature of a text file is that it can be opened up in a text editor such as Windows Notepad or Unix: vi Editor and viewed and edited in a meaningful fashion.

Transformation

The Oracle Database supports the indexing and ability to summarize most document formats. The database does not offer any abilities to transform, edit, or convert the documents. It's not possible to convert a DOCX file to PDF. Though you can convert the document formats to HTML, there is no support for the extraction of an image or other digital objects embedded within them. Oracle also does not support the transformation of an individual page into a JPEG image (for thumbnail display). Some of these capabilities are obtained by integrating OpenOffice and its batch manipulation routine.

Digital object composition

A digital object can be thought of as just more than just one single image. It can actually become a complex structure in its own right, even growing to the point of having its own hierarchical structure.

The starting base – NULL object

There are two types of digital objects within Oracle that could be classified as NULL.

A NULL value can have numerous meanings, but in the relational world, a NULL value is one which is unknown and not just blank. A number that is NULL can be considered to be zero, but a true NULL value is one that is unknown and has the potential to be any value.

When it comes to dealing with objects, an object can be created and just given the value NULL.

```
myimage ORDSYS.ORDIMAGE
...
begin
myimage := NULL;
```

An object can also be initialized as a composite, meaning its object structure is set up. As an object can be composed of multiple types, the initializing involves setting up the individual values.

```
myimage ORDSYS.ORDIMAGE
...
begin
 myimage := ORDSYS.ORDIMAGE.init();
```

This is the equivalent of performing the following code:

```
myimage ORDSYS.ORDIMAGE
...
begin
 myimage := ORDSYS.ORDImage(ORDSYS.ORDSource(empty_blob(), NULL,NULL,N
ULL,SYSDATE,1),NULL,NULL,NULL,NULL,NULL,NULL,NULL);
```

Most of the subtypes are set to NULL, but some can be given default values. Though from an object-oriented perspective, the two cases are intrinsically separate, they still raise the issue of when an object is truly NULL. This book will not take up that point, as it is distracting from looking at the issue of treating a digital object.

The focus of a digital object is the unstructured data within it. This could be multimedia or some future structure yet to be determined. The metadata around the object just supports it and helps define it for now. It is realistic in the future that a digital object will not need any metadata, as the digital object itself will contain sufficient information to define it. The metadata can be seen to be like an indexing structure, which is there to improve performance and to make it easier for someone to find the digital object. It is there as a supporting structure. It is not the digital object.

So, the NULL case for a digital object can now be raised. It's an initialized object structure that might have metadata but does not yet have unstructured data associated with it. The NULL case is one that says that this digital object has the potential to take any value. It could be a photo, an audio file, a video, a text file, or many of these.

It's important to put the focus on the unstructured data that could be contained within the digital object and not the data (referred to as metadata) that supports it.

The original image

Most digital objects start with an original image. This is the core image. All other images attached effectively are to accompany or support it. The original can be a photo, an audio file, a video, or any unstructured data of any size.

> The original image is never modified. Derivatives can be created from it, and the image can be indexed.

As with all digital objects, there are exceptions to the rule as to what the digital object is and how can it become fuzzy. Once a camera takes a **DNG (Digital Negative)**, the original is never modified. The exception comes when modifications that the photographer makes to the image are stored; they are just stored as changed data within the original. So the original might be changed and enhanced, but behind the scenes, all that is stored is the original with the change vectors stored separately. On accessing the DNG, the original raw image is opened and all changes are then applied. So even though the original DNG is not modified, the actual DNG file is modified, as the change vectors effectively result in the core file being changed.

Indexed digital object

The goal of indexing a digital object is to improve performance. A traditional index found in relational databases will improve performance when searching and performing queries. In some cases, an index can be used to enforce referential integrity (enforcement of the primary key).

With an index on a digital object, the goal is to improve retrieval or delivery time. A digital object can be quite large, whereas a relational record is typically small. The time to retrieve a 10 MB of digital photo can be in seconds or minutes depending on the network speed. If a user was displaying a page with 100 digital objects shown on it, with each one being shown smaller (less pixels) to enable all of them to be viewed on the screen, then the total download could be 100 x 10 MB or 1 GB. Scale this up to 100 concurrent users and most networks (even internal ones) will be struggling to deliver the images. Add on top of it that public sites can pay for a cost for download (for example, Amazon charge a fixed rate per GB retrieved), and it becomes obvious that retrieving the original of the digital object is not cost-effective.

The important point to stress here, which is the key for scalability and differentiates the unstructured database from the relational one, is that the focus for tuning is heavily around the speed of delivery, not the speed to perform a query.

Pyramid index

For a number of digital objects, scalability is achieved via a pyramid index. In the traditional index, a thumbnail is created, which is a much smaller version of the original. For audio and video, this thumbnail can also be referred to as a snippet. The thumbnail can vary in size. For a digital image, it can be between 80 and 140 pixels in length. It can be created just by shrinking or reducing the image. For organizations that have varying sized images, they can create a postcard thumbnail. This is one where a key area of the image that best portrays the information in it is cropped out and then shrunk down in size. A thumbnail will typically be between 1 k and 10 k in size.

Using the previous example, if a user now requests 100 images, and if each thumbnail is 10 k in size, this means that only 1 MB of data is delivered. This is a major improvement.

The pyramid index takes one or more (there is no limit) reduced, cropped, or resized images of the original and enables those to be delivered to the user on request. This enables the user to effectively zoom in and view larger details of the original.

The pyramid index can become quite sophisticated and hundreds of variations of the image can be created at different resolutions, each smaller than the original. When it is set up correctly, it allows the user to quickly zoom in to different areas of the digital image without ever downloading the original.

As with any index, performance is gained at the expense of storage, and the more sophisticated the pyramid index, the more storage is required. For most organizations, having a two-level structure is sufficient. This involves creating a thumbnail and web quality image. The web quality is a larger version of thumbnail that is created for optimal viewing on most computer screens. The web quality is typically 600 pixels and between 100 k to 1 MB in size.

For a video object, the snippet might be of a low-quality extract by 10 seconds of a key scene within the video itself, while the web quality equivalent might be a 60-second extract (or compilation) at a slightly higher quality. Movie trailers would be classified as being part of the pyramid index. A video object might also have digital image thumbnails representing it as well as the snippets. The digital image thumbnail might be of a key scene, while the web quality would be the snippet.

Each digital object type has its own characteristics and methods for what the thumbnail is and how it should be represented. A document might have a thumbnail being a digital image of the first page, or it could be an abstract covering what the document is about.

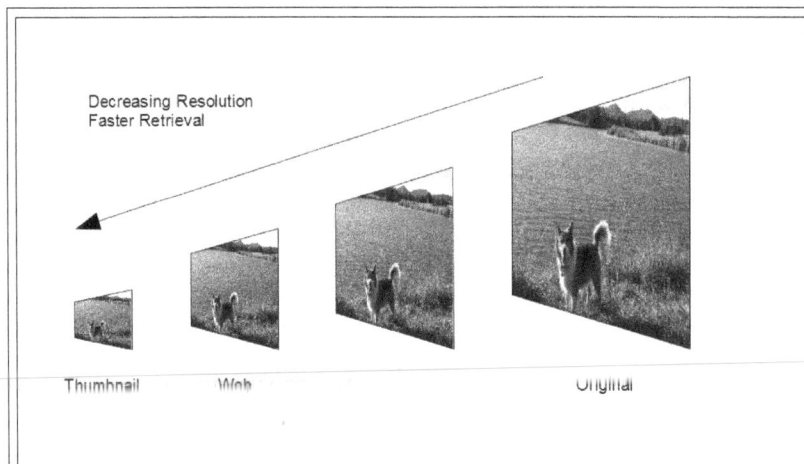

Derivatives

A derivative is a digital object that has been transposed, transformed, compressed, and/or converted for the purposes of digital image delivery. An indexed image such as a thumbnail is created for the purpose of performance. One or more derivatives can be created. For a digital image, it could be an image that has attributes that make it ideal for being embedded in a PowerPoint. Another one could be created with a CMYK color space embedded in it to make it suitable for printing. For a digital video, a derivative might be one with a h264+ codec and another with an MPEG-4 codec. For a document, a PDF derivative could be created.

In some cases, the derivative and indexed image can overlap. A high-quality web digital image could be used for image delivery.

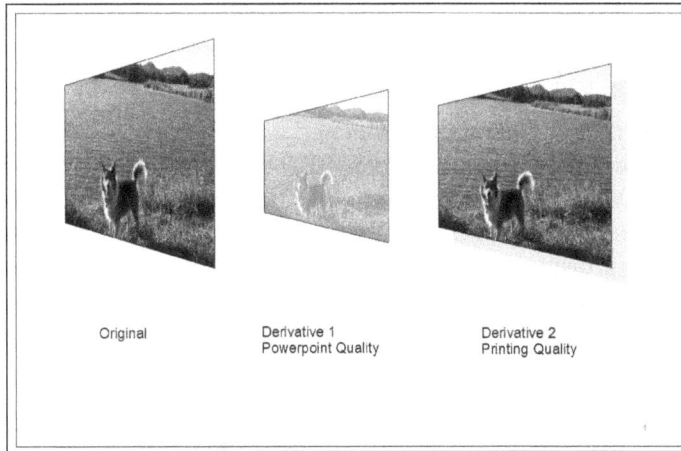

Original

Derivative 1
Powerpoint Quality

Derivative 2
Printing Quality

Masters

A digital object might be a digital photo of a vase. The object itself represents the vase. Multiple digital photos might be taken of the vase from different angles. Each one of these is referred to as a master. One of these can be marked as the representative master, and from it, the thumbnail presented to the user is the one shown. There is no limit to the number of masters a digital object has. A master can also have many derivatives. This can result in a digital object having a large number of digital images contained within it.

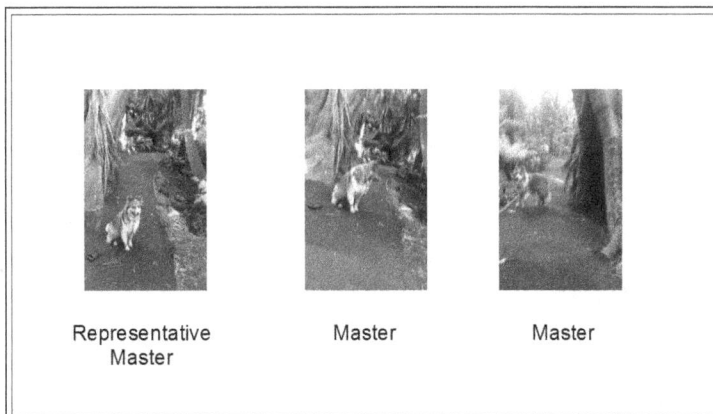

Representative
Master

Master

Master

Components

An individual digital object can be composed of many components. If a digital object has many masters, and each master has many derivatives, as well as indexing the actual digital object will have many components within it. This will increase the size of the actual digital object.

The digital object can have metadata associated with it. Each master can also have metadata associated with it (for example, EXIF, XMP, or IPTC values). Though it's possible to store metadata within a web quality image or thumbnail, as they are used for indexing by not storing metadata within them, the size of the digital image will be reduced, making it faster to retrieve them.

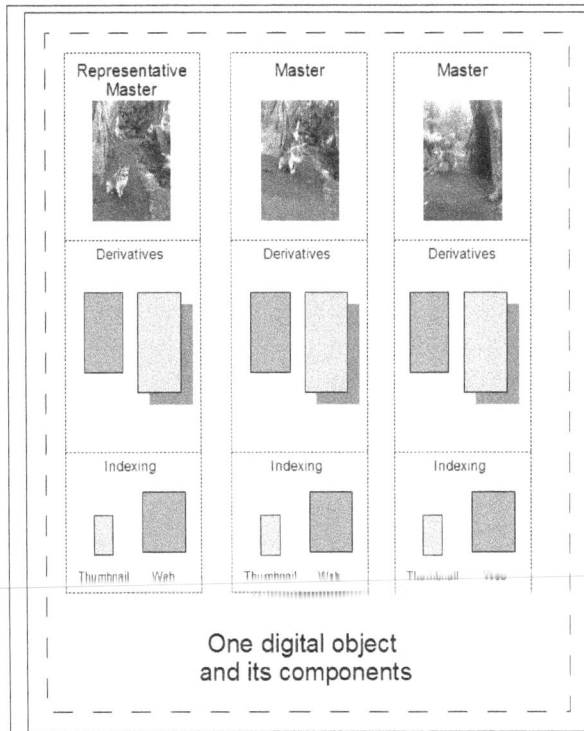

Representative Master	Master	Master
Derivatives	Derivatives	Derivatives
Indexing	Indexing	Indexing
Thumbnail Web	Thumbnail Web	Thumbnail Web

One digital object
and its components

Version hierarchies

When a digital object is modified, previous versions can be kept. These versions can be stored inside the same digital object similar to a master. The difference is that a master is a different view about the same digital object, and the version is the same image that has been modified. As different people can be editing different parts of the object or even different masters, a hierarchy can be formed containing all the different versions and who modified them.

For a version hierarchy, the challenge is the storage required to store all the different versions. Even if one byte in metadata embedded in the image is modified, then a new version is required to be stored. What database vendors need to start looking at doing is using techniques for optimally storing these versions. It's possible using the technology used for MPEG compression for version hierarchies. In this case, each version is like a frame and only the differences between the versions are stored in a compressed manner. Though no database vendor offers this capability, such a feature would have major storage ramifications and enable more versions to be stored.

Though an original should never be modified, as explained with a DNG, it's possible to modify the original while keeping it unmodified. One just changes the metadata around it. When it comes to video and audio, this goes into gray territory, as the original might need to be digitally edited before it becomes the official original. As is always the case with unstructured data, once a rule is established, it does not take long for exceptions to the rule to come to light. The changing nature of this means that a fuzzy attitude needs to be adopted when dealing with all unstructured data.

Relationships

A relationship is an association or link between any two or more digital objects. This is covered in greater detail in *Chapter 3, The Multimedia Warehouse*. A relationship can be used instead of the master concept. It can flatten the structure of the digital objects that are presented. The decision as to whether a master concept or a relationship concept is used is one that is based on the business requirements of the organization.

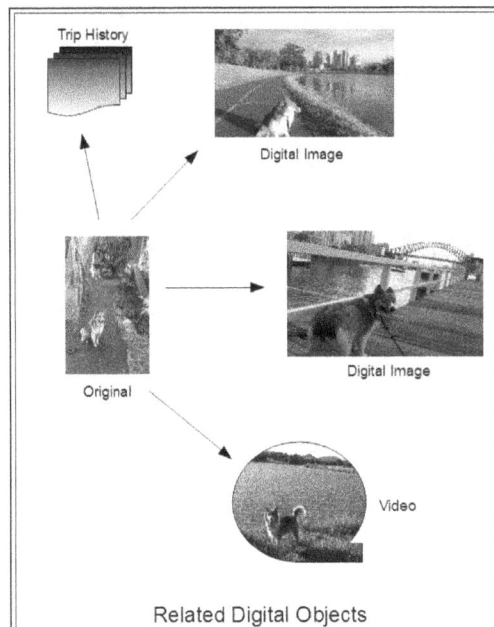

Unstructured data business cases

Only with the increase in uptake of social media and the introduction of devices, such as the iPad or Android, has the focus on data that has started to change from structured text to the one that involves multimedia or other types of unstructured data.

It is fair to say that most organizations have not considered the business need for managing their unstructured data until a strong business imperative has emerged; in this case, a reactive approach has been taken to its management. In fact, most business organizations need in place some form of digital image or asset management database, just like they need databases to manage their structured data.

The following are examples of businesses that may have a requirement for digital object management.

Sporting club

Any club involved in sport will have digital photos taken, videos of events, newsletters, interviews, or promotion of their club.

Charity

Charities may require digital object management for marketing or promoting their charity. A charity involved in finding homes for pets would have photos of those animals along with a case history of each. A charity involved in selling second hand clothes or furniture would have e-commerce requirements. Charities involved in assistance programs would have requirements to store a variety of data, including photos, audio, and documents.

Neighborhood watch

Neighborhood watch was a community-based social organization focused on monitoring and assisting policy within the neighborhood. Digital images of vandalism, property destruction, or even of good works done by the community are needed to be distributed across the neighborhood, as well as given to the local authorities.

News

Any organization involved in print media has requirements to store and manage all news stories and articles created. It is like having a digital object warehouse of information (which is covered further in *Chapter 3, The Multimedia Warehouse*).

Food

Any organization involved in food or beverages has a large focus on marketing and promoting that product. Managing, and more importantly, having a tight control over all the digital objects that are used in promotions or adverts is an important requirement.

Government

Every government organization (local, state, or federal) has requirements to store digital images, documents, videos, and any form of multimedia. Digital video can be used for training, digital photos for marketing, promotion, or as a way of managing assets. Even government departments that focus on tax collection need marketing tools and digital image management for internal use in brochures or for public education.

Summary

There is a lot more to understanding digital objects than most people realize. Each type has certain characteristics and behaviors, which can make manipulating and controlling it complicated. Because of the large size of digital objects, most employ their own compression methods. In some cases, data (information) is lost on compression. The data can be stored as characters, bytes, or instructions. There are a number of standards that exist for each digital object type, and for each type, there are numerous formats available, each with their own characteristics, making them well-suited for their own environment.

Chapter 3, The Multimedia Warehouse covers the concepts of what a multimedia data warehouse is and how a business can load and manage the large number of digital assets that might acquire.

Exercises

These questions are designed to have the reader go beyond the traditional method of answering questions. They involve using the concepts designed in the chapter and doing additional research on the Internet to come up with the best solution to address the questions raised:

- Define the attributes of a digital type that would be used to be a three-dimensional representation composed of a set of scanned images of a real-world object, like a vase in a museum or a wrecked car in a crime scene.

- With the huge rise in the popularity of multi-player gaming, there will come a time when matches between players will be stored, just like sporting match videos are stored. Though video of these matches can be used as a simple capture method, it doesn't capture the players themselves or the multi-view capability these games offer. It also would not allow searching, like finding the scene where player A discovered the ambush of player B. It should also be possible to search for all games that featured player A winning against player C. Detail a digital object structure and its data types that can not only capture digitally all this information, but allow for it to be easily searched against historically and against abstract concepts.

- Describe the compression method invented by Kodak called V-mail during the Second World War. Was it lossless or lossy? Can this technology be adapted for use by any digital systems today?

- With robotic space exploration, a cost-effective and popular method for discovering what is on distant planets, planetoids, asteroids, and comets is via autonomous robots. Describe a universal type, including the compression method for sampling the chemicals found in the atmosphere. Of importance is that the sampling is continuous over multiple locations and is the must factor in any local weather conditions. As it's continuous, it must be accurately time-stamped, factoring in that the time on remote locations will not match to earth time. It must also handle data loss due to solar activity or partial data transfer, with the notion that it's better to get some data, uncompress it, and get some results back rather than nothing.

- When looking at postcard images, the pixel dimensions are fixed. Determine an algorithm to create a postcard image when the images themselves are based on objects of unusual size. In particular objects such as a tapestry, which might have original dimensions of 1000 x 60 and is square in shape.

3
The Multimedia Warehouse

This chapter covers the basics of what a multimedia warehouse is, what it's useful for, and how it compares to a traditional data warehouse. A key focus will be on the importance of metadata and how it must be correctly managed, as well as covering categorizing techniques of digital objects and the different ways of dealing with data consistency.

Comparing

A multimedia warehouse is based on the same concepts as a data warehouse but can vary dramatically, because the nature of the digital objects stored within it enable new capabilities and concepts. Most multimedia warehouses employ to some data transformation, cleansing, and cataloging to make them more efficient to query and report on. Additionally, they might transform the images, summarize, combine, and restructure them. The most popular usage is to web enable the frontend, enabling it to be queried and accessed via a web browser by the general public.

The data warehouse

The idea of a data warehouse has been around for a long time, and specialized software vendors have come about purely to address the needs of it. The data warehouse evolved from a number of different directions simultaneously. Academics then formulated more official rules governing what a data warehouse really is.

For some, the data warehouse came about to solve the performance issue of ad hoc queries causing havoc with the performance of a transactional database. A user running one badly-formed query could shut down the database. The need to enable users to run these queries meant moving them to a copy of the database. From this grew the need to perform **Extract, Transform, and Load (ETL)**[1] against that copy. Various database features grew from this to enable the efficient movement of data from the primary databases to the data warehouse. This ensured that the data warehouse had information that was up-to-date.

Other needs arose, which include the requirement for managers to be able to query a number of different databases. From the requirement to produce summary information grew the concept of business analytics referred to as **online analytical processing (OLAP)**[2]. The introduction of OLAP also opened up the idea that the data itself did not have to always be up-to-date and an exact copy of where it originated from. OLAP produced summary data focusing on different data dimensions (for example, geographical location, departmental sections, and time), which were useful for performing complex aggregate queries. When time-based summary queries were performed, the need to have completely up-to-date information was not required, especially when historical queries were done. This concept is missed by most database administrators and relational academics, who have been trained and brought up to believe that a true database is always consistent. The data warehouse threw this concept out and changed some of the rules. For OLTP, it was true that the data had to be consistent, but for data warehouses, there were new rules, and data consistency wasn't high on the agenda. For a multimedia warehouse, this same concept is equally true. A multimedia warehouse works to a different set of rules. The way the data is loaded, queried, and secured involves a different focus.

Data consistency

Data consistency[3] summarizes the validity, accuracy, usability, and integrity of related data between applications and across an IT enterprise. Data consistency is an important topic and is central to a relational database. For the user, consistency means that when they view data, the data has to be accurate and correct. It hasn't been changed by the disk or corrupted. It's a core concept of computing and the Oracle Database has a lot of features built into the database to ensure consistency.

Data consistency is heavily emphasized in the relational model, and the notion of primary keys, foreign keys, and constraints were made available to enforce consistency. The consistency in the relational model is real time at the transactional level (called *atomicity*[1]). As the model is mathematically based, it cannot be faulted. It is well-proven and tested.

There is a tradeoff. To enforce this level of consistency requires more computing resources and high-speed networks. The real-time nature of the consistency starts to fall apart in distributed systems. If an application is distributed across multiple databases at different sites, it can be quite difficult to keep them in sync and consistent in real time. Oracle replication initially tried to address this issue by offering synchronous (real time) and asynchronous (delayed) replication. With the introduction of replication via the redo logs (a common replication feature of most databases), asynchronous replication became stock standard. The notion of a delay existing between when the data is changed and when that change is eventually reflected in other areas, negated the real time requirement of consistency and introduced the idea of *eventual consistency*[5].

With the power of computer systems today, real-time application consistency has scalability limitations. Attempting to enforce foreign keys and a multitude of other constraints can prove to be resource-intensive, as the size of the database grows, as well as the number of users. With the rise in popularity of *NoSQL*[6], also came the notion of eventual consistency. It doesn't dispute the concept of data consistency at the transactional level. It says that the need for the data to be always consistent in real time isn't a mandatory requirement in all cases. For a financial system, it's most likely to be a mandatory requirement to always be consistent, but a social network application doesn't always require the data to be immediately consistent. By introducing eventual consistency, a number of previously encountered scalability and performance issues were overcome-enabling applications, such as Facebook and Google, to scale to hundreds of millions of users.

A data warehouse can make use of eventual consistency to achieve some of its performance requirements. The materialized view structure that can be used within the database is one such example. A data warehouse has different requirements on top of this and introduces a new concept, which traditional data consistency doesn't fully address.

Logical Data Consistency

Consistency is currently broken up into three sections:

- **Point-in-time**: This type covers disk and software. It checks whether the database writes data to the disk correctly.

- **Transactional**: This type ensures that a set of data items (logical unit of work) are consistent. Within the database, this ensures whether it's consistent when failure occurs.

- **Application**: This type ensures whether data across multiple transactions are consistent.

Each section expands on the capabilities of the previous one to enhance it.

What is missed is the accuracy and consistency of the data itself. In transactional consistency, the model doesn't care if a field containing an integer has the value 10 or 20, provided all other columns that reference it (primary keys, foreign keys) match.

Logical data consistency focuses on the data value themselves and their accuracy. It overlaps with eventual consistency. A good way of highlighting this is with a name field. A name field typically contains a first name and last name, but when a value is entered in, is it logically correct?

What if instead of John Smyth, John Smith is typed. Does it appear to be incorrect? The immediate answer is no; except that the consistency model can't tell if this is right or wrong. Even if the name John Smyth is entered, it still might be incorrect, because the person's full name wasn't entered. Should the name John Paul Smyth have been entered instead? At what point when entering in a name is it correct? The same can be said for address or contact details. What if person changes their name or phone number? In this case, the entered value might have the illusion of being correct when, in fact, it's now incorrect.

Another way of looking at this is with dates. If a person enters in a date, which relates to the period of time they were born, is the year sufficient? If they enter in their birth date, is that date actually correct? A more valid date is the one that includes a time. But, is it time with hour and minute, or hour, minute, and second? Also, what about a hundredth of a second? The precision of the date stored varies based on the context in which the date is used.

True consistency implies accuracy in the data, that is, being able to trust the data and trust the results when it's queried. It has been shown that we can't trust the data, as there is a fuzziness to it, a range of trust values. With the birth date entered, we might trust the year, month, and day, but not the hour, minute, and second.

If a person enters in an e-mail address, is that address a valid one? Is that e-mail address the one that belongs to that person and will it only belong to that person? Some applications can achieve a high degree of comfort in determining that the e-mail matches the person, but to maintain this over time can be difficult. There is a degree of accuracy and trust to be obtained here.

Most of the time, these fuzzy issues with data items are glossed over, as they are too difficult to understand, control, or are beyond the boundaries of the application (fuzzy data is data, which has a range of values and its logic refers to the mathematical manipulation of the fuzzy data). We have learned to accept logical inconsistency in data as that's par for the course. It's now taken for granted so much that it's instinctively ignored in a lot of cases. Yet most data items have a degree of fuzziness to them. Any data item defined as an integer indicates that the precision required is not the same as a real number. Dates, timestamps, even spatial co-ordinates have degrees of precision, where we accept a certain level of accuracy, but except that it doesn't have to be fully accurate.

The relational system might have a mathematical model behind it, ensuring the consistency of the data in the transactions, but it can't control whether the data values themselves are fully correct. It can't mathematically enforce that the name entered is 100 percent valid or matches the person's true identity. For a name, its very hard to even ensure that it has been spelt correctly.

When we take real-world data, it's translated and messaged to fit the computer system. Obvious errors can be corrected against (if an invalid date is entered), but we are never going to get full precision and full accuracy on all data entered. All that can be done is to achieve a level of trust with what is entered.

In a multimedia warehouse, the concept of trying to achieve logical data consistency is not attempted, as it becomes apparent that the amount of data that is fuzzy forms the bulk of most of the digital objects. The goal is to achieve a level of precision based on each data item and then, understand the implications of that precision.

In a warehouse that uses OLAP, when statistical queries are run over larger items, minor issues in the precision of the data can be factored out (averaged). In other cases, data that doesn't fit within the standard deviation can be excluded as anomalous and ignored. Those who work heavily with statistics will know the adage, "Lies, damned lies, and statistics"[7]. By manipulating the database, especially when you know the precision of the data isn't high, can enable some users to adjust the results of the queries to better fit their expectations or goal. The results can be fudged.

Multimedia warehouses take the logical data consistency issue further when it comes to classification of a digital object. Is that John Smith in the photo? Is that a lyrebird singing in the audio track? Is that a photo of a chair? Is this person in the video? Is this digital photo identical to this photo? Is this document a photo? As is covered in this chapter, multimedia databases utilize fuzziness extensively. Data is never accurate. It only has a degree of accuracy that is fluid. It can change based on the circumstances, or even how the query is phrased.

Those used to the traditional data warehouse, especially one based around relational concepts, can have a lot of trouble dealing with the fuzziness of multimedia and the fact that it is not accurate. This can lead to almost comical attempts made by people to classify it:

This PDF file is a document if it contains more than x number of words, but it's a photo if it contains one digital image and less than y number of words.

In most cases, it just doesn't make sense to try and match the relational world to the multimedia one. The two are very different. It has been shown that probability theory is a subset of *fuzzy logic*[8], meaning that dealing with the fuzziness of data is mathematically sound and a natural extension of data management.

I have experience with a number of people who just want to avoid all unstructured data and require it to be ignored and not stored in the database (just keep it in the file system and out of harms way). Based on my personal experience, the large amount of resistance in the computing field to working with multimedia and any form of unstructured data is quite worrying. In a number of cases, it's attributed to just being too difficult to understand. For others, this type of data pushes their knowledge based beyond the traditional comfort zone of relational, which is well-understood.

Computer science is a constantly changing environment. New technology and advances in it cause major rethinks in the interface use, performance, and data management at least every two years. A newly released database introduces new features and replaces old concepts. Database administrators have to relearn new concepts and ideas at least every two to three years. In computing, you can't be conservative and dream of staying in your comfort zone. Yet, talking about the fuzziness of multimedia, the ways it impacts the database, and the ways to work with it, is constantly ignored. Ironically, that conservatism is found in database vendors including Oracle. In their case, I have stated many a time to a number of product managers that it's easier to (insert my valid witticism) than it is to convince Oracle on the benefits of multimedia in the database. Interestingly, when looking at the psychology behind this conservatism, one can use a positive aspect of it for designing and tuning databases. This is covered in *Chapter 9, Understanding the limitations of Oracle Products*, on tuning and why the greatest cause of performance problems is caused by management. So many tuning issues are missed because fuzzy concepts are ignored.

Dilapidated warehouse

As the data warehouse concept grew, the idea of just throwing any data into a central repository appeared, especially, if it originated from older systems where not much was understood about its original structure. It was certainly easier and cheaper to just grab the data, copy it to a central store and say to the users "here it is, do with it as you want". Unfortunately, this concept failed because the data warehouse was driven by the database administrators. It was soon learned that a data warehouse was only successful if it was driven by the users themselves. They had queries and questions that needed to be answered. The data warehouse had a key business requirement and function. If that focus was lost, the data warehouse becomes a Dilapidated Warehouse and an expensive dinosaur. A number of data warehouses have suffered this fate.

But even in this case all was not lost, as from it came the concept of data mining, where patterns within the data and between the different data items could be calculated automatically. Having a data warehouse, which didn't have a core business requirement was not a death sentence. It was still possible to get useful information from it.

Data warehouses have numerous challenges to deal with. The most important ones are security, performance, and preventing information overload.

Security

As more users access a data warehouse, it's important to ensure that only authorized users can access the data they are allowed to. For a security warehouse, information could be marked with different security clearance levels. This can require security to be implemented at the individual row level.

Unfortunately, just restricting access to the data could result in the data warehouse becoming unusable. In a population census database, users doing queries can get summary information about regions (for example, a suburb) but are not allowed to access the data coming from individual households because of legal privacy requirements. Restricting access to these records would mean that the summary queries cannot be performed. The security needs to be configured to resolve this dilemma.

One solution to address security is to use the concept of a data mart. A data mart is the access layer of the data warehouse environment that is used to get data out to the users. The data mart is a subset of the data warehouse, which is usually oriented to a specific business line or team. Go to `http://en.wikipedia.org/wiki/Data_mart` for more information on data marts.

The use of a data mart enables the warehouse data to be tightly restricted to a well-defined set of users.

As access to summary information can become important and strategic to the business, especially if business decisions are based on it, the requirement to be able to audit what is queried and what a user actually views also becomes a key component.

Performance

Data warehouse queries can become very resource hungry and expensive to run. Database systems have been constantly evolving over time to deal with the performance issues. Some of the performance solutions include parallelization, materialized views, smart caching, partitioning, and high-speed intelligent hardware (for example, Oracle Exadata). As the amount of data grows, so does the complexity of queries users run because, simply, they now can. This means the performance requirements of the data warehouse are always changing.

A data mart can also be useful for performance, as it allows the data warehouse to be partitioned and each data mart can be tuned to the requirements of the set of users using it.

Information overload

As more and more data is moved into the data warehouse, it can become very hard to work out what sort of queries can be run and how best to run them. To resolve this data maps or data dictionaries are created; providing a road map for the users to enable them to query intelligently against the data. Additionally, data marts allow for the key data items of interest to be made available to the user, as well as hiding structures they have no need to see or access.

The multimedia warehouse is different and has many faces. It can be seen as an extension of the existing data warehouse with the proviso that the focus is mainly on digital objects and not as much on the data. A multimedia warehouse is a super set of a data warehouse. It can contain all the traditional data warehouse elements and then contain all the digital objects. In reality to design and create an efficient and effective data warehouse, it's best to start with the digital object as the core and then load in data relating to it.

Like a data warehouse, a multimedia warehouse should be driven by having a business need. For multimedia warehouses that have an intelligence gathering focus, the requirement for data mining becomes very important.

There is no one type of multimedia warehouse, just like there is no one type of data warehouse, as each exists to satisfy a business requirement. They can be grouped into a number of different types, each with its own characteristics. The location of storage used for the multimedia warehouse can be referred to as a repository.

Types of multimedia warehouses

The following information describes some types of multimedia warehouses. This list does not cover all possible variations and will change as the technology changes.

Traditional

The traditional multimedia warehouse is based around the same concepts of a data warehouse. The goal is to be able to provide a repository of digital objects and data that has originated from different sources. The data and the objects themselves go through an ETL process. This process would include the need to establish valid relationships between the data and the digital objects.

In a data warehouse, the data itself can be summarized into a layer, with that data itself summarized, and so on, into numerous parent layers. The standard example is creating a layered data summary structure of sales data, based on regions within a city, the state, a state regional area, and the country. Region is just one dimension of many in which the data can be grouped and summarized. Another dimension is time. Data might lend itself to be moved into these dimensions and summarized, but digital objects do not. That doesn't mean that a similar summary process can't be achieved. Digital photos can be combined together into a montage, snippets can be extracted from video and combined, key pages in different documents can be extracted, and then combined. Oracle Text can use its gist capability to automatically summarize a document or extract the key themes about the document.

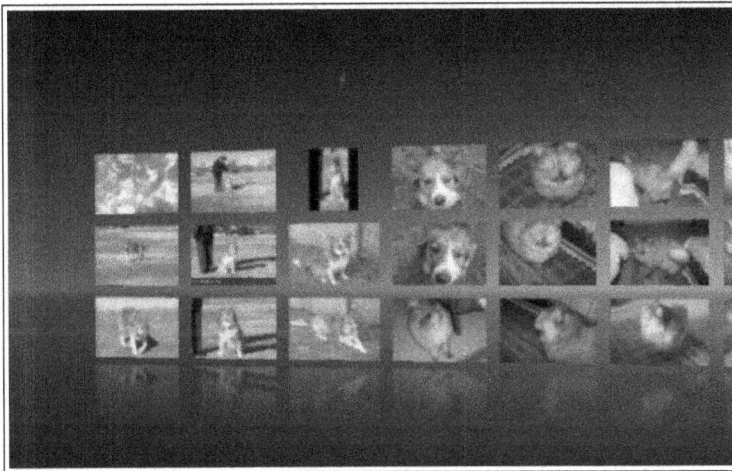

The product Cooliris (http://www.cooliris.com/) summarizes photos onto a three-dimensional wall. The website Midomi (http://www.midomi.com) will try and recognize and match a tune that is hummed or sung.

As the repository contains digital objects, the tools used to perform queries need to be enhanced to not only intelligently query these objects but to also display them. For video, this can be quite difficult, especially if the videos have originated from a variety of different sources.

Part of the ETL process for dealing with digital objects involves transforming them into a universally accepted format, enabling all tools accessing them to display them correctly. For digital images, this might involve converting them to JPG. For video, it might involve converting them all to MPEG. For audio, it might involve converting them to MP3 and for documents, converting them to PDF. These formats have the greater likelihood of being viewed or played by most applications and tools.

In a standard data warehouse, even though data can be summarized across multiple dimensions when displayed, the data is typically displayed in one dimension. Meaning that only one key piece of information is conveyed within the summarized view. A summarized bar chart might display sales total within one region. The one dimension of data conveyed is sales.

In a multimedia warehouse, the display requirements and methods for displaying inherently encourage multiple dimensions of information to be displayed. These concepts can then be taken back and used in a data warehouse. A chart can use colors to convey one dimension of data, while the shape of the graph can be another dimension. Converting the output into three-dimensional enables more dimensional information to be shown including the size, movement, icons, and a changing perspective based on the view angle. Even audio output can be integrated in. Google maps utilizes the integration capability by allowing data such as public utilities, traffic information, points of interest, and road conditions to be overlaid and integrated into one map. Applications can even overlay their own dimensions of data. Another example is a tag cloud (covered later in this chapter), which uses the font size of a word to indicate additional information about its usage.

As one key goal of the data warehouse is to extract and process summary information, it soon became obvious that when reading raw figures from the database, it was easier to understand, comprehend, and find useful patterns in the data if it was converted into a visual form. Graphical OLAP tools became popular in the market to address this need. The human mind can absorb a lot of information quickly if it's presented in a visual form compared to presenting it as raw data.

A multimedia warehouse, by the nature of the digital objects that are stored in it, encourages the use of visualization tools to view and process it. There is a temptation for warehouse architects to convert the digital objects into raw data and use that for displaying the information, rather than using the strength of the underlying medium to create a more powerful and visual environment for the warehouse. This temptation originates from a lack of understanding and skill in with working with multimedia and trying to treat it as raw data just like a data warehouse, because that is the comfort zone of the architects.

Multimedia is referred to as rich media for a reason. It can greatly enhance and add intelligence to a warehouse. It should not be seen as raw binary data that might be useful to occasionally create a visually appealing interface. The warehouse should have at its core focus, the digital objects with the metadata around, that is used to drive the summarization and perform analytical queries.

Image bank

In an image bank warehouse, the goal is to provide a central repository, which all digital objects and applications can access. The metadata is stored in applications outside the warehouse and these applications then just reference the digital objects in the warehouse. The only metadata stored with the digital objects is physical attribute information about the digital object. For a photo, this would be the EXIF metadata.

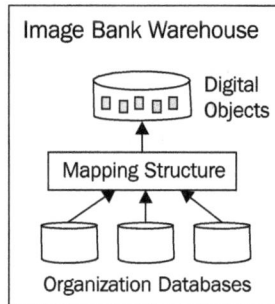

An important goal of the image bank warehouse is to store the digital object once and have a repository that can be tuned to the special requirements of multimedia. In this environment, it is still reasonable to create a data warehouse, with values in the data warehouse referencing the image bank warehouse. The advantage is that traditional data warehouses do not have to worry about the management and nuances of dealing with multimedia. They do not have to worry about the storage requirement or trying to handle and detect duplicated digital objects that might result, when different applications migrate parts of their data into the data warehouse.

The disadvantage is that the relationship between the data in the application and the digital object is loosely defined. It's typically a many-to-many relationship, meaning that one digital object can map to zero or more data items in other applications. Also, a data item in an application can map to multiple digital objects. In this scenario, it's possible to get orphaned records if an image is deleted or changed. In addition, the object relationship has to be configured. All the relationships need to be defined. If there are hundreds of thousands of digital objects and hundreds of thousands of data items across many applications, then it can be a very expensive process to build the relationship structure. When digital objects from different application systems are merged, it can be quite complex to look for duplicates, determine which digital object is the correct one, and then adjust the existing application to reference the master digital object.

So, even though an image bank warehouse can offer a lot of benefits, its strength and its weakness centers around the object relationship table, how well it's managed, and how accurate the relationships are within it (see *Appendix E, Loading and Reading,* which can be downloaded from the link given in the Preface.).

Data mart

In a multimedia data mart, the goal is to take a controlled subset of digital objects, which can originate in a multimedia warehouse, possibly transform them, and then make them available for consumption. A popular method is to make these digital objects publicly available, where they can be manipulated, utilized, and even enhanced. Crowdsourcing methods can be applied to these images with the results cleaned and fed back into the parent multimedia warehouse.

The concepts behind a multimedia data mart are very similar to the traditional data mart, where the existence of it is created to address security, performance, or information overload issues.

Another use is to take a well-defined subset of digital objects with a simplified subset of metadata and then locate them on a high-end server (a computer with a lot of resources). The digital objects are then made available within an organization for querying and display.

Public

In a public warehouse, the goal is to take digital objects from one or more internal systems and place them in a database, which can be accessed by the general public. The use of crowdsourcing (covered later) enables the general public to attach metadata to the images. When the digital objects are migrated to the public warehouse, they may be transformed into postcard sized ones. This transformation loses information within the image but provides consistent width, height, and quality giving a more aesthetic and user-friendly interface.

The public database servers housing the digital objects can be treated like a Bastion host (Bastion host is a special-purpose computer on a network specifically designed and configured to withstand attacks[9]).

The queries performed in a public warehouse are a mixture of course and fine grain based on what the core focus of the warehouse is (the definition of course and fine grained queries is covered later in this chapter). Some warehouses are designed for researchers, others just to enable the general public to better understand what the organization offers (see *Appendix E, Loading and Reading*).

eSales

In an e-Sales warehouse, the primary goal is to enable a form of e-commerce selling of the digital objects or what the digital objects represent. The delivery and configuration is detailed in *Chapter 5, Loading Techniques*.

For this multimedia warehouse, the digital objects are collected from one or more internal systems. The use of metadata is key for driving how the images are found and subsequently purchased. This means that the metadata around the image has to be transformed, cleaned, and made suitable for public consumption. The metadata, which is not suited, needs to be removed (see *Appendix E, Loading and Reading*).

Intelligence (security/defence)

A very powerful form of multimedia warehouse is the one used for intelligence gathering. Government departments, defense organizations, police agencies, and security firms can use multimedia warehouses.

The politics within a state or country can encourage the development and use of a multimedia warehouse. Police agencies in different states in a country have a reputation for not trusting the other. This can stem from perceived corruption, personality clashes, or conflicting security procedures. The result is a hesitation to share information in solving a case. Governments then create new agencies with new directives to try to resolve this impasse. They collect the information, transform it, and create an intelligence database. In some cases, they can create a data mart focusing on a particular criminal area of interest such as drugs, sexual offenses, and organized crime.

Information which is collected, cleansed, and stored in the central warehouse can come to it in both, a structured or unstructured format. Structured would include data, where the meaning for each value is well-known. This can include case information.

Unstructured can include surveillance video, audio from phone conversations, crime scene photos, and documents such as financial ledgers. The information might not have been digitized or fully cataloged. A crime scene photo might be labeled with a unique ID, ensuring its relationship to a case is established, but it might not be cataloged, where all information in the image is identified. As previously covered, computer systems are still not at the point, where they can easily analyze an image or video and determine what or who is in it.

Audio conversations, if clear and of a high quality, can be translated automatically but auxiliary information in the audio such as background noises or other simultaneous conversations, are not cataloged. To complicate the handling of audio conversations, a translator might be required if a different language is used. As covered in more detail later in this chapter, an automatic translator could be used, but the resultant translation might result in misinterpretation of the original conversation. The more information extracted, the greater the overall intelligence of the whole warehouse. Improvements in technology will ultimately overcome these limitations.

Additional information captured and stored includes biometric. This covers fingerprints, voice patterns, DNA, and blood types.

Information can come from a variety of sources, including internal systems and the Internet. All types of information can be captured including public biographies, company histories, and specialized databases (such as entomological databases, furniture, carmakers, and pharmacy information). With storage now being a lot cheaper and increasing in capacity, more of these databases can be captured and stored, enabling more complex and intelligent queries to be performed. The use of robots to trawl for data is a feature that search engines use.

An intelligence warehouse is intrinsically object-focused. An object can be a person, car, or piece of evidence. Information is then captured about the relationship between those objects.

Information also has to be cataloged as to how trustworthy it is. Information gleaned from a blog would not be trustworthy, because it's likely to be just hearsay and personally biased. Whereas, information coming from an internal system may be highly trustworthy. Generic queries when run need to use a fuzzy matching system taking into account the inherent trustworthiness of the data, and ensuring that the causal false relationships are not formed because of untrustworthy data. A query when run might need to perform that query a number of times, each time looking at different dimensions and using different fuzzy algorithms to do the match. The different result sets can then be merged with the aim of producing a result set that is indicative of the original question being asked.

The intelligence warehouse is a prime candidate for data mining, especially using a *data mining*[10] tool that can identify relationships between the different objects that might not normally be obvious. This can include:

- **Association rule learning**: Looking for relationships in the data
- **Clustering**: Looking for groupings in the data
- **Anomaly detection**: Looking data of interest that does not seem to fit

The intelligence warehouse is not limited to just its repository. One which can cross reference its results with Google, Wiki, and other external sources can provide additional information that might return unexpected relationships that may not normally have been considered.

The intelligence warehouse has a security requirement that separates itself from the other multimedia repositories. Such a huge and important amount of information requires securing the warehouse in a number of key areas:

- **External hacking**: Depending on the sensitivity of the data, there might be a requirement for external but authorized-only access to the warehouse. Police officers in the field might need to be able to run queries from remote locations. As soon as the system is made available on the Internet, it is open to potential hacking. To protect from this requires numerous security systems and authentication methods. In addition, encryption at a high level should be done on all data. Always keep in mind that, for a hacker, they use the easiest way in. There is no need to take a sledgehammer to a front door when the back door is wide open. The back door in most cases is one vulnerable to social engineering.

- **Social engineering**: This is an often neglected and not well-understood form of illegal access. The process simply involves getting the access to the data using any means other than trying to break through the firewall through brute force. A common method is for a hacker to pose as the local IT person and they ask the manager for their password. The only way to combat social engineering is to train all staff, including numerous practice sessions, into how to avoid not giving away information. To combat this, social engineers target new employees, who have not been trained, or staff in other companies that might have access. Hackers and social engineers are highly adaptable and adjust their strategies on a continual basis to new technology.

- **Internal theft**: This involves a staff member inside the organization stealing the data or performing a query and passing on the results to an external party. This can be done for ideological reasons or for financial gain. Although a potentially hard to combat system can use its own data mining tools and focus them internally on to the queries the staff perform, looking for anomalous or out-of-ordinary queries, and then flag them. Restricting access to data is also important. Additionally, all queries performed and the results returned should be audited and periodically reviewed. A staff member, who is aware that all queries they perform are audited and checked, is knowingly in a harder position to commit theft.

- **Modification**: This involves modification of internal data causing search queries to miss correct results, or setting up bogus information and sites with false data, which are then incorporated into the core warehouse. It's not enough to just protect the warehouse, but the source system, where the data comes from also needs to be protected. Modification can be deliberate but can also happen accidentally due to human error. Computer systems normally uses check sums to ensure that their internal data is not corrupted and is valid. When a person is involved in translating an audio tape or identifying objects in a photo or video, mistakes can be made. The only way to utilize the equivalent of a check sum is to have one or more people validate the data entered in. Unfortunately, this can be quite an expensive operation to do, especially if there is a huge amount of information to be ingested and translated and limited resources available to process it. This is where it becomes important to establish the trustworthiness of the data. In addition, its trustworthiness, where it originates from but also to its processing accuracy.

- **Trojans**: This method has been used more often as security becomes tighter and better enforced. It basically involves fooling someone internally in to installing a Trojan on their computer. This is traditionally done via scam e-mail messages purportedly designed to look official, to trick someone into plugging a malware-infected USB drive into a computer. This technique has been well-documented as used by companies or government agencies in different countries to spy on the other.

Structures

A traditional data warehouse will usually not contain structures within it. The data will be stored in tables and joined together and queried as required. Summary and dimensional tables are also built to improve performance and give dimensional views of the relational data.

With a multimedia warehouse, the focus is different. Each digital image is viewed as an object with its associated metadata describing that object. The objects are still queried in an ad hoc fashion, and dimensional and summary tables are still built, but the objects are put into structures to help manage and control them. For the user querying the warehouse, these structures might be hidden, or they might be used to add intelligence or control to the queries performed.

The following describes some of the structures that can be deployed into a multimedia warehouse. Whether these structures are actually used is dependent on the type of objects being stored and the purpose of the multimedia warehouse.

Collections

A collection is a group of digital objects. An object typically belongs to one collection but can live in multiple collections. Attributes can be assigned to a collection, including security, metadata, and categorization structure.

A museum would have multiple collections. Each collection could equate to a physical section in the building (objects in the east wing or handel building), a time period (16th century art), or objects similar in type (pottery, paintings, tapestry).

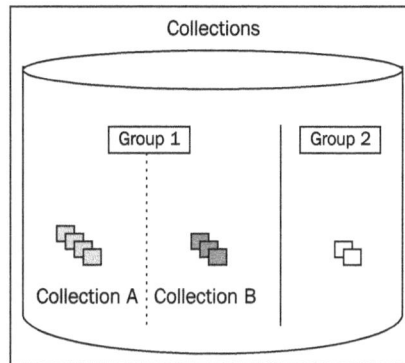

A government department might equate each collection to a department.

A photo laboratory might equate each collection to a photo shoot (the Jones wedding, the university student photo shoot of 2012, the motocross race).

In most cases, a collection has an owner who is the manager of the set of objects. Grouping the digital objects together enables actions to be done en-mass to the whole collection. Each digital object might have its security set or its metadata updated.

A collection can be assigned a name, enabling it to be easily referred to.

Groups

A group is a set of collections. Groups can be nested and contain other groups.

If a government organization sets up each section to have its own collection, then it might group these sections into a branch and each branch into a department.

A photo laboratory might group multiple collections (where each one is a photo shoot) into a photographer, where that photographer owns all the digital objects.

A museum might create a group for public digital objects, where all the other groups, which are marked as private, contribute their public images to the group.

Like collections, having groups makes it easier to classify digital objects and work on them en-mass. Security attributes can be applied to the whole group. A group can be taken offline.

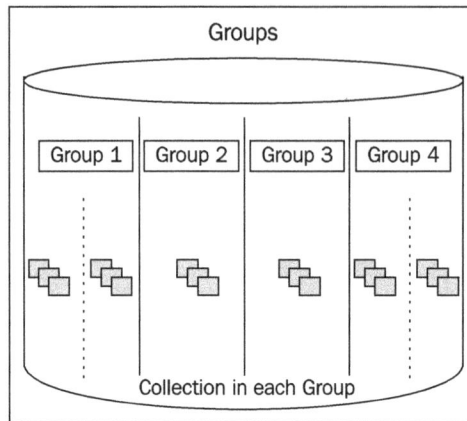

Categories

Within a collection, digital objects can be stored in a hierarchical structure called a category. The aim of the category is to enable these digital objects to be classified and provides an alternate method for finding and viewing digital objects.

A digital object can belong to multiple categories. A category can be nested. Though a category structure is typically hierarchical, there is no requirement for this to be adhered to.

Category structures can have security attributes and rules associated with them to make them easier to manage. A digital object can inherit the security roles of the category when assigned to them.

Even though a digital object can belong to multiple categories, for management, it's best if it belongs to a primary category.

A category can be compared to a file system structure. A category structure can map exactly to a file system structure but not necessarily the reverse. Categories transcend the limitations imposed by file system and enable more creative and flexible methods of handling digital objects.

Categories can be virtual or dynamic. They can be based on attributes of the image. A good example is date on which the image was created. The dynamic category structure enables a hierarchy to be built using year, month, day, and hour.

A category can also be based on the metadata in the image. If the metadata within a digital object includes address, this can be linked to *Google Maps* [11] and, the address can be reversed engineered into spatial co-ordinates. These co-ordinates can then be used to enable a category structure based on location, including country, city, suburb, and street.

There is no limit to the type of categories that can be created virtually using metadata or physical attributes of the digital object.

Lightbox

A lightbox can be described as a play area or holding area for images. Lightboxes can be private or shared with others. Nearly identical in structure to a category (and could even be called a type of virtual category), a lightbox is slightly different; in that, it is created by the user and images are put into it manually. It's also similar in concept to a shopping basket. A shopping basket is primarily private and session specific. A lightbox can be just for a session or kept permanently. Some other unique characteristics of a lightbox include:

- A lightbox contents can be manually ordered. Depending on the interface, a lightbox contents can be sorted in three or more dimensions (one additional dimension being time).

- A lightbox can be shared with others, even though other users don't have permission to access the images. Permission is inherited via the lightbox. This, of course, is a feature that might not be suited for some secure multimedia warehouses.

- Actions can be performed on a lightbox. Its contents could be printed or e-mailed to a person. A request might be put in to transform, convert, or fix the contents of the lightbox. Additionally, mass editing of metadata can be done against all the images in the lightbox.

- Lightboxes can be merged or set operations performed on them. Find the intersection of two lightboxes, meaning find the images common to both. Also, take one lightbox and minus another lightbox from it, meaning find the images in the first lightbox that do not exist in the second one.

- Lightbox contents can be checked out or in. The check-out process puts a lock on the digital object, saying it's been exclusively locked for modification by a user. Check in releases that lock. The lock should not be confused with a database lock, which is part of a transaction. A check out lock is independent of the status of the database and immune to database restarts. Check out locks can have expiry dates and override locks on them to make it easier to manage them.

The visual metaphor for a lightbox is a person taking a set of photographs, putting them on a table, and sorting through them and keeping the ones they want. Historically, a lightbox was a plastic box with a back light that photo laboratories used for sorting out images for a photographer and determine which ones were suited for printing.

Relationships

A relationship is a many-to-many link between two digital objects. The type of relationship can be used to describe characteristics. Information can be stored in the relationship and that can adapt over time, resulting in network intelligence.

Standard relationships include:

- **Master**: This is the official or best-quality image in relation to all the other images. This relationship links multiple images together and specifies that one is the master to be used for viewing or printing. It's assumed the other images are similar in relationship to the master.

- **Duplicate**: This is the opposite of the master. If one image is the master, the other can be referred to as a duplicate. It can also be thought of as a backup.

- **Parent/Part**: One image in the relationship is marked as the parent. This might be a complete view of the digital object. The part images are subsets of the image. There might be different views of that image. A part can also be a master with its own duplicates. A part can also be referred to as a child.

- **Related**: In this, two images look similar but are not the same. This is like a see also. Two images might be related because they were taken by the same photographer, or there might be pictures of objects made by the same artist.

- **Dynamic**: Relationships can be derived based on analysis or ad hoc pieces of information. In a criminal investigative multimedia warehouse, digital images of different people might be associated with each other based on the fact that they were in the same place at a particular time.

Relationships can be time-based. Meaning that they are valid for a set period of time or can change over time. It should be possible to perform queries based on time.

Using basic neural network algorithms, relationship information can change over time based on usage. A simple counter might be used when a relationship is created. As this relationship is reused, this counter increases conveying information about its importance.

Google uses this concept in its search algorithm to establish the importance of a web page based on how many other pages access it. In this case, the relationship is between two web pages, and the counter increases for every page referencing it. Pages with relationships with large counter values are deemed to be important.

In the case of a criminal investigative multimedia warehouse, the counter can be used to note every time two people either met or were in the same vicinity of each other (if surveillance is used). In such a scenario, patterns of behavior can be ascertained based on the strength of the relationship. The strength is subjective based on the counter value.

In a museum warehouse, relationship information can be stored based on how often an image is clicked on and linked to a search. Or how often an image is accessed if other images are also accessed. In this case, the relationship is established. If other people click on the same image combination, the strength of the relationship is increased.

The way the counter value increases can be linear or geometric. It can also be time-based and relationship strength values can decrease over time if not used.

Though not a true neural network, a large amount of information can be captured between digital objects based on usage and access by users. Intelligence can be added to the multimedia warehouse, which might not be possible using conventional means. This concept adds value to the warehouse.

Thesaurus

A thesaurus can be described as a set of terms linked together based on similarity. The terms belong to a controlled vocabulary. This is important, as new thesaurus terms cannot be added without clarification by an authority. A thesaurus can be hierarchical but does not have to be. A thesaurus conforms to a defined standard. There are numerous standards with a popular one in usage being the Z39.19-1993 monolingual thesaurus.

The terms in a thesaurus are linked together using relationship constructs. The most common two are broader term and narrower term. The following are examples:

- **Geography Thesaurus**: Broader term is Australia. Narrow terms are New South Wales, Queensland, Australian Capital Territory, Victoria, South Australia, Tasmania, Western Australia, and Northern Territory.

- **Furniture Thesaurus**: Broader term is Bedroom. Narrow terms are bed, clock, radio, mirror, chair, and wardrobe.

Relationships are one way, but common usage indicates bi-directional support. Terms can be self-referencing, and it's possible to have circular references, but this is discouraged.

A digital object can be mapped to one or more thesaurus terms. A user can navigate through the thesaurus, then perform a search for all digital objects that match the term. Searches can be hierarchical, and do not have to match exactly to a digital object. For example, a digital object can be mapped to Victoria, but should still be returned if a search on Australia is done.

A digital object can be manually mapped to a thesaurus term or mapped dynamically using its metadata. A manual mapping is required if there is no sufficient or accurate metadata to determine which thesaurus term or terms the digital object belongs to.

Additional thesaurus concepts include Used For, Related Term, and Use Reference.

Taxonomy

A taxonomy is similar to a thesaurus, with the addition that it contains preferred terms and is used mainly by science. It is a classification whereas a thesaurus is a store of related terms. The terms are contained within a hierarchy and the terms conform to a well-defined vocabulary. A taxonomic hierarchy is also well-controlled. In the life science taxonomy, different levels in the hierarchy are fixed and equate to values such as genus, species, and subspecies.

Taxonomic examples include taxonomies for fossils, plants, psychology, and even business. Taxonomic structures can vary in their meaning, use, and strictness of adherence. Most major taxonomies conform to an internationally agreed standard to ensure that the structure remains consistent and accurate. As there is meaning in the structure, knowledge can be associated with the results that are returned. Ensuring the taxonomic structures are correct can be considered to be very important.

Due to the well-structured nature of a taxonomy, ad hoc queries performed against digital objects can be returned in a taxonomic structure.

Metadata standards

Metadata when conceptualized into a shared standard can be said to be part of an ontology. An *ontology*[12] renders shared vocabulary and taxonomy, which models a domain with the definition of objects and/or concepts and their properties and relations.

By grouping together metadata and defining a standard from it is useful for searching and understanding what a digital object is. It is now common practice for all digital cameras to capture and store metadata about the photo in metadata fields conforming to the EXIF standard. This can include aperture, focal length, brightness, and GPS co-ordinates of the image.

Most metadata is stored in the XML format, which is an easy-to-use and flexible data storage format. The definitions of the metadata within an XML format can be described using the XMP standard, which is also in XML.

The popularity, simplicity, flexibility, and wide-spread use of XML has resulted in nearly all metadata being stored in the XML format. Even older formats are being coerced into this format where possible. A good example is IPTC, which is one of the first metadata standards used for TIFF images. It used a propriety format, but in the latest version of TIFF images, it is being stored in the XMP format.

Digital images

This section details some of the most common metadata formats based on the multimedia image type.

IPTC

International Press Telecommunications Council (**IPTC**) enables the exchange of news. It was originally formulated in 1990 but only became popular with the adoption by Adobe. It was one of the first standards put together and does not use XML but rather a propriety format embedded in the header of the image. In 2001, Adobe extended IPTC to be incorporated into XMP, enabling large values to be stored. It currently supports both XMP and IPTC to be stored in the digital image at the same time. Each metadata item is called a property and has a fixed type of value. Internally, a unique numeric code was assigned to each value to identify what type of value it is.

Examples of some of the properties that can be found with their identifying number are:

5	IMAGE NAME
10	PRIORITY
15	CATEGORY
20	SUPPLEMENTAL CATEGORY
22	LOCALE
25	KEYWORD
40	SPECIAL INSTRUCTIONS

55	CREATED DATE
60	CREATED TIME
65	ORIGINAL PROGRAM
80	BYLINE
85	BYLINE TITLE
90	CITY
95	PROVINCE STATE
100	COUNTRY
103	ORIGINAL TRANSMISSION REFERENCE
105	HEADLINE
110	CREDIT
115	SOURCE
116	COPYRIGHT
120	CAPTION
122	CAPTION WRITER

The standard can be found at `http://www.iptc.org/std/photometadata/specification`.

IPTC values are found in TIF images. Oracle can extract IPTC information from an image.

EXIF

This is a standard designed for still-image cameras and comes from an exchangeable image file format. First published in 1996, it has been enhanced to also include audio.

The EXIF standard is more designed to capture information about how the camera took the image. This includes values such as aperture and focal length. As digital cameras today are embedded in mobile phones, smart devices and devices such as an iPad, they can also capture more information on top of this, including who took the photo and where it was taken.

In that regard, some of the values in EXIF overlap with IPTC, but the standard does not replace IPTC. Information is stored in tags in a tightly controlled but flexible structure, enabling each tag data type to be identified. The standard can easily be expanded on as technology changes.

The standard is flexible and is growing. A large amount of information can be captured about the image. Some example values include:

- APERTUREVALUE
- ARTIST
- BATTERYLEVEL

- COLORSPACE
- COMPRESSION
- COPYRIGHT
- DATETIME
- EXIFIMAGELENGTH
- EXIFIMAGEWIDTH
- EXPOSURETIME
- FOCALLENGTH
- GPSALTITUDEREF
- GPSLATITUDE
- GPSLONGITUDE
- IMAGEDESCRIPTION
- IMAGELENGTH
- IMAGEWIDTH
- MODEL
- ORIENTATION
- PIXELXDIMENSION
- SHARPNESS
- SHUTTERSPEEDVALUE

The standard can be found at `http://www.exif.org/specifications.html`.

EXIF values are found in JPEG and TIF images. Oracle can extract EXIF information from an image.

XMP

Extensible Metadata Platform (XMP) is a standard designed to be used in a digital object and is pioneered by Adobe.

XMP uses XML and has been designed to incorporate other standards. This includes IPTC and EXIF. Its usage is more determined by the camera manufacturer, as the standard is controlled by Adobe. It is extensible and adaptable, and the values that can be extracted are constantly changing. As it uses XML, the details about the items are stored as attributes in the XML along with the data making it easier to define new values and embed them in the XMP.

An XMP example extracted from a camera can be found in *Appendix A, The Circa Data type*.

XMP values can be found in JPG and TIF images. Oracle can extract XMP information from an image. It can also write XMP back to the image. Even though Oracle easily extracts the XMP, it only extracts the XML component. The XML Schema available in Oracle is needed to extract the various attributes and values from the XML. This is covered in *Chapter 12, Customer Case Studies*.

The XMP standard can be found at `http://www.adobe.com/products/xmp/`.

Audio

Unlike video, which has a large number of competing standards with new standards emerging every year and changing in popularity based on which devices can best play them, for audio, the most popular standard is MP3. This standard has won out, because in the early days, when smaller files were more important, it would compress audio files dramatically with loss of quality that was varying and acceptable. An audio CD could only hold 70 minutes of music, whereas an audio MP3 could hold 10 times or more music. This huge difference in storage resulted in it being used extensively and most manufacturers adopting it.

Audio compression standalone is slightly different to audio being stored in a video file. In that case, the popularity of the codec is driven by quality and how easy it is to sync to the frames in the video. Standalone audio is associated with music albums and podcasts, which require metadata to help understand the content. With audio embedded in a video file, the album concept and the need for metadata is not required. So, even though an MP3 codec can be used in a video file, its usage is more determined by the video.

ID3

The ID3 metadata standard (ID short for identifier) first appeared in 1996. The first version format was simple and stored 128 bytes of data in the header of an audio MP3 file (which initially had no support for metadata being embedded in it). The standard was designed to hold information regarding music, but with the increase in popularity of podcasts (radio show style audio), the standard was coerced into working with it.

It contained information including the artist name, album, speed, and genre. Its limitations led to a new compatible version referred to as ID3v2, which can store more information. With the use of iTunes and other music stored, the ability to tag music become important for managing and categorizing.

The ID3 data is not stored in an XML format. The market at the moment still has the ID3v2 as the popular standard to use and the Adobe XMP standard, which supports MP3 as still to be adopted. Only when major music stores start using the XMP standard will it increase its popularity. With ID3v2, album covers (jpg thumbnails) can be embedded in the track.

The following table lists the most common ID3v2 values used:

ALBUM	This is the name of the album the audio track is on. For a podcast, it can refer to the name of the podcast show.
ARTIST	This is the name of the persons, group, or organization that created the audio track.
COMMENT	This explains description or additional information regarding the audio track.
COMPOSER	This is the author of the music item or the writer of the script for the podcast. This does not have to be the same as the artist.
COPYRIGHT	This provides information regarding usage and intellectual property of the audio track.
DETAILS	This provides information about the audio track, for example, 44100 Hz Stereo, 128 kbps, playtime 04:54.
ENCODED_BY	This provides information about who and how the audio track was created.
FORMAT	This provides information about the encoding of the audio track for example MPEG 1 Layer 3, Joint Stereo.
GENRE	This is vocabulary indicating the type of music or whether it is a podcast. For music the vocabulary is well defined and used by products such as iTunes.
SUBTITLE	This provides additional information regarding the title of the audio track.
TAGS	This is a set of keywords used to help when searching. It can also be used to indicate what ID3 standards are supported, for example, ID3v1, ID3v2.
TITLE	This is the name of the audio track.
TRACK	If this is a musical item, then the track refers to the position in the album in which it exists. This could be 3/11, or third track in the album where 11 tracks exist.
YEAR	This is the year of creation or publication.

The standard can be found at `http://www.id3.org`.

ID3v2 values are found in MP3 audio files. Oracle can extract property information from an MP3 file but not the ID3 values.

Relational

Standards for storing text data have existed for a long time. Botanical systems have been using taxonomies for hundreds of years. In addition, Botanic systems have been trying to classify the names of the people who identified and classified the plants. This was done before computers existed and employed a flexible form of grammar and syntax to classify names[13]. For example, Betula alba L. 1753, nom. Rej.

With the rise in popularity of XML and the understanding that data can be grouped together and attached to an object, numerous standards began to appear to control the attribute names and how the data would be grouped. The goal being twofold:

* To allow data to be intelligently searched on (for example, find me all authors whose name ends with Smith)
* To allow data for objects to be interchanged between different systems

In the 1990s with the increase in usage of relational databases, the need arose to be able to interact with these standards and convert data from the relational format into the XML format and back again.

In this scenario, relational refers not to a relational database but the potential to store textual data in a relational structure via XML.

CDWA Lite

Categories for the Description of Works of Art (CDWA), the Lite version, is an XML-based schema using CDWA as a base. Its goal is to provide an easy-to-use standard to enable data transfer between museums[14].

CDWA uses the concept of a piece of work, which is an object. When digitized, it becomes a digital object. Some of the values used include:

culture	This shows the name of the culture, people, or nationality from which the work originated.
dateQualifier	This shows what the date means.
displayCreationDate	This includes a description of the date or range of dates. It can be in circa format.
displayCreator	This includes the information about the creator of the work.
displayMaterialsTech	This shows what the work is made of. This can include values such as gold, lacquer, silk, leather.
displayMeasurements	This explains the physical dimensions of the work.

`extentMeasurements`	This gives an explanation of the part of the work being measured. Its values conform to a well-defined list.
`measurementsSet`	This explains, for measurements, what units or values are used. This can include metric values like mm or kg.
`earliestDate`	This gives the earliest date for when the work was created.
`latestDate`	This gives the latest possible date for when the work was created.
`locationName`	This gives the name and physical location of the organization, group, or place that is responsible for the work.
`nameCreator`	This gives the names of people or organizations that were involved in the creation of the work.
`nationalityCreator`	This gives the nationality of those responsible for the creation of the work.
`objectWorkType`	This is a well-defined value indicating what work type it is. This can include values such as painting, armor, or photograph.
`recordID`	This is a unique ID for the work that has come from the originating site. This can be referred to as an object ID and refers to a unique internal key to identify the work.
`recordSource`	This shows where the work was sourced or originated from.
`recordType`	This specifies whether the work is an individual item or many (such as a series, group, or collection).
`roleCreator`	This is the role played by the person who created the work. Its standard value is artist.
`title`	This is name of the work, typically values as assigned by the creator of the work.
`vitalDatesCreator`	This provides information including birth and death (lifespan) of the creator of the work.
`workID`	This is an accession number of the work.

The Dublin Core® metadata Initiative

Dublin Core[15] is a metadata standard used to describe resources for the purposes of discovery. Initially adopted by museums, the standard can be used by most organizations. It is composed of two levels, simple and qualified.

The simple level consists of these values:

- Title
- Creator

- Subject
- Description
- Publisher
- Contributor
- Date
- Type
- Format
- Identifier
- Source
- Language
- Relation
- Coverage
- Rights

The values and overlap with the CDWA standard are the ones described earlier. An actual description of each value can be found at `http://dublincore.org/ documents/dces/`. Each value would relate to a metadata value.

As the standard is primarily designed for discovery, search engines can make use of the individual metadata fields to perform advanced searches. Searches can be done on just the artist name, location, or period of time in which the work was created.

An example of Dublin Core data in XML format is:

```
<metadata
xmlns:xsi="http://www.w3.org/2001/XMLSchema-instance">
<dc:title>Hockey Stick</dc:title>
<dc:creator>Margot Donte</dc:creator>
<dc:subject>abstract art</dc:subject>
<dc:description>Cubist work of art depicting the essence of sport and
life</dc:description>
<dc:publisher>Acme Publishing</dc:publisher>
<dc:contributor>Harold Smith</dc:contributor>
<dc:date>circa 1920</dc:date>
<dc:type>Painting</dc:type>
<dc:format>Canvas</dc:format>
<dc:identifier>M.23.32</dc:identifier>
<dc:source>Australia</dc:source>
<dc:language>English</dc:language>
<dc:relation>see M.23.32.b</dc:relation>
<dc:coverage>Pre 1930's Depression</dc:coverage>
<dc:rights>Public Domain</dc:rights>
</metadata>
```

The goal of the qualified Dublin Core level is to provide a well-defined vocabulary or exemplary qualifiers. These are additional structured actions to be applied against the value. When a value is qualified, it can still be read as if it was as a standard sentence. This can include adding structure to a sentence such as "Is Version Of" or "Is Part Of".

Darwin Core

Darwin Core[16] is an extension to Dublin Core. It intended to facilitate the sharing of information about biological diversity by providing reference definitions, examples, and commentaries. The focus is taxonomy for biological disciplines. The standard includes coverage of:

- **Occurrence**: This a method of uniquely identifying the record.

- **Event**: This is an action that occurs at a place and during a period of time.

- **Dublin Core location terms**: This is a region or physical spatial location. By overlapping with Dublin Core, which already defines this, allows for integration of data between different systems.

- **Geology**: This includes geological classification, covering concepts such as geochronologic era, chronostratigraphic erathem, and the stratigraphic horizon.

- **Identification**: This includes information regarding how the identification of the taxonomy was made.

- **Taxon**: This includes the taxonomy (phylum, class, order, species, or genus) of the organism.

- **Relationship**: This includes the details about the relationship between resources.

- **Measurement (or fact)**: This includes the value, type, method, creator, and date of information collected.

Media Art Notation System

Media Art Notation System (MANS) is a System of Formal Notation for Scoring Works of Digital and Variable Media Art. It is an attempt at coming up with a standard that uses XML for the categorization of multimedia. It uses **Digital Item Declaration Language (DIDL)** that allows for greater, more granular descriptions of a multi-component digital object[17].

Image tagging

For organizations that first digitize their assets, the initial problem of categorizing and identifying them becomes apparent. This is a time-consuming task requiring expertise and consistency. A digital object that has been incorrectly identified can be lost in the system. For organizations with hundreds of thousands of digital objects, the classification can become an expensive and difficult task to achieve.

The notion of image tagging has been around for some time. This involves a person adding a metatag and using it to identify the digital object (in this case, a tag is just shorthand for metatag). The tag is usually just one characteristic of the digital object and usually not a complete identification of the image (which would include author, security, copyright, and licensing). A tag might be an attribute, which lists all the items in a digital photo, or a set of words, that best describe the digital object.

Adding a tag in this case becomes useful when searching to find the digital object. One or two curators having to view, identify, and classify tens of thousands of digital objects are likely to make mistakes, as well as possibly introducing a bias into the tagging, resulting in the digital object becoming hidden.

To help overcome this issue, some businesses have opened themselves up to the general public and empowered authorized users to do the tagging for them. In such a case, all the curators need to do is to vet the results and verify that the descriptions provided are valid. It's much easier to validate a tag against a digital object than it is to do the tagging.

The challenge is to get people with sufficient skills to tag the images, while at the same time, ensure the digital objects are not vandalized or corrupted. Additionally, if users with insufficient skills badly tag images, this might result in more damage being done than if a curator tagged the image themselves. The idea of opening up the site to the general public and allowing them to add intelligence to the digital objects via tagging is a form of crowdsourcing.

Crowdsourcing

Crowdsourcing[18] is a distributed problem-solving and production model. In the classic use of the term, problems are broadcast to an unknown group of solvers in the form of an open call for solutions. With crowdsourcing, there is a balancing act between ensuring good quality data, ease of use, and recognizing correctly tagged values.

A well-structured computer system that manages the tagging and vetting can automatically track how well a user is doing with their tagging effort. Vetting is done under the assumption that it is easier to review a digital image and confirm that the tags are correct, versus the effort involved in determining what the tags should actually be. The vetting process involves a workflow for accepting a tag:

- The user attaches one or more tags to the digital object
- The digital object is the unmarked to be vetted
- A manager then reviews the tags against the digital object to verify that there is a match
- The digital object is marked as being vetted
- The new tags are made available for searching and reviewing
- The user is then informed of the result of the vetting

Crowdsourcing can be a useful technique for the translation of tags. An organization can request that a set of tags are translated into one or more languages. This technique is likely to produce better, more accurate results than attempting to use automatic translation through a *Babel* translation tool[19].

Gaming techniques

By adopting the competitive nature of some individuals and putting it into a constructive environment, a form of game can be formulated that not only encourages correct identification of an object but makes it fun for the person doing the tagging. This can result in a higher, more accurate throughput of the digital objects being tagged.

There is a cost involved in producing and maintaining the game versus doing the tagging manually. This cost has to be factored in to determine whether it is worthwhile doing it. Adding a game might also restrict the target audience, who will be willing to be involved in it. It might also give the appearance of cheapening the site. If the target group are teenagers to those in their twenties, the gaming aspect might make it more interesting to participate in, especially if there is a monitory prize involved.

To make the gaming site more attractive and competitive, leader boards can be set up, with even monetary or equivalent prizes given to the most successful taggers.

It's possible to adapt popular games to the tagging process. The space invaders game, which is well-known by most people, when adapted would have the aliens coming down equating to digital objects being tagged. If a user tags a digital object, the alien is destroyed. As it's a time-based game, the user is encouraged to not linger and tag as many images as possible. Like the *word association* game[20], the fast, spontaneous reaction to assigning tags could result in creative tag associations being formed.

Data types

All metadata is text-based; in that, it is composed of characters from a well-defined character set or sets. To ensure consistency when copying or moving data, the same international standard as used for XML, which is UTF-8, should be used minimally. There is UTF-16 and other supersets of UTF-8 that can also be used.

As was covered in *Chapter 1, What is Unstructured Data?*, data that is stored as raw text is in effect, unstructured. This is due to the fact that there are no rules or controls that govern it. Though text-only metadata is flexible in its entry, it is easy to introduce errors. A good example that most museums encounter is representing the date in a text field.

In the following list, determine the actual dates:

- 12-Dec-01
- 10/11/12
- 19 June
- 30th February 2010
- Februry 10th 1870
- 50-60a.d.

In addition, how easy would it be to do a date search range on these values?

The following are the issues identified with the previous dates:

- It is not clear what the year is. Is it 2001, 1901, 1801, or some other year? Shorthand for years is what resulted in the year 2000 issue.
- Is it the 10th November 2012 or 11th October 2012? The date format dd/mm/yy versus mm/dd/yy always results in confusion, and neither date value is internationally accepted.
- Is the value 19th June or 19th July? Shorthand for months can result in confusing dates.

- This is not a valid date. It's very easy to enter in a non-existent date as there is no date validation.

- February is misspelt. This can make it impossible to determine what the correct date is.

- This is a circa date, not a correct date. Circa dates are of a different data type.

It is possible to break down text values into sub types, which have their own domain rules. Some of these are well-defined and conform to standards, others such as circa are still in the process of being defined. By breaking down the metadata into types, it becomes possible to do intelligent searches on the data and more importantly be guaranteed that the data is accurate.

The classic definition of a relational database is one in which all the data is perceived to be a set of tables. How the data is stored or managed is separate to the core concept that all data is being accessed using the SQL statement and modified using **Data Manipulation Language (DML)**.

For metadata and all the data types, the same holds true. The data can be stored in an XML database, relational database, NoSQL data store, embedded in a digital object in a proprietary format, or a raw text file. When using Oracle, storing the data in an object/relational structure makes it easier to manage, secure, and control. What has been shown with social networks is that it is not necessary to store it in a traditional relational database. How it's stored is a matter of implementation based on the available software, technology, and business requirements.

The following lists some of the more popular and well-known data types. Some storage systems can handle these data types transparently and others cannot easily be represented.

Text

Even though all other data types are based around the text one, not all metadata fits naturally into a data type. In which case, it remains as text. Text fields are commonly seen described in databases as `varchar` or variable character fields. Text data can still have some domain-boundary rules associated with it:

- **Fixed domain list**: A validation rule can be applied to a text field that forces it to belong to a set of well-defined values. This is also referred to as an enumerated type, for example, text metadata values belonging to the set of compass directions, such as north, south, east-west, north-east, south-west, and so on.

- **Repeating value**: This is a concept that is forbidden in traditional relational databases and removed when a database is normalized to first normal form. With the introduction of object types in Oracle 8, repeating fields were reintroduced as `varrays`, as they were a natural feature of objects. As metadata is attached to a digital object, repeating values became a natural fit. An object can have a text field of keywords describing it. One or more values can be assigned. Max limits to the number of entries and the width of each entry can additionally be assigned. Text values can also be grouped together with other data types into a repeating group of values.

- **Fixed size**: The length of characters or bytes is limited in size, for example, a text field has a maximum length of 100 characters. It's important when working in the UTF-8 (or greater) character set to differentiate between a character length and byte length. Certain non-traditional characters can be represented using 1 to 4 bytes in UTF-8, resulting in the number of bytes used to represent the text field exceeding the number of characters.

Date

The DATE data type is one that is stored internally as a number. Date is one of the most varying data types and what drives it is the precision required. Oracle internally supports date and timestamp.

Domain rules include enforcement of a valid date. Typical search options include the ability to find all digital objects created within a date range. As the data is stored internally as a number, it becomes quite easy to perform the date arithmetic, including adding a date and date interval together or subtract two dates. There are a large number of date functions available. Traditionally, date and time are stored together with a fine level of precision for time storage.

Date management gets complicated when time zones and daylight savings are factored in for international databases.

For some scientific or astronomical systems, the traditional DATE type is not flexible enough especial when relativistic motion has to be taken into account when doing calculations.

Interval

Oracle supports the concept of intervals being stored, which is essentially the difference between two dates.

Time

Time is generally included in the date, but there are situations where only the time is needed and not the date. For a botanical database, it might be important to note the time of day when a flower blossomed, but there is no requirement to store the date. Oracle does not support time being stored separately and usually requires the time to be filled with a dummy date value. By doing this, standard domain rules for time can be enforced and time calculations can be done.

Season

This data type is generally ignored, but for some systems it can be important. There are four traditional seasons – summer, autumn, winter, and spring, It's not correct to state that one can derive the season based on the date. If I say what season is it if it's 1st January? If you answer winter, the answer is correct in the northern hemisphere, but in the southern hemisphere, it's summer. Additionally, locations near the equator do not have the traditional four seasons, and generally have two, the wet season and the dry season.

Botanic systems need to store the season for describing the plants, flowers, or seeds. For searching, it's also reasonable to query all plants that display some activity in a particular season.

Circa

A circa date is an approximate date. It can include an approximate date range. When museums date old items, they might not know the exact date and use the term circa to denote the approximate date it was created.

When looking at geological dates, the date period can extend back hundreds of millions of years. When looking at astronomical dates, it can go back billions of years. Geology and astronomy generally don't use circa but their own terminology. The concept of using an approximate date is still the same.

Interestingly, the approximation varies geometrically originating from the current date. A circa date of 2000 would be accurate to about plus or minus 1 or 2 years. Whereas, a circa date of the 1900s might plus or minus be 3 or 4 years. A circa date from the 1600s might be plus or minus 10 or 20 years. The further back in time one goes, the more the degree of accuracy diminishes.

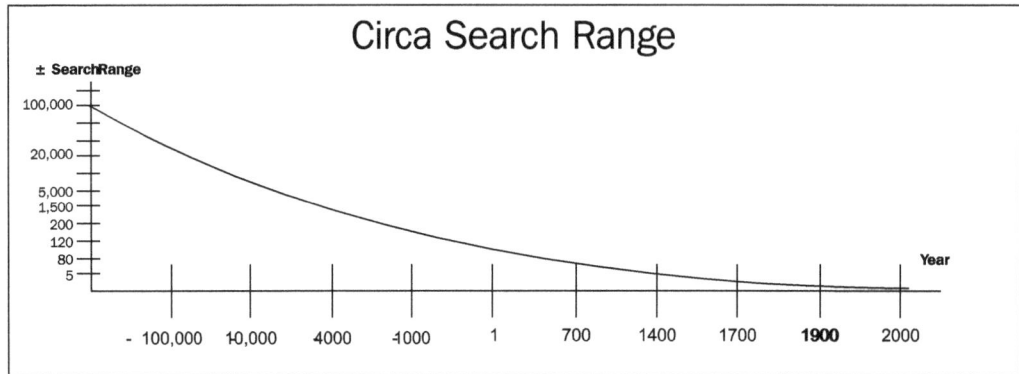

Circa Search Range

The approximation and degree of accuracy is determined by the dating method used, the type of item, and the length of time.

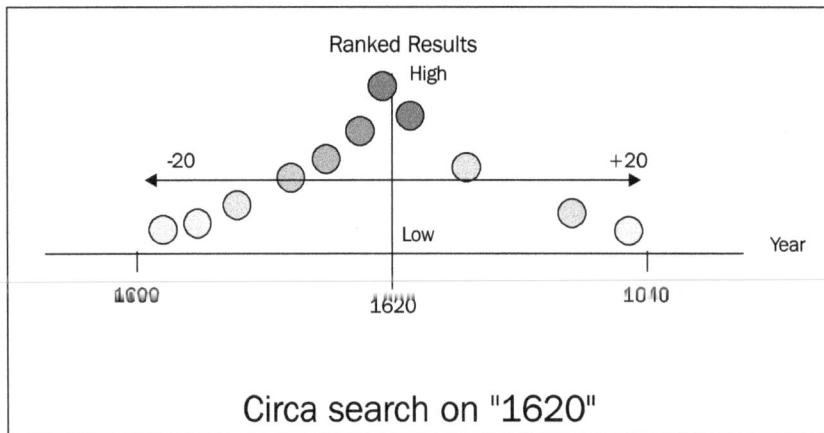

Circa search on "1620"

When searching on a circa date, a fuzzy logic algorithm is best used, and it needs to be flexible enough to factor in exact date and circa dates. If a person is searching for pottery in 1620, the search engine should query circa dates for anything that overlaps 1620 using fuzzy techniques. If the 1600's period was determined to be plus or minus 20 years, then any object with a circa date of 1600 to 1640 would match. Ranking now becomes important, as the closer the circa date is to the actual date, the higher the ranking.

If a person searches on circa 1620, then they are requesting a broader search range. In this case, it is from 1600 to 1640, meaning any object from 1580 (1600 minus 20) to 1660 (1640 plus 20) would match. Again ranking is important and objects matching closer to the number would have a higher rank.

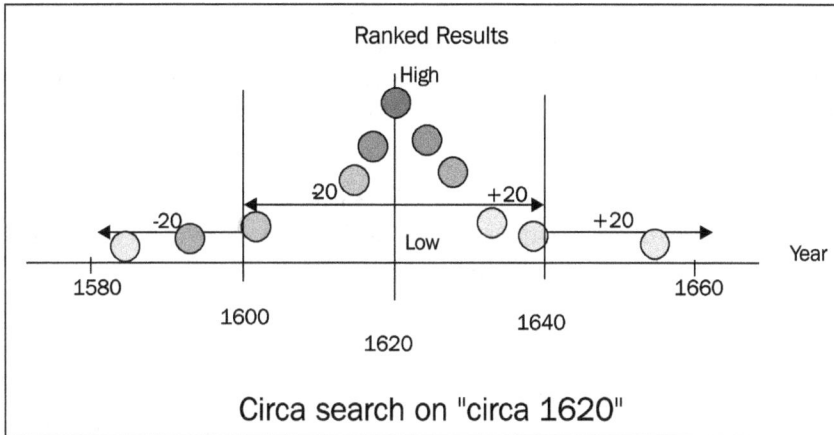

Circa search on "circa 1620"

There is no official circa standard and the text is free flowing. To address this, a formal syntax for circa has been described and can be found in *Appendix D, Chapter References*.

Boolean

A `boolean` value is traditionally thought of one that has two values, TRUE or FALSE. Sometimes, phrased as yes or no. Computationally, they can be represented as 1 and 0.

It's important to consider that the traditional thinking of `boolean` being binary doesn't hold up well in the real world and the NULL case needs to be correctly addressed. As such, a trinary logic system for dealing with `boolean` needs to be handled. In this case, the values are TRUE, FALSE, or NULL.

For metadata, this might be a tag that indicates whether the digital object is publicly available. The null case being that it hasn't yet been decided what it should be.

When using `boolean`, the set of domain functions available enables complex searches to be performed, for example, find all images that are publicly available but not yet licensed.

Number

The `number` data type is a type that has changed over time to handle the increasing power of computer systems. By default, a number is a real number. Real numbers[21] can be thought of as points on an infinitely long line, called the number line or real line, where the points corresponding to integers are equally spaced. Unfortunately, not all real numbers can be stored in a computer system. Transcendental numbers are ones with an infinite number of decimals (for example, π and e), and some numbers such as `i` (square root of negative 1) cannot be stored except as a formulaic representation.

What limits the range of numbers that can be stored is their precision. The precision[22] of a value describes the number of digits that are used to express that value. The number of digits also includes decimal values.

In a computer system, storage determines the precision. As a computer system is based on binary, the precision is linked to the number of bytes made available to store the number. When programming, the precision can be limited by the size of the registry values (not to be confused with a Windows registry). Computer chips that are 64 bit have a greater precision than those that are 32 bit. The EXIF metadata standard makes extensive use of numbers to represent a variety of values. The standards indicate what the precision is for the value.

Most database systems today can handle numbers 264 or ± 232.

Although it is commonly done, storing a number as a text limits its usage. It becomes very hard to validate or to perform arithmetic expressions against it. Storing as text also consumes more storage, which can make it harder to tune queries performed against the database.

Metric and imperial

Numbers are used extensively for storing scientific metadata. The challenge is then to use a universally accepted standard. The most common standard used by all countries in the world, except three, is the *metric system*[23]. As the U.S. still uses imperial, this can cause issues when it comes to understanding what a number actually means.

If a metadata value of 5.0 is stored for length, is this in meters or yards? Without knowing what system is used, major errors in calculations can be made[24].

As the accepted international standard is metric (except for altitude), and even as the U.S. has accepted the use of this standard but been unable to implement its usage in the country[25], it should be a fait accomplice that metric is always used for. Experience has shown that this is not realistic. For museums and organizations that are decades old, the data they have might be in the imperial system, even though they are using the metric system.

Rather than trying to force a change to metric, it's best when storing numbers to first determine whether it is metric or imperial. This is easily achieved when using XML, as it is just another attribute. When using a relational database, this requires the value to be stored in another column to indicate whether it's metric or imperial. A possible solution is to create a specialized scientific data type, which has as its attributes, whether it is metric or imperial, and another attribute to store the number. This is an effective strategy but makes it hard to make use of a lot of built-in functionality that is available, when only a number is used. In this case, methods would have to be written to handle number processing. This might not be a cost-effective strategy.

Ultimately, an organization should determine for each of its data types whether they are to be stored in metric or imperial, and then enforce this on ingestion.

Accession number

Most museums use the term accession number to describe the primary key of the object. This is a unique value or number that identifies the digital object. What makes the accession number more robust is that information can be encoded into the number using dot notation. The number might not just be limited to numerics (the digits 0 to 9) but might also include characters.

The term originates from the idea of creating a unique key using a number system that increases by one for each new object. Though this is still possible, over time the characteristics changed.

In a registry system (a system that manages physical files, again not to be confused with the Windows registry), numbers are assigned sequentially to each new file. The full accession number is prefixed by the year, and reset to one at the beginning of the year. Special characters are used to separate the year from the number, but the year and the sequential number combined make the accession number, as only the two combined together form a unique value.

The following are examples of accession numbers based on a year system:

- `2010/00023`
- `2008.1234`

As the year is coded into it, it's immediately apparent when the object was cataloged.

For objects that can be represented in multiple ways, then additional notation can be used to identify it. So, if the object is a car, then pictures can be taken of it from different angles. In this case, these additional shots can be expressed as an additional number with a letter is assigned to it.

The examples given in the following list are all the digital objects that reflect different views of the same object:

- 2011.1234a
- 2011.1234b
- 2001.1234c

or if number dot notation is used

- 2011.1234.1
- 2011.1234.2
- 2011.1234.3

There is no right or wrong way for determining whether numbers or characters are to be used. Those with a computer background will likely gravitate towards numbers, as this is traditional for computer systems, whereas curators will gravitate towards letters as visually it's clearer what the relationship is. The letters stand out more in comparison to the numbers.

It's also possible to encode additional information in the accession number. The digital object can be prefixed using a character such as A (audio), V (video), P (photo), or D (document). Again dot notation can be used, or numbers can be associated with each type.

- A.2012.1234a
- P.2012.1234a
- P.2012.1234b

This indicates that the three digital objects are all based on the same object. Where, the first is an audio of it, and the other two are digital photos of it.

Using the dot notation relationships can be encoded between multiple objects. In the following example, the accession number does not use the year, but rather uses a three-tier concept to categorize the object.

- 14.5329.498
- 14.5329.499
- 14.5329.600

Those digital objects that are related share the same middle number. In artwork, this could be used to indicate that the same artist was used to produce the artwork (for example, Da Vinci or Monet). This, of course, gets more complicated when multiple artists work on the same digital object and the accession number starts to encounter limitations.

The information stored in the accession number hierarchy of dot notation is not limited in the length of information that can be stored in it. There are no exact universal standards that have to be conformed to. The format of the accession number is typically managed by the guidelines of software vendor. There are some accession number standards in some fields, such as bioinformatics, library science, and medicine.

With an accession number, what is important is being able to accurately and clearly define the rules about how the accession number is formed. Unfortunately, a number of well-aged museums have over time employed multiple and conflicting standards for the accession number, with a lot of exceptions to the rules employed within it to get around the changing nature of technology.

It's unfortunate that the concepts behind normalization were never realized by the architects of those who manage accession numbers. When *normalization*[26] occurs, the goal is to identify fields with multiple values in them and to break them out into separate columns. If this was done, the accession number would become a simple key that uniquely identifies the object and is a unique number. All other information such as the year and relationships between objects would be extracted and stored in other columns. The reality of the real world though doesn't always meet with the neat solution that normalization can bring. Museums display their works to the general public and label them. Those labels have limited spaces and being able to encode additional information in them, they can be of great use to those researching, identifying, and finding objects. So even though one can explain the benefits that normalization can bring to managing digital objects, the accession number will not disappear or be replaced by a normalized structure. There is nothing stopping one utilizing the best of both world's concept and using an accession number and having its information being additionally stored in a normalized or object structure. This feature can be covered in Oracle using a number of other features including materialized views and embedded functions in SQL. This is covered in greater detail in *Chapter 4, Searching the Multimedia Warehouse.*

Name

Name is a specialized data type used to identify an individual. This can be the person who created the object, took the photo of the object, who last edited details on it, or who is responsible for its copyright.

There are a lot of attributes of name, and it can be stored in a number of ways. It's typically stored as a text field in the format – first name, last name. Other attributes can include title, middle name, birth date, death date, and gender.

Like accession number, it's possible to store multiple attributes for name into the one field, giving added meaning to it. When looking at the person who first classified a botanical specimen, the representation of the name can include values such as first name, middle initial, last name, date classified, date reclassified, and name of person who reclassified[27].

For a museum, where the name is associated with a digital object, it is important that sufficient information is stored to ensure that false positives (covered in Chapter 4, Searching the Multimedia Warehouse) do not occur when a search is done.

If a digital object has the name of John Smith, then it's likely to be retrieved when someone searches for John Smith. But, is it the right John Smith? As there are so many potential false hits that can come back from this, the search is not accurate. This is where a name matching algorithm is needed.

Such an algorithm would have to apply fuzzy techniques and ranking based on the initial information entered. In the example of a memorial that has photos over a 100 years old with basic information identifying the individuals in them, then the name-matching becomes more complex. It needs to factor in values such as the middle initial or name, birth date, death date, nationality, and even death location. If some of these values are not available, then guesses (ranked accordingly) can be made.

For photographs containing multiple people, the circa date can be used along with the relationships in the group. If, for example, the photo is of John Smith, Fred Hangle, Harold Mills, and it was taken at the Somme in 1916 in World War 1, then a search looking for Smith, Hangle, and World War 1, should bring this up (World War 1 should translate to a circa date).

Additional attributes for name can include occupation, address (which is a type within a type), membership number, and contact details (phone, e-mail, mobile). What is important to note is that the information that is captured and managed within this type is determined by the context in which it is used. It is not appropriate to request the sex of a person in an e-Commerce system, as this is confidential medical information. For further information regarding name, sex, gender, and title data types refer to https://sites.google.com/site/sgtndata/.

Address

The address data type, like the name data type is composed of a number of varying attributes. The attributes used are based on the context in which the address is needed. Breaking down an address into country, city, suburb, and street enables geographical-based queries to perform. By using the Google address web service, an address can be translated into the spatial latitude/longitude co-ordinates. Keeping the country attribute system enables e-commerce systems to distinguish between local and international, for purposes of determining the currency for orders and shipping costs.

When used as part of the name data type, address is typically treated as a repeating group, as a person can have one or more addresses. When used in an e-commerce system, address can be used for shipping, billing, and delivering to different addresses, in the case of a gift. Address can also be used with name for matching and searching.

If a history of addresses is stored, then it's possible for security agencies to use time-based queries to establish approximate locations of individuals.

Filename

Most digital objects have a representation of themselves stored in a digital file, which is stored in a location controlled by the operating system. This is commonly referred to as the filesystem. Each file within the filesystem has a name, known as the filename.

The filename can include its physical path or directory structure, especially if the filename is not unique. Information can be stored in this structure and can be used to further identify or be used as metadata for the file. If, for example, the parent directory was the year the photo was taken, then it's valid to capture and extract this information from the filename.

It's also a realistic option for the accession number to be used as the filename. In some cases, a variation of this number can be used, especially if special characters are used and the storage media cannot handle it.

Filenames and their paths can be controlled and limited by the storage they are on. The paths can vary depending on the operating system. When a network drive is used, then understanding the path can get quite tricky. It's possible for a file to be stored on a **Network Attached Storage** (**NAS**) and be accessed simultaneously from Unix, Windows, and Mac. The access path to this file can vary in its structure.

In the following table, the same file stored in the same directory could be accessed using different methods. Each one using a different file path syntax for accessing it. If the server stores the Unix path, then a Windows user trying to use that same path is not likely to be able to access it. It will need to be translated.

Windows	Traditional	`c:\mydir\myfile.jpg`
	UNC	`\\mydomain\mysite\mydir\myfile.jpg`
Unix	UFS	`\u01\mydir\myfile.jpg`
Browser		`file:///C:/mydir/myfile.jpg`

By storing the digital objects in the database, the need to use or reference the path once loaded is not an issue, as the object can be served straight to the user from within the database. For organizations using a mixed environment, ensuring a consistent file path can be a challenge.

Digital files are not just limited to the two most used operating systems (Unix and Windows). They can also appear on mobile devices such as an iPad and more mature operating systems such as MVS.

A digital file is not necessarily unique, though most operating systems enforce the notion that the name must be unique within its home directory. Even this can get complicated when links to files are used. In this case, the same file can exist in multiple spots with different paths.

As discussed later, the challenge that most multimedia warehouses will experience is matching the files to existing relational (or equivalent) metadata.

It's also possible for searches to be performed against filenames and their paths. In some cases, the path might need to be translated to match the operating system knowledge level of the user. Most users are more familiar with Windows than Unix and users might actually only access a file via a Windows share. If the Unix path is stored, this might be of no use to the user, especially if the Windows share hides some or most of the path name.

Spatial co-ordinate

The traditional view of spatial co-ordinate is one which is a geographical location, such as latitude and longitude. In this case, the co-ordinate is just a point location. A set of co-ordinates can be combined into shapes, such as circles, squares, or polygon to represent an area. By adding additional dimensions, such as altitude, depth, or height, then a three-dimensional co-ordinate can be established. Incorporating time, as well as the planet, the co-ordinates that are based in can add extra information to the position.

As a spatial co-ordinate can be of any shape, it can be of any size. Once a spatial co-ordinate is stored, it's possible to perform spatial queries against it. A common one is find all the images within 5 km of my current location. A spatial co-ordinate lends itself well to being stored in XML, enabling it to be integrated with other images. Integration with Google Maps is a cost-effective solution for taking latitude/longitude points and visualizing them on a map.

A polygon spatial co-ordinate can be used to identify the path of a car under surveillance. A spatial query can then be used to correlate that co-ordinate with others and produce related digital objects. This could be photos or video of physical objects near them.

Spatial queries typically employ fuzzy search concepts such as finding images near us, or finding any digital object in this approximate area.

Even though latitude/longitude with geographic location are the most common applications seen for a spatial co-ordinate, it's not just limited to this. This data type can be used when the point of reference is not geographical but a virtual concept. In an intelligence data warehouse, the ability to create a spatial map of relationships between people, is a useful tool for analysis.

Summary

A multimedia warehouse is a superset of a data warehouse. It can include within it a standard data warehouse but contains additional digital objects. The focus in a multimedia warehouse is the relationship between the digital objects. Metadata is a key element for enabling searching between the digital objects.

Chapter 4, *Searching the Multimedia Warehouse* will cover how to search against the objects in a multimedia warehouse. It will cover the different search methods, dealing with false positives and how to format and display the results.

Exercises

These questions are designed to have the reader go beyond the traditional method of answering questions. They involve using the concepts designed in the chapter and doing additional research on the Internet to come up with the best solution to address the questions raised:

- Define an XML standard for a museum that is based around the history of dog collars
- Design a multimedia warehouse that has the core focus of providing forensic information to a large number of police agencies
- Define a data type that handles international telephone numbers (including mobile, and fax), include the domain rules, and search rules

4
Searching the Multimedia Warehouse

This chapter covers how to perform search as and queries against digital objects in a multimedia warehouse. It includes the different ways a multimedia database can be searched and the different types of search that can be performed. It will cover how to interpret and understand what is returned, as well as how to intelligently display the results that come back.

Multilingual data

Not all countries in the world or organizations use one language. Some are bilingual, others support multiple languages. Data coming in from other sites might be in a different language. Museums around the world regularly share items, and the digital information relating to them might be in a different language.

The challenge for all these organizations is how to handle this data in the best way. The issues can be broken down to the following:

- Storing
- Displaying
- Translating
- Searching

All spoken languages can be represented in text; some phonetically, others in a representative structure. Different languages use different symbols to represent the pronunciation. Some languages use one symbol to represent a sound (phonetic), others use a mixture of one or more to represent the different sounds. Languages such as, English have introduced a large number of exceptions to this, so much that dictionaries need to include a pronunciation guide. English also has multiple symbols representing one base symbol (uppercase and lowercase). The different symbols are used to control the grammar.

Languages evolve and change over time and most can be traced back to certain regions in the world. As such they have a common base. Most European and American languages share a similar character set revolving around one called *Latin*, which was based on *Greek*. Asian, Middle Eastern, and African have completely different character sets.

Within those languages that use character sets based around Latin, the characters (referred to as a grapheme) can look similar but have additional characteristics used to control the pronunciation. In English the letter A is used, but in other languages in addition to A we can also use Ā, Á, Â, Ä, Å, À, Æ. In this case a special character referred to as a *glyph*, is added to the character. In some cases it's referred to as an *accent*. When this is done, the result is a character that is called a *diacritic*.

Storing

The character set used by XML is UTF-8. With the increase in popularity of XML for data transfer (web services), database systems had to conform to it or a superset of UTF-8 (the next one being UTF-16). UTF-8 can store most of the character sets that represent most languages used in the world. The challenge is loading in and retrieving without losing the translation.

Diacritic

Accuracy in searching is important, so when a person searches for the word "entree", should results that have the word entrée also be included? If a person searches on entrée, should results with entree be included?

The commonly accepted view is that the diacritic should not be taken into consideration when searching even though there is a chance that a *false positive*[1] (see the *False positive* section for more details) could result. The diacritic is normally used to control the pronunciation of the word and not its meaning. This is different than a *homonym*, which is a word with the same pronunciation but has different meaning. When a user searches on the word "passed", are they searching for an approval or someone who moved on (went by) or did they mistakenly confuse it with *past*, as in before now?

The result is that searching when there are diacritic characters should be ignored, and the diacritic be converted to a base character. So if the character was Ë when searched on, it would be converted to E. When displaying the character the original value should be displayed. So even though a search was done on E, if the result included the character Ë then this value should be displayed.

Multiple languages

The next issue is if a organization is bilingual. Do they have two completely different storage structures for each language? So if a `meta` tag was called `Artist Comment`, then two versions of this value would be stored, one for each language. The user would only see the value relating to their language.

Though this seems like a reasonable direction to go in, it's not always practical, especially for systems with hundreds of thousands of objects each with potentially hundreds of `meta` tags. If a digital object has not been translated then the image might be lost to someone looking for it but using another language.

This issue can be broken down into two problems:

- When searching, does a user only search on words within their language or are they able to search across multiple languages?

    The goal here is to avoid false positives. It's possible if a user searches on a word in one language it might be spelt identically in the other language but have a different meaning. This is called a *false friend*. In this case a user might retrieve the wrong digital object. This is useful if the user is doing a fine-grained search (covered in the *Searching* section), but if they are doing a course-grained search then this could be a limitation.

    The best solution in the end is to enable the user to choose which action they want.

- If the digital object has not been translated (and only one language exists for it), should the object still be allowed to be accessed even though it means showing the object using a language the user might not understand?

    The answer to this can be country dependent. In Canada, which is bilingual (English and French), all government organization have to support both languages. In this case a digital object would not be shown unless both the French and English versions existed.

In the United States, which has English as the main language, some regions have a large Latino population. In those areas, organizations can offer bilingual services especially when it makes good business sense to do so. In this case it's likely not all the digital objects would have been translated. So in such case the English version would be shown if a Spanish equivalent was not available.

Translating

With the introduction of babel fish various sites have become available that offer computer translations from one language to another (for example, `http://babelfish.yahoo.com/`). It's tempting to believe that by using this technology one can automatically translate metadata from one language to another. People who have used babel fish quickly realize that even if the words are translated the context isn't. The result being that the translations become nonsensical. Sometimes the translation partially works but the grammar is awkward and not user friendly.

The result is that automatic translation still has a long way to go. It has its uses and when used with its limitations factored in, can help those who need a quick translation, to get a basic idea of what the original meant. It is not suitable for organizations that wish to be multilingual and want to convert their data quickly to the other language. In the end the best translation is done using humans, and especially using humans who are trained in the semantic structures and nuances of the environment the organization is in.

To complicate it with translation even more, different business types use different languages which can make it hard for a person to translate unless they are well versed in it (also referred to as business jargons). For example, legal terms can have different meanings to ones used in the intelligence community, botanical, the physical sciences, and museums.

Security

The most efficient way of controlling which users should be allowed to access images is best done via roles. A role is a very simple concept but a lot of people who have never used them struggle to understand what they do.

A role enables fine-grain access to a set of images. It enables security to be configured based on the business requirements. Roles also enable security to be changed very quickly and easily.

With security one has to always remember that it's a balancing act. The more restrictive and tighter the security, the less chance there is of unauthorized access. The tighter and more restrictive the security is, the harder it can actually be for a user to do their job, to perform queries, or do things quickly. The less security, the greater the chance of a digital object being stolen or damaged. One goal of a warehouse is to allow users to do ad hoc and complex queries without the burden or restrictions of an OLTP environment. Each organization is different and has their own security requirements, but an overly eager security manager, or a very paranoid one can easily go to the extreme and make it near impossible for a user to do their job and access the environment. In these cases the security administrator can cite hypothetical or real-life scenarios where lax security resulted in data loss. But again, the security administrator has to understand the business requirements of the user. If the user can't do their job properly because of overly burdening and restrictive security, then the warehouse can quickly become a *Dilapidated Warehouse*. A well trained and experienced security manager should be able to balance the business needs with the user needs.

The simplest security system is to not have any security (in all cases it is still assumed that security such as firewalls and effective password management is used). In this environment, all digital objects have public access and everyone has identical access to all data. For a data mart that acts as a bastion host (covered above), this might be a reasonable solution to embark on, but for the vast majority of sites they will require security that is more controlled.

The next simplest security system involves introducing a checkbox indicating whether the image is public or private. In this case if the image is public any user can access it. If it is not public, then only a user who is defined as authorized can access it. As more collections are added with more digital objects the need to limit access becomes more important and a natural hierarchy of access is formed. It grows from a simple public/private scenario to one of the public, defined users, managers, or administrators scenarios. From this, the security will likely grow as a manager might want to control which users access their objects.

In an intelligence warehouse security might be based on top secret, secret, and so on. However, there might be additional secret levels based on whether a contractor is accessing the data. In addition, if the warehouse is shared by joint forces (for example, navy, air force, and army) then the security levels might vary between the different organizations, with each one controlling who is classified as top secret or secret.

Eventually the security requirements grow to a stage where only by using roles can the security methods be fully addressed.

A role is incredibly simple. It is an object (but to make it easier to comprehend refer to it as identifier). If a user is given a role, they can access any digital object that also has that role. A user and a digital object can have more than one role. A real-life analogy could be like having a security pass (a security pass being like a role). That security pass can give you access to certain rooms in a building (each room being a digital object). If that room has the security that matches your pass you can enter the room (access the digital object).

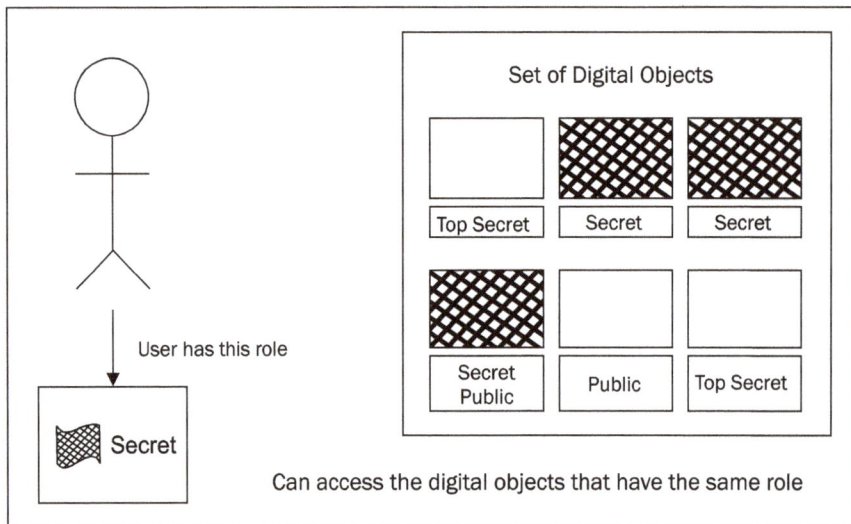

Like anything simple, it can become incredibly complex when used in a complex environment. All SQL databases use roles as it is an ANSI standard. The implementation of roles though in a SQL database is unfortunately limited and organizations invariably have to build their own equivalent concept to overcome these limitations.

In the base case with roles it's a simple match from a user with a role to a user with a digital object. That concept can be expanded to include the following:

- Roles can be used to control access to image derivatives. You might have a role that gives you access to the core image, but you might want to control whether the user can access the original and/or some of its derivatives. You might want to set up an environment for low level security. Users can only access a low DPI version, whereas top-secret users might have access to the original image which has a greater quality. A recent example of this was when the US publicly released satellite images. The images had a lower resolution so that when you zoomed in on them it made them blurry. They kept the higher resolution ones for internal use.

- Roles can be used to control the access to metadata. A digital object might have a hundred metadata fields. Some might contain sensitive or confidential information. Some might contain propriety information or administrative notes that other people should not see. Roles can be used to access the image and a different role can be used to control which metadata values the user can access.

- Roles can be used to limit access to categories. An equivalent to categories is operating system folders. A role can be used to control which categories a user can see. This enables a structure to be created with categories for confidential data and ones for public. In a hierarchical category structure the question that arises is that if a user has access to a child category but not the parent ones, can they still access the category? Different operating systems when looking at folders handle this in different ways. In most cases the answer is no unless you can specify the full path to the child category. This only makes sense in a command-line environment (such as, DOS or a Unix Shell) but doesn't work very easily in a graphical environment. In this case the solution is to allow the user to see the parent categories but see them in a very restricted fashion. This might even include not being able to see their names, though this makes it hard to perform additional functions such as, copy or move. Especially if these tools require the full path to correctly access the digital object.

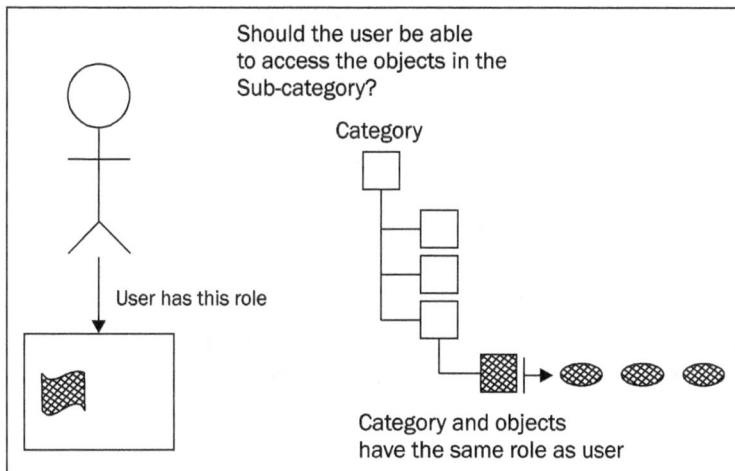

- Roles can be used to determine which users can access a purchase order and either review it or edit it. This is covered in greater detail in *Chapter 5, Loading Techniques*. If a purchase order requires it to be authorized by a manager, then that manager needs permission to see it. By attaching a role to the purchase order, if the manager has the same role, then they can review or edit it.

- Roles can be used to determine which accounts can review and edit other accounts. If a user has an account with a role (indicating that it's of a management level) mapped to it, then if a manager has that same role they can then edit or view the user account.

Role security can be enhanced even more to include the following capabilities:

- A role can be associated with an IP address to restrict where a person can access the data. If the user who has logged in has an internal IP address (indicating local access) then they can be automatically assigned a role with greater access. If they are external then they might be given limited access. This is useful for organizations that enable remote login. It's harder via a remote login to control which digital objects a user sees. During a remote login, a user could show friends/family the images. Where as if they were on an internal network might not be able to do that just because of the physical limitations of the environment.

- A role can be enabled to only be active during certain times of the day, or days of the week. This can be used to ensure that a user can only access sensitive information during controlled periods.

- It is possible for a role to be granted to other roles (parent-child granting). This is a form of inheritance. If you have a parent role, then you automatically have access to the child roles. This setup is useful for sites that use a large number of roles and after a while it becomes unwieldy to manage them all. It does add to the complexity of controlling access as the role (parent-child) hierarchy has to be well understood.

- Roles can be inherited from other systems. A user accessing a multimedia warehouse using LDAP can inherit the roles from their LDAP account.

- Roles can be password protected. A user, at log in, might be given access to a number of roles, but has to provide an additional password to enable them. For a consultant working on site for a short term this can be a useful feature. They might have a long term account because they do occasional on-site jobs for the organization. Their base account though has minimal access, but their security is set up with password protected roles and is ready to go (they don't need to request a new account and authorization every time they go to the organization). This saves time. To access digital objects a manager gives them the password to enable the role or roles. The password is changed on a daily basis. If the consultant works in different areas, access can be given on demand and rescinded by simply changing the password.

Roles can be used to add new security scenarios to an environment. If a user creates a lightbox, they might add to the lightbox ten images for which they have a legitimate access. If the role security allows it, they can give another user access to their lightbox. That user can then see the images in the lightbox even though they do not have the roles to access those objects.

A role can also be given additional privileges including select, insert, update, delete, and alter. Such a concept is well detailed in SQL databases, but in a multimedia database this access can be used to control metadata manipulation. A user can be given a role with *select* access, giving them read only access to the metadata. If the user was given a role with *select* and *update* access then the user can read the data and modify it. If the user is also given *insert* access, it means they can assign new data to an image, or maybe create a new image. If the user has *delete* access then they can delete a metadata value or delete an image.

To change the structure or definition of the image, the *alter* privilege is used. If a user is given alter access it means they have the ability to manipulate the image. This might include resizing it, creating a new thumbnail, or other forms of physical manipulation. If its metadata, it might mean they can change the attributes of the parent meta tag, including changing the meta tag name. Alter access has a lot of capabilities and should only be assigned to users with the correct skills and understanding to use it. Alter is different to update. Alter involves changing the structure of the image, where as update applies to changing the metadata attached to the image.

If a user is given a role without select, insert, update, delete, or alter access, it means the user can search for an image but cannot see the metadata nor see the digital object itself. However, they can see that a digital object was returned from their search request. They might only see the digital object name or some piece of public information on the object. In this case they know their search returned a result, but they can't see anymore information on it. In this case the system might request that they get the correct authorization to see the object.

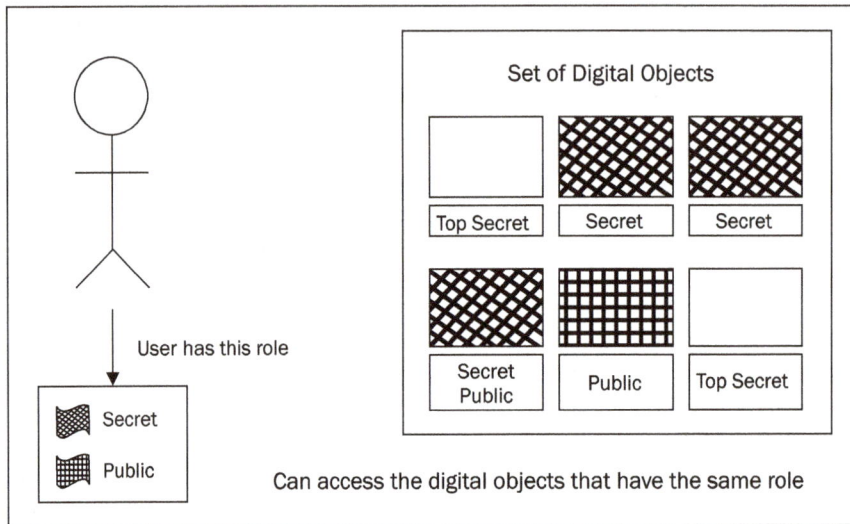

Roles can also be assigned with or without administrative privileges. Again this feature is common in SQL databases and basically says that if a role is assigned to a user with administrative privileges it means that user can assign that role to another user. This enables hierarchical security where authority is passed to another trusted user.

Searching

When it comes to searching, most people have a Google or Bing mentality. This means they have been inadvertently trained in search behavior because of their extensive usage of these search tools. They are used to typing in a word or two and have the results come back in a ranked order. This type of search is a **course grained** search. It is effective when you are blindly reaching out trying to find a match. Users then look at the results and narrow down their search manually by checking the results to see if it was what they were after.

This type of searching is very effective when the information is spread across a large number of systems. It is not effective when more refined or **fine grain** search methods are requested. These search systems are also based around the concept of HTML page being the only type of digital object being searched on.

A number of these search engines struggle or just cannot handle fine grained queries. If a user wanted to find all images that were portrait and were not rotated correctly, it would involve looking at the physical attributes of the digital image and its EXIF value for rotation.

If user wanted to do a fuzzy query using a `circa` datatype, these search engines can't even begin to handle them, primarily because the metadata types are not extracted or calculated.

The major search engines use the HTML page as the core digital object. Its importance is based on relationships or links from other pages to this one. The text within it is treated as raw text and for some, they might extract the HTML `<meta>` header information and use it to assist in searching. The engines do not focus on the meaning of the data in the pages.

Another limitation of these course grain search engines is that they assume all data is public. There is no security. There is no ability to restrict what is accessed based on a role. Making the assumption that everything is public simplifies the focus of the search engine, enabling the engine to focus on the data and what it has been trained to think is important for queries. The only security protection in place involves protecting the privacy of the user doing the queries and trying to hide their search history from others.

Course grained search engines are notorious for returning false positives (discussed later in this chapter), effectively returning the wrong HTML document. Most users are now aware of this and what separates the different search engines now is the algorithms they use to ensure greater accuracy in what is returned. Because these search engines are working primarily with HTML which uses tags to markup the pages and not describe the data, they have a challenge to understand what the data in the pages means. To overcome this, the major search engines also integrate with other systems, such as, Wiki, online dictionaries, and popular databases. When they do this they can extract data and gain a greater understanding of what it means.

Because the course grained search engines have limited security and focus at the HTML document level, it enables them to scale to handle hundreds of thousands of requests spread across tens of thousands of servers.

Fine grained queries are more complex, requiring more accurate and context sensitive queries which can be very resource intensive to run. A fine grained search engine should produce accurate and consistent results.

An analogy for a course grain search engine is a top-down query. Where as a fine grain search engine uses bottom-up query. It's possible to merge the two together. In Oracle, the product *Oracle Text* can be viewed as a course grain search engine (even though it allows fine grain queries). When an Oracle Text SQL query is used with additional relational `where` expressions, a mixture of both course and fine grain querying can be done.

Oracle Text Query

select m.raw_document, ctxsys.SCORE(10) vrank   Course grain clause

from mydocument m

where contains(m.raw_document,'car and boat',10) > 0 and

document_type = 'PDF';   Fine grain clause

The following section on searching covers the various fine grain methods that can be used to search based on the context of the data warehouse application. It also covers how to represent results and techniques for searching.

Indexing performance

An often overlooked aspect of course grain versus fine grain searching is the speed at which changes are reflected in the index. The *course grain* search engine looks for changes to data and indexes or re-indexes them. A *fine grain* search is updated as the data is updated. As such the fine grain search engine is always up to date and there are no delays. When a transaction is performed against the data in the warehouse that change is immediately reflected in the index. When a user does a query, they are doing a query against the most up to date version. There is a performance cost involved in doing this. The course grain search engine utilizes the concept of *eventual consistency* with delays of minutes, hours, or days occurring from when the changes are made until they are reflected in the search engine results.

For course grain engines, such as Google, it is impractical to implement real time consistency so eventual consistency is the only solution. As most web pages are static, the user community is accustomed to not seeing changes in pages being instantly reflected back in the search engine. Google offers a flexible crawl rate for the search engine robot. When the robot, also referred to as a **bot**, accesses a page for indexing it's called a **crawl**. In effect it crawls around the site. As indicated on their website[2]:

> *"Google has sophisticated algorithms that determine how much to crawl each site. Our goal is to crawl as many pages from your site as we can on each visit without overwhelming your server's bandwidth."*

Data warehouses typically employ the use of *eventual consistency* as they are dealing with summary data. As covered when reviewing the different types of multimedia warehouses, a multimedia warehouse might have different business directives resulting in the need for real time consistency. In that case, how the search engine indexes the data has to be taken into consideration.

Oracle provides a built in search engine called **Oracle Text**. This engine can index documents and generate themes and summaries of that document. The resource intensive nature of that indexing process makes it impractical to index the document in real time and routines are provided to enable indexing, in bulk, in batch. Though the Oracle Text search engine can act as a fine grain search engine, its delayed indexing capabilities puts it in between the described course grain and fine grained search engines. As the technology and software changes, the behavior of the search engines will also change resulting in the search engines being ranked, at various points, between the two extremes.

Metadata based

The simplest method for searching is to query its metadata. As the data is text based, search algorithms have been in the market for decades and are well suited for querying against it. Using SQL at the backend enables incredibly sophisticated queries to be written. To scale upwards to handle hundreds of thousands of concurrent requests, alternate technologies to SQL need to be used. One of these is NoSQL which enables more concurrent queries to be run but usually with major limitations (these are discussed further in *Chapter 8, Tuning*).

Image structure

When searching against multimedia, its physical structures can also be queried. This includes width, height, size, duration, and all other characteristics. To simplify the process, this information can be replicated into metadata, enabling a standard metadata search.

Electronic commerce

For e-commerce multimedia warehouses, additional attributes are needed to be searched on. This includes availability, price, customer information, and price item details including price dimensional information (size, color, and style). This is covered in greater detail in *Chapter 5, Loading Techniques*. It's reasonable to search for all digital images that are black and white, in stock for under $20 and that can have a wooden frame attached to them.

False positives

One of the greatest challenges in dealing with search is trying to determine if the result that came back was correct. If it isn't it's called a **false positive**. A **false negative** is when an expected result does not come back. In statistics a false positive is a Type I error and a false negative is a Type II error. A simple example of a false positive is if you search for a car and a picture of a boat comes back. An example of a false negative is if you search for a car but only three pictures come back but you know there is a fourth. A false negative can be harder to detect as it involves having a good understanding of the data.

Sometimes though, there might be a gray area between what is returned and what the query is. A search on car might return a boat, but the metadata attached to the boat might include the phrase "A car towed the boat to the waterfront". In which case technically the answer is correct because the digital object has metadata which contains the word car, but semantically it's not what was intended.

In other cases if a complex query is asked with a mixture of search items coupled with join expressions, such as *and* / *or*, when the results come back it might be important to actually check, what was the original question that was asked. When using the SQL language this is a common practice that seasoned developers use. If there is any reason to doubt the results, first check the question that was asked.

The challenge of all search engines is to first of ensure the results do not contain false positives and secondly to ensure that the results semantically match the original query. Ensuring no false positives are returned is more an algorithmic coupled with programming issue. Ensuring the results semantically match is an ongoing and challenging issue for all search engines. This capability is only in the early stages of development, with each search engine offering different methods for dealing with it. Course grain search engines deal with it differently to fine grain ones. A researcher using a fine grain search engine might determine the results of the query are not all semantically correct. They might then use additional search attributes to fine tune the query, maybe restricting the metadata fields searched against or forcing the search to only use trusted metadata values.

Stop words

Stop words are designed to help prevent some false positive cases. A set of stop words are a list of words that are to be ignored. Standard words include the, and, or, about, and then. A full list of common ones can be found at:

```
http://www.textfixer.com/resources/common-english-words.txt
```

A digital object containing a stop word will not fully index the stop word. When a search is performed the stop words are filtered out. So a search on *car then boat*, will do a search on *car boat*. The stop word "then" will ignored.

It is important to stress that stop words should not always be filtered out. When an exact match is requested (for example "car and boat"), the search being requested is to look for that exact phrase which might include the stop words. The search engine needs to know to distinguish between searches on words and exact phrases.

The living search

The concept of a **living search** is an idea that is useful for fine grain search engines. The idea is that once a search is run it is always alive. If a new object is added or deleted, then the search result immediately reflects that.

This is different to a course grain search. Here the aim is to run the search once and then review the results. The living search is designed more for researchers.

For fine grain search engines, when a query is run the results are stored in cache. The cache can then be accessed by the user to display the results and to search within the results. For a course grain search engine, the number of results that are returned can be incredibly large. Searches on Google can indicate millions of hits. Most users when searching never advance beyond two or three pages. The issue that needs to be addressed is when a user does a query and retrieves thousands of results; what should the behavior be when the user navigates between the sets of results? In the scenario where a page displays ten results, when the user navigates to the next page is it more efficient to:

- Store the results in a cache and use that for navigation
- Redo the query and retrieve the next set

Redoing the query is simpler to implement but is not efficient if the queries are complex and consume a lot of resources. For a course grained engine, such as Google, it makes sense to not cache and just redo the query. The challenge with managing a cache is that it requires the result to be stored. This consumes physical storage and if there are hundreds of thousands of concurrent users this requires a lot of storage.

Having a cache offers major performance benefits for fine grain searches. The performance overheads of navigating the cache are small compared to the performance issues related to having to rerun the query just to deal with page navigation. A cache is useful for performance because running a complex fine grain query can be expensive on computer resources. If a user runs a query it is stored in the cache. If the user reruns the same query then the cache can be accessed rather than the query being rerun. If another user with the same security privileges runs the same query then they can also access the cache.

The living search is designed to work with a cache. Once the query is run, if the user navigates between pages then the pages and the results might change if new objects are added or removed. The results are always accurate.

For those with database knowledge they might be tempted to conclude this is the equivalent of a **dirty read**[3]. Oracle has implemented at its core, the concept of read consistency. This feature, which most developers now take for granted, enforces the idea that when a query is run, the results of that query are accurate at the time when that query started running. New rows are added or deleted or ignored. Oracle uses its database rollback segment and internal **SCN (system change number)**. These are internal numbers used to automatically handle this. This is a very powerful feature and ensures queries are accurate when run. This is crucial for banking systems where if a query, when run, might take more than an hour, the answer will be valid because the database ensures the results are correct at the time of it running.

The living search though is slightly different. When the query is first run the result will be accurate as of the time it runs. The differentiator is that the result set stays alive and adjusts itself to match the status of the database. For a dirty read the user can access data that is not yet committed (saved). This isn't a living search query. Here the user can only access saved data, never dirty. Additionally, the query is not fixed to what read consistency offers.

The temptation is then to state, why not just rerun the query (force a cache refresh) and see what is new? This act requires the user to initiate the re-query. For the living search, the user doesn't have to do this because when they navigate and access the results, they are always accurate. The living search concept turns the idea completely around. It changes the attitude that the user has to always refresh to get the latest result. With the living search, the one initial query is always alive and accurate.

This feature is useful for multimedia warehouses that focus on policing or criminal detection. A user can enter in a complex query that might take a lot of resources to run. The user can keep the query alive and through different interfaces review the query for changes to the results. New hits or changes are immediately available to the user.

The challenge for those implementing a living search is to do this efficiently. The quickest method is to have a batch program go through all queries marked as living searches, rerun them, and update the cache. This gives the illusion of a living search query but is not accurate. It is also not effective performance wise. If there are ten thousand queries and each one needs to be rerun on a regular basis, then the server will very quickly become overwhelmed with running complex queries, even when the resultant cache might not change.

What is required is a core rewrite of the underlying search engine to handle this feature. This means that on every digital object addition, modification, or deletion all the queries need to be validated against this digital object to see if the cache needs changing. This validation has to be done efficiently. One has to be aware that even a slight change to the metadata around a digital object or even its core physical attributes, can cause a query result to change.

Shared caches offer major performance gains as only the one query needs to be managed and a lot of users can access the one result. For sites with public access to their collection, the need to rerun the same queries, when the same public user is doing the query, is removed. The challenge then becomes when a user wants to change the order in which the results appear.

Course grain search engines typically return the results in a ranked order. Their strength is how they best match the rank result to the query. The rank engine can be improved if the search engine keeps a history of the user and can make assumptions using this history on the type of query the user is performing.

For fine grain search engines, ranked results is just one of many possible ways of having the results returned. The user might want the digital objects sorted based on the filename, the data loaded, or even a particular metadata value. The results might be grouped based on taxonomy or within a thesaurus. It's important to remember that the result set is not limited to ranking, which is what most users have been unwittingly trained to accept when using the course grain engines.

To enable a user to change the ordering of the results, the temptation is to look at the cache and sort it based on the request of the user. This falls down when caching is used as the same cache can be used by multiple users each wanting a different sort order. Session based or shared ordering is needed. This requires enabling the cache to be stored in different sort orders.

The living search offers a powerful tool to the repertoire of search tools available to users in a multimedia warehouse. Though it's not a mandatory requirement to have it, its adoption will change the focus of search engines to be more query centric and not result centric.

Currently the only vendor that offers support for the living search is Piction.

Data mining

As we have covered already, data mining involves looking at data and trying to find patterns or relationships in the data. With a multimedia database, as the focus is more on digital objects, a key goal with data mining is trying to find relationships between those objects. This can involve looking at the metadata elements and using a number of matching techniques (including fuzzy matching covered a little later in this chapter) to ascertain how well matched two digital objects are.

The data mining tool might need to go through all digital objects and then compare them to every other object in the warehouse and determine what relationship it has to it. For a warehouse with a large number of digital objects this could be a time consuming process, but the advantage is that it can run in parallel in batch.

Data mining can be done on all the digital objects in the multimedia warehouse, or individual ones can be data mined.

Big O notation

Big O notation is a method for simply describing the number of operations required to perform a task. In computing this notation is often used for database tuning and to emphasize how expensive a computing task or operation is. Its use first came to light in the eighties when it was used to highlight the search result set sorting problem. Sorting algorithms used algorithms that were O(n2), meaning if there were 10 rows (n is equal to 10), then the number of operations required to achieve these task would be 102 or 100. As the number of rows grew so did the amount of effort required to do the sort. As sorting is such an important feature used not only in SQL, but many internal functions, the goal was to reduce it. Eventually algorithms came out which managed to reduce it O(log n), and in the case of an *interpolation*[4] search, it has been further reduced to O(log log n). Big O notation is covered further in *Chapter 9, Understanding the limitations of Oracle Products*

For data mining, to establish all the relationships using Big O notation is $O(n^2)$. This can be reduced to O(n) by limiting how the relationships are established and the surreptitious use of indexing.

Representing the results

A key goal in having a warehouse is to be able to perform analysis. The output can be just raw data, similar to what is found in a spreadsheet. Different tools in the marketplace provide a wide variety of ways of querying and handling this data. As the goal is analysis, the more data that can be processed by the user, the more effective the analysis.

The challenge is that most people cannot handle or digest large amounts of raw data and make sense of it. The very nature of multimedia in the database encourages the use of display interfaces that offer a more vibrant and interactive system enabling large amounts of data, produced from analysis, to be displayed. This section covers a number of visualization methods available in the market that are designed to take advantage of the unique characteristics of multimedia.

Interface

Currently most interfaces are limited to two dimensional flat screens with audio. With the recent introduction of 3D TV and gaming consoles it is inevitable that this technology will make its way into mainstream usage. Additional devices such as cameras that can interpret hand gestures as well as body sensitive clothing (initially seen as gloves), enables both input and sensory feedback to be achieved adding new dimensions for dealing with the data. In addition the recent introduction of Siri and Iris, voice responsive applications have again pushed the boundaries between computers and human interaction, enabling intelligent voice control. When adapted for the multimedia warehouse, the goal will be to ask the computer the question, rather than trying to navigate through GUI screens attempting to formulate the query. The challenge in the early stages with this technology will be confidence and trust factor of the data that is returned. Has what I verbally asked for been answered correctly by the computer system?

Ultimately what makes an interface useful is how efficiently and quickly it can handle input and output requests.

Visualize the results

The goal is to visualize and make sense of as much data as possible to achieve an end goal. Such a concept is just not possible with structured data warehouses as all that could be returned is text. By combining and overlaying images, using color coding schemes with tactile feedback screens, enables large amounts of data to be amassed and absorbed in a way that humans can understand and interpret it.

Tag cloud

A **tag cloud** enables typically two and sometimes more dimensions of information to be displayed to a user. The first dimension is a word and depending on the application can be calculated from a search result, a statistic (be it a frequency or aggregation) or size. Simply, it's some form of metric that can be applied to the word. The strategy is to allow more information to be seen and viewed in a way that enables intelligent interpretations of the data.

The second dimension is font size used to display the word. The larger the font the greater the statistical meaning. If in an intelligence warehouse a search was done on an individual name, the results that come back might be known associates of that individual. The larger the font could be used the indicate the greater the association. A visual look at the tag cloud immediately shows who the major associations are.

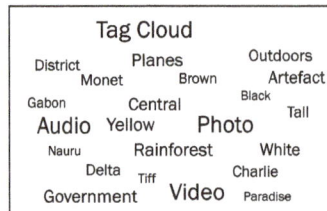

A tag cloud makes it easier for people to absorb larger amounts of information and to establish patterns or correlations in them.

Other dimensions can include color, where each word can have a color associated with the font. Using the previous example, if family members are given a color, personal friends another color, work colleagues another color, and casual acquaintances another, the tag cloud can now easily show more details on the relationships. This makes it easier to visually rule out close friends and family and allow the person doing the query to easily focus on which casual acquaintances are the most popular.

Another dimension could include the position of the words to each other. In the preceding example, the position could relate to time between the last contact between the individual and the associate. The closer to the individual the more recent the last contact.

When a tag cloud is used, as in the previous example, it can provide a wealth of information enabling the user to understand and absorb information quickly and to make new decisions based on the data retrieved.

When the tag cloud concept is extended to multimedia, the concepts for the tag cloud remain the same except rather than the focus being on a word, instead it's on a digital object. A good example is found at http://www.ted.com/.

The size of the image indicates information about a metric concerning it. In the www.ted.com case, the size is indicative of how frequently the digital object has been accessed.

In the original example, if an individual search is replaced with an object search, then results can include associated or other types of digital objects, such as cars or physical locations.

Like a tag cloud, additional dimensions can be displayed using color and relative position. By moving to a third dimension for the display, these dimensions can become more obvious. Frame borders around a digital image, sound and animation can also be used to display extra dimensional information.

A new concept with the display which utilizes video motion can also be used to display additional dimensional information. By having the objects move at different speeds or even behaving erratically is another method which can be used to highlight dimensions of those objects.

In the example, if a digital object starts to jitter it could be used to indicate that the associate is a known criminal or that the object has been used in a recent crime. The more skilled and adept the user is at absorbing the information, the greater the chance that patterns can be seen that previously might have been missed.

The danger with an image cloud is information overload, where too much information in too many dimensions is shown resulting in important patterns being overlooked. Its important that a user can control and manipulate the dimensions ensuring they absorb the data at a pace that matches their skill level. This is covered in more detail in *Chapter 11, chapter name*, covering **CHI (computer human interaction)**.

Infinite zoom

This concept, immortalized in the movie Blade Runner, introduces the idea of a digital image storing all information in it. Within the image one can zoom to unlimited depth. A number of vendors have taken this concept down different paths. One shows how a whole book can be stored in one image with the viewer able to maneuver around the whole book using a hover concept and zoom in/out, right down to the letter. The other is to stitch thousands of images together into one large image, enabling a digital photo with a large depth. Google earth is another example of this in action.

For the user looking at the image, the impression is that there is just one image and one is continually zooming in and out. Behind the scenes though the technological implementation is done using complex indexing, revolving around a pyramid index (covered further in *Chapter 6, Delivery Techniques*).

Though the infinite zoom is not truly infinite in the depth it offers, it does provide to the user a simple front enabling quick access to parts of the image. By overlaying metadata, and even integrating other views, multiple perspectives can be added to the digital image. This then offers a powerful way of combining, viewing, absorbing, and understanding large amounts of information.

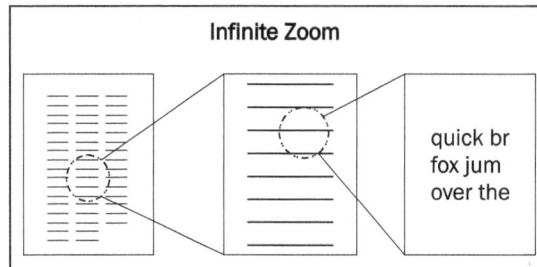

Complex social network

For those who work extensively in a multimedia warehouse, the need to identify and store relationships between the digital objects becomes apparent. It can be seen as an important component, enabling analysis beyond the traditional OLAP. Relationships between the digital objects can be as simple as relating similar accession numbers. The relationships can be manually defined or created using the metadata. How the relationships are formed can be based on a myriad of factors, some even being related to the unique characteristics of the digital objects themselves.

For a digital image, relationships can be established based on the content in the digital image or even images that look the same. The strength of the relationship can be determined based on the type of relationship. Two digital images might be related because they both contain buildings in them. The strength would be low. But if the digital images contained paintings of Van Gough then the relationship would be high.

The strength of the relationship becomes important. It can be increased if there are additional common components. Maybe the two digital images were created by the same person. Maybe they were created on the same day. Additionally they could be created using similar cameras or even in a similar location. The dimensions of data that can be used to create the relationships can dramatically vary. The more relationships discovered between two digital objects, the stronger that relationship becomes.

The digital objects and the relationships begin to closely correlate to the behavior of a *social network*[5]. Graph theory has been used to document social networks and how analysis based on the patterns, can be used to extrapolate new relationships. It can also be used to highlight key relationships between digital objects.

The simplest starting point for the visualization of this is to start with a circle and to place points on the circumference all the digital objects. Lines are then drawn between the points, with each line indicating a relationship. As more relationships are entered it becomes visually obvious which digital objects have the more important relationships.

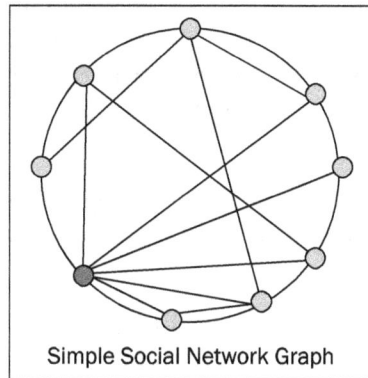

Simple Social Network Graph

The use of the circle has certain advantages and is simple to configure. A simple SVG program can easily produce a graph. It only offers one perspective of the relationship and can miss other relationships. A three dimensional one using a sphere rather than a circle can be additionally color coded to contain more information. While two dimensional flat screens are used, the attempt to represent the three dimensional sphere is limiting. The recent introduction of three dimensional screens will hopefully overcome these display limitations.

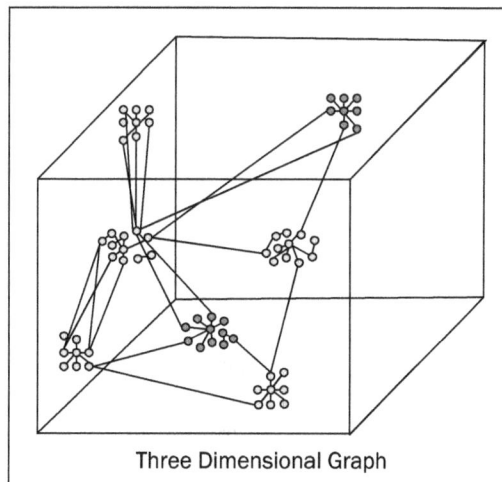

Three Dimensional Graph

Tree map

A **tree map** interface is a dynamic interface that enables causal relationships between digital objects to be discovered dynamically and visually displayed back to the user. The user starts with a digital object (a node) represented as a shape on the screen. This can be a circle, but based on the type of object can be any shape. Context sensitive parts of the object enable additional information such as metadata or digital images to be displayed. Once the user has the base digital object, the tree map looks for related objects and displays them as nodes around the first node. It links them together using a line (or a branch), giving the illusion of a tree structure. It is in effect a type of data-mining tool.

The strength of the relationship can be shown using colors or the thickness of the branch. The user can then access the related nodes and branch out from those to find additional relationships.

The goal of the tree map is to enable the user to find the relationships between digital objects. Using the *six degrees of separation* concept[6], it is anticipated that most nodes should be within six branches (relationships) of the other nodes. Whether the actual figure of six is achievable is based on a number of factors. Graph theory shows how a network of relationships only needs a small number of seemingly random connections to achieve the goal of six.

As the six degrees concept has become ubiquitous, the intuitive nature of the tree map is easier to grasp for most people enabling the interface to exploit this concept.

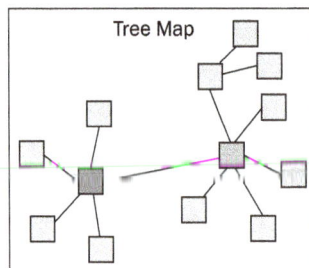

Lightbox

Again, another technology immortalized in a movie (in this case, the Minority Report) which due to the excitement it produced, has spawned a number of devices moving in the direction of being able to achieve some of the features highlighted in the movie. With lightbox, the direction is an interaction of touch and screen.

This concept takes the idea of using finger gestures to manipulate and control multiple digital images, integrating concepts like infinite zoom. The lightbox as described here is not the same as lightbox already defined. It's just a case of the same term being coined with multiple meanings.

The starting point is a screen full of images which are displayed randomly. The user can then rearrange, resize and control/categorize them using finger gestures only. Now available on the iPad; a larger version was first pioneered by Microsoft using a table computer. Sign language reading computers enable the whole touch screen concept to be removed and replaced with a more advanced display.

VRML and SVG

There are two well known markup languages available to visualize data in a HTML environment. They are as follows:

- **Scalable Vector Graphics** (**SVG**): This is a markup language for creating two dimensional vector graphics. Defined in 1999, it was largely ignored because it was not natively supported in the browser. SVG can be used to draw graphs, animation, and fonts. It supports the use of color and can be interactive. As of 2011, most of the popular browsers have agreed to natively support it. Firefox 9 and Chrome support it. Internet Explorer has indicated it will support SVG. Enhancements in the markup language over the next couple of years will result in additional functionality enabling a number of the visualization tools discussed to be represented in SVG[7].

- **Virtual Reality Modeling Language** (**VRML**):. This is a markup language designed for creating interactive three-dimensional vector graphics. It was defined before SVG but had performance issues when rendered on computers in the mid 1990s. The large amount of XML data required to render a three-dimensional graphic also made it very difficult to download over telephone lines. This led to it being ignored by browser makers. With the popularity in SVG growing, the direction VRML takes will still need to be determined. It can either be absorbed into SVG, remain separate or SVG can be enhanced to enable the three dimensional aspects of VRML[8].

Irrespective of the direction, VRML offered a way of visually displaying in three dimensions, large amounts of data simply. Like SVG it is an ideal tool for multimedia warehouses. With the huge improvement in rendering speed, network bandwidth, and the ability to compress data dynamically, VRML is an ideal tool to visualize multimedia data and relationships.

In addition to VRML, there are competing standards for rendering three dimensional objects including X3D (http://www.web3d.org). Until natively supported within the browser, neither VRML or X3D will be adopted and will be limited to specialist sites and applications.

Synchronized Multimedia Integration Language (SMIL)

SMIL's goal was to enable multimedia presentations to be embedded within HTML. It uses XML and has the ability to display text, video, and audio. It can do this while retrieving the multimedia from different devices. They key capability of SMIL is to be able to control not only what is displayed, but when it is displayed. The timing capabilities add a unique aspect to this which is not found in the other markup XML display languages, which are mostly passive by nature.

SMIL[9] is used to enable animation in SVG. As SVG is available in Chrome and Firefox, SMIL is also supported. As of IE9, SMIL is not supported. Though SMIL is not a replacement for Microsoft PowerPoint or Open Office presentation, it is only a matter of time before these programs enable the export of SMIL presentations so they can be viewed in the browser. Currently the method utilized involves generating images of each slide and then using HTML and/or JavaScript to handle slide timing and transitions. Naively handling it will improve the functionality and ensure cross platform consistency.

Once SMIL is bundled in with IE9, developers will be able to take advantage of its capabilities and its multimedia capabilities will start to be fully realized.

In this example SMIL displays three videos simultaneously:

```
<smil>
 <head>
  <layout>
   <root-layout width="1200" height="800"/>
   <region id="vid_left" width="360" height="240" left="0" top="0"/>
   <region id="vid_center" width="360" height="240" left="360"
top="0"/>
   <region id="vid_right" width="360" height="240" left="720"
top="0"/>
  </layout>
 </head>
 <body>
  <par dur="50s">
```

```
    <video src="move1.mpg" clip-begin="1.12s" region="vid_left"/>
    <video src="move2.mpg" clip-begin="0s" region="vid_center"/>
    <video src="move3.mpg" clip-begin="1.12s" region="vid_right"/>
  </par>
 </body>
</smil>
```

HTML 5

HTML 5[10], at the time of writing, is the latest incarnation of the HTML markup language. Its key strength is the ability to work better with multimedia objects. HTML 5 is covered further in *Chapter 5, Loading Techniques*.

HTML 5 came to attention when Steve Jobs (former CEO of Apple) ensured there would be no support of the product Adobe Flash on any iPad or iPhone. Until then, it was assumed that Adobe Flash would be the de facto multimedia display product for browsers and mobile devices. The desire to offer an open standard, that would seamlessly work in the browser, which had no perceived security issues, effectively cornered the Adobe Flash product. Its long term future is still up for debate.

HTML 5 provides greater play capabilities for audio and video. One of its key goals was to get around one of the biggest drawbacks for dealing with multimedia, which was the difficulty in finding and installing plugins for the browser so that it could play audio or video. The huge range of audio and video codecs made it hard to get consistency and uniformity when dealing with audio and video. Unlike digital images which had agreed standards of display (JPEG, PNG, and GIF) which all browsers supported, there was no agreed standard in display for video. Although there still is no agreed standard for audio and video, what HTML 5 does offer is the ability to deal with the different codecs and ensure that there is greater chance of being able to view the multimedia. They also enable the designer of the HTML page greater control over the customization of how the player looks and behaves.

HTML 5 alone cannot provide animation within web pages. Either JavaScript or CSS3 is necessary for animating HTML elements. Animation is also possible using JavaScript and HTML and within SVG elements through SMIL, although browser support of the latter remains uneven as of 2011.

Adobe Flash

Adobe Flash[11] is a plugin for web browsers that has a multimedia focus. It was first released in 1997 and was quickly accepted as the premier tool for multimedia visualization on the Internet. By 2012 a lot of sites that required video playback, audio playback, animation and Internet gaming used the Adobe Flash product. In 2011 it was openly attacked by Apple citing concerns about it being open, its performance, its security, and it not supporting the video format used on Apple mobile devices (which was also propriety).

Adobe Flash is still extensively used on the Internet but with the introduction of browser support for HTML 5 along with SVG and SMIL, the necessity to develop applications in Flash is now being debated.

Voice XML

Voice XML[12] is an XML format which is an audio browser integration that uses human speech as its primary focus. Its design is to enable speech synthesis (computer generated voice) and voice recognition. It's currently supported as a plugin for browsers and is not natively supported. When the Voice XML standard eventually becomes stable and the market can see a need for it to be bundled in with browsers (like video, audio has been in HTML 5), then this interface to the computer using audio will enable a new and exciting dimension to how multimedia data is accessed and viewed.

Other devices

So pervasive is the use of two dimensional flat screens to represent data that other devices are completely missed.

Braille devices

This device enables a dynamic tactile view to be achieved. Currently two forms exist in the market. The first is designed for the visually impaired to read braille via a device which can simulate braille characters. The other form is a glove which when worn can stimulate the skin providing the sensation of feeling an object. The glove when combined with a 3D visual device will enable the user too feel and manipulate 3D digital objects. Gaming devices are already pioneering the technology, as can be seen with the Peregrine Gaming Glove (http://theperegrine.com).

Audio

The use of audio can supplement a visual display. Sounds can be made to add extra information or provide warnings. A simple beep can be used to indicate a user has navigated to a security sensitive area. Text to speech can read key data summaries preventing too much visual information being displayed on the screen.

Search features

As a number of the visualization concepts described are still in their technological infancy, standard search techniques using text data will take center stage in the foreseeable future. With the focus on research, analysis, and data mining, this section covers some of the standard features expected from a search engine in a multimedia warehouse. It is important to keep in mind that compared to the traditional data warehouse, querying the multimedia warehouse involves a more object focused mentality crossed with traditional warehouse querying.

Summary groups

Also referred to as a dimensional summary, the summary group provides a cross reference on the results returned. A typical method is to break down the search into the core multimedia types, such as photo, audio, video, and document. Users can then quickly query these summary groups to look at the results specific to the media.

There is no limit to the types of summary groups that can be returned. Examples include the following:

- Date loaded or created. Using year and/or month.
- Distinct metadata values. This involves grouping the results.
- Object shape.
- Duration of audio or video.
- Mimetype
- Search engine type. This is if a query is run against multiple search engines and the results have been combined together.

Calculating a summary group can be an expensive operation to perform. If it involves metadata, it requires doing a separate query to retrieve all the distinct values. If the query result set is large, this operation can be machine resource intensive.

Workarea

Like a lightbox, a **workarea** is a query result which has been saved. The workarea allows the user to move results into it and even do queries within it. The workarea can be saved, assigned a name, and cataloged. The workearea can be combined or a new workarea can be created based on the intersection of one or more workareas.

Having support for a workarea also means that users should be able to do query within query. That is, run a query against a result set.

Non discriminatory search

For a multimedia warehouse containing a mixture of digital objects, it's important that the one search can query all the objects. Some off the shelf search engines have restrictions on what they can search against. Having to run two or more queries against different search engines (where each one searches against the capabilities of the multimedia) and then manually combining those results, is not effective and likely to result in errors. It also limits the ability to do complex queries. If it has to interrogate multiple search engines it should seamlessly integrate the results while still allowing complex queries to be run.

A search engine should be media and data agnostic. It should be able to query against digital images, video, audio, documents, spatial, and metadata. It should be able to interrogate external search engines (such as, Google and/or Bing) and integrate the results in with the initial query.

Result notification

For long running search queries, users should have the option of running the query in background (or batch mode). Users can also be emailed the results of queries, or if a living search option exists, being able to have new results matching their query sent to them.

Restrict the results

When a user performs a query they should have control over the number of results returned. They might just be interested in the top ten results, even though ten thousand might be returned. This feature is useful when a workarea is created based on the results of a search.

Control the output

A useful feature is to allow the search to return the data in a variety of formats. Some of these include:

- **Comma Delimited Format (CSV)**: This allows the result set to be loaded into a spreadsheet.
- **XML**: This allows the result to be shared between computer systems. An advantage is if the XML can conform to one of the metadata standards mentioned.

Audit search

For intelligence and secure multimedia warehouses it's important to be able to have full auditing of all queries run. This will mean storing a large amount of result data. In the event of a security breach, this information can prove to be invaluable. It's important to not only trap the query a user performs, but the actual output sent and displayed on the screen. In a number of countries, it's not sufficient in prosecution to be able to prove a user performed a query illegally. It needs to be proven that they actually saw the results. As data changes, the result from when the user ran the query might change a day later. A user under suspicion of performing an illegal query can say that when they ran it, no data was returned.

For police systems this auditing is very important, as potential corruption can be investigated if a police officer starts to query the results of a police investigation being performed by a different unit. Even though the security model in place might allow them to access the data, they shouldn't be accessing it unless approval is given. Secure checksums need to be stored against the screen captures and stored separately to ensure these checksums are not tampered with.

Designing a search language

An organization might initially use an off the shelf course grain search engine for their multimedia warehouse. Eventually they will come to the conclusion that to do complex queries, research queries or queries that are unique to the particular characteristics of the digital objects, they will need to build their own fine grain search engine. This will allow them to control and ensure the answers they require can be phrased within the limitations of the engine.

Search context

Most search engines behave differently when it comes to obvious search constructs. The context that the search engine has to decide to use is ambiguous. If I access a search engine and search on: car boat bike, what exactly is the request I am searching on?

Is it one of the following:

- Car AND boat AND bike
- Car OR boat OR bike
- "car boat bike"
- Car AND boat OPTIONAL search on bike

There are more variations on this search. The Google search tries to match all words and then rank the results based on the number of results. If the value being searched on contains *car boat* next to each other and contains *bike* near it, that intuitively should rank higher than one where the three words are randomly distributed throughout the document. But what if the result contains *boat car*, in reverse order? The position of the results, based on the initial context in which the search was done, now has relevance. However it might not because different users might have completely different goals when searching.

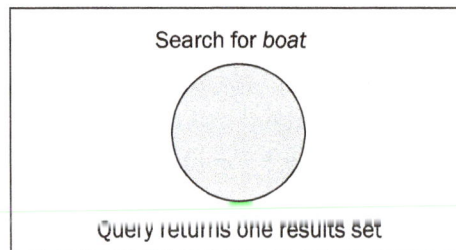

This is why course grain search engines must differ from fine grain. In a course grain search engine, the engine has to make attempts to guess the context of the search and do its best to rank the results based on that. For a fine grain search engine, result ranking might not be important. The default behavior might be to interpret that when a user enters in a number of search words then the goal is find all of them (using AND). It might allow the user to configure, via the preferences, what the default behavior should be.

A singular search is one that involves the search on one word for example, car. A singular search can also be done on a fixed set of words typically enclosed in quotes for example, "car boat". No boolean operations are done between them. A boolean operation is one which involves AND, OR, NOT. The result of a singular search is a query result set. When multiple search terms are used and boolean operations are involved, then multiple query result sets need to be combined using the concepts based on set theory.

Set theory primer

All search engines involve the same basic core concepts which are centered around set theory. Set theory involves dealing with the following actions:

- **Union**: The English equivalent is OR. If you do a search for boat or car, the result set is a union of the two. A union will return a unique set of values.
- **Intersection**: The English equivalent is AND. If you do a search for boat and car, the result set is an intersection of the two.
- **Minus**: The closest English equivalent is NOT. If you do a search for boat not car then the result set is the first set minus the second set.
- **Union all**: Simply appends the two result sets without looking for duplicates.

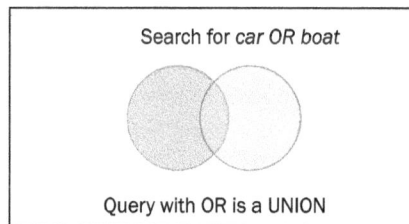

Search for *car OR boat*

Query with OR is a UNION

Order of precedence

If the search term is car AND boat OR bike, how should it be evaluated? There are actually two choices:

- Car AND boat. Then get the result set OR bike.
- Boat OR bike. Then get the result set AND car.

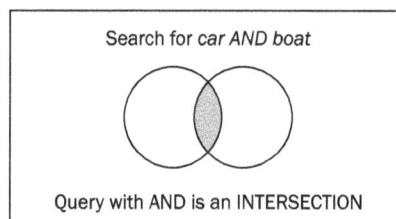

Search for *car AND boat*

Query with AND is an INTERSECTION

Order of precedence is used in mathematics when an expression is ambiguous. In mathematics some operations have precedence over others.

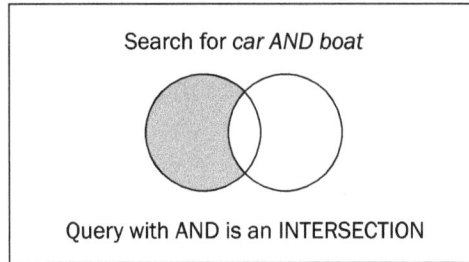

Search for *car AND boat*

Query with AND is an INTERSECTION

So if the expression is as follows:

5 + 6 x 7

The result would be as follows:

- 77 if the precedence is + over x
- 47 if the precedence is x over +

In mathematics, multiplication has precedence over plus. The same holds true in computing but can vary between languages. In set theory, AND traditionally had precedence over OR. To enforce precedence round brackets are used. Most search engines support the use of round brackets to force precedence. What is enclosed in the brackets is performed first.

The following examples show how the same query can vary just by rearranging the clauses in the statement as well as using round brackets.

```
Sql 1> select count(*) from dict where table_name like 'USER_%' and
table_name like '%S' or comments like '%bs';
 COUNT(*)
----------
      287

sql 2> select count(*) from dict where (table_name like 'USER_%' and
table_name like '%S') or comments like '%bs';

  COUNT(*)
----------
      287
```

```
sql 3> select count(*) from dict where table_name like 'USER_%' and
(table_name like '%S' or comments like '%bs');

COUNT(*)
----------
      281
```

In statement 1, we see that 287 rows are returned. The order of precedence of AND is proven when in the second statement round brackets are put around the AND statement forcing it to run first. This is highlighted in the third statement where the OR is forced to run first with the results having an AND run on them.

By rearranging the statements we can get different results:

```
Sql 4> select count(*) from dict where table_name like '%S' or
comments like '%bs' and table_name like 'USER_%';

COUNT(*)
----------
     1226
```

```
sql 5> select count(*) from dict where (table_name like '%S' or
comments like '%bs') and table_name like 'USER_%';

COUNT(*)
----------
      281
```

```
sql 6> select count(*) from dict where table_name like '%S' or
(comments like '%bs' and table_name like 'USER_%');

COUNT(*)
----------
     1226
```

In the fourth statement we rearrange the clauses, because the AND is done first, it now does a different query compared to the AND in the first statement. In the fifth statement, the brackets ensure that the OR is done first, with the result that the query performs identically to the third query. By putting brackets around the AND the result then matches the fourth query, again showing AND is evaluated first.

What this highlights is that with a search engine, the position and ordering can impact what is returned. In some cases it can completely change the whole meaning of the query. As most users are not familiar or comfortable with having to know about the order of precedence, the assumption made is that statements are evaluated left to right in the order in which they appear.

When looking at the two popular search engines Google and Bing, we can deduce that Google always evaluates left to right and ignores round brackets. Bing also evaluates left to right but enforces the use of the brackets to enforce precedence.

Search Query	Google	Bing
car and boat or bike	About 81,200,000	124, 000, 000
(car and boat) or bike	About 81,200,000	124, 000, 000
car and (boat or bike)	About 81,200,000	122, 000, 000
boat or bike and car	About 81,700,000	123, 000, 000
boat or (bike and car)	About 81,700,000	127,000, 000
(boat or bike) and car	About 81,700,000	123, 000, 000

There is no right or wrong way when it comes to precedence, just a way of ensuring the users doing the query are aware of it. Due to the popularity of the search engine, along with the technology being integrated in with so many other engines, its method of completely ignoring precedence will likely win out. The general public will unknowingly be trained to accept this as the only behavior for a search engine.

Specialized query terms

This section covers advanced concepts when performing a search.

Spelling mistakes

Mistakes happen when entering in a search term. It can be a spelling mistake or just a guess at what the spelling of a word is. Some search engines detect the mistake and offer to correct it.

Some examples are as follows:

- With *Google* if you type in carrx, it will respond with "Did you mean: carex"
- With Bing if you type in carrx, it will respond with "Including results for car. Do you want results for carrx?"

Fine grained search engines have the ability to not only offer corrections, but can cross check their database and see what words could match the potential mistake, offering results back to the user that will produce results. It's not efficient for a search engine to offer carex as an alternate to the mistake carxx, if there are no values with carex in the database.

Sounds like

There are instances where a search is required to find a value that sounds like the value you want. Databases offer *soundex* capability which allows a user to find words that sound like the one you want. So a search on smith, will return values of smith as well as smyth, smythe.

A search with a soundex capability requires additional smarts to handle it.

With multimedia searching, soundex is just the beginning and additional search capabilities might be required using a similar context:

- Digital images: Find images that look like this one
- Audio: Find music that sounds like (audio sound, not to be confused with pronunciation)
- Video: Find a video similar to this one
- Find digital objects related to this one

Searching on multimedia can involve new search terms and specialized terms. It can involve searching for lists, object shapes, cross reference queries, queries looking for missing data, bad objects, objects loaded based on date as well as specialized searches on accession numbers, and names. The implementation of these search capabilities are likely to come at a cost in performance and impact the scalability of the search engine (in terms of how many concurrent queries it can process).

Stem search

Stem search is a feature useful for fine grained search engines. It tells the search engine to look for words that have a similar structure to the word being searched on. So a search on the word car, might also look for cars.

By linking a stem search to a thesaurus, the stem can perform intelligent queries using the thesaurus as a base. So a search on car linked to a thesaurus, might also search on caravan, motorbike, Ford, Holden, engine, and so on. When searching on a regional area, the stem might include the states within that region, maybe even the cites.

A stem search can intelligently broaden the width of the search, allowing more results to be returned. It might also increase the number of false positives. This is where *ranking* becomes important.

Ranking

If a search is done on three words, such as automobile, boat, and car (represented as A, B, and C) then the results that come back can be returned in a ranked order based on how well they match. The order of the results returned could be returned as follows:

- "A B C": Look for an exact match on all 3 words and they are next to each other.

- "A C B", "B A C", "B C A", "C A B", "C B A": Look for a variation on all three words, and all three are next to each other.

- "*A B C*": Look for a match where the words can be contained within other words.

- "A B" and C, "A C" and B, "B A" and C, "C B" and A: Where two words are next to each other and the third word is contained nearby. Ranking can be improved by word proximity.

- A and B and C: Where all the three words exist.

- "A B", "B A", "A C", "C A", "B C": Where two of the words exist and are located next to each other. There is no match for the third word.

- A and B, A and C, B and C: Where two of the words exist but there is no match for the third word.

- A or B or C: Where one of the words match.

The ranking can be fine tuned with the addition of *stem* and *soundex* in the results. A smart ranking, as identified above, will return results that in most cases will typically return what the user is requesting.

As the number of words used in the search increase, so does the number of permutations that need to be searched on. This will increase geometrically the number of sub queries that need to be performed. A well designed search engine could, on indexing, factor this into consideration reducing the search time.

In the Google search, the ranking notion is different and uses a similar concept to the ranking specified. With Google, the challenge is more focused on what to do with results that are ranked the same. How do you differentiate them? Because of the huge volume of data in Google, a search can return over 100,000 results. It's possible that in such a search the first 1000 all match the first requirement where all 3 words appear in that order next to each other.

To rank those that have the same result, Google employs a ranking algorithm that is well suited to the Internet. It ranks based on popularity of the page. The more popular the page (as in, how many other pages link to it), the higher the rank result. Google takes this rank result further by enabling it to push ahead of other ranks. So a very popular document that just contains the three words A, B, C in any order might become ranked higher than a document matching "A B C", but is not as popular. Google also uses other techniques such as ranking some sites automatically higher than others. This includes Wiki and You Tube. The exact ranking algorithm that Google uses is propriety to the company and is far more complex than has been described. For more information see `http://en.wikipedia.org/wiki/PageRank`.

A concept similar to this method can be used to enable intelligent searches to be performed. In an intelligence multimedia warehouse, a query on a person, a car, or any object of interest might produce a large number of results. By factoring in the number of associations or references made to the object it could enable the search engine to adjust its rank, attracting the attention of the person performing the query to digital objects which might have a greater relevance. Though this method would use a concept similar to what Google uses, its actual implementation in a multimedia warehouse would be very different.

Mandatory and other terms

Additional search options can be employed to add intelligence to the result. The plus symbol "+" traditionally refers to mandatory, meaning the term must exist in the search result. For example, +car and boat, looks for car and optionally boat.

The minus symbol "-" indicates the term must not be included in the result. This can be useful to reduce the number of false positives. For example, +car -boat, means look for anything containing car but it cannot contain boat.

The semi colon ";" means find terms near each other. So car ;boat would search for digital objects with both these terms in it, and within a small number of words of each other. The closer they are together the higher the rank.

Word frequency

A search typically looks to see if a digital object contains the search term. If the digital object contains the search term but it's repeated multiple times, then this repetition can be used as justification to increasing the ranking of the result. The justification being that the more often a word is repeated in a document the more important it must be. The search engine needs to factor this into consideration and in addition to indexing the word, store the frequency of the appearance of the word, so that it can use this value to adjust the ranking.

The trouble with documents

For a multimedia warehouse containing a large number of documents, searching using these terms can be useful, but it can also produce a large number of false positives. A user searching on bike might get documents returned that might casually reference the word bike, but they might not actually be about bikes.

This is an issue with most course grain search engines. They generally do not know what the page is about. In a HTML page keywords can be contained in the `<meta>` tag which are user supplied, and provide a summary of what the document is about. This is designed to add extra information to a page enabling searches to use this information to rank it higher. The challenge with the search engines is to realize that this information can easily be manipulated, and fool the engine into returning a page when the document is not really about it. In the early days of the Internet this was once a tactic used by companies trying to sell products and have their pages pushed higher in the search ranking results. It was because of this manipulation that Google came up with the idea of using links to pages to drive ranking. This was based on the assumption that the more useful a page is having information in it, the greater the likelihood that other sites will link to it. HTML pages containing sales information are unlikely to be linked to. The strategy was effective because it was hard to defeat and typically produce results containing information useful to the person doing the query. So for Google, when a user does a query against the search engine, the result that comes back is one which is likely to contain information of relevance to the user. It is not always guaranteed that it will be the best one. Although, it is hoped that best one is the one that comes back. For a course grain search engine which could not guarantee perfect answers, very good answers sufficed.

In a multimedia warehouse where the content is controlled, the users are more than likely to want the best answer. For a warehouse that contains documents, the contents of the documents are more than likely controlled and will not contain deceiving information. They can contain noise though. The larger the document the greater the chance of noise. The noise refers to the probability that a document contains a word being searched on which is not relevant to the document. A document with 20,000 words in it will contain a large number of distinct words in the English language (vocabulary). The greater the number of words, the larger the Vocabulary and the greater the chance the word searched on happens to be in it.

For documents, the idea of blind word searching loses its appeal when searching with a small number of terms. When using a complex search with a number of terms, the likelihood of getting a false positive is reduced. But for a simple search the likelihood grows with the number of documents and the size of them. The solution that Oracle incorporated into the database in Oracle 8, and then bundled in seamlessly in Oracle 10, was to incorporate technology that could determine what the document was about. This involves looking at the grammar, patterns of words, and usage of words to deduce what the document is about. It creates a set of themes that can be searched on. If a user searches against the theme they are likely to get a result that closely matches what they are searching on. Combining the theme results with a standard document search, and giving the theme matches a much higher ranking, allows a user to do both simple and complex searches and retrieve results that are very close to what they requested in their search.

Autosuggest

A recent new addition to most coarse grain search engines and one which is also proving popular for fine grained searches, is the ability to suggest the search as the user is entering it in. This is referred to as an **autosuggest** and involves querying the database for popular matches as the user is typing in the search terms. With the speed of most networks and servers now, the ability to remotely query, return results, and display them as users are typing in, is now viable. This was not a realistic option ten years ago.

As the user is typing they can look ahead and see potential search values they might want. They can then choose the value and fast track the search.

The challenge is to do this quickly and to return an intelligent set of results. For search engines that track users previous searches and preferences, they can even factor this into the search.

Search engine scalability

Scalability is used to indicate whether the search engine can expand to handle an increase in concurrent and complex searches, as well as the storage of all the data relating to the search. Scalability is covered in greater detail in *Chapter 9, Understanding the limitations of Oracle Products*.

As previously discussed, course grain search engines achieve their scalability by sacrificing flexibility in how they search, to achieve very short response times. The architecture enables the engine to be distributed across a large number of servers, offering the ability to handle more queries and return results consistently, in under a second.

A fine grained search engine is designed to offer greater search capabilities, with the ability to fine tune components of the query. As we have already covered, this includes the ability to search on well defined metadata values, do flexible searches on accession numbers, dates, numbers, and to look for relationships between the digital objects. A fine grained search engine will not have the requirement to scale to handle the number of concurrent users that a Google search engine has to deal with. If the search engine is run within an organization, the user base is well defined and can be controlled.

If the organization opens up its multimedia warehouse to the general public for querying then the issue of scalability becomes important. As the number of concurrent users grows, the capacity of the server might be exceeded. A fine grained search is unlikely be able to scale transparently just by plugging new servers in. Oracle has its flagship product Exadata, which is designed to scale and to handle an increase in the number of users and queries. This product might not be cost effective if the organization has a limited budget. Also, even though the Exadata server can scale to theoretically handle over a thousand nodes, it cannot scale to handle the tens of thousands of nodes that the Google search engine has.

So for an organization to scale their multimedia warehouse, it will have to make a decision as the popularity grows to either limit the growth or switch over to a course grain engine and sacrifice functionality. One has to keep in mind that it's not always a course grain or fine grain choice. It's feasible to actually offer both services concurrently. The general user population doing base queries can use the course grain engine, and those requiring fine grain queries can do them, but have them put on a request (batch queue) and have the results returned to them, or be willing to wait a little longer for the results.

The challenge is integrating the two search engines, but if the user interface is HTML based then this is usually a minor programming and configuration issue. Ultimately it is reasonable to be able to scale the search engine in a multimedia warehouse and achieve good results for a large number of concurrent queries.

Federated search

A **federated** search is a method for the aggregation of results of searches from multiple databases and sources. The idea is to be able to do searches across the whole environment, looking for any digital object. A federated search has limitations with what it can retrieve because of security. So even though it's a course grain search, the type of queries that are run and how the results are managed are identical to a fine grain query. It's just like taking a fine grain query and extending its search range to cover other databases and environments.

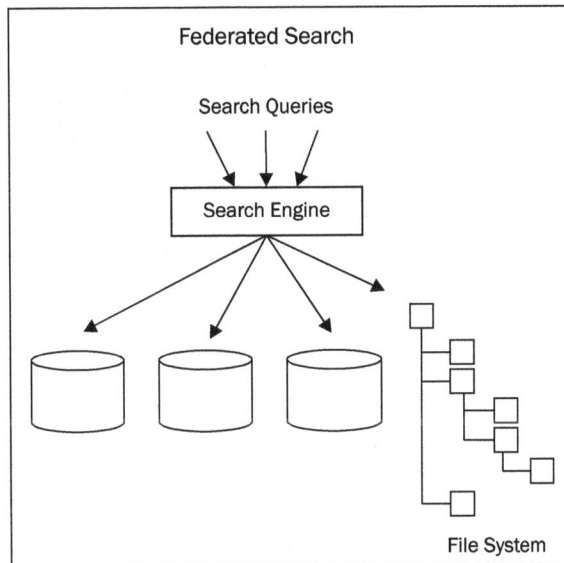

Fuzzy searching

As discussed in *Chapter 1, What is Unstructured Data?*, the idea of exactly matching two images leads to an issue of what exactly is a true match? The idea behind a fuzzy search is to try and address the issue of looking for two digital objects that are identical to each other. The aim is to produce a grading scale of likeness based on a number of characteristics. The resultant search produces a fuzzy result.

When doing a fuzzy search, the search is turned around. Rather than asking for two objects that are identical, the notion of identical is completely abandoned, and the aim is to find images that are as similar to each other as possible. The result can suffer from observer bias, where two different people looking at the results, might interpret the results differently.

This is highlighted by using music as an example. Pick a well known song and try to find another song that matches it as closely as possible. Different people will match it using different characteristics. Some might look at the chorus, some the person singing it, and some might focus on the lyrics. Observer bias indicates that the resultant match might be disputed by different people. In which case the characteristics used in determining the match must be factored into the answer.

It comes down to: "Here is the answer, now what is the question?"

Are these pictures identical?
One is a mirror image of the other.

In the case of a video, the query might be: find the scene with the chair in it. For a human observer the question is straightforward, but for a computer, trying to define what a chair is becomes incredibly difficult. Is it an object with four legs, maybe also three legs? Is it a chair if no one sits on it? Is a plank of wood sitting on two bricks a chair? We start to move into gray or fuzzy areas trying to even classify a chair. Traditional computing algorithms have immense trouble trying to determine what a chair is, let alone identifying one in a video where the perspective of the object can change. It can be obscured by other objects or even be covered by objects such as a blanket. Computer systems using logic can via brute force (make use of immense computing power), look for key features, and make a guess at what a chair is. Computers using neural nets (modeled on the neural structures of the human brain) can do pattern matches more efficiently, but require immense effort to train them to recognize a chair. Even then, when the chair is obscured the network struggles to recognize it as a chair.

Fuzzy searching isn't limited to digital objects, it can also be applied to metadata. As previously covered, the name and address data types can require fuzzy matching. Is the digital object with the name John J Smith identical to the one with the name John James Smith? The answer is maybe. Fuzzy matching can assign a degree of fuzziness indicating how close the match is factoring in other values in the name like date of birth, address, or contact details.

Even though fuzzy searching concepts have been around since the early 1990s, they have not attracted much support because the mathematics behind them was not well described. In the last ten years, with a large push from Japan and proven implementations using fuzzy logic algorithms, along with more papers published covering fuzziness; has fuzzy logic started to be accepted? The problem is the understanding of it is not well known and not encouraged, with the result being that most programmers do not consider using the principles behind it when programming[13].

Collaboration search

Is a search allowing multiple separate search engines, which can be managed by different organizations, to perform a search and combine the results. An example given previously already involves a search engine accessing the local database and then querying Google to add additional results.

For organizations that offer a public system, they might consider creating a web service front end to their database, allowing other organizations to query their database and do a collaborative search.

The advantage of a collaborative search is that it can offer more results, which for analysis can be very useful. That means, for an organization allowing others sites access to do their own collaborative search, that the organization loses control over the data. If the other organization doesn't reflect the originating source, it might result in copyright issues. For digital images that are returned, it could lead to licensing issues. In addition, the organizations need to trust the data they are querying. As they have no control over it, there has to be a trustworthy element associated with the results returned.

Summary

Searching within a multimedia warehouse requires an understanding of fuzzy concepts and being able to effectively visualize the results. An effective search engine for querying multimedia needs to factor in the need for course grain and fine grain searching. As most digital objects are described using metadata, the search engine needs the capabilities to query against it. In addition, the search engine needs features to perform queries specific to the attributes of the type of digital object. Most search engines which have a relational data centric focus, lack the capabilities to do enable these advanced querying features. The search engine also needs to be able to adjust its search behavior based on the data types of the metadata. This includes being able to do fuzzy searching against circa data and intelligent querying against accession and object numbers.

Exercises

1. Design a metadata structure that supports searching on video.

2. Design a search algorithm for searching on animal sounds in audio files.

3. Design a search engine for researchers that enables collaboration, in that different researches can contribute to the search results and share that information between other researches. New results added are highlighted and their reasons for addition are included. The search engine might involve finding all historical information on a particular painting, meaning the search engine has to work across multiple sources.

5
Loading Techniques

Loading in digital objects can be as simple as just taking them from a directory and storing them in the database. In most businesses, the loading gets more complicated as there is a need to attach metadata to the digital object, to process and transform it, and to even verify and validate the metadata being transferred into the digital object. This chapter covers loading methods, the issues encountered in loading, as well as strategies for attaching metadata to digital objects.

Loading methods

In Oracle, the following are utilities or programming environments available for loading digital objects into the database:

- SQL*Loader
- PL/SQL calling Oracle Multimedia
- PL/SQL calling `dbms_lob` package
- Java
- Oracle Spatial
- XML DB
- External language (some examples include C and PHP)
- Oracle Database File System
- External application (Photoshop, Word, which uses an API call to save straight to the database)

Though these methods are heavily programmatic, they rely on the notion that the digital objects already exist in the file system. There are potentially other locations, which could be considered as sources for loading into the database:

- FTP (and sFTP)
- E-mail (as attachments or embedded in the e-mail)
- Other databases
- Websites (HTTP)
- Web services (Multipart MIME)
- Embedded in Powerpoint or documents

The digital objects might come in a variety of formats, which require processing before they can be loaded into the database. Some include:

- ZIP (Gzip)
- RAR
- TAR
- Encrypted

Finding the images

The situation most business find is that their digital objects are sitting on one or more drives, and they need to find them all. They might want to sort out the good images from the bad ones before loading. If they were copied over from a Apple Macintosh computer, then the Mac header information will be copied as another file, in effect creating a ghost version of it.

If the Mac file is called `myimage.jpg`, then when transferred to Window or Unix, the file `.myimage.jpg` will also come across. This file is not a digital image but contains Apple Macintosh's specific-header information. It needs to be ignored.

A business might also want to ignore digital objects below a certain size or ignore those of a certain type. The challenge is sorting out the wheat from the chaff.

Unfortunately, Oracle does not provide any database utilities that can help the business achieve this. In fact, to get a directory listing of a file system it should have one of these options:

- Shell out to the operating system using Java, then capture the results, and store them in an Oracle table. This requires setting up Java with special privileges to shell out and access the operating system. On Windows, shelling out using Java results in case-sensitive queries.

- Shell out to DOS/Shell using Java or Oracle Scheduler, and write a script to do the directory listing. Have the script direct its output to a text file. Then, on return from the shell out, use `utl_file` to read in the text file, process it, and store the results in an Oracle table.

- Develop an Oracle Cartridge in C that when called accesses the operating system directly, which performs the directory listing and inserts the resultant data into an Oracle table.

These methods work well when processing a directory with thousands of objects in it. It fails when an attempt is made to look for a small subsection of digital images that could be spread across multiple drives, where hundreds of thousands of digital objects are stored. In this case, a directory listing isn't the best solution. Rather, an operating system search is needed. Better still, if all the digital objects in the operating system were indexed, then it would be even easier to find a small subset of objects by calling the search utility responsible for the operating system index.

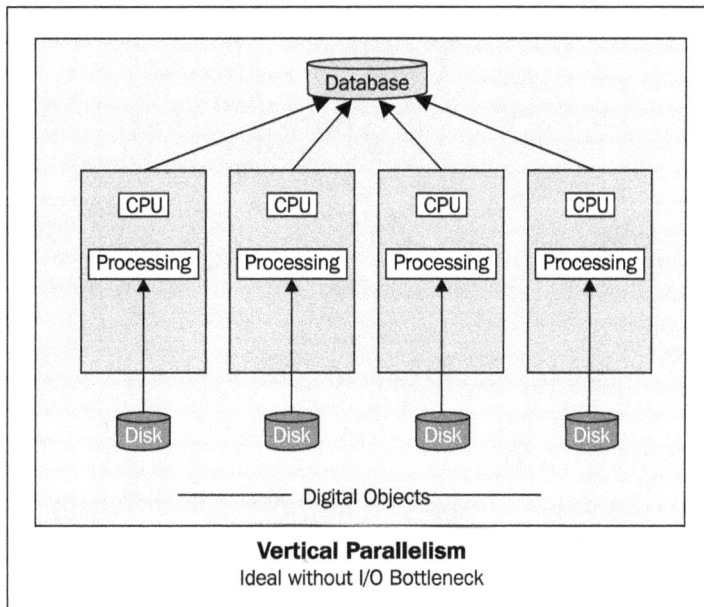

Vertical Parallelism
Ideal without I/O Bottleneck

SQL*Loader is designed for relational data, and even though it can be loaded in digital objects, its limitation is that it cannot easily locate them. So, telling SQL*Loader here is the parent-starting directory on a disk; finding all images within that directory structure and then loading them in is just not possible. SQL*Loader is also not integrated with Oracle Multimedia. The result is that trying to load digital objects using SQL*Loader and then extracting and processing the metadata (or even watermark, rotate, or create derivatives) is just not possible.

Pull method

To do a directory listing and then load images into the database, while processing them, requires a programmatic approach. With the PULL method, a program runs inside the database. This is typically going to be PL/SQL working with Java, Java working with PL/SQL, or each of these languages working on their own inside the database. The program shells out to find all the images to load. It then locates them and initiates processes to create derivatives of them. This can be done outside the database or after they are loaded. The processing decision is based on what action is required and whether Oracle Multimedia can perform the task. Once processed, the images are then pulled into the database. Metadata can then be extracted. This load can be done in parallel using a number of methods.

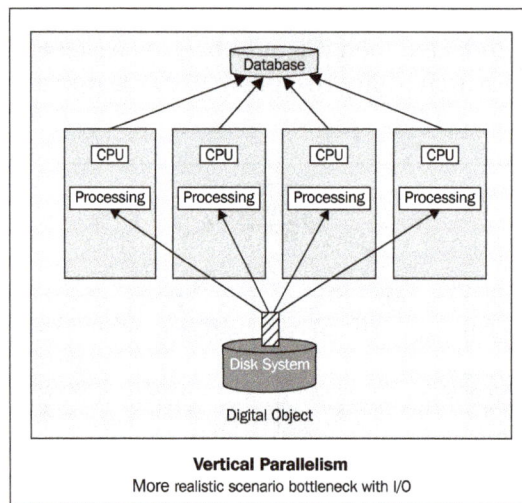

Vertical Parallelism
More realistic scenario bottleneck with I/O

Vertical parallelism

This uses parallelism on sets of images. It's intuitively the obvious option. For a job, you just break it up into tasks and assign a CPU to each one. For example, with Parallel 4, four jobs run, each independently processing their own set of images. When one job finishes, it will typically not be able to assist the other jobs. This form of partitioning works best when the server has the same number of CPUs (or cores) to work with each job. It is also effective if each job can work against its own disk. This ensures that there are no disk bottlenecks.

Ultimately, vertical partitioning suffers from the problem of I/O bottlenecks, making horizontal partitioning a better option. With digital object loading, I/O can be very intense as objects between 10 MB to 10 GB are processed and read in from the disk. Normally, memory cannot be used to assist, as the size of the digital objects can exceed the volume available on the server. Even the act of processing a digital object might involve a lot of disk I/O, especially, if it's a video. Having multiple parallel processes working aggressively against the same disk will ultimately result in the disk becoming congested and the parallel jobs competing for resources. The result is that they will run as slowly as if there was no parallelism.

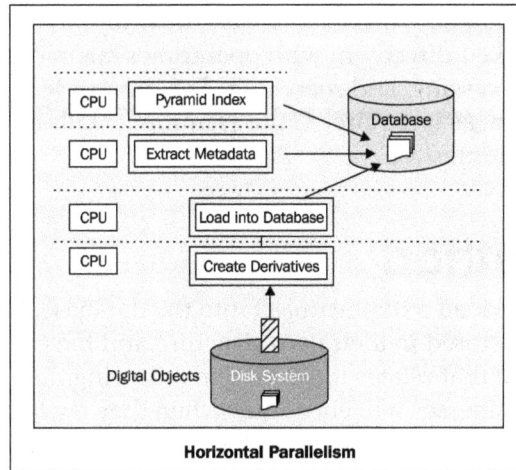

Horizontal Parallelism

Horizontal parallelism

Horizontal Paral involves parallelism in stages. This is very similar to how Oracle SQL runs its parallelism. One or more CPUs are assigned to each stage in the process. Processing of the digital objects is handled in a similar way to an assembly line. One process can be responsible for shelling out and creating the derivatives, another for loading the derivatives into the database, another for extracting the metadata, and another for creating the pyramid index (thumbnail and web quality). As one tasks finishes its job, it starts on the next one that is assigned to it. This is usually done using a set of queues. Each process is a specialist in its own task. The downside is that if a process is delayed, the whole assembly line could be slowed down, as processes sit idly by waiting for work to do.

Push method

This method involves using an external program such as PHP, Perl, Ruby, C, or VB. It runs and does a directory listing and determines which images are to be loaded. It then processes them using its own processing capabilities or invokes a third-party tool (such as ImageMagick) to process them. It can also extract the metadata. Once done, it then pushes the images into the database. It can do this via an INSERT statement, or it can invoke a PL/SQL module and just pass the pointer to the blob (which is the digital object) to it. The PL/SQL program then does any additional database processing before loading the image into the database.

Cartridge method

In this case, a specialized Oracle Cartridge is built in C. The program does the directory listing, finds the images, and processes them before inserting them into the Oracle Database. This method is the fastest, because the cartridge is a C compiled program that is tightly linked with the database. In addition, the cartridge has the capabilities of being linked directly in with operating system objects, enabling it to do directory listing, processing, and searching. The downside is that it's the hardest to develop and maintain, as it requires C programming skills and knowledge of Oracle OCI (Oracle Call Interface).

Loading method

There is no right way to load a digital object into the database. Each business will have the digital objects stored in their own structure and the challenge is to work out where all the data is that relates to them. The following describes some of the situations that most businesses will encounter when they try to determine the loading methodology to use that best meets their business requirement.

Metadata matches to digital object

The scenario is that not all digital objects yet exist, some need to be scanned in, and some need to be taken by a photographer. There is thorough metadata for all the digital objects. This is a scenario found in museums or other organizations, where they manage collections. In this case, the following rule applies:

- Metadata: Master list of all objects
- Digital object is attached to metadata

The metadata can exist in another database, in XML format, or CSV format. It is loaded in first, effectively becoming a relational record (as covered in *Chapter 3, The Multimedia Warehouse*). They form a master. As digital objects are found and loaded in, they are matched to these records and attached to them. The method for matching is covered in the next section.

Based on the storage structure used, it might be feasible that the same metadata attaches to one or more digital objects. This is covered further in a later section in this chapter.

This methodology works well in a global map that needs to be captured and what hasn't yet been can be easily calculated. It's even possible to let users see what digital objects have yet to be captured, and enable them to initiate a workflow requesting it to be digitized as a high-priority task (or even as a paid for additional task).

For public users, it might not be friendly to see the metadata for the digital object without actually seeing that object. For users doing research, being able to see the metadata, irrespective of whether the object is there or not, can be a good thing. In the end, the business has to decide on what type of user they are catering for. If the business is in the process of selling digital objects, then users should not see records without a digital object attached. As covered in *Chapter 6, Delivery Techniques* e-commerce sometimes requires abandoning traditional commerce notions and looking at different avenues. So as covered, there could be money made by adding an option for users to pay a premium to buy an image that is not yet digitized.

Digital object matches to metadata

The scenario is that the digital objects exist, but the metadata might not exist. In this case, the digital objects are all loaded in. Metadata might be extracted from the digital object if it's embedded in it. Metadata might be matched to it from external systems. The same metadata might match to one or more digital objects. As the metadata comes from different systems, the quality might vary and overlap.

Mixed digital object and metadata

In this scenario, it is unknown if the metadata is the primary list or if the digital objects constitute the primary list. In this case, both are loaded in separately into the system. Once it is inside the database, attempts are made to match the metadata to the digital objects or digital objects to metadata. The results could be merged together. This scenario works well for a multimedia warehouse, where the digital objects and metadata come from disparate systems, and part of the goal of the warehouse is to match the two together and look for patterns.

Digital object no metadata

In this scenario, the digital objects are loaded into the database. The metadata is then manually added to the digital objects. This can be done via a workflow, where different people in the organization are responsible for adding different parts of the metadata to it. By using crowd-sourcing, it's even possible to open up parts of the metadata attachment to the general public.

Many masters

In this scenario, there are numerous digital objects that are related closely to each other. As they are loaded in, rather than loading them as separate digital objects, they are loaded in as one digital object, with one of them being marked as the primary master, which is the one that is primarily seen by those viewing it. The other masters can be treated as the equivalent of related digital objects. Each master can have its own set of derivatives. This could include a PPT version, A4 version, and low-quality. The result is that one logical digital object could have hundreds of masters with its own derivatives. So, one logical digital object behind the scenes could have hundred of physical digital objects. They could be mixed. There could be digital images, video, audio, and documents all associated with it.

On loading, the challenge is to identify which images are tightly related to each other and need to be stored as many masters. This is covered in the *Digital object matches to metadata* section later.

If the many masters option is used, then a search will only return the one digital object. It is possible to develop a search routine that enables the many masters option to be used, but when searched on, it flattens out the results. The business needs to decide from a frontend user perspective, which is friendlier and best matches the business needs of the user.

Derivatives

A digital object can be processed, and the derivatives are created from it, which are the result of the digital object being transformed. The traditional transformation includes creating smaller versions for digital images and PDFs for documents. There is no limit to the number of derivatives created.

An organization might want to consider the opposite of the many masters option when storing derivatives. In that, they might store each derivative separately as its own digital object. This concept is called **flattening**. The equivalent in the relational world is to convert a table with rows and columns into one containing two columns and many rows (also known as **name-value pairs**).

For a public site, this might simplify the search-and-view process. In doing this, the same metadata needs to be replicated across all the derivatives come digital objects. When a user searches for a digital object, all the derivatives will match and will be seen in one search.

Matching existing data to images

When loading multiple digital objects into the database, the challenge most organizations will face is how to match similar objects (combine them into one), to match metadata to the digital object, or to match the digital object to the metadata.

The standard approach is to use the filename to match. If a digital object resides in the filesystem, then it will have a filename. For Windows and Unix, the name will have an extension (.jpg, .doc, .mov, .tif) indicating its type (file suffix). On a Mac, as already covered, the file type is stored in a separate file.

The file type is very important, as it determines how the operating system should treat the digital object. If an attempt is made to open it, the file type will match to an application in the computer, which then knows how to handle it. When using a web browser, the equivalent of the file type is mimetype, which is embedded in the header of the digital object as it's downloaded. The browser then has a set of applications that it uses to map mimetype to an application. Most browsers now have built-in applications for displaying the most common file types such as JPEG, GIF, and PNG.

Besides the file suffix, the rest of the filename can contain useful information for matching the digital object to the metadata. Ultimately, there are four ways of matching a digital object to a separated metadata:

- Information is encoded in the filename. This could be the accession number or an image name. It can also contain additional information about the image indicating whether it's a derivative, thumbnail, web quality, or which range of digital objects it matches to. A digital object can map to exactly one metadata record. It can also map to many metadata records. It could be a picture of two or more museum items, each with their own accession numbers. It could also be part of a set of digital objects. Digital images of artwork might contain multiple images of different parts of the item, especially if the item is three-dimensional, large, or spread over a large space (as found with Modern Art). With the key being stored in the filename, an algorithm is needed to process the name and extract/convert the key into a value that can be used to match to the metadata. A filename also has to be unique within the directory it resides in. So, if a digital object has multiple derivatives, then each filename has to be different. This can complicate the naming standard.

- Information is encoded in the file system directory the digital object resides in. In cases where there are multiple digital objects, which belong to the same master (are derivatives), then rather than encoding a key in the filename, the key can be encoded in the directory the digital objects reside in. This results in one directory structure per digital object. The filenames in the directory can then be descriptive about what the actual digital object is. This can be useful if there is no metadata in the digital object.

- Information is encoded inside the digital object. For a digital image, this could be in the IPTC, EXIF, or XMP tags. For audio, it could be inside the ID3 tag. As there are no official standards for defining which value is the official primary key, different organizations can use different values. In fact, a large set of digital objects could use a mixture of standards with different digital objects having their key being stored in different tags.

- Metadata contains the actual filename. In this case, the location/file/area that contains all the metadata to be matched to the digital also contains the actual filename (and maybe directory) of the digital object. This is the easiest matching scenario as it's an exact match.

So, matching comes down to one of these scenarios:

- Matching a key in the metadata to the filename or directory the digital object resides in

- Matching a key in the metadata to a key embedded in the digital object

- Matching a filename with a possible additional directory name to the digital object filename

The last two points are easily handled for matching and will not be covered. It's the first one that deserves the most attention, as it can be the most complex to achieve. To start, there are limitations in the filenames that need to be highlighted:

- Filenames cannot normally contain special characters. This includes single and double quotes, slashes, ampersands, asterisks, exclamation mark, and the at symbol. For some operating systems, it's possible to enclose and reference filenames containing special symbols inside single or double quotes.

- Space can be an enemy. Most operating systems in their scripting language use a space as a delimiter for commands. Spaces complicate matters. In the following example, determine the result:

  - `dir my filename*`
  - `ls my filename*`

- Depending on what is entered, the result might be an error or an undesired effect. The solution most operating systems offer is to capture and reference the name in quotes:
    - ◦ `dir "my filename"*` or `dir "my filename*"`
    - ◦ `ls "my filename"*` or `ls "my filename*"`

- An additional issue with spaces is the double space. This can be visually very hard to spot (font-dependent) and deceptive when debugging and trying to determine why a digital object will not load. If the metadata contains a single space and the filename has a double space, then it will not match. The solution is when matching to remove all spaces or to enforce a standard where double spaces are just rejected.

- Filenames have a maximum length. This was once 30 characters, but most operating systems have since allowed a much larger value. For Windows, in the latest operating system versions, it's around 260 characters. In Unix, it is 255 characters. The value can vary depending on the underlying filesystem used. If one assumes a maximum of 250 characters, then a large amount of information can be stored within it.

- Unix filenames are case-sensitive. Windows filenames are not case-sensitive. This means, on Unix, a digital object with the name `M.200.100.jpg`, is different to `m.200.100.jpg`. Even `m80.jpg` is different to `m80.jpg`. This can add to a level of complexity when matching with relational data as case-sensitivity might need to be factored in. It can also be used to one's advantage. If the key to match is called `M21ABC`, then files with the name `m21abc.jpg`, `M21abc.jpg`, `M21Abc.jpg`, and `M21ABc.jpg` will all match to the same key by using only the simple function of uppercase checking. Such a capability is not possible in Windows.

Filename encoding

For museum systems, the primary key can be the object ID or the accession number. As the accession number is more curator-friendly (as covered in *Chapter 3, The Multimedia Warehouse*), it's typically embedded in the filename. For other types of businesses, similar analogies hold. The following are some examples of filenames and the equivalent accession number:

- `m200.100.tif`: `M.200.100`

- `A_80_154.jpg`: `A.80.100`

- `B100_300det54.jpg`: `B.100.300` (detail #54)

- `retaken_100-345a.tif`: `100.345.a`

In the previous examples, a casual look at the names can determine what the key (or accession number) is. A computer program is needed to parse the name, removing prefixes and suffixes, convert underscores and dashes to full stops, and even add full stops if needed. In the following example, finding the key gets more complicated:

- `M100_200a-f.tif`

- `300_500,510,520.tif`

- `A80_50a-g B50_60 M100_200g-h.tif`

- `john_smith-jane_doe-canberra_department_local_services_ july_2012.tif`

In the first case, the one digital image relates to any keys with accession number `M.100.200.a` to `M.100.200.f`. This could include `M.100.200.b` and `M.100.200.c`. Not all these accession numbers might even exist.

In the second case, three accession numbers `300.500`, `300.510`, and `300.520` are found in the one digital image. It could be a digital image showing all three objects in one photo.

The third case is a mixture of the first two, and states that the image contains accession numbers `A.80.50.a` to `A.80.50.g`, `B.50.60` and `M.100.200.h` to `M.100.200.h`.

The fourth case has no key but identifies information about who is in the digital image and where it was taken. The key is a combination of each of the names and location.

The number of variations and permutations for indicating which keys are found in the filename can become more complex, as attempts are made to reflect the keys in it.

It's also possible to store relationships between digital objects in the filenames. If brackets are supported in the operating system, then the following filename indicates that the accession number is `100.200.300`, and it has two related items, `100.200.310` and `100.200.320`. For example, `100_200_300 (100_200_310, 100_200_320).jpg`.

So, the following information can be stored in the filename:

- The key used to match the digital object to the metadata (which can be an accession number, object ID, or generic primary key such as a name, number, or code).

- Whether the digital object replaces the existing one (using words, such as taken, reshoot, reload in the filename).

- Whether it is a thumbnail, web quality, derivative (using values such as tnail, web, deriv).

- Whether the digital object is a composite of many other digital objects.

- Whether the digital object is part of the main digital object.

- Relationships between the digital object and other digital objects.

- Metadata about the digital object; this could include keywords, location, or photographer's name. With a 250-character limit in the filename, the amount of data would be limiting.

For a business that is digitizing objects, it can be an on-going process. The best solution is to embed the keys in the metadata inside the image. This will ensure that there are no mistakes made when matching the digital object to any supporting metadata. For digital images, there are a number of tools in the market place (such as Adobe Photoshop) that support the processing and then data entry of metadata into the digital object. For audio, it involves using a tool that can embed metadata into the header (using ID3 or XMP formats), and for video, it becomes more difficult, as each video format has different supporting standards.

For a multimedia warehouse, it's likely that most of the objects have already been digitized, and the goal is to load them in to the database and match them to any metadata if possible. In addition, relationships are calculated between the digital objects. In this case, the key might not be embedded in the metadata in the image. It might be in the filename or the metadata might have the filename associated with it. In this case, one or more of the methods outlined might need to be used.

Data cleansing

As covered, there are two key steps when loading a digital object. They are to load the digital object in and to match existing metadata to it. The ordering can be done either way and the match of the existing metadata is optional.

When the digital object is loaded, it needs to be processed. This includes creating derivatives as well as watermarking or general image cleanup (cropping, sharpening, adjusting, censoring).

Once the meta is attached to the digital object, it might need to be cleansed. The concept is similar to what happens in a data warehouse. Some basic cleansing processes include:

- Converting `varchar` (sets of characters) dates into proper dates. A date might be stored in a `varchar` field. The dates might be of a mixed format, such as 12th Jan 2010, 10/12/08, Jan 15th 2000. They need to be translated into a standard date format.

- Converting `varchar` numbers into numbers.
- Ensuring there are no orphaned relationships (all keys storing relationships match to valid digital objects, which is similar to primary key and foreign key integrity in relational databases).
- Validating names and addresses.
- Verifying spatial co-ordinates.
- Validating field lengths.
- Removing double spaces and converting to uppercase or lowercase as required.
- Verifying key words (tags).
- Converting comma delimited fields into repeating groups, or converting repeating groups into comma delimited fields (there is no right or wrong option here, it's what ever best matches the business needs).
- Converting imperial measurements to metric.
- Updating free form values to conform to a standard display (when displaying audio bit rate, ensure the acronym is `nn Mhtz`, where `nn` is a valid number).

Data cleansing can also involve populating empty fields with default values and deriving fields from other fields (separating name into first and last name).

Loading decisions

When loading digital objects, the following issues need to be addressed as part of the load process:

- Where are the digital objects found?
- Can the database access them? (security)
- Is there sufficient storage to handle them?
- If archiving is enabled, is there sufficient storage for the archives?
- Will there be different types of digital objects (audio, video, images, documents)?
- For each type, what are the processing rules? (watermark, cropping, rotation)
- For each type, what derivatives are needed?
- For the processing, which server should it be performed?
- If the digital objects are loaded singularly, how long will the load take to run? Will it run in a realistic time frame?

- Should the load be broken up into separate tasks, which can be run independently and in parallel?
- Are the digital objects going to be stored in the database or kept in the filesystem?

Depending on what the objectives are for having the digital object determines the answers to the previous questions. This, in turn, impacts how best the load should run.

Types of loading

In addition to the questions asked earlier, there are additional ways of loading based on the answers to these questions:

- Are the digital objects to be loaded in en-mass or piece meal?
- Will there be an initial ingest of thousands of digital objects?
- Will they be loaded in one at a time via a browser, or via e-mail or through a hot folder?

The digital objects can be loaded in via one of these methods:

Batch

A batch process runs and finds the images in:

- The filesystem
- FTP location
- Mail server (POP3 or equivalent)
- Web trawl (HTTP access a site, look for digital objects on the pages, and load them in)

Hot folder

As a user puts a digital object into a nominated directory, a process is triggered (awoken), which then loads the digital object in. The hot folder can check for new digital objects at fixed time intervals or when a new object is added. Attributes can be given to hot folders indicating processing options. This allows the user to add their digital object to different hot folders, each one architected to perform a certain function. One might create a number of derivatives when added, another might extract the metadata and then assign certain security roles to the digital object.

Integration API

This is a feature unique to Oracle with its Database File System. In this case, the file system is integrated with the database, such that when the user saves the digital object to the filesystem, they are, in fact, saving it in the database. Though, currently, only available on Linux (Windows and Solaris offer partial support but not to the same level as Linux), this tight level of integration enables loading as easy as copying the files to the filesystem. APIs can be built in PL/SQL so that when the digital object is inserted, a program is triggered, which can do all the processing. This can include metadata extraction and image transformation.

The downside of this method is that it encourages the storage of the digital objects in a hierarchical or filesystem architecture. One might consider this flexible, but in reality, it's quite limiting and constrains the usage of the digital objects to a rather outdated and archaic structure.

Manual

The user pushes the digital object into the database via a browser or application. It's possible to integrate object libraries in with Photoshop, Open Office, and Microsoft Office. These libraries can enable the user to save the digital image, document, or other digital object straight into the database. They can bypass the operating system entirely.

Loading step-by-step

When loading objects in, from the filesystem, the following are the steps required to load that digital objects in:

- **Find the images**: This involves looking across one or more file systems in multiple directories. It might involve looking for them in an FTP location or on remote websites.

- **Filter the results**: This involves removing redundant images based on filename, suffix, and even directory location.

- **Extract metadata**: Used when matching the metadata embedded in a digital object with an existing metadata. This is an optional step and can be done later. It might need to be done at this point in case the digital object needs to be rejected if there is no match, or if there is no match to be passed to another area for separate processing. In which case, rather than extracting all the metadata, only the meta value needed to match to the key is extracted.

- **Matching, combining, or replacing**: If the previous step is not performed, then based on the image filename, can information be extracted from it to determine if there is an existing metadata that can be matched to it? Also, based on the filename, has this digital object already been loaded in? If a similar digital object has been loaded in, should it be loaded in as a new one, or combined using the many masters concept?

- **Image processing**: The original image is processed and transformed. For a digital image, this can involve creating the pyramid index (thumbnail and web quality) as well as derivatives (maybe A4, PPT, printer quality). For a video, this might involve sending it to a transformation server for conversion or creating a snippet of it.

- **Full metadata extraction**: If it wasn't extracted previously, or if not all the metadata was extracted in the early steps, it's best done at this stage. At this stage, data cleansing can also occur.

- **Finalization processing**: This involves adding security, looking at relationships, attaching copyright, and cataloging the digital object.

Error handling

In any loading process, errors can occur and need to be handled. There could be failures due to:

- Lack of disk storage
- Invalid digital objects (an object is marked as a tif image, but it's not one)
- Corrupted digital objects (due to disk error or program error)
- Invalid metadata (if the XMP is not stored correctly, it will return an error when being processed)
- Server memory errors (video and digital image processing consumes a large amount of memory; if it's not freed correctly, then memory creep can occur resulting in the server eventually running out of memory and failing)
- Hardware errors

The loading program needs to be able to correctly trap, handle, and report on any of these errors as they occur. One error on load should not cause the entire loading process to fail. It should be robust to continue running on failure. Like SQL*Loader, there should be options for it to be able to cleanly fail if too many errors are encountered.

Logical errors

If an algorithm used to parse a filename, and if determining the key (or accession number) isn't robust enough to handle all variations or just has a bug in it, then it might incorrectly match or reject the association of metadata to a digital object. In this case, a false match might occur or a match that should have occurred won't (false positive and false negative).

In either case, the loading utility needs to be able to handle these logical errors and do a cross-check post load and validate all data entered to ensure it is correctly matched.

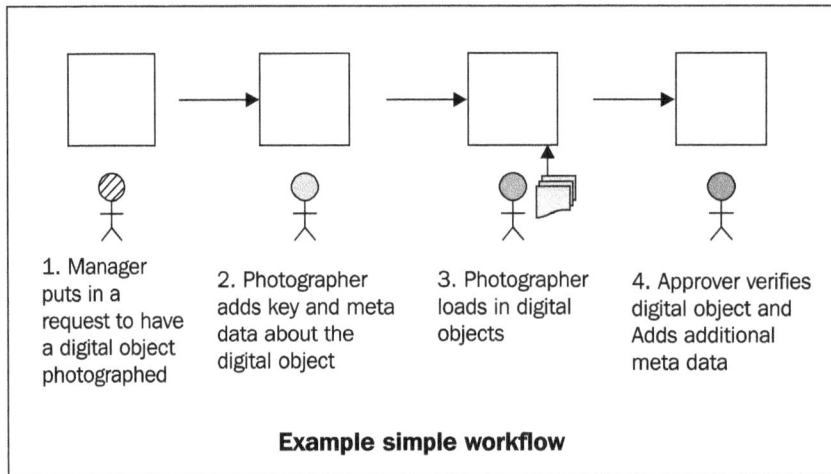

| 1. Manager puts in a request to have a digital object photographed | 2. Photographer adds key and meta data about the digital object | 3. Photographer loads in digital objects | 4. Approver verifies digital object and Adds additional meta data |

Example simple workflow

Loading via a workflow

In the cases of manual loading the business might want greater control over how the digital object is loaded in. To ensure quality control, security of the image and accuracy of the metadata added, the digital object might go through a workflow process before even being loaded into the database.

The workflow might initially prompt for metadata to be specified, which is very similar to a data form entry screen. The data entered is validated before going to the next step of adding one or more digital objects. Once loaded, the workflow might result in another person verifying whether the image matches the data. Another person might then assign copyright.

Summary

Loading digital objects into the database can involve a number of process steps. Based on the type of business, the steps might be as simple as just loading the images in. It might grow to include matching metadata to digital objects or digital objects to metadata. The challenge is working out a method for correctly matching the digital object to the metadata. Loading can be done in bulk with the challenge here being to locate where all the digital objects are, as they could be spread across different disk systems or even be located on websites, ftp sites, or e-mail servers. In some cases, a workflow process might be needed to ensure the digital object has the correct metadata attached to it.

Exercises

These questions are designed to have the reader go beyond the traditional method of answering questions. They involve using the concepts designed in the chapter and doing additional research on the Internet to come up with the best solution to address the questions raised:

- This chapter has covered a number of locations where digital objects can be found. This includes the filesystem, mail server, ftp, and via HTTP on websites. Identify another type of location and determine if the digital objects found there could be loaded into a database.

- Define a filename syntax (EBNF or Railroad) that can be used to match a digital object to its metadata. It should be able to deal with the variations of names, relationships, digital object types, and can also include instructions on loading, such as this is the master digital object, or the sRBG colorspace should be used when processed. Keep in mind the maximum file length of 255 characters.

- Determine a loading strategy for parallel loading for:
    - Loading in 10,000 videos of FLV format, each of 1 GB in size. Also required is a video snippet of 30 seconds and an MPEG derivative to be created. The database is on a server with 16 cores but runs on a SAN. Determine if horizontal or vertical parallelism works better.
    - Assume a five node cluster with each node containing 8 cores (Oracle RAC).

There is a requirement to load in 1 million digital images, each in size of approximately 10 MB. Each digital image requires a web quality and thumbnail to be created as well as metadata embedded in the image to be extracted. The digital images reside on a SAN in a deeply nested directory structure. Describe a strategy for setting up the Oracle Database to load and process in all one million digital images. Work out ways for dealing with the disk I/O bottleneck issue and to maximize use of all four cores in the server.

6
Delivery Techniques

This chapter covers the concepts of how to deliver digital objects to a customer. It focuses primarily on e-commerce and covers digital rights management and all the copyright issues one has to typically deal with when delivering an image. It includes post metadata processing and embedding, dealing with multiple image types, workflow processing of images and designing a set of flexible business rules for dealing with the changing nature of the market.

Securing an image

Before any attempt is made to sell a digital object, the first question that a business will raise concerns about is managing the security of the delivery of all the digital objects. A singular issue such as security might not seem too daunting to deal with, but in a number of cases, the attempts to address it are so challenging that many e-commerce projects have not made it past the design stage. This is because an adequate security framework cannot be established.

Protection from theft

When dealing with digital objects, theft takes on a whole new meaning. A shop theft generally focuses around the undetected, removal of a physical object from the store. This is usually an identifiable cost to the business. Using a variety of security methods (including cameras, security guards, electronic tags, cabling, and mirrors) items in the store can be secured from theft.

In the digital world, the concept that is based around theft or stealing has a number of different interpretations.

Is it really theft?

When a digital image is copied from a site, we are accustomed to the idea that it is theft, as this is what we have been led to believe (see any DVD header talking about piracy). Therefore, we now perceive it as if it was the theft of a physical object.

In reality when a digital image is copied, all that is really taken are a set of 1's and 0's. In fact these 1's and 0's aren't taken, they are converted into a signal which is then transferred to another site. When looked at it this way, nothing is taken. In fact when a digital image which appears in your browser is saved locally, then all that is done is a set of 1's and 0's are transferred from memory in your computer to disk storage in your computer. It's already there. It was arguments similar to this that inspired the hacker community and led to the idea of open source. It was a view that nothing was really being stolen, so there was no damage.

> *"Open source is a philosophy, or pragmatic methodology that promotes free redistribution and access to an end product's design and implementation details".*

In the real world there is an analogy which closely matches what is happening in the digital world and is worthwhile covering. It concerns books.

If a book is copied and reproduced, then nothing is physically stolen in the initial instance. The reproduction of the book is done independently of the original. How and what it's reproduced on is immaterial. The ink used, the font style, anything else is not important and doesn't detract from the issue that the book has been stolen. In reality what has been stolen is the intellectual property and not the physical medium the book is on. In the case of digital images, it's not the 1's and 0's which are important, it's what they represent which is. It's the effort in how they are assembled and the unique pattern which is a combination of 1's and 0's that form character sets, which then form words and subsequently text in a book.

The book analogy sounds good and seems to cover the basic concept of theft. It centers around the idea of intellectual property. However, this is not always the case with multimedia, just when you think you have it covered, a whole new nest of vipers hidden underneath rears its head. Given the notion centered around intellectual property, are the following situations cases of theft?

- A person goes to a library and borrows a book. They read the book. They have consumed its content. What difference is there here to someone illegally downloading a book, printing it out and reading it?

- Most modern libraries now allow you to borrow a DVD for one or two nights at no cost. This allows you to watch it without paying for it or reimbursing anyone for the use of the intellectual property. Even though if I went to a store I would have to pay for it there.

- I buy a DVD. I decide to have a movie night where a whole lot of friends come over and watch it. Each of those friends are not paying to view it. The business that owns the intellectual property of the DVD is not getting compensation for the fact that my friends have seen it but not paid for it. So lets say that one of my friends has now viewed the DVD. If they had downloaded it from the Internet and viewed it, then that would be considered to be illegal. A theft of intellectual property. Yet the result is the same. In both cases they have consumed the intellectual property. In both cases the owner did not get royalties for it. Yet one case is perfectly legal and in the other case it's illegal and there are active campaigns to prevent it.

  In most countries, if I charged my friends to view it, then that would be considered to be illegal because I am collecting monies for it without reimbursing the original owner of the intellectual property.

- I buy a DVD. I watch it and give it to a friend. I know full well that I will never watch it again. My friend is now the owner of the DVD but has not paid the business that owns the intellectual property of the DVD anything for this. They have in their possession a legal DVD, yet if they download the exact same movie from the Internet then that is considered illegal. The end result is still the same as the person has consumed the same intellectual property without payment.

In the last two years in the US, UK, and Australia the notion of a DVD Kiosk has appeared. At the Kiosk you purchase a DVD on the understanding that you will return it after a period of time. You provide a credit card and it's billed per night. If after a period of time you don't return it then you are charged full price and you own it. You have in your possession a physical item. The material and cost of assembly is very low. You have not purchased the DVD but more what the DVD represents — the intellectual property on it.

It might be considered that rather than buying a DVD you are buying a right to be entertained. This notion which is similar in concept to an amusement park, has separate issues. Compared to buying an item of clothing, what you are actually buying in this case is a variable. Initially you are renting the DVD and then potentially buying it if you don't return it. If you watch it once, but forget to return it for a couple of days, the price to you goes up. Whether the DVD is returned after 1 hour, 1 day, or 1 week is not important to the kiosk, as it can produce replacement DVDs at a very low cost which doesn't match the cost which you paid.

Yet the DVD kiosk is accepted as a valid location for purchasing movies because in the end one is paying for the convenience. The rent/buy mechanism is there because the rent price is less than the buy price. A consumer who watches a lot of DVDs might realize that the concept of ownership is not cost effective. A movie might be watched once every five to ten years, or maybe never again depending on its quality. In the end the consumer is buying the use of intellectual property over a period of time with the agreed right to own it outright after that time.

One still has to be careful here. Because at no point does the consumer own the actual intellectual property. They in actuality own the intellectual property that resides on that physical medium and no others. The agreement being that even though they own or are renting it, they are renting it on that physical medium—that DVD only. This is important, as the DVD itself now has an important meaning. It physically represents the intellectual property that the consumer has purchased.

So with the kiosk, the security in place is that the kiosk has the users credit card which is used to control the behavior of the consumer. It's a balancing act between compensating the owner of the intellectual property and coming up with a satisfactory method for the consumer to use that intellectual property, that is best managed based on the type of medium it is produced on. The rules for dealing with digital objects are still evolving and in the marketplace a number of different methods are being tried.

It's because of this evolution that a number of businesses being are now hesitant to put their toes into the cold waters of digital object consumption and just consign it to the too hard basket, hoping that one day it will get resolved. These businesses have lost out because of this reluctance and are now struggling to catch up and effectively compete.

When it comes to securing a digital object there are a number of factors that need to be taken into consideration that are beyond the usual theft that most people know about.

Modification

A digital image, such as a photo, document, video, or audio can be modified. When such an object is used as evidence in a court of law, if modification is detected it becomes tainted. Even the failure to adequately protect it could taint it even though it might not be modified. Advances in photo-editing tools have allowed people with basic skills to perform complex manipulation and editing of photos, in effect changing their meaning.

Modification can also involve the equivalent of a graffiti attack. This might involve a website or images on the website being overtly or subtly modified. The overt method is usually a form of protest graffiti, where the original images are hacked then modified with a message. The subtle modification involves the changing of areas of the site to mislead those who go there. This could include changing the meaning of sentences on the web page or even the careful replacement of digital images with ones with a different meaning. Such activities can be done to manipulate how a company is perceived, to obtain a competitive advantage, or to use it to cause confusion for political gain.

Securing in these cases involves firstly protecting access to the site containing the digital objects. This includes firewalls, strong password protection, and physical protection of the computer servers themselves. Secondly, the digital objects can be protected using checksums that are stored in a separate location. Periodic validation of the current digital objects and the website, versus the stored checksums, would quickly highlight if there has been any modification. A checksum can also be used in criminal cases to verify the accuracy of the digital object and guarantee it has not been modified. A checksum can only check if the digital object has been modified, it can't protect it from modification.

In some cases, it might be prudent to encrypt the digital object and control access to the key used to decrypt it. Such an action is CPU intensive and will slow down access in retrieval, but will guarantee that the digital object is not modified.

Storage of digital objects in the database is a good step to prevent modification, as access to the digital object in the database can be firmly controlled. Having it stored in the file system relies on file system security to protect it.

Disruption

The equivalent real-world analogy to this is a group of protestors picketing the entrance of a business and preventing customers from entering. In the digital world, disruption is normally referred to as a DOS or Denial of Service Attack. Here a set of computers are typically hijacked (referred to as zombie computers). These computers can be located anywhere in the world and in some cases can number in the millions. The computers are then directed to send requests to the server, in effect swamping or overloading it with requests. Regular customers accessing the site are blocked from getting in.

When DOS attacks first appeared, smart routers could usually intercept the requests and bounce them before they were sent to the server. With an upgrade in the sophistication of the attacks, they are now designed to be random, look legitimate, and originate from sites that are typically considered safe. This makes dynamic prevention very difficult when a server is attacked. Most routers are now designed to handle small-scale DOS attacks.

A defensive tactic when a DOS attack occurs is to disconnect the server from the network just in case the overloading of it causes either physical damage, or enables a backdoor hole in the frontend to be opened up (usually attributed to the incorrect handling of failure code), enabling a hacker entry into the server.

The best preventative methods of protection from disruption are to invest in network technology that can detect a small scale DOS attack.

Copying

Copying is commonly known as pirating. This involves taking the original digital object, copying it, and then reselling or redistributing it. Well known for all types of digital objects but especially with DVDs and music. Prevention of this requires a completely different approach to the whole concept of e-commerce and is covered later in this chapter.

Theft

Theft is similar to copying except the goal is more directed at personal or local use, rather than pirating which involves the wholesale reselling and retribution of the copied digital object. Downloading MP3s from an illegal site is technically theft. Reselling them would be classed as pirating. The large entertainment companies would claim there is no difference between the two as the end goal in both cases is a loss of reimbursement to the owner of the intellectual property.

As mentioned earlier, there are some key and important differences between the two. This hasn't stopped a number of companies from attempting to prosecute individuals who download but do not resell. The goal of this prosecution is to send a message to the marketplace that theft is not tolerated. In practice, this has caused more harm to the image of the company doing the prosecution. The current attitude of consumers in the marketplace is "most of us are doing it, we don't see it as wrong, so you as a company are just being mean". Such heavy handed tactics have failed to even slow down theft, so clearly a new tactic in dealing with it is needed, one which involves thinking outside the box and changing the rules. It requires abandoning the idea of treating a digital object just like a physical object. Consumers already know the two are very different. This is covered in greater detail later in this chapter.

Forgery

Forgery or counterfeiting involves taking a digital object, reproducing or remanufacturing, and claiming it as your own. This is different to copying where that claim is usually not made. Forgery is also done selectively, usually focusing on just one digital object and using it. It's typically done when there is a perceived high rate of return on the counterfeit object. In the real world a forgery or counterfeit looks and behaves like the original but it isn't. In the digital world the same concept applies, but because of the easier copy capabilities it's slightly different. A person wants to buy a high-quality copy of a rare Ansel Adams photo (a famous historical nature photographer who specialized in black and white photos). They might go to a site, pay a large price, and expect a very high resolution image. What they might get is a scanned image taken from a camera of a person who went to the museum and took a picture of it. The scan is of mixed quality and not an accurate representation of the original. It is though claimed to be the real copy of it. This is a forgery.

Preventative measures against this are covered in the following sections.

Destruction

Destruction is the deliberate destruction of a digital object. In a legal case this could be to prevent it being used as evidence. In other cases it could be done to cover up embarrassing pictures. Tabloid magazines usually take digital photos of celebrities in awkward situations. In a lot of cases most would like these photos destroyed. Protecting an image from being destroyed is similar to *modification*.

Plagiarism

Plagiarism involves copying a digital object, then modifying it and claiming it as their own. Unlike forgery, plagiarism doesn't involve the selling of the digital object. This is different to *fair use*, which is a term used to enable companies and individuals to take an extract of a digital object and then use it in their own site. The *fair use* is restricted to a particular length of time, and is usually quite small.

The law regarding what constitutes plagiarism gets quite complex. For digital objects it initially involves proving the alleged plagiarist has been able to access the original digital object. This requires a comprehensive audit trail.

Document plagiarism has been around for a very long time and universities and schools spend a lot of time preventing and detecting it. Software now exists which can analyze two or more documents and determine if they are similar. A student plagiarizing now has access to the Internet and a wide variety of information which they can copy from, introducing a variety of plagiarized pieces of work. The result is that it makes it hard for the person marking the paper to determine if it really is authentic. The same person marking it also has access to the Internet and can easily check sentences to see if they have been published, simply by doing a standard search on them.

For images it gets more complex as it becomes subjective. A photo of a sunset is such a popular picture with millions available on the Internet, that if one is stolen and slightly modified, it would be near impossible to prove that, unless the image had a unique characteristic in it. The aim is to prove that the plagiarized image is based on an original one.

There are a number of methods covered later in this chapter for protection in this case. Protection usually comes at a cost, especially if the digital image is designed to be sold. The cost being that the quality of the image is reduced.

Illegal access

Illegal access involves accessing a digital object at a site which a person is not entitled to access. This could be via the standard hacking technique of using a user account obtained fraudulently, or by having a valid login then using URL injection to retrieve digital objects. Sites which store images outside the database are particularly vulnerable to this. All the digital objects are stored in directories which the web server can access. An incorrectly configured webserver could easily allow a person to manipulate the URL and retrieve images. Objects stored inside the database can be protected more easily.

Replace

Replace is similar to modification except the goal is to replace, undetected, a digital object with another one. In a legal case the goal could be to substitute evidence exonerating the suspect. It could be used as a form of deception in espionage or it could be used to remove an incriminating piece of information (such as a person's face) from a publicly available photo.

Accidental

Accidental is unintentional damage. A customer has a license on a digital image and continues to use it beyond it's expiry date. A web browser caches an image and a person using it in a public setting legitimately views a digital image, but the cache is not cleaned out. The next person using the public computer might then accidentally access the digital object.

The real world analogy is someone losing an item and someone else finding it and then keeping it.

In the digital world, the most common reason is due to program error. A fault in the search program or cache enables a user to view a digital image even though they are not allowed to. There is no intent by the person doing the viewing. In fact they might not even be aware they are viewing a digital object they are not entitled to.

Harvesting

Harvesting is a common tactic used by search engines and raises a number of ethical issues. If the digital object resides on a site and is publicly available, does another company have the right to copy and keep it?

In the case of a search engine, they might harvest the images to build up a public image index. Most search engines already do this for HTML pages, so by extension they are allowed to do it for any digital object found on the page.

A museum though might not be too impressed to know that the image they have made available to the general public with the data which is designed to encourage them to go into the site and buy additional objects, has been captured by a search and viewed in it. The search engine is likely to do a bland display or have it displayed out of context. It could even ruin the interpretation of the image.

So although harvesting is allowed and the large search engine providers allow robot control files to be embedded in home pages which can give instructions on what can be accessed, it's really up to the harvester to decide whether they want to adhere to those rules.

Other

A virus or Trojan can be embedded in any digital object. It's just whether the program which displays the digital object can be manipulated to run the virus when invoked. In programs, such as Word, which uses a macro language, a virus would be written in the same macro language and invoked on opening. Most digital object display programs do not use macros. This doesn't mean that this will always be the case.

Adobe Photoshop with the DNG format embeds within it XML commands to process the image automatically on opening. It uses these commands to add post modifications to the image so that the original does not need to be modified. This is not a macro language so it's not susceptible, but it does highlight the case of using macros is starting to grow. As digital objects become more widely used and advanced user friendly features are added to them, the requirement to start to use macro language will become more popular. If not correctly designed, they could open the door to macro viruses, Trojans and spyware.

A feature which some vendors would like to push for is the automatic deletion of digital objects once its expiry has been reached. At the moment the thought of autodeletion is not palatable to most users so it's not being attempted. The work around is to encrypt the digital object then provide a propriety player which can decrypt and play the content. The player determines whether the digital object has expired, and if it has it will not play it.

Protection methods

The following defines some of the methods available to protect images from theft or damage. Undoubtedly as technology improves, new methods will start to appear in the market. Different vendors will attempt different methods to protect their digital objects, but hopefully in the next ten years, a consensus will be reached on what the preferred methods are. These methods will have match the needs of the business versus the expectations and desires of the customers who consume those digital objects.

Such is the speed at which this market can change, consumers will accept or reject disruptive technologies and allow one type of technology to dominate the market for a short period of time, only to move on to the newest technology a short time later. A lot of technologies are being tried out, each hoping that theirs is the best one.

For the general business which is just trying to do basic protection of their digital objects there are some methods available that can protect them.

Visible

The standard method in this scenario is to use a watermark on the digital object. For a digital photo this could be a semi transparent watermark or the use of heavy compression so the quality is just not there. For a video it can involve a ticker type banner on the video or reducing the quality to detract from the idea that this digital object is worth copying.

This method is the first most photographers and businesses use as it's the simplest and easiest to do. It's also the most obvious and easiest to explain. The market reality says that doing this is not conducive to being a good business practice. The simple reason follows the *what you see is what you get* idea. If a digital image looks bad, it's less likely to be purchased. If the image has a large watermark right in the middle of it, potential customers will not know exactly what is in the image. The result is general consumer dissatisfaction. In a competitive situation where one business watermarks and the other doesn't, the business without the watermark is likely do better. It goes against the logic most are used to, but e-commerce purchases rarely conform to the traditional commerce model. If it did conform to it, we would be shopping exactly like we do in a shopping mall. Experience gained from the last 20 years of online shopping on the Internet has proven otherwise.

With audio, a good example is with iTunes. All their audio previews are of a high quality and are thirty seconds to a minute long. However, using this scenario, a business manager may still fear that a customer could play the previews over and over again, effectively listening to a good portion of the music track and the whole album and never buy it. The reality of the market has proven otherwise and consumers have demanded higher quality previews. In fact, the use of higher quality previews has improved sales of the music as it encourages purchasing, because if they like the album they will want to purchase it fully. The desire to also have the music local, so it can be played on portable devices, is crucial in this decision process.

So, high quality previews are important for selling effectively. Minimal or no watermarks are also important, so that the appearance of the digital object is not lost and the customer knows what they are buying.

What about theft? If a high-quality image is viewed then what is stopping it from being copied? Most computers, even the iPad, allow screen capture. If a customer sees an image they like and want to copy (but not pay for), then there is nothing that can be done to stop it. Even an image with a watermark on it can be edited out using photo-editing software.

The solution is to change the rules for dealing with digital objects. In cases where photos are taken at an event and then resold online, one can turn the whole concept of theft around and encourage it. In this model, a photographer attends an event to take photos (maybe at a restaurant, sporting event, school formal, concert, or public function). They are paid an upfront fee for taking the digital images. The images are then put online and sold by actively encouraging people to download them for free. The photographer at the site then offers additional services. They might offer framing, special effects, maybe photo's on a t-shirt, mug, plate, or poster-size versions. But they allow the images to be copied and distributed without royalties. The idea is to use this to market the site and the images to other people. If the photos are of a good quality, then the hope is that the customer will buy the extra features that upsell the digital image.

In this model, the photographer doesn't have to be concerned about theft, the extra time to manage copyright, or putting on watermarks to protect the images. This is a cost saving to the business.

This model changes the thinking strategy for dealing with digital objects and incorporates some of the ideas introduced by open source. Sometimes making things available for free can improve the business and not cause it to lose out.

Google are the pioneers of this model by always offering their software for free, from using their search engine, to providing desktop search engines, free document editing environments, e-mail, and Google Earth with street view. They are a successful company because they have worked out where the money is to be made when they sell. None of the business models they came up with would have ever worked in the real world. No economist would have ever dreamt of implementing it based on their traditional thinking paradigm.

This is why it is so important for any business doing e-commerce to not be hampered by traditional commerce rules, but be willing to try new ideas. The reverse though has shown that a large number of companies have failed when they did try other business models, hoping theirs would be the new way of doing things only to discover failure. During the 1990s, the Internet was abound with a huge range of business models, each offering new ways of doing things. The result was massive failure and the infamous dot-com collapse of 2000-2001.

The trick is to be adaptable and be willing to switch to a new business model when it appears that the old one isn't working. An analogy is the **Zui Quan** martial art's style which is referred to as drunken boxing. Here the fighter is always in an irregular and off-balance state. Though hard to master, the ability to always be in an off-balance state can lead to a variety of maneuvers not available in the traditional fighting stance. The F-22 Raptor fighter plane has been deliberately designed to not be stable, requiring a computer to control and fly it, with the pilot simply guiding it. Its inherent instability allows it to make turns and moves other fighter planes cannot match. In the e-commerce world, a business that adopts similar models and one that can adapt quickly and turn around when the market changes, is more likely to succeed than one which is stable. Even large companies have been able to achieve this, especially ones that are stable in their traditional selling platform. Microsoft turned a number of their product ranges around very quickly when the threat of open source code looked to grow into their market space. They rebuilt, replaced, and redesigned core products to compete, realizing that if they didn't move and adapt quickly they would lose access to the whole market space. As a result they have managed to stay in the search indexing and document management market spaces.

Preventive

Preventive involves creating an environment in the computer system that makes it very hard to copy a digital object. As already covered, some large scale businesses are encrypting their digital content and then using specialized programs to decrypt and play them. This works well with video, as it's very hard to capture a video playing in these devices. Unlike a digital image which can be captured using a screen grab, video is harder to capture. Audio can also be captured by redirecting the audio out on a computer and feeding it back in using a normal analogue-capture tool. Such a method is a bit clumsy but still very effective. For video, the idea of mounting a video camera in front of the computer screen and capturing the video is rather messy.

When the video is fed in via the browser, then browser plugins such as **UnPlug** are able to intercept, capture, and save these videos to a local file.

Other preventative measures include encrypting the URL that a user clicks when retrieving their digital object. This prevents it from being modified. A simple hack technique is URL modification, so if the URL to retrieve a digital object was:

```
http://www.site.com/img/download_image?pk=10234
```

Then an obvious technique to access other images is to just modify the URL and see what happens:

```
http://www.site.com/img/download_image?pk=10235
```

A variation on this technique can be seen in the movie *The Social Network*, it shows that in the early days of the Internet, how easy it was to download all the digital objects from another site.

By encrypting the URL it can't be modified unless the hacker knows the key:

```
http://www.site.com/img/download_image?enc_pk=AOD34DA2456BB2
```

It's also possible to include an expiry timestamp in the encrypted value which ensures that the link expires after a period of time. This prevents the URL from being passed on to other people as after a period of time it will expire. A potential downside with this method is that the URL cannot be bookmarked.

Bookmarking

It's worthwhile covering bookmarking at this point as it raises a number of design questions when building an e-commerce system. A **bookmark** is effectively taking a copy of a URL, storing it in the browser or in a central repository (such as www.digg.com), and then referring to that URL at a later time. Such a feature can be either good or bad for a business as it all depends on the context in which the bookmark is used. Bookmarks can also be used to embed parts of a website into another website.

An organization, such as a museum, which offers access to digital objects might want to ensure that when digital objects are accessed, they are accessed in the correct context. An organization might try to create a super museum website and capture all the URLs to digital objects from museums around the world. They then present them in their own site. Such a concept is not illegal but the practice is discouraged as it can be misleading to the customer. It is in effect a form similar to plagiarism. Because the content is not actually copied but just referenced then it goes into some very gray territory. Some HTML features dealing with frames (in HTML it's referred to as an **iframe**) prevent access to other sites just to ensure the person viewing the site is not deliberately misled about the owner of the content.

The problem with websites capturing URLs and redisplaying them is that they can completely change the context in which the digital object is viewed. They can change how it appears (color, background) and even change the definitions or metadata around it. For the owner of the digital object this can be seen as the equivalent of vandalism or even theft.

So an organization building a website which enables digital objects to be viewed, needs to factor in the ramifications of bookmarking. If there is no business issue by having it, then the URLs that appear at the site should allow them to be copied. Alternatively most sites now offer a sharing widget on the site which enables the attaching of the URL to other sites.

The following two screenshots show different variations of popular widgets designed for taking a bookmark and publishing it, or storing it, in a central repository for future reference.

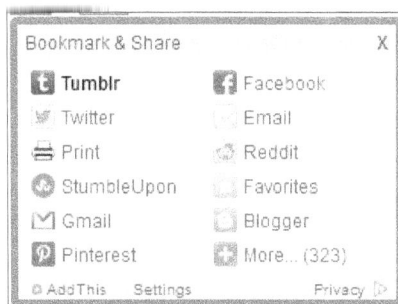

If a business decides that offering the capability is not a good business objective, then they will need to encrypt it with an embedded expiry into the URLs. This will prevent any URL, if copied, from being able to be used at these share sites.

Reactive

In some cases a more reactive approach to security is needed. Prevention might not be enough. What is needed is to actually track and even trap a perpetrator who is attempting to access objects they are not allowed to.

The reactive case involves putting in a monitor program which will SMS or e-mail when an incursion is detected. An incursion might be an attempt being made to modify the URL. Once the incursion is detected then a number of steps can be done by the business to detect who the person is.

Auditable

In addition to monitoring, it is crucial that access to all images is audited. This includes tracking search results and logging when a customer downloads an image. It should include it even if they have just viewed it. In security agencies, it can be also important to screen capture what a user has actually seen on the screen. A search result might not be sufficient. If a search returns 20,000 results, it can be hard to legally prove that a user navigated through hundreds of pages of images to view a particular digital image which they were not allowed to. Dynamic HTML has advantages here in that the whole output can be redirected to an audit trail before being returned to the user. This will result in a large audit trail, but in the case of providing legal proof that a user viewed an image can be crucial in securing a conviction.

Self destruction

As previously covered, the idea with self destruction is that the digital object destroys itself after a period of time. This is currently being used by subscription providers as a way of protecting the digital objects intellectual property if the user stops paying for the subscription.

In some cases having a program delete data from a user's computer might be considered to be akin to a virus and to be treated as such. This has resulted in the idea being unpalatable to a number of companies. So rather than delete, the idea is to disable access. This involves encryption of the digital object and using a program to control access to it.

Accept

An interesting and different approach which as been touched on is to abandon the whole idea of trying to protect the digital objects from being copied, and turn the tables around and encourage it. In some cases, such a radical change in business direction can pay off. Although, for a business dealing with digital objects it all centers around, how do they make money from it? A well know real world analogy to this is the one concerning McDonalds (the family food restaurant), where the point is made that McDonalds is not in the business of food but in the business of real estate. Though not really true as the real estate they have is an asset and does not contribute to cash flow, it does highlight that for some businesses the method for making money can come from areas they might not have considered.

In the case of the music business, there are a lot of aspiring artists and only a very small proportion of them make it seriously in the industry. TV shows, such as "The Voice" or "Idol" push this idea where only the best will succeed. The standard business model is that a musician composes the music, cuts it to a CD, which is then sold and they make money from it. The focus is around the CD. What is shown is that only those who make the big time make any serious amounts of money from the sale of CDs. A similar point can be made for authors writing books. The large majority do not make much money from the selling of them.

If the focus is changed and the CD is turned into a marketing item rather than a sale item then the rules for selling change. As the CD now falls under marketing, it makes sense to push it so it's copied and distributed to as many people as possible. The aim is to reach a large target audience. The musician then has to look at making money from other areas. This can include performing at concerts, gigs, and other places. Selling extras to the music can also be done, including merchandise, such as T-shirts, jackets, and personalized albums. The list of items that can be sold is quite large and well supported in the industry. The e-commerce site would encourage the downloading and distribution of the album with the encouragement to purchase merchandise, as well as, having a tightly integrated venue and ticketing system to ensure that fans can buy tickets and attend gigs. This view is similar to open source which prescribes the philosophy that all software should be free (all music should be free) and money is made from services (merchandise, playing at events) around the software.

A number of musicians are moving down this path and achieving success from it. In some cases they offer albums to be purchased on iTunes but if you go to their website you can play and download their music from there.

The large music companies of course do not like this business viewpoint because it impacts on their bottom line. A similar directional compromise in the marketplace is likely to be reached just like it has with open source software. The fear ten years ago was that all businesses would have to go down the open source path to compete, which would destroy the sale of software and ruin the industry. What has happened is that a lot of businesses have adopted open source in part or in its entirety. Oracle offers a mixed model (mainly due to acquisitions), where they offer products, such as Java for free (but not open source), whereas MySQL is an open source.

For most consumers there is no difference between open source and free. It's just free. Oracle provides free software, such as Java and Oracle XE but it is not open source. They require the need to protect their intellectual property as well as ensuring the stability of the product. Open source and stability is a mixed bag and really does depend on the skill of the group of individuals supporting it. In some cases it can be well argued that open source is better supported and has a faster turnaround for fixes and enhancements because it is not locked into a vendor.

In the music industry, musicians offering their music for free has not impacted the market. In fact, it has resulted in it being forced to become more consumer focused and deliver equivalent concepts. One in particular is the subscription model, where a customer pays a certain amount of money per month and can then get unlimited access to all the music in that businesses library of music. Another model incorporates advertisements, where a customer has access for free to the business site, but will get an advert in between music plays (they can pick which ever music they want to listen to). If they do no want to listen to the advertisements then they need to pay for a full member subscription.

What open source has done, just like musicians offering free music, is to force the larger companies to be more consumer focused and adapt to the rapidly changing technology in the marketplace.

Legal proof

Cases where it is suspected that an image may have been copied, and resold require legal proof that can be used to prosecute the alleged perpetrator.

This can be quite hard to do and typically involves a number of steps:

- Request that the alleged perpetrator delete the suspected copy
- Show that the alleged perpetrator was actually at the site and had the opportunity to copy the digital object
- Prove that the digital object is in fact a copy

The last point can be done a number of ways. If the digital object was simply copied then a byte-by-byte comparison would prove that it is a copy.

If the image was modified, then this can be harder to prove. Embedding a hidden watermark into the image is one method (see `http://en.wikipedia.org/wiki/Digimarc`). If the watermark can be extracted from the modified image then it can prove that it was copied. The challenge with this software is to ensure that the watermark does not impact on the visibility of the image, cannot be detected by the perpetrator and be removed, or be accidentally removed through digital object modification.

Although it can get more complicated. With video and audio, rather than copying and stealing the intellectual property in the image, it can instead be licensed for use. In the movie industry all audio sound tracks have to have a legal license proving that they are legitimately obtained and not just copied. This automatic enforcement has ensured that all artists are correctly compensated when their intellectual property is included in someone else's content.

Licensing involves managing copyright and intellectual property. The implementation of it is covered later in this chapter with the concept of a pricing calculator and user fees. Even music made available for free on a website might have licensing restrictions on it. On download it might be made available for personal use only and not for business use.

This subtle but important change, impacts on the whole idea of open source. Open source also has variations in its licensing. One model says that the open source code can be used by a business that, provided that, when used their code is also made open source. Some allow a business to embed the open source code into theirs and then resell it.

In the music industry the strategy is to allow music to be used with unrestricted use by the general public, but cannot be used by a business. The idea being, if that business makes a profit from the use of the music, then the musician should be compensated accordingly.

With licensing the implementation of it moves down a couple of paths. The first is to ensure that if a business makes money from the use of the digital object then the owner should be compensated. The protection of the intellectual property can also be important to ensure that when it is used by a business it is used in the manner, in which, the owner of the digital object is happy for it to be used in. In the United States, recent cases of politicians using musicians soundtracks in their advertisements has resulted in some requesting the advertisements to be removed because there was no agreement with them for the use of it in that manner (especially if the musician disagrees with the views of the politician).

License enforcement usually rests with the owner of the digital object. It is their responsibility to monitor and confirm whether the license is being adhered to. They are also responsible for following up and attempting to rectify the situation if they determine there is a misuse of the license. Only as a last resort is it taken to court. The challenge for the business is that the cost of going to court might outweigh any costs arising from the license agreement. Also, the cost of monitoring and enforcement for a small business might not be cost effective, in which case the business hopes and expects their customers to conform to the license.

A look at different business situations

This section covers some of the issues that might arise when looking to sell digital images.

Copyright

A business might want to purchase access to a digital image for a specific purpose. It might include a portion of a video in a documentary (requiring access to historical footage for example), or a digital image to be included in a book, or audio on the soundtrack to a video.

In these cases the requirement is to deal with the issue that "you giving me access to your digital object will enhance my business". The pricing model solution to dealing with this is highly subjective and involves user fees and copyright. Once the fee situation has been calculated the copyright owner gives permission for image use. The user fees along with a pricing calculator can be used to determine what the cost is to use the digital object.

There are a large number of dimensions or factors that might need to be taken into consideration. An educational institution are likely pay less in comparison to a business. A student doing a thesis might be allowed very tightly controlled and limited access at no cost. For use in a book, the print run number might be important. For a video the potential viewing audience or even time of viewing might impact the price. Volume discounting and frequent usage discounts are just some of the considerations that should be taken into account when the final price is determined. The actual method for calculation is going to be based around the perceived value of the digital object, which can be determined by its age, rarity, and popularity. Popularity can result in the digital object price being reduced or alternatively increased.

Greeting card

A greeting card enables a customer to e-mail one or more people a digital image, which has been enhanced with the goal of celebrating an event. From the business side, they are using the customer to sell their image. From the customer side, they receive a service (typically free) that adds value to their experience and enables them to share the digital object with others.

The result is that the idea of an electronic greeting card is to provide a service. What type of service is dependent on the owner of the digital object. A photographer might offer a greeting card to promote the sale of key digital images in the site. If it's a wedding, then those who attended the wedding might send greeting cards to friends and family. The end result is to expand the potential pool of customers who might purchase the image. It's a free service designed to entice and encourage additional purchases.

For a site where the digital images are free to access, then the concept is still the same. The goal is to offer a value added service with the result that it will encourage others to come to the site. Even for the sites that offer Christmas, birthday, or special event cards the goal is still the same. Use this service to expand the customer base.

Variations include being able to add special effects, animation, and music to it, to enhance the experience of the card and take it beyond the standard idea of it being just a message with a simple picture.

From a security perspective, the challenge is to allow the distribution of the digital image to a potential large set of unauthorized users without losing control of the actual digital object. In essence how do you make an image publicly available but still keep it private?

The easiest method is to not allow the digital image to be e-mailed out. Instead a link is provided, such that when it's clicked on, it takes the user back to the site. An expiry can be built into the e-mail link. Though this seems to provide an adequate solution, most e-mail clients view such links as dangerous and actively discourage the user from clicking on them. Firewalls and virus protection programs, especially ones found in a business, might reject the URL even if the user clicks on the link in the e-mail. In which case it defeats the service goal of having it. Sometimes it's easier to go with the basic concept and send a greeting card image either embedded in the e-mail or as an attachment. This is likely to be accepted and viewed by the customer.

Music

This has already been covered but by doing a simple business review, it's apparent that when it comes to selling music digitally there is more involved than just the standard selling of CDs. There are a number of models and it's all based around the popularity and success of the musician.

- **For very popular musicians**:

    The best method is still to sell CDs. Licensing rights to the music and merchandise are a good way of earning additional monies.

- **For musicians who have had limited success**:

    The profit made from CD sales is not great. There is a greater likelihood of monies to be made from licensing the music and selling merchandise. If the brand name of the musician is well known, then attending music gigs is also a potential source of revenue.

- **For new musicians**:

    There is not much money that can be made from selling CDs. A better model involves making money from first establishing a loyal fan base by using the CDs to market themselves, then attend venues making money from ticket sales and merchandise sold.

When looking at music and what is involved in audio digital objects, it becomes important to determine what is actually being sold. Is it the digital object, or the brand name behind the digital object? In the case of music, the brand name is the name of the musician (or band). If one steps back, looks at the bigger picture and attempts to sell the brand name first, then there are more opportunities for making money but also more risks. If the digital object is treated as just a marketing device to help sell the brand name then the traditional prime source of sales income is lost. For new musicians this is a worthwhile risk as there is not much that can be lost. For well established and popular musicians this can be an unacceptable direction.

By taking the lessons learnt from the music industry into the domain of other digital objects, such as video and digital photos, then does the selling of the brand name continue to hold true? For one off videos the concept doesn't hold. There is no real concept of a brand for a digital video. For TV shows, it has the potential to still work but with modification. For a long running TV show, such as "The Simpsons", the brand has been sold well. Rights to the TV show enable toy and other manufacturers to sell a variety of goods about the show. At some point, it might even make sense to make the episodes available for free to keep the licensing profitable.

For digital images the answer varies and doesn't match well to the music industry. With the exception of a small minority of famous photographers, the idea of selling the brand just doesn't fit well.

In the end when looking at the four main types of digital objects; digital images, audio, video, and documents, the methods for selling might overlap but they are all distinct in the approach that is best used. In all cases, the lessons learnt from open source should be considered as it does offer potential new business directions. Though it's a highly competitive market, the competition which is appearing focuses around coming up with killer methods for how the digital object is sold versus competition about the quality of the product. This has been seen recently with the introduction of subscription services, giving unlimited access to content. What is delivered is secondary, what is important to the customer is how it's obtained.

Electronic commerce

The e-commerce store is a digital frontend, web-based shop, focused around the selling and delivery of digital objects. As the business requirement can overlap so tightly between digital and physical objects, both are defined and described in this section.

The e-commerce system can be hosted anywhere in the world. It can allow anyone to browse and buy items, or it can enforce the need to create an account with the shop to perform transactions.

The interface should be HTML based or use a web service layer to integrate with it. For mobile devices, such as an iPad or Smartphone, then a specialized application is required. In these cases the shop should be looking at providing a HTML storefront first followed by Smartphone applications.

It's important that the shopfront is integrated. It should offer the one interface to buy any items and mix different item types in the one purchase. A customer should (if the business sells it) be able to buy a digital photo and download it, a book about the author of the photo, a soundtrack on CD to go with it, and a ticket to a local venue where the photo is displayed-all in one purchase.

Not all browsers are the same

Over time the interface used to access e-commerce systems has changed as the technology has changed. When flash was popular there was a huge push for all sites to use it as it offered a user friendly interface. With improvements in JavaScript the interface can now become more user friendly with drag/drop capabilities and helpful widgets. The challenge is not all browsers run JavaScript the same, and the solution has been the development of JavaScript frameworks guaranteed to work on a set of browsers. With HTML 5 now being integrated in to most browsers and offering consistency in behavior as well as advanced functionality, the need to use JavaScript has diminished. It's important to note that JavaScript will never be replaced by HTML. It offers features and capabilities that HTML will never look to adopt. JavaScript can utilize web services providing enhanced navigation and data validation which HTML just cannot do.

The e-commerce system should work across all browsers as well as browsers on Smartphone devices.

IP address country tracking

At times it's important to know approximately where in the world the customer originates from. This can be useful for limiting content which might be restricted to certain countries of the world. Video is a prime example. Some businesses in certain countries have been able to obtain rights for enabling controlled viewing (meaning adverts are included in it, or it's a paid subscription) of the video. The limitation is that it's for that country only. That has resulted in potential customers in other countries not being allowed to view it. As annoying as this is for international customers, the complex nature and fluidity of the copyright model, has resulted in some of these country limiting behaviors.

The conclusion then is that the e-commerce system has to be able to track the location of the customer. Asking the customer which country they come from is not going to work. If customers realize they are denied access because of their location, then they will just indicate they belong to the country where they are allowed to view it (they will lie).

The solution is that the IP address of the customer needs to be reverse engineered to the country. This is actually possible as IP addresses are assigned in blocks to different countries and this information is made publicly available. Provided the customer is not spoofing their IP address (changing it or having it redirected from other servers), the reverse engineer should return the correct origin of the customer. It can actually be used to even narrow it down to a region in a city.

Order lifecycle

A customer purchase order will go through many states as it progresses from an initial order to a completed one. In a transactional database system, the typical direction to go down is one where the transaction happens (is committed/saved) or it doesn't happen (it's rolled back). In an e-commerce system a transaction could be done in one click or go on for longer than a couple of days and involve legal paper work.

In reality an order follows a fuzzy logic path and it goes through various stages. Some stages are halfway points and could equate to the degree in which the order is completed. Each business has different requirements for dealing with an e-commerce order, but most follow a common set of stages.

The following is a list of the most common states a purchase order can go through. At any point in the cycle a customer can leave and not return.

Status	Definitions
Pre-order - No order made	The customer has accessed the application but has not yet attempted to make an order. This is the NULL case.
Pre-order	The customer has accessed the part of the e-commerce application and are adding items to the basket. The order has just been created.
Pre-order confirmed	The customer has progressed beyond the "add items to basket stage", and is now actively trying to finalize the purchase. This can be important to know as it separates customers who just browse and want to know the total, versus customers who it looks like are serious in making a purchase.
Pre-order bank	The customer is using a credit card payment and is at the point where they are communicating with the bank to make it. This could be a redirect where the customer is taken to the bank, or where the e-commerce site takes the credit card details and passes them securely to the site. Failure can occur at this point. A customer who is redirected to the bank might make the payment, but the bank fails to pass this information back to the e-commerce site, leaving the order in a partially completed state.
Awaiting authorization	The customer is requesting access to the image and is awaiting for the owner to grant approval.
Ordered	The order has been made.
Order paid	The order has been made and payment has been received. In the case of a credit card payment this can be done in one step. For a cheque or phone order, payment can be delayed while the monies are cleared.

Status	Definitions
Order authorized	For an order waiting authorization, the order has now been authorized by the owner. This can become more complex if the order is composed of many items, with each item requiring approval from different authorizers. Final authorization only occurs when all the items have been processed and accepted or rejected.
Order completed	The order has been made and sent to the customer. For a digital order, payment, and delivery can be done in the one step. For delivery of a physical item this can take longer to fulfill.
Order customer canceled	The customer has made the order and then at some point canceled it. When the order has been paid for, a cancel will then trigger a refund.
Business canceled	Order is canceled by the business. Depending on the state of the order, this might trigger a refund.
On hold	The order has been put on hold for business reasons.
Processing	The order requires a set of post purchase workflow tasks to be done before delivery. This could be acquiring stock or production of the item.
Problems	There has been a problem identified with the order and it requires intervention by the business.
Archived	The order has been completed, delivered and finished. Rather than being deleted, it is archived purely for reporting purposes. Archiving puts it out of the way and in an area where it will not cause any impact with other orders (false positives when searching).

Payment methods

There are multiple methods currently available that an e-commerce site can use.

- **Merchant**: This is payment by credit card. This is the most popular method as it is the simplest and payment is usually instant. It's also well controlled by the banks and audited. Merchant payment requires the use of SSL (encryption of the data between the customer and the bank). In most cases, the site should never capture the credit card details, but rather send them to the bank (via a secure SSL transaction) or be redirected to the bank where the customer makes the payment and the business is then credited with it.

  A business might keep the credit card details for recurring payments. If a business does this, then they will be required to conform to a strict set of digital and physical security requirements. It has been shown historically that internal fraud or break ins to a business can occur just to steal credit card numbers. Credit card numbers need to be stored using the highest level encryption possible with access tightly controlled and fully audited.

The recommendation is that a business should not store credit card numbers. This is a job best left to the bank. Most banks now offer a facility to do recurring payments without the need for the credit card details to be kept with the business. A business storing credit card numbers is advertising itself as a rich target for hackers.

Customers accessing a site that uses this has to establish a level of trust with the business and hope their card number is not misused or intercepted.

- **Central merchant**: Popularized by PayPal, this is similar to payment by credit card except it ensures the safety of the credit card number. The idea is that the customer makes a secure, safe, and guaranteed credit card payment to the central site. The central site then pays the business. The idea is that the customer can trust the central site and not have to worry that the business they are buying from might acquire their credit card number.

- **Phone order**: The customer rings up the business via a phone and transcribes their credit card number to an operator who then processes the transaction. This was a popular method prior to online merchant facilities. With the improvements in safety of online merchant, this method has dropped out of favor by many businesses as it's labor intensive and the credit card number could still be recorded with the business.

- **Cheque** (alternate spelling is check): The customer makes the order and payment is made using a cheque. This is a slow process and can take days or weeks to complete. It also requires manual intervention and is an additional cost to the business as they have to handle and process them. Also the order might not be considered ready even though the cheque has been received. It might have to be cleared first.

- **Barter** or **trade**: Popularized by Bartercard (www.bartcard.com), involves the concept of using trade dollars equating to businesses goods and services. This can then be used as a credit. This method of payment is designed more for businesses.

- **Billing**: A customer establishes a line of credit with the business and can then spend against it. Typically used by businesses who do online shopping, it is based on a trust between the customer and the e-commerce site. The billing method gets around the delays that can be caused when payment is made by cheque. With Billing payment is instant (like credit card), but the customer can then send a cheque later to cover one or more purchases.

The challenge for the business is to determine at what point is the payment considered made? A customer might buy an item, but because it hasn't been delivered yet, should the amount be deducted from their line of credit?

- **Store credit**: A customer buys credit for use in the business. This is equivalent in concept to a debit card, because the customer will never owe the business any monies, they are just using monies they have already given to the business. A business might offer discounts if a customer purchases store credit.

- **Gift certificate**: Is similar to store credit except the credit is designed to be given to someone else. Also with a gift certificate, the customer is encouraged to use it quickly by attaching an expiry on it.

- **Frequent shopping points**: Popularized by airlines and now used by credit card companies, this method allocates a set of points based on the amount spent at the business. The points can be redeemed for goods or for discounts on subsequent purchases. The idea of the point system is to encourage customers to return to a site and make further purchases. In some countries, the tax department can view these points as equivalent to cash and it has to be treated as such. (It's subject to the local tax code and conversion rate. It's this reason why a number of sites equate $1 to 1 point as it makes it easier to deal with the tax department.)

- **Cash**: The universal and traditional method. For an e-commerce system this is not an ideal solution because it involves getting the cash to the business and the business then safely dealing with it. It's a manual method and doesn't work well with automated e-commerce systems. Cash can be easily stolen or lost.

- **Authorization**: Here there isn't an actual monetary payment. Instead access to the digital object is given by a third party. The cost is free but the key point is that permission must be given.

- **Milestone**: It is used when a service is purchased (provided). In this case when the service has reached an agreed milestone (step in the project) payment is made.

- **Mix**: Payment isn't always just using one method. For an expensive order a customer might have to use multiple credit cards. They might also mix by using a cheque and a credit card. If they are using billing and their limit is exceeded then they might pay the difference using a credit card.

A comprehensive audit trail

A key component of any e-commerce system is being able to track and audit all changes made to an order. This is important from a legal view. It's also needed to determine if there was administrative error. Has a basket item been deleted when it shouldn't have been? Has the price been changed or a discount been given incorrectly? An audit trail is also a bonus in that it provides a complete click through history of how the user has navigated through the system and how they have used it. Such information is important to improving the order workflow and seeing where users encounter choke points or areas where they just give up and leave. It can also be useful to know which items are added then removed from the basket and how long users take to navigate between pages.

The traditional development method for an audit trail is to keep a separate table or tables, that are populated with information as the main tables are updated. So if a customer adds an item to the shopping basket then this initiates a trigger routine which adds a timestamp and record to the audit table indicating this has happened. It is up to the application to determine what triggers the audit update and what information is transferred to it. The downside with this type of audit table is that it's very hard to calculate a history of how the user has navigated and used the system. This system also prevents the idea of rolling back an order to a point in time or rolling it forward.

The solution is to create an architecture that uses some of the concepts found in an Oracle database, and come to terms with the issue that a lot of relational storage is going to be used. The idea is to discard the whole notion of audit tables, use the concept of a **System Change Number** (**SCN**) with the adoption of a never delete attitude.

The base concept is simple. When an order is first started it is assigned an SCN of 1. A timestamp is associated with this SCN. As the customer steps through adding items or providing details about shipping and delivery, then the SCN is increased and *all the information with the changes* is inserted. If a basket item is deleted, then as all the information is reinserted the deleted basket item is just not included (see the following example).

SCN	1	2	3	4	5	6
	Item Added					
		Second Item Added			Item Deleted	
			Pricing info and discounts applied $$	$$$	$$	Shipping information specified $$
				Third Item Added		

With each action the SCN number is increased by 1 and the previous history is kept exactly as it was. The constant frequent data inserting lends itself naturally to an object oriented design.

The downside with this method is that extra relational data is stored. Functionality is gained at the expense of storage. With a multimedia database, the volume of relational data is going to be quite small in comparison to the volume of multimedia data. So such an increase in additional storage, which might seem large for a database administrator used to managing relational data, is in fact quite small in volume.

Storage efficiency can be gained by introducing a global SCN and breaking up the different tables used in an e-commerce system and using a local SCN on each. So if a customer updates their delivery details, then the basket information is not re-inserted, only the delivery detail information is. The global SCN ensures that all changes are kept in sync.

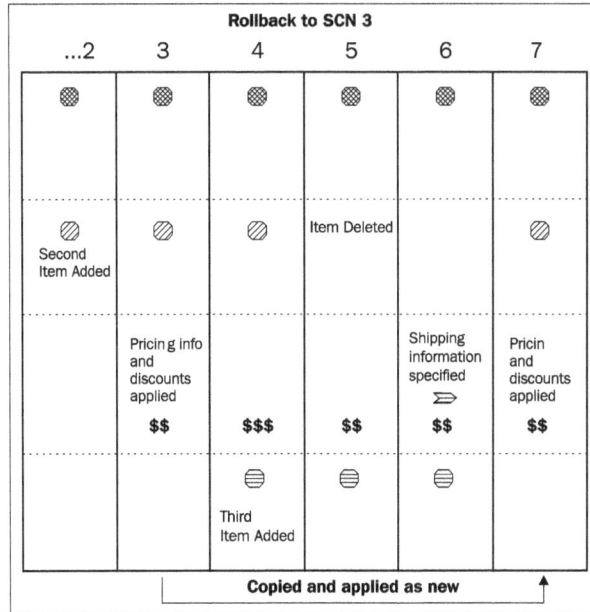

Storage recovery can be made by reviewing any transactions, extracting analysis and summary information, then deleting any of the rows, which contain SCNs that are not being used.

To rollback a transaction involves looking at the data at a particular SCN, which completely represents the state of the e-commerce transaction at that time. That information is then copied and inserted in with a new SCN, greater than the largest one. That way the transactional data is rolled back, but the audit history is kept. The natural temptation for rolling back is to delete all the data to the SCN. This in effect deletes part of the audit trail, which is not an acceptable solution.

Locking down the price

The analogy when using a relational database is you start with a car. You break it down into its individual parts (wheels, seats, and engine) and those are the tables. When doing a relational query, you just assemble the bits together to get the desired result.

In the e-commerce environment, this involves putting all the pricing information into a price book with price items. When a customer makes an order, they reference the items in the price book.

The problem with this design is that if a customer picks an A4 print for $20 and they buy it, then if an administrator comes in and changes the price to $25 or changes the name, the next time the customer sees their order the price and/or name will have changed. The relational side assembles the purchase order from the base pieces which means referencing the price book.

A solution is to prevent updates on price items. Effectively a new one needs to be created when something changes. The old one is locked in and the new takes effect. This way the customer will never see a change on their order. Unfortunately this solution gets more difficult to implement when digital objects are factored into the pricing. If a customer buys a digital image then they will see a thumbnail of it and hopefully this thumbnail will appear on their receipt page, making it friendlier and easier for them to know what they purchased. What happens if the thumbnail is modified or if the metadata around the digital image is modified? If that metadata is used to drive a pricing calculator or workflow then the order could become corrupted. In this case the solution is to lock down everything in an e-commerce system and prevent any changes. This isn't practical to achieve.

The better solution is to sacrifice storage for order reliability. In this case when a customer adds an item to the basket all the details about that item are captured and stored with it. This includes the thumbnail, the metadata around it and the price book information. The result is that if an item is ordered a thousand times its information is copied a thousand times. As it's mostly relational data and even the thumbnails themselves are small, the total volume of information is not large when it's compared to the total volume of all the digital objects. It's this point that needs to be considered. If the total size of the digital objects is 5 TB, then 100 GB of storage for relational data and an e-commerce system (based on on a base size of 5 GB of core digital thumbnails, metadata, and price book information) is small.

Post processing issue

A very crucial performance issue that has to be taken into consideration with an e-commerce system that delivers digital objects, is when it comes to the delivery of image derivatives. This might be the delivery of post card images, ones that are for PowerPoint, are for printing (CMYK color space), or a certain size (A4) or type (High quality Tiff). Metadata might be embedded in the image on delivery.

The business decision that has to be made is to either create all the derivatives at ingestion, or create them on demand. The following describes advantages and disadvantage for each.

- **Create on ingestion**:
    - ° More storage is needed to hold all the derivatives
    - ° Backup storage is larger because of the additional database storage
    - ° Ingestion takes longer due to the processing requirements of each image
    - ° If metadata is to be embedded in the image, it has to be done at the time of processing, or at periodic intervals if it's known that the metadata has changed and this change needs to be reflected in the derivative

- **Create on demand**:
    - ° Storage is kept to a minimum (only one digital object is kept)
    - ° Metadata, if embedded in the image will be up to date
    - ° A dedicated transformation server or a server with a lot of spare CPU capacity is needed to process the image on delivery
    - ° Delivery time is impacted due to the processing requirements
    - ° A popular image will require processing for every delivery, resulting in the same processing steps to be repeated often

A potential third option uses a combination of the two. The idea is to use the create-on-demand option. The difference is that once the derivative is created, it is stored with the digital object as per the create on ingestion. This means initially the storage footprint is low, but will grow. Popular images do not need to be processed again. This method acts like a permanent cache and it's more complex to implement.

There is no right or wrong solution. Ultimately it comes down to a business decision based on storage volumes, server capacity, and delivery requirements. Even as server capacity grows along with storage, it's anticipated that the benefits and disadvantages of each method will remain the same, with neither one becoming the better option.

In cases involving video, the transformation currently is so processor heavy and in most cases can take hours to perform, the recommendation would be, to create any derivatives on ingestion rather than on demand. Over time the processor power available in CPUs will grow (especially with the tighter incorporation of Graphical Processor Units or even special purpose CPUs designed for video conversion), making it cost effective to create video derivatives on demand.

What are you buying?

With a digital object this is actually a valid question to ask. This section covers most of the different types of options that can be bought. Over time, as new pricing models start to appear this list will grow. The important point is that any business needs to be flexible and be willing to change their business model in the situations where the market changes. Adaptability is crucial to business survivability.

Price books

The current thinking for shopping is similar to the Amazon store, in that a customer buys a physical product. This could be a book, clothes, DVD, or any item. The item is then shipped to the customer. With iTunes, there are no physical products to buy only digital ones. This means the item on purchase is digitally downloaded and its usage is controlled via iTunes.

When it comes to the type of items that can be defined in a price book and purchased, they can be broken down into the following types with characteristics:

Item type	Deliverable	Characteristics	Postprocessing
Physical image	A physical representation of the image (digital object). This can be a print, a poster, or other variations. For audio it can be a CD and for a Video a DVD. It can be a combination of other images.	It is delivered using a postal system (courier, freight, shipping, or hand delivery). Postage is required to be calculated and included in the total price.	The digital object might need to be printed, cut to DVD, or physically transformed. In some cases the original digital object might not yet have been digitized or might exist in a form not suitable for postage.
Digital image	A downloaded, electronic (digital) version of the image (digital object). This can include streaming delivery(video on demand).	It is delivered via the network. A cost might be needed to be factored in for bandwidth usage.	Copyright management and enforcement of monitoring and correct usage.

Item type	Deliverable	Characteristics	Postprocessing
Physical item	This is any item that is not a digital object. It could be a book, a postcard, a souvenir, clothing, food, or electronics. Typically they are items that complement the digital object. A person buying a digital image of a museum object might also want to purchase a book on it.	Similar to a physical image for delivery. Might include gift wrapping. Will have metadata associated with it, similar to a digital object. Used to help search for and link the item to digital objects.	Stock management. Determining if the item is available, how many are left, should more be shipped in. Alerts and warnings if out of stock. Basic stock control.
Donation	A customer donates money to an organization (for museums this can be "friends of" the association). The donation might result in discounts on subsequent purchases.	Has different tax implications and calculations. Is usually a one-off cost, but could be agreed to be re-occurring.	An official tax receipt. Possibly might include access to private images or be entitled to discounts on items.
Membership	Similar to a donation except membership comes with agreed privileges. This could include physical items (a book), access to a wider range, or quality (high res) of digital objects.	Is usually an agreed yearly or monthly payment. Membership can come in different tiers.	Is specific to the membership requirements agreed on.
Subscription	This is similar to a membership but implies access to content for an agreed period of time. This could be a newspaper, or magazine. A digital subscription might give access to digital objects, content (online magazines), or access to high resolution digital objects or full length videos.	Items can be physical or digital. The key point is the agreed payment entitling the customer access to content.	For physical items, stock management and control. For digital items, management and enforcement of copyright.
Time and materials	This is payment for a service of an individual or company. This can be a consultant, contractor, laborer, or part-time employee. The service can be performed remotely.	Also referred to as *T&M*, this is usually an hourly payment for a person doing and following an agreed work schedule.	Contractual arrangements, monitoring deliverables, and agreeing to work that is to be performed.

Item type	Deliverable	Characteristics	Postprocessing
Credit (gift)	This is purchasing an alternate form of currency. This can be a gift certificate or store credit.	The credit can be used as an alternate payment method. In the case of gift certificates it can expire after a period of time.	Security and protection of the credit against fraudulent use.
Service	This is the opposite of a digital image. Here the customer pushes their digital object to the organization for it to be processed and serviced. This could include photo correction, digital video editing, audio mixing, adding special effects, and banner pages.	The customer owns the digital object, not the organization. The object is never made public. The serviced digital object is then returned to the customer.	Workflow and quality control to ensure the service provided is as agreed with the customer.
Request	This is a customer paying for an action to be performed. This might be to perform a search against a set of items in a government department. It might be to conduct a family history study or research into a particular person in a museum (as part of a project or business study). What is delivered is usually the results in document form.	The request is unique to the needs of the organization. A library of archives that is not digitized might offer librarian search type services. Memorials might offer historical tracking and research services. The request is well defined.	Workflow tracking and monitoring. Quality control to ensure the request is delivered as agreed.
Ticket	A customer purchases a seat at a venue for an event. Events can be public (no arranged seating) or private (fixed seating).	Prices can vary based on the time of the event, the location of the seats at the venue and even if the event has added extra features.	Delivery is typically a ticket or electronic signature (barcode or number) proving access is legitimate to the event.

Item type	Deliverable	Characteristics	Postprocessing
School Booking	A school books a program at a business. Similar to a ticket at an event, complexity is introduced due to the varying nature of school requirements, the number of attendees and that a program is repeated on a calendar. The business provides a service to the school when they arrive (for example, a guide, interactive experience). Typically used by museums, memorials, parliament buildings, historical societies, zoos, botanical gardens, and local municipalities.	A program can be shared between multiple schools attending or per school. A program can be self guided. Here the business doesn't provide an official representative as a guide, just guaranteed access to the facility.	Involves a tightly focused and structured training plan designed around the unique capabilities of the business, the different age groups, and needs of the school. Mainly designed with education, it can be used equally by the general public.
Auctions	Can be broken down into a number of different types, each with their own characteristics. An auction generally involves multiple customers, the concept of bidding, and is time based.		
Customer	This is the eBay concept. Here a customer makes an item which they own, available for sale. For digital items, this could be a photograph, access to a video they own, or even their own services.	The customer determines what is being sold. What the starting price is, reserved price, and how long the auction runs for.	Delivery becomes problematic as the exchange of monies and agreed delivery of goods needs to be properly handled.
Store	This is similar to a clearance sale. The business offers key items up for auction. Similar to a customer auction, the store auction is more controlled and can be used to auction key items in a collection.	Key items can be made available for the auction or just sold as is.	Delivery is less problematic as the store which owns the e-commerce system is responsible for the shipment of goods.

Item type	Deliverable	Characteristics	Postprocessing
Print Media	Takes the store auction concept one step further enabling a bidding structure to happen to enable exclusive access to a digital object. A tabloid photographer might configure an auction for exclusive rights to one paparazzi type photo for three days. The winner gets to use it exclusively. After the time period, the photo can be purchased by anyone. This auction is designed for the print media (newspapers, magazines), where the age of the photo can dictate its price.	This introduces the concept of short-term ownership and temporary copyright access. It's time based and rights are automatically relinquished at the end of the agreed time period.	Delivery is more simply handled as it's digital, but in some cases for security, might involve the shipment of the images directly to the customer.
Reverse	Involves a group of customers uniting together to obtain a bulk discount price. This auction is targeted initially at tradespeople who by banding together can purchase items such as building equipment, electronics, or clothing in bulk.	The customers agree to purchase a quantity of a particular item, and do this within a fixed time period. The greater the quantity purchased the lower the price becomes.	Delivery of items is standard postage and shipment. Each customer is shipped to separately as if they made the order on their own.

Pricing options

There is a difference in the business focus for the pricing of physical items versus digital ones. A physical item is either sold as is (like a book) or can have a set of dimensions associated with it to provide the customer with choice and variation on purchase (for clothing dimensions this can include size, color, and style; for food it could be flavor; for a DVD it could be the region it's destined for).

For a digital object, especially digital photo's, there are a lot of options available. Postprocessing can change it and result in the object being converted into any form. Framing, sizing, and even the medium the digital photo is printed on can impact the price and range of options. When factoring in copyright, usage fees rules and even the requirement to use a pricing calculator, then the complexity of purchase options starts to grow.

Pricing for time based multimedia isn't necessarily limited to a one off cost. It can also be expanded to include varying pricing based on length of time. A customer might want a snippet of a video between two timestamps. Pricing can be calculated on a per second rate. A similar concept can hold for audio. For documents, pricing could be done per page.

Pricing can also vary based on who the customer is. An internal customer might be able to buy the item at cost and different price values can be linked to the roles a customer has (which can be linked to subscription or membership discounts).

A business which sources their items from a manufacturer might also want to link their prices to the manufacturers with a profit margin percentage. That way if the manufacturer increases their price, the price the business offers is automatically increased.

Complex items might also be linked to an internal table in the database, which offers a similar capability to a manufacturer but is linked to an existing financial system. This ensures a central area for price management.

An item being sold might also be discounted. Discounts can be due to a customer being a member, having a subscription or because they have purchased on volume. It's likely some items might need to be protected from this, especially if that item is being sold at cost (maybe due to a promotion). Large shopping chains do this frequently. They will offer an item at a dramatically reduced price, at cost or below (at a loss) to entice customers into the store. The reduced item cannot be discounted anymore.

The reverse of this option has also made a recent appearance. Customers can nominate (via a subscription) a set of items, such that when they purchase just those items they are entitled to a discount.

Understanding the business rules

An e-commerce system focused on digital delivery needs to be one that is flexible, adaptable, and can be easily configured and adjusted to the changing requirements of the business. This is achieved by using the concept of business rules.

In an e-commerce system there are three key areas:

- The price book. This contains pricing information.
- The digital images with their associated metadata.
- The customers and security (roles) they have. A customer can be public, an authorized account or an internal account.

A set of business rules combine these areas together. The business rules define the relationships and indicate the flow of purchase. An e-commerce environment might have a variety of business rules. One might be for public customers, another might be for internal customers. Each might have different characteristics covering tax, payment, and customer information. The business rule assigned to a customer has to be dynamic and can be based on a role the customer has or even their physical location. For an international e-commerce system, different business rules can be used depending on the country the user comes from. This can be used to control the display of pricing (dollar symbol, pound symbol, or euro symbol), availability and pricing of products. It can also control which merchant banking to use as well as how the tax is calculated.

A business rule is comprised of a set of e-commerce rules. There are a number of them available with each one handling a different aspect of the behavior of the e-commerce system.

Tax rule

Tax calculation can be one of the hardest steps in an e-commerce system to determine as each country, even states in a country can have different and sometimes conflicting tax rules.

The following lists some of the considerations that need to be factored in when designing the rules for an e-commerce system:

- Tax might have to be calculated on where (country and state) the order was physical dispatched from.
- Donations or charity groups might be entitled to a tax exemption.
- Overseas (international) orders might be considered duty free (Tax exempt).
- In countries that offer goods and services tax (France, Australia, and Canada), the tax calculation might be simpler to perform, but postage might be considered to be a service. In which case tax might have to be calculated on it.
- Tax might need to be calculated on any administration charges imposed on using a merchant facility (credit card) as it's considered to be a service.
- In countries that have a sales tax, the tax might vary between different types of items. A book might have a different sales tax compared to a DVD, print of a physical image, or even the purchase of a digital image.

In the United States when shopping, tax is added at the point of purchase. In countries that offer a GST, tax is bundled into the price. For e-commerce systems the standard rule is to offer the item with the tax included in the price. This is to make it user friendly. Offering an item online without specifying the tax might be perceived by customers as an act of deception, in that costs are just being added later and they are not seeing the true value of the item.

In general, the rule most e-commerce sites follow is to list the price with all taxes included. Additional taxes on administration charges for credit cards have to be clearly spelt out before payment is attempted. Following this method ensures all customers from around the world, will be able to follow a consistent and simpler method for purchase.

Offering the price inclusive can prevent international customers from claiming tax exemption on purchase. An e-commerce site can just simply ignore this issue, indicate that the items are not tax exempt because of local laws or try and offer a manual service to the customer enabling them to claim the tax back from the tax department.

A friendlier solution is to create a number of different tax rules. One rule for local and the other for international customers. On logging in to the site, the appropriate tax rule is attached to the user. Prices are then calculated based on this. The customer still sees the price with the tax included in it.

In addition, most countries insist on a sales receipt that includes a tax report, which all customers are entitled to. All tax extracted needs to be clearly identified on the receipt even if it's inclusive, with the actual amount shown. A side issue that can still add complexity is if the tax is inclusive, when calculated is the amount rounded up or down to the nearest cent?

Download rule

Central to the e-commerce store is the ability to buy and download a digital object. Though an e-commerce system doesn't have to offer this capability, for those that do, there are some business issues that need to be factored in:

- For a digital image what is being purchased? Is it the original or a derivative? If a derivative, then which one? Or is it a set of them? Is metadata included in the derivative? If so, which set of metadata?

- Are there copyright and legal terms and conditions that have to be accepted before the digital image is downloaded?

- How does the customer perform the download?
    - Are they directed to an FTP site?
    - Are they sent the digital image in an e-mail? (Read receipted)
    - Are they sent a link to download the image in an e-mail?
    - Are they directed to a website where they can login and download it?
    - If the download fails, how many attempts are they are allowed to download it?
    - Is the download resumable on failure?

- Is there an expiry on the download? If so, what business action should occur when it's reached?

- Is the download available on multiple servers (distributed globally) ensuring the customer has access to a download that is closest and therefore fastest for them?

- For multiple downloads, can they be combined into the one ZIP file (not compressed, but combined)?

Pricing rule

The pricing model used within an e-commerce system forms the backbone of the whole system. Pricing methods have been discussed but additional factors need to be considered:

- **Rounding**: When discounts are calculated or prices adjusted should the item itself be rounded up or down to the nearest cent? Should the rounding happen at the final order total stage instead?

- What happens if the same item is added to the basket more than once? Is it kept as a separate item, deleted (assuming customer error) or merged in (quantity is increased)?

- How is the price displayed? What is the format mask and currency symbol to use? For international orders is the price converted to local currency? Are all prices converted to local currency?

User fees rule (pricing calculator)

For some types of digital objects and how they are being used, the actual price is calculated on a set of conditions. The digital object is then purchased and copyright restrictions are defined. The purchase conditions might fall under the situation where the digital object is leased for a period of time and constrained in its usage. As covered in the *Copyright* section, the user fees can be based on a number of dimensions, including what type of business the customer is in, the volume being purchased and the intended use of the digital object (for example, is it used in a book, in a movie, or in a soundtrack?).

Different types of dimensions can apply to different types of digital objects (video is different to photos), so ultimately a flexible set of rules is needed. The rules can also be based on metadata and even the roles assigned to a user (internal users might have different rules compared to external users).

Very complex rules can invoke a pricing calculator, which is a purpose built program designed to handle the complexity. The pricing calculator will include an auditing and review component which clearly explains to the customer how the calculation was made and what copyright limitations there are, based on the options they have chosen.

Postage rule

Calculating postage can be one of the most difficult tasks to achieve when building an e-commerce system. Postage can add a significant cost to the total order especially if the customer wants a high speed delivery. Postage is usually calculated on the following dimensions:

- **Delivery location**: Can be as simple as just local or international, or can be as complex as postal zones, with each zone having a different cost and relating to different parts of the country and/or world.

- **Size**: The larger the object, or the more unwieldy the shape, the greater the cost in delivery. Size can be independent of weight.

- **Weight**: The heavier an item is, the greater the delivery cost. Most shipping companies try to mix weight and size together to come up with a more uniform and simpler cost. *For $10 we will ship the item if it's less than 500 G and no larger than A4 with a 2 cm max height.*

- **Speed of delivery**: The faster the delivery time the greater the cost. Delivery next day can be three times more expensive than standard delivery which might take four or more days.

- **Delivery method**: This is related to the speed of delivery. It might involve delivery by truck, train, plane, or ship. Delivery by truck might be slower but it might reduce the cost.

- **Insurance**: Expensive, valuable, or fragile items might need to be insured in case they are damaged in transit. A digital image that is printed and framed in glass, might require insurance. Adding insurance is customer friendly but unless a good insurance plan is used, it can add a lot of additional costs to administering it.

- **Receipted**: This is usually an additional cost and requires the customer to sign or indicate that they have received the goods. If this feature is enabled it has to be factored into the workflow, as the delivery is only correctly calculated when the customer has indicated that they have received the goods.

  A similar concept holds true for digital delivery. The customer has to indicate that they have received the digital download.

Mixed orders

Postage calculation gets more complicated when multiple items are purchased in the one order. Postage might have to be calculated on each item, a set of items, or all of them. A mixed order of digital items and physical items should not result in postage being unintentionally calculated on the digital items.

Split orders

To add complexity to the order processing, a customer might want to have their order split, with some items being shipped high speed and others at normal delivery speed. Some items might even be delivered to a different location. This feature is customer friendly as the customer only works with the one order and not many. Building this capability in is very complex as there are a lot of rules and variations in it.

Combining items

If a customer buys three items, should the postage be calculated on each item or on the total size of the items combined? The answer is dependent on the types of items purchased. If postage is $1 for a basic print (hardcopy of a photo) and five are ordered, then postage shouldn't be $5. It should be $1 as the five items combined still result in the one postage cost. If three items are purchased, one is a print, the other a hardcover book and third an A3 sized glass framed print, then the postage options available vary:

- Postage is calculated on each individual item. Resulting in three separate postage charges and is the most expensive for the customer.

- Postage is calculated on the largest item and the hope is the other items can be bundled in with the larger item. In this case, the postage is based only on the A3 sized glass framed print.

- Postage is combined where possible. The A3 glass framed print has its postage calculated, and the book is combined with the print for its own calculation.

The number of permutations with postage possibilities grows with the number of items purchased. The result is a potential 3 layer deep postage structure:

- **Layer 3**: Postage is calculated per individual item
- **Layer 2**: Similar items are grouped together and postage calculated for the set
- **Layer 1**: Postage is fixed at one price for the whole purchase order

In this case initially all items purchased fall into the first layer. Unless they need to be separately calculated in which case they would fall into the third layer. Alternatively, if they can be grouped together they will fall into the second layer.

Free postage

An e-commerce system can offer free postage in a number of cases:

- When the order total exceeds a certain amount (encouraging customers to purchase more)

- When certain items are added to the basket postage is exempt (as part of a special promotion)

- Frequent shoppers can be entitled to free postage

- A subscription service might allow customers on sign up to be entitled to free postage

Free postage usually implies standard delivery, but with a subscription service it might include high speed delivery.

Pick up

Even though postage might be calculated on an order, the customer might request that they pick it up from the place of manufacture. This means that the postage is then exempted. If the business is local, it might be easier for the customer to pick it up themselves especially if the order is large.

Negotiated

For large size orders, the customer could negotiate delivery to help reduce the cost. In which case the item is delivered to their city but not their shipping address. The customer then picks up the item from the depot of the postal service.

This method can sometimes be required if the customer is not going to be in a position to receive the item (they might be away on holidays), and just want the item kept at the depot until they are able to pick it up.

Delayed

When a large order of mixed items is made, it's possible for delays to occur in one or more of the items. This could be due to manufacturer issues or even delays in receipt of stock items. In which case the e-commerce system needs to factor in what should be done:

- Wait for all items to be available before doing the shipping: The order is delayed (hopefully the customer is notified), but the order is shipped as per the postage agreement made with the customer.

- Do a partial shipment: Ship the items that are currently ready, and ship the remaining items as they become ready. This will result in a cost to the business but it will ensure the customer receives some of their ordered items.

- Customer choice: The customer is contacted and asked if they are happy with the delay or do they want the items shipped as soon as possible in a mixed load.

- Automatic customer choice: If the customer is identified as a frequent shopper, if they have a subscription service or if their original order exceeded a cost threshold, then the order might be automatically split if there is a delay. This is to ensure there is a high level of customer satisfaction maintained, with the potential for repeat business. Sometimes the bigger picture is more important than small cost savings.

Monitoring

It's important for a customer to be able to track the status of their delivery. They should be informed when the item is dispatched for delivery and, if possible, have the ability track it with the postal service.

Payment rule

Methods to pay have already been covered. The payment rule defines these payment methods and sets up the environment to use them:

- Should international customers always have to pay by credit card?
- For phone orders, if it's outside working hours, should the option be disabled?
- For cheque orders, should processing occur on receipt of the cheque or when payment has been verified?
- If the order is considered paid, should it be locked down to prevent subsequent modification?
- Is partial and mixed payment allowed?
- Can an order be processed even though it has only been partially paid (equivalent of a deposit)?
- At what point in the payment processed workflow should an official receipt be generated?

Customer information rule

This is a rule that covers all the different data entry fields a customer has for entering in information. This can include their name, address and e-mail address. Different businesses have different requirements and therefore, different ways of handling this information.

The rule needs to be flexible so that different rules can be used on different types of users. An internal user who works for a government department might need to enter in section, branch, department, rather than a physical address. International customers might need to provide additional information compared to local ones. Examples of some of the most popular fields include:

- Name or first name, and last name
- Salutation (the title: Mr, Ms, Mrs, and Dr). Should be a free form field not a combo box as there are a large number of titles possible
- Address or P.O. box, street, suburb, city, country, postcode/zip
- Phone (work, home)
- Mobile
- E-mail address (work, home)
- Date of birth
- Fax

- Pager
- Business URL
- ABN (unique business identification number)
- Permission to receive e-mails, notifications from the business or their business partners
- Section, branch, department, and project code

Customer trigger rule

This is a set of rules designed to trigger and notify the customer when an event has happened. The customer might want to be notified when the order has been shipped. If there are order and delivery problems the customer might need to be sent an e-mail.

The trigger rule sets up a condition and action, with the goal to notify and inform the customer about the order. This can be an e-mail, SMS, or a workflow that is initiated to have someone ring the customer.

Discount rule

A discount can occur in a variety of situations. A discount can be on an item level or order level.

Issues to cover with item level discounts:

- Is it set for an individual item? For example, this digital image is 30 percent off.
- Is it set for a price book item? For example, those who choose an A4 print will get 20 percent off.
- Is it based on a meta tag value? For example, any digital objects with the meta tag value of armor gets a 10 percent discount.
- Is it triggered when another item is purchased? For example, if you buy this book with the digital object you get 25 percent off.
- Is it time based? For example, this item is on special on the 24th and 25th of July.
- Is it volume based? For example, if you buy 10 items you get 30 percent off, but if you buy 50 then you get 50 percent off.
- Is it immune from being discounted? For example, all items with the meta tag value of ship get 20 percent off unless it's marked as immune from being discounted.
- Can an item be discounted below its cost price?

Order level discounts apply to the sub total of the order. Some issues to cover include:

- Is the discount applied when the order total is greater than a certain value?

- Does the discount apply to all the items in the basket or if some are discount immune, are they included or not included?

- At what point is the discount applied, is it before or after tax/postage is calculated?

- Can a discount be applied manually by the sales administrator?

Refund rule

In a number of situations a customer might have paid for an item but due to issues such as, product defect, product unavailability, customer dissatisfaction, or just overpayment by a customer, then a customer might be due a refund in monies.

Refund payment via credit card payments can be done, but can be difficult to perform. For a business, the refund procedure is likely require a workflow to not only manage it, but ensure the refund is justified and authentic (protection from internal fraud).

Each bank, each e-commerce system, and each merchant facility offers different services for refunds. In some cases due to the complexity and hopefully infrequency of refund requests, the simplest method can be manual. This involves having an operator process the whole refund request.

For most e-commerce sites, the refund process goes through a number of stages:

- Refund requirement is identified. This can be driven by the customer or initiated when an item cannot be delivered.

- Customer is notified that a refund is due. They can then be given a choice for how they want the refund to be handled. Some options include: Giving the customer in store credit or a gift certificate. They could be sent a cheque or an attempt could be made to refund their credit card.

- Refund is approved. For accounting purposes (and to ensure there is no fraud), this is likely involve an independent person in the business reviewing the refund and confirming its validity. For small amounts, the refund approval could be automatic.

- Steps are enacted to perform the refund. This might be invoking a program that talks to the bank and performs the refund, or it might be as simple as writing a cheque and sending it to the customer.

- The e-commerce system is updated to indicate the refund has taken place and the order is modified to reflect it. Order totals, receipt pages, and other parts of the order need to be updated to reflect the change, especially if a partial refund has been made.

Ticketing rule

In the case of digital payment of a venue or event, the notion of ticketing is introduced and is covered using a separate business logic. In particular:

- What is the maximum capacity of the venue?
- What happens if a minimum capacity is not reached by a certain time?
- Are seats fixed or open (fixed being on purchase, a seat number is assigned to the customer, open being there is no fixed seating, there might not even be seating).
- Is the ticket price varying based on the seating position, or section within the venue?
- Does the ticket price vary based on the proximity to the event start date?
- Is the event repeating (for example, is it a regular show held at the same time, or is it a one off)?
- Will the customer get an e-receipt (SMS or e-mail) on purchase?
- How is the customer informed if the venue date/time is changed?
- Is there reserved seating?

Integrated stock management

When physical items are purchased, the requirement for automated stock management is introduced. In this case the following needs to be factored in:

- Is the item marked as unavailable if not in stock? Is it hidden if there is no stock?
- At what point is the item debited from the stock list? Is it on addition to basket, on purchase, or on delivery? Each option has different points of failure.
- When the stock inventory falls low, who is notified and what happens?
- Is there an automated stock/supplier capability enabling new stock to be automatically purchased from the supplier when the inventory falls low?
- If stock is purchased and it's not in the inventory, what happens?

- Is their reconciliation done between the physical stock and what is claimed in the inventory?
- If stock is located in different physical locations, or if the same stock item is located in different cities, is the customer given a postage discount because one item is physically closer? How is the order then sent to the customer if the items are in different locations?

Post-purchase workflow

Even though a digital object might be available for digital download, on purchase it might not have yet been digitized. This means a post-purchase workflow is needed to assign a photographer to photograph the item, or someone to scan it in if it's a print. For older medium such as film, glass slides, and negatives, the process might involve a number of steps to locate it and digitize it.

The workflow in this case would involve locating the item to be photographed, finding a photographer, checking the item out, taking the photo, loading it in to the system, performing quality control on it, then attaching it to the order so it can be downloaded (this might result in an e-mail being sent to the customer with the download link).

In cases such as purchasing physical shop items, inventory management needs to be handled via a workflow. Where the item in the order is tracked, packaged, and then shipped. At each stage the workflow is checked and handled by one or more different people.

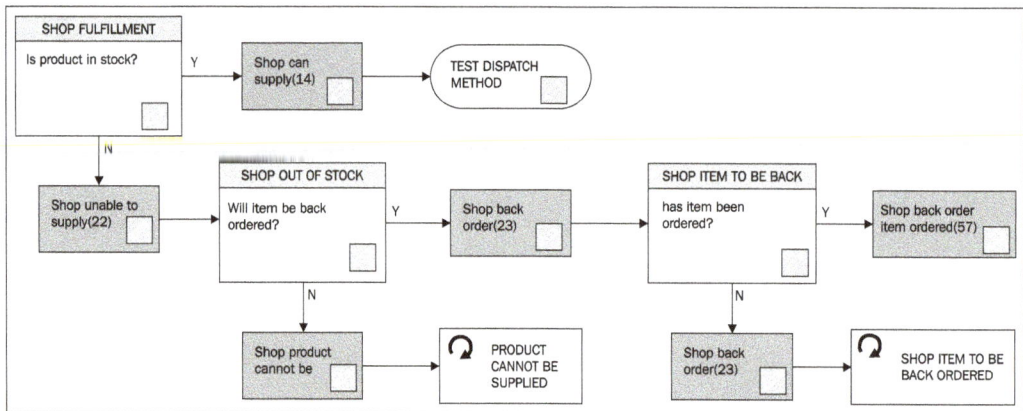

A workflow follows a set of process steps, usually resulting in a question being asked, and based on the question, the item in the workflow progresses to another stage. The metadata attached to the item might also be used to determine where and to which group the item moves to.

For complex workflows, the flow could be broken up into parallel tasks (or threads). Where each thread performs certain activities before being merged back in with the main order at later stages.

Summary

With this rise in the usage of digital objects, the business requirements for an e-commerce system has grown dramatically. A business needs to be adaptable and change quickly when the market changes. To achieve this, a business needs a system that utilizes dynamically adjustable rule sets, each performing different business requirements.

Image purchasing, pricing, and control of the order process are best handled and centered around metadata and roles. This focuses the whole process around the data and gets away from rigid structures which might be hard to adjust when the need arises.

An e-commerce system should work equally well on the Internet via a HTML browser as well as on portable devices using applications and web services, such as the iPad, iPhone and other smart-phone devices.

In *Chapter 7, Techniques for Creating a Multimedia Database*, focus now moves to how to configure an Oracle database to manage and store multimedia.

Exercises

1. Define a pricing model for a subscription based service, offering unlimited access to digital movies, with varying pricing for different countries in the world.

2. For an auction, determine some of the business actions that can be implemented to stop or discourage the behavior of bidding in the last 60 seconds.

3. Define some methods for delivery of digital images that improve on the speed of the digital object being delivered.

4. Group images. Describe a business model for how multiple digital objects can be purchased and grouped together for a print (for example, combine five photos onto the one framed print).

5. For a mixed or multi-type purchase, define what other types can be effectively purchased besides these ones: Digital photos, audio, video, documents as well as physical items, such as merchandise and tickets for venues and subscriptions for services. For these new types how easily do they fit into the e-commerce model?

7
Techniques for Creating a Multimedia Database

This chapter covers the technical aspects of setting up a database to use Oracle Multimedia. It contains tips, codes, and useful techniques for setting up and managing an Oracle Database and covers the core storage capabilities of the Oracle Database. The goal is to enable the database administrator to make correctly informed decisions about the physical structure of database storage objects, in particular tablespaces, datafiles, and database capabilities.

Tier architecture

The rules surrounding technology are constantly changing. Decisions and architectures based on current technology might easily become out of date with hardware changes. To best understand how multimedia and unstructured data fit and can adapt to the changing technology, it's important to understand how and why we arrived at our different current architectural positions. In some cases we have come full circle and reinvented concepts that were in use 20 years ago. Only by learning from the lessons of the past can we see how to move forward to deal with this complex environment.

In the past 20 years a variety of architectures have come about in an attempt to satisfy some core requirements:

- Allow as many users as possible to access the system
- Ensure those users had good performance for accessing the data
- Enable those users to perform DML (insert/update/delete) safely and securely (safely implies ability to restore data in the event of failure)

The goal of a database management system was to provide an environment where these points could be met. The first databases were not relational. They were heavily I/O focused as the computers did not have much memory and the idea of caching data was deemed to be too expensive. The servers had kilobytes and then eventually, megabytes of memory. This memory was required foremost by the programs to run in them. The most efficient architecture was to use pointers to link the data together. The architecture that emerged naturally was hierarchical and a program would navigate the hierarchy to find rows related to each other. Users connected in via a dumb terminal. This was a monitor with a keyboard that could process input and output from a basic protocol and display it on the screen. All the processing of information, including how the screen should display it (using simple escape sequence commands), was controlled in the server.

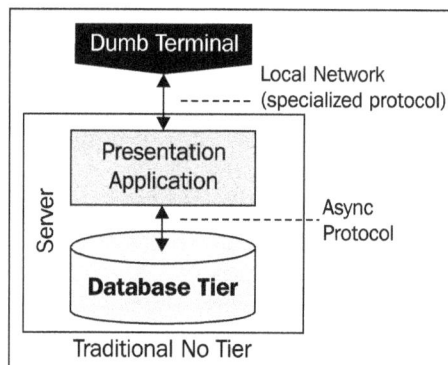

Traditional no tier

The mainframes used a block mode structure, where the user would enter a screen full of data and press the *Enter* key. After doing this the whole screen of information was sent to the server for processing. Other servers used asynchronous protocols, where each letter, as it was typed, was sent to the server for processing. This method was not as efficient as block mode because it required more server processing power to handle the data coming in. It did provide a friendlier interface for data entry as mistakes made could be relayed immediately back to the user. Block mode could only display errors once the screen of data was sent, processed, and returned.

As more users started using these systems, the amount of data in them began to grow and the users wanted to get more intelligence out of the data entered. Requirements for reporting appeared as well as the ability to do ad hoc querying. The databases were also very hard to maintain and enhance as the pointer structure linked everything together tightly. It was very difficult to perform maintenance and changes to code. In the 1970s the relational database concept was formulated and it was based on sound mathematical principles. In the early 1980s the first conceptual relational databases appeared in the marketplace with Oracle leading the way.

The relational databases were not received well. They performed poorly and used a huge amount of server resources. Though they achieved a stated goal of being flexible and adaptable, enabling more complex applications to be built quicker, the performance overheads of performing joins proved to be a major issue. Benefits could be seen in them, but they could never be seen as being able to be used in any environment that required tens to hundreds or thousands of concurrent users. The technology wasn't there to handle them.

To initially achieve better performance the relational database vendors focused on using a changing hardware feature and that was memory. By the late 1980s the computer servers were starting to move from 16 bit to 32 bit. The memory was increasing and there was drop in the price. By adapting to this the vendors managed to take advantage of memory and improved join performance.

The relational databases in effect achieved a balancing act between memory and disk I/O. Accessing a disk was about a thousand times slower than accessing memory. Memory was transient, meaning if there was a power failure and if there was data stored in memory, it would be lost. Memory was also measured in megabytes, but disk was measured in gigabytes. Disk was not transient and generally reliable, but still required safeguards to be put in place to protect from disk failure.

So the balancing act the databases performed involved caching data in memory that was frequently accessed, while ensuring any modifications made to that data were always stored to disk. Additionally, the database had to ensure no data was lost if a disk failed. To improve join performance the database vendors came up with their own solutions involving indexing, optimization techniques, locking, and specialized data storage structures. Databases were judged on the speed at which they could perform joins.

The flexibility and ease in which applications could be updated and modified compared to the older systems soon made the relational database become popular and must have. As all relational databases conformed to an international SQL standard, there was a perception that a customer was never locked into a propriety system and could move their data between different vendors. Though there were elements of truth to this, the reality has shown otherwise. The Oracle Database key strength was that you were not locked into the hardware and they offered the ability to move a database between a mainframe to Windows to Unix. This portability across hardware effectively broke the stranglehold a number of hardware vendors had, and opened up the competition enabling hardware vendors to focus on the physical architecture rather than the operating system within it.

In the early 1990s with the rise in popularity of the Apple Macintosh, the rules changed dramatically and the concept of a user friendly graphical environment appeared. The **Graphical User Interface (GUI)** screen offered a powerful interface for the user to perform data entry. Though it can be argued that data entry was not (and is still not) as fast as data entry via a dumb terminal interface, the use of colors, varying fonts, widgets, comboboxes, and a whole repository of specialized frontend data entry features made the interface easier to use and more data could be entered with less typing. Arguably, the GUI opened up the computer to users who could not type well. The interface was easier to learn and less training was needed to use the interface.

Two tier

The GUI interface had one major drawback; it was expensive to run on the CPU. Some vendors experimented with running the GUI directly on the server (the Solaris operating system offered this capability), but it become obvious that this solution would not scale.

To address this, the two-tier architecture was born. This involved using the GUI, which was running on an Apple Macintosh or Microsoft Windows or other Windows environment (Microsoft Windows wasn't the only GUI to run on Intel platforms) to handle the display processing. This was achieved by moving the application displayed to the computer that the user was using. Thus splitting the GUI presentation layer and application from the database. This seemed like an ideal solution as the database could now just focus on handling and processing SQL queries and DML. It did not have to be burdened with application processing as well. As there were no agreed network protocols, a number had to be used, including named pipes, LU6.2, DECNET, and TCP/IP. The database had to handle language conversion as the data was moved between the client and the server. The client might be running on a 16-bit platform using US7ASCII as the character set, but the server might be running on 32-bit using EBCDIC as the character set. The network suddenly became very complex to manage.

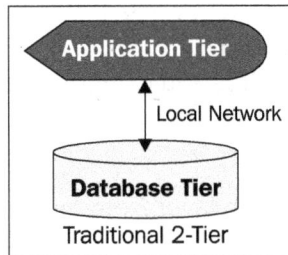

Traditional 2-Tier

What proved to be the ultimate show stopper with the architecture had nothing to do with the scalability of client or database performance, but rather something which is always neglected in any architecture, and that is the **scalability of maintenance**. Having an environment of a hundred users, each with their own computer accessing the server, requires a team of experts to manage those computers and ensure the software on it is correct. Application upgrades meant upgrading hundreds of computers at the same time. This was a time-consuming and manual task. Compounded by this is that if the client computer is running multiple applications, upgrading one might impact the other applications. Even applying an operating system patch could impact other applications. Users also might install their own software on their computer and impact the application running on it. A lot of time was spent supporting users and ensuring their computers were stable and could correctly communicate with the server.

Three tier

Specialized software vendors tried to come to the rescue by offering the ability to lock down a client computer from being modified and allowing remote access to the computer to perform remote updates. Even then, the maintenance side proved very difficult to deal with and when the idea of a three tier architecture was pushed by vendors, it was very quickly adopted as the ideal solution to move towards because it critically addressed the maintenance issue.

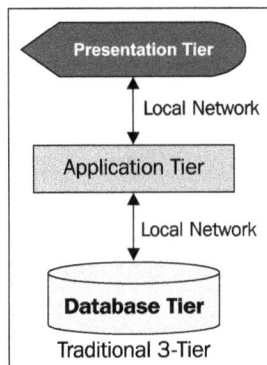

Traditional 3-Tier

In the mid 1990s the rules changed again. The Internet started to gain in popularity and the web browser was invented. The browser opened up the concept of a smart presentation layer that is very flexible and configured using a simple mark up language. The browser ran on top of the protocol called HTTP, which uses TCP/IP as the underlying network protocol.

The idea of splitting the presentation layer from the application became a reality as more applications appeared in the browser. The web browser was not an ideal platform for data entry as the HTTP protocol was stateless making it very hard to perform transactions in it. The HTTP protocol could scale. The actual usage involved the exact same concepts as block mode data entry performed on mainframe computers. In a web browser all the data is entered on the screen, and then sent in one go to the application handling the data.

The web browser also pushed the idea that the operating system the client is running on is immaterial. The web browsers were ported to Apple computers, Windows, Solaris, and Unix platforms.

The web browser also introduced the idea of standard for the presentation layer. All vendors producing a web browser had to conform to the agreed HTML standard. This ensured that anyone building an application that confirmed to HTML would be able to run on any web browser.

The web browser pushed the concept that the presentation layer had to run on any client computer (later on, any mobile device as well) irrespective of the operating system and what else was installed on it. The web browser was essentially immune from anything else running on the client computer. If all the client had to use was a browser, maintenance on the client machine would be simplified.

HTML had severe limitations and it was not designed for data entry. To address this, the Java language came about and provided the concept of an applet which could run inside the browser, be safe, and provide an interface to the user for data entry. Different vendors came up with different architectures for splitting their two tier application into a three tier one.

Oracle achieved this by taking their Oracle Forms product and moving it to the middle application tier, and providing a framework where the presentation layer would run as a Java applet inside the browser. The Java applet would communicate with a process on the application server and it would give it its own instructions for how to draw the display. When the Forms product was replaced with JDeveloper, the same concept was maintained and enhanced. The middle tier became more flexible and multiple middle application tiers could be configured enabling more concurrent users.

The three tier architecture has proven to be an ideal environment for legacy systems, giving them a new life and enabling them be put in an environment where they can scale. As is covered in greater detail in *Chapter 8*, *Tuning*, the three tier environment has a major flaw preventing it from truly scaling. The flaw is the bottleneck between the application layer and the database. The three tier environment also is designed for relational databases. It is not designed for multimedia databases. In the architecture if the digital objects are stored in the database, then to be delivered to the customer they need to pass through the application-database network (exaggerating the bottleneck capacity issues), and from there passed to the presentation layer.

Those building in this environment naturally lend themselves to the concept that the best location for the digital objects is the middle tier. This then leads to issues of security, backing up, management, and all the issues previously cited for why storing the digital objects in the database is ideal. The logical conclusion to this is to move the database to the middle tier to address this. In reality, the logical conclusion is to move the application tier back into the database tier.

Virtualized architecture

In the mid 2000s the idea of a virtualization began to appear in the marketplace. A virtualization was not really a new idea and the concept has existed on the IBM MVS environment since the late 1980s. What made this virtualization concept powerful was that it could run Windows, Linux, Solaris, and Mac environments within them. A virtualized environment was basically the ability to run a complete operating system within another operating system. If the computer server had sufficient power and memory, it could run **multiple virtualizations** (**VMs**). We can take the snapshot of a VM, which involves taking a view of the disk and memory and storing it. It then became possible to rollback to the snapshot.

A VM could be easily cloned (copied) and backed up. VMs could also be easily transferred to different computer servers. The VM was not tied to a physical server and the same environment could be moved to new servers as their capacity increased.

A VM environment became attractive to administrators simply because they were easy to manage. Rather than running five separate servers, an administrator could have the one server with five virtualizations in it.

The VM environment entered at a critical moment in the evolution of computer servers. Prior to 2005 most computer servers had one or two CPUs in them. The advanced could have as many as 64 (for example, the Sun E10000), but generally, one or two was the simplest solution. The reason was that computer power was doubling every two years following Moore's law. By around 2005 the market began to realize that there was a limit to the speed of an individual CPU due to physical limitations in the size of the transistors in the chips. The solution was to grow the CPUs sideways and the concept of cores came about. A CPU could be broken down into multiple cores, where each one acted like a separate CPU but was contained in one chip. With the introduction of smart threading, the number of virtual cores increased. A single CPU could now simulate eight or more CPUs.

This concept has changed the rules. A server can now run with a large number of cores whereas 10 years ago it was physically limited to one or two CPUs. If a process went wild and consumed all the resources of one CPU, it impacted all users. In the multicore CPU environment, a rogue process will not impact the others. In a VM the controlling operating system (which is also called a **hypervisor**, and can be hardware, firmware, or software centric) can enable VMs to be constrained to certain cores as well as CPU thresholds within that core. This allows a VM to be fenced in. This concept was taken by Amazon and the concept of the cloud environment formed.

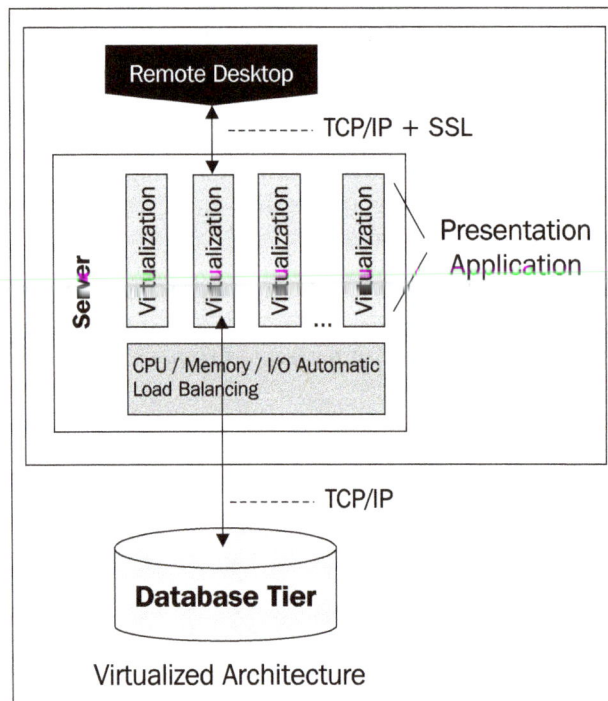

This architecture is now moving into a new path where users can now use remote desktop into their own VM on a server. The user now needs a simple laptop (resulting in the demise of the tower computer) to use remote desktop (or equivalent) into the virtualization. They then become responsible for managing their own laptop, and in the event of an issue, it can be replaced or wiped and reinstalled with a base operating system on it. This simplifies the management. As all the business data and application logic is in the VM, the administrator can now control it, easily back it up, and access it.

Though this VM cloud environment seems like a good solution to resolving the maintenance scalability issue, a spanner has been thrown in the works at the same time as VMs are becoming popular, so was the evolution of the mobile into a portable hand held device with applications running on it.

Mobile applications architecture

The iPhone, iPad, Android, Samsung, and other devices have caused a disruption in the marketplace as to how the relationship between the user and the application is perceived and managed.

These devices are simpler and on the face of it employ a variety of architectures including two tier and three tier. Quality control of the application is managed by having an independent and separate environment, where the user can obtain their application for the mobile device. The strict controls Apple employs for using iTunes are primarily to ensure that the Trojan code or viruses are not embedded in the application, resulting in a mobile device not requiring a complex and constantly updating anti-virus software.

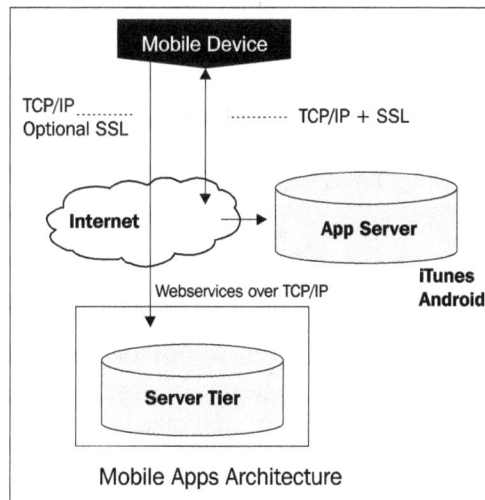

Mobile Apps Architecture

Though the interface is not ideal for heavy data entry, the applications are naturally designed to be very friendly and use touch screen controls. The low cost combined with their simple interface has made them an ideal product for most people and are replacing the need for a laptop in a number of cases. Application vendors that have applications that naturally lend themselves to this environment are taking full advantage of it to provide a powerful interface for clients to use.

The result is that there are two architectures today that exist and are moving in different directions. Each one is popular and resolves certain issues. Each has different interfaces and when building and configuring a storage repository for digital objects, both these environments need to be taken into consideration.

For a multimedia environment the ideal solution to implement the application is based on the Web. This is because the web environment over the last 15 years has evolved into one which is very flexible and adaptable for dealing with the display of those objects. From the display of digital images to streaming video, the web browser (with sometimes plugins to improve the display) is ideal. This includes the display of documents.

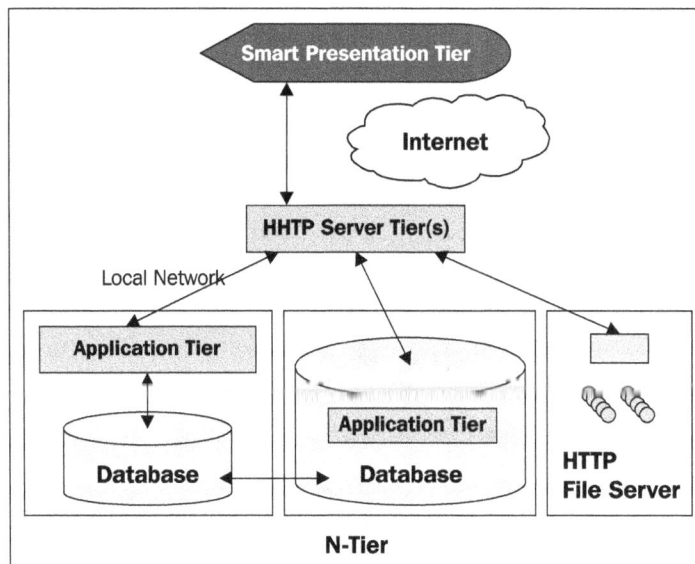

The browser environment though is not strong for the editing of these digital objects. Adobe Photoshop, Gimp, Garage Band, Office, and a whole suite of other products are available that are designed to edit each type of digital object perfectly. This means that currently the editing of those digital objects requires a different solution to the loading, viewing and delivery of those digital objects.

There is no right solution for the tier architecture to manage digital objects. The N-Tier model moves the application and database back into the database tier. An HTTP server can also be located in this tier or for higher availability it can be located externally.

Optimal performance is achieved by locating the application as close to the database as possible. This reduces the network bottleneck. By locating the application within the database (in Oracle this is done by using PL/SQL or Java) an ideal environment is configured where there is no overhead between the application and database.

The N-Tier model also supports the concept of having the digital objects stored outside the environment and delivered using other methods. This could include a streaming server. The N-Tier model also supports the concept of transformation servers. Scalability is achieved by adding more tiers and spreading the database between them. The model also deals with the issue of the connection to the Internet becoming a bottleneck. A database server in the tier is moved to another network to help balance the load.

For Oracle this can be done using RAC to achieve a form of transparent scalability. In most situations as covered in *Chapter 8, Tuning*, scalability at the server is achieved using manual methods using a form of application partitioning.

Basic database configuration concepts

When a database administrator first creates a database that they know will contain digital objects, they will be confronted with some basic database configuration questions covering key sizing features of the database.

When looking at the Oracle Database there are a number of physical and logical structures built inside the database. To avoid confusion with other database management systems, it's important to note that an Oracle Database is a collection of schemas, whereas in other database management the terminology for a database equates to exactly one schema. This confusion has caused a lot of issues in the past. An Oracle Database administrator will say it can take 30 minutes to an hour to create a database, whereas a SQL Server administrator will say it takes seconds to create a database. In Oracle to create a schema (the same as a SQL Server database) also takes seconds to perform.

For the physical storage of tables, the Oracle Database is composed of logical structures called **tablespaces**.

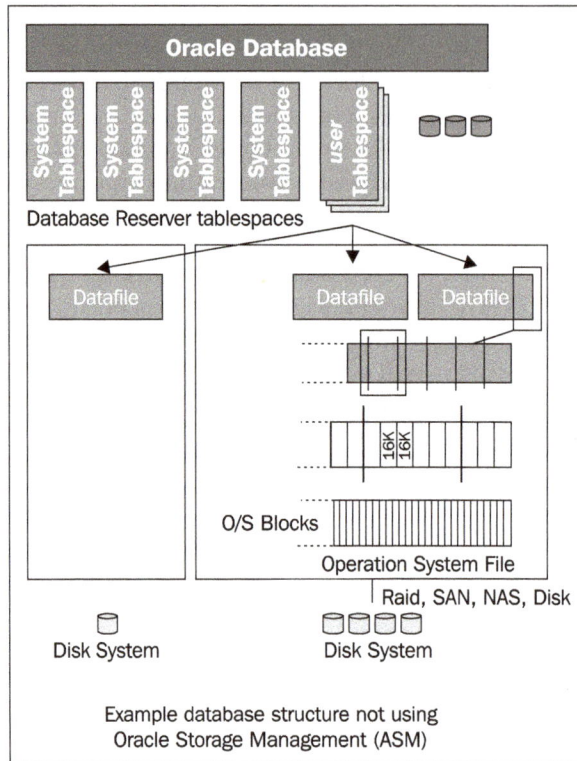

Oracle Database

System Tablespace · System Tablespace · System Tablespace · System Tablespace · user Tablespace

Database Reserver tablespaces

Datafile

Datafile   Datafile

16K · 16K

O/S Blocks

Operation System File

Raid, SAN, NAS, Disk

Disk System

Disk System

Example database structure not using
Oracle Storage Management (ASM)

The tablespace is designed to provide a transparent layer between the developer creating a table and the physical disk system and to ensure the two are independent. Data in a table that resides in a tablespace can span multiple disks and disk subsystem or a network storage system. A **subsystem** equating to a Raid structure has been covered in greater detail at the end of this chapter.

A tablespace is composed of many physical datafiles. Each datafile equates to one physical file on the disk. The goal when creating a datafile is to ensure its allocation of storage is contiguous in that the operating system and doesn't split its location into different areas on the disk (Raid and NAS structures store the data in different locations based on their core structure so this rule does not apply to them). A contiguous file will result in less disk activity being performed when full tablespace scans are performed. In some cases, especially, when reading in very large images, this can improve performance.

A datafile is fragmented (when using locally managed tablespaces, the default in Oracle) into fixed size extents. Access to the extents is controlled via a bitmap which is managed in the header of the tablespace (which will reside on a datafile). An extent is based on the core Oracle block size. So if the extent is 128 KB and the database block size is 8 KB, 16 Oracle blocks will exist within the extent. An Oracle block is the smallest unit of storage within the database. Blocks are read into memory for caching, updated, and changes stored in the redo logs. Even though the Oracle block is the smallest unit of storage, as a datafile is an operating system file, based on the type of server filesystem (UNIX can be UFS and Windows can be NTFS), the unit of storage at this level can change.

The default in Windows was once 512 bytes, but with NTFS can be as high as 64 KB. This means every time a request is made to the disk to retrieve data from the filesystem it does a read to return this amount of data. So if the Oracle block's size was 8 KB in size and the filesystem block size was 64 KB, when Oracle requests a block to be read in, the filesystem will read in 64 KB, return the 8 KB requested, and reject the rest. Most filesystems cache this data to improve performance, but this example highlights how in some cases not balancing the database block size with the filesystem block size can result in wasted I/O. The actual answer to this is operating system and filesystem dependent, and it also depends on whether Oracle is doing read aheads (using the `init.ora` parameter `db_file_multiblock_read_count`).

When Oracle introduced the Exadata they put forward the idea of putting smarts into the disk layer. Rather than the database working out how best to retrieve the physical blocks of data, the database passes a request for information to the disk system. As the Exadata knows about its own disk performance, channel speed, and I/O throughput, it is in a much better position for working out the optimal method for extracting the data. It then works out the best way of retrieving it based on the request (which can be a query). In some cases it might do a full table scan because it can process the blocks faster than if it used an index. It now becomes a smart disk system rather than a dumb/blind one. This capability has changed the rules for how a database works with the underlying storage system.

ASM—Automated Storage Management

In Oracle 10G, Oracle introduced ASM primarily to improve the performance of Oracle RAC (clustered systems, where multiple separate servers share the same database on the same disk). It replaces the server filesystem and can handle mirroring and load balancing of datafiles. ASM takes the filesystem and operating system out of the equation and enables the database administrator to have a different degree of control over the management of the disk system.

Block size

The database block size is the fundamental unit of storage within an Oracle Database. Though the database can support different block sizes, a tablespace is restricted to one fixed block size.

The block sizes available are 4 KB, 8 KB, 16 KB, and 32 KB (a 32 KB block size is valid only on 64-bit platforms). The current tuning mentality says it's best to have one block size for the whole database. This is based on the idea that the one block size makes it easier to manage the SGA and ensure that memory isn't wasted.

If multiple block sizes are used, the database administrator has to partition the SGA into multiple areas and assign each a block size. So if the administrator decided to have the database at 8 KB and 16 KB, they would have to set up a database startup parameter indicating the size of each:

```
DB_8K_CACHE_SIZE = 2G
DB_16K_CACHE_SIZE = 1G
```

The problem that an administrator faces is that it can be hard to judge memory usage with table usage. In the above scenario the tables residing in the 8 KB block might be accessed a lot more than 16 KB ones, meaning the memory needs to be adjusted to deal with that. This balancing act of tuning invariably results in the decision that unless exceptional situations warrant its use, it's best to keep to the same database blocks size across the whole database. This makes the job of tuning simpler.

As is always the case when dealing with unstructured data, the rules change. The current thinking is that it's more efficient to store the data in a large block size. This ensures there is less wasted overhead and fewer block reads to read in a row of data. The challenge is that the size of the unstructured data can vary dramatically. It's realistic for an image thumbnail to be under 4 KB in size. This makes it an ideal candidate to be stored in the row with the other relational data. Even if an 8 KB block size is used, the thumbnail and other relational data might happily exist in the one block. A photo might be 10 MB in size requiring a large number of blocks to be used to store it. If a 16 KB block size is used, it requires about 64 blocks to store 1 MB (assuming there is some overhead that requires overall extra storage for the block header).

An 8 KB block size requires about 130 blocks. If you have to store 10 MB, the number of blocks increases 10 times. For an 8 KB block that is over 1300 reads is sufficient for one small-sized 10 MB image. With images now coming close to 100 MB in size, this figure again increases by a factor of 10. It soon becomes obvious that a very large block size is needed. When storing video at over 4 GB in size, even a 32 KB block size seems too small.

As is covered later in the chapter, unstructured data stored in an Oracle blob does not have to be cached in the SGA. In fact, it's discouraged because in most situations the data is not likely to be accessed on a frequent basis. This generally holds true but there are cases, especially with video, where this does not hold true and this situation is covered later. Under the assumption that the thumbnails are accessed frequently and should be cached and the originals are accessed infrequently and should not be cached, the conclusion is that it now becomes practical to split the SGA in two. The unstructured, uncached data is stored in a tablespace using a large block size (32 KB) and the remaining data is stored in a more acceptable and reasonable 8 KB block. The SGA for the 32 KB is kept to a bare minimum as it will not be used, thus bypassing the issue of perceived wasted memory by splitting the SGA in two.

In the following table a simple test was done using three tablespace block sizes. The aim was to see if the block size would impact load and read times. The load involved reading in 67 TIF images totaling 3 GB in size. The result was that the tablespace block size made no statistical significant difference. The test was done using a 50-MB extent size and as shown shown in the next segment, this size will impact performance. So to correctly understand how important block size can be, one has to look at not only the block size but also the extent size.

Details of the environment used to perform these tests is detailed in *Appendix E, Loading and Reading*.

```
CREATE TABLESPACE tbls_name BLOCKSIZE 4096/8192/16384 EXTENT
MANAGEMENT LOCAL UNIFORM SIZE 50M segment space management auto
datafile 'directory/datafile' size 5G reuse;
```

The following table compares the various block sizes:

Tablespace block size	Blocks	Extents	Load time	Read time
4 KB	819200	64	3.49 minutes	1.02 minutes
8 KB	403200	63	3.46 minutes	0.59 minutes
16 KB	201600	63	3.55 minutes	0.59 minutes

UNIFORM extent size and AUTOALLOCATE

When creating a tablespace to store the unstructured data, the next step after the block size is determined is to work out what the most efficient extent size will be. As a table might contain data ranging from hundreds of gigabytes to terabytes determining the extent size is important. The larger the extent, the potential to possible waste space if the table doesn't use it all is greater. The smaller the extent size the risk is that the table will grow into tens or hundreds of thousands of extents. As a locally managed tablespace uses a bitmap to manage the access to the extents and is generally quite fast, having it manage tens of thousands of extents might be pushing its performance capabilities.

There are two methods available to the administrator when creating a tablespace. They can manually specify the fragment size using the UNIFORM extent size clause or they can let the Oracle Database calculate it using the AUTOALLOCATE clause. As covered in *Appendix E, Loading and Reading*, tests were done to determine what the optimal fragment size was when AUTOALLOCATE was not used. The AUTOALLOCATE is a more set-and-forget method and one goal was to see if this clause was as efficient as manually setting it.

Locally managed tablespace UNIFORM extent size

Appendix E, Loading and Reading, covers testing performed to try to find an optimal extent and block size. The results showed that a block size of 16384 (16 KB) is ideal, though 8192 (8 KB) is acceptable. The block size of 32 KB was not tested. The administrator, who might be tempted to think the larger the extent size, the better the performance, would be surprised that the results show that this is not always the case and an extent size between 50 MB-200 MB is optimal.

For reads with SECUREFILES the number of extents was not a major performance factor but it was for writes.

When compared to the AUTOALLOCATE clause, it was shown there was no real performance improvement or loss when used. The testing showed that an administrator can use this clause knowing they will get a good all round result when it comes to performance. The syntax for configuration is as follows:

```
EXTENT MANAGEMENT LOCAL AUTOALLOCATE segment space management auto
```

Repeated tests showed that this configuration produced optimal read/write times without the database administrator having to worry about what the extent size should be. For a 300 GB tablespace it produced a similar number of extents as when a 50M extent size was used.

As has been covered, once an image is loaded it is rare that it is updated. A relational database fragmentation within a tablespace is caused by repeated creation/dropping of schema objects and extents of different sizes, resulting in physical storage gaps, which are not easily reused. Storage is lost. This is analogous to the Microsoft Windows environment with its disk storage. After a period of time, the disk becomes fragmented making it hard to find contiguous storage and locate similar items together. Locating all the pieces in a file as close together as possible can dramatically reduce the number of disk reads required to read it in. With NTFS (a Microsoft disk filesystem format) the system administrator can on creation determine whether extents are autoallocated or fragmented. This is similar in concept to the Oracle tablespace creation. Testing was not done to check if the fragmentation scenario is avoided with the AUTOALLOCATE clause. The database administrator should therefore be aware of the tablespace usage and whether it is likely going to be stable once rows are added (in which case AUTOALLOCATE can be used simplifying storage management). If it is volatile, the UNIFORM clause might be considered as a better option.

Temporary tablespace

For working with unstructured data, the primary uses of the TEMPORARY tablespace is to hold the contents of temporary tables and temporary lobs. A **temporary lob** is used for processing a temporary multimedia object. In the following example, a temporary blob is created. It is not cached in memory. A multimedia image type is created and loaded into it. Information is extracted and the blob is freed. This is useful if images are stored temporarily outside the database. This is not the same case as using a `bfile` which Oracle Multimedia supports. The `bfile` is a permanent pointer to an image stored outside the database.

```
SQL>
  declare
    image              ORDSYS.ORDImage;
    ctx                raw(4000);
  begin
   image := ordsys.ordimage.init();
   dbms_lob.createtemporary(image.source.localdata,FALSE);
   image.importfrom(ctx, 'file', 'LOADING_DIR', 'myimg.tif');
   image.setProperties;
   dbms_output.put_line( 'width x height = ' || image.width ||
                         'x' || image.height);
   dbms_lob.freetemporary(image.source.localdata);
  end;
  /
  width x height = 2809x4176
```

It's important when using this tablespace to ensure that all code, especially on failure, performs a `dbms_lob.freetemporary` function, to ensure that storage leakage doesn't occur. This will result in the tablespace continuing to grow until it runs out of room. In this case the only way to clean it up is to either stop all database processes referencing, then resize the datafile (or drop and recreate the temporary tablespace after creating another interim one), or to restart the database and mount it. The tablespace can then be resized or dropped and recreated.

UNDO tablespace

The UNDO tablespace is used by the database to store sufficient information to rollback a transaction. In a database containing a lot of digital objects, the size of the database just for storage of the objects can exceed terabytes. In this situation the UNDO tablespace can be sized larger giving added opportunity for the database administrator to perform flashback recovery from user error. It's reasonable to size the UNDO tablespace at 50 GB even growing it to 100 GB in size. The larger the UNDO tablespace the further back in time the administrator can go and the greater the breathing space between user failure, user failure detected and reported, and the database administrator doing the flash back recovery.

The following is an example flashback SQL statement. The `as of timestamp` clause tells Oracle to find rows that match the timestamp from the current time going back so that we can have a look at a table an hour ago:

```
select t.vimg.source.srcname || '=' ||
       dbms_lob.getlength(t.vimg.source.localdata)
from test_load as of timestamp systimestamp - (1/24) t;
```

SYSTEM tablespace

The SYSTEM tablespace contains the data dictionary. In Oracle 11*g* R2 it also contains any compiled PL/SQL code (where `PLSQL_CODE_TYPE=NATIVE`). The recommended initial starting size of the tablespace should be 1500 MB.

Redo logs

The following test results highlight how important it is to get the size and placement of the redo logs correct. The goal was to determine what combination of database parameters and redo/undo size were optimal. In addition, an SSD was used as a comparison. Based on the result of each test, the parameters and/or storage was modified to see whether it would improve the results. When it appeared an optimal parameter/storage setting was found, it was locked in while the other parameters were tested further. This enabled multiple concurrent configurations to be tested and an optimal result to be calculated.

The test involved loading 67 images into the database. Each image varied in size between 40 to 80 MB resulting in 2.87 GB of data being loaded. As the test involved only image loading, no processing such as setting properties or extraction of metadata was performed. Archiving on the database was not enabled. All database files resided on hard disk unless specified. Additional performance metrics, setup, and server details can be found in *Appendix E, Loading and Reading*.

In between each test a full database reboot was done. The test was run at least three times with the range of results shown as follows:

```
Database parameter descriptions used:
Redo Buffer Size = LOG_BUFFER
Multiblock Read Count = db_file_multiblock_read_count
```

Source disk	Redo logs	Database parameters	Fastest time	Slowest time
Hard disk	Hard disk 3 x 50 MB	Redo buffer size = 4 MB Multiblock read count = 64 UNDO tablespace on HD (10 GB) Table datafile on HD	3 minutes and 22 sec	3 minutes and 53 sec
Hard disk	Hard disk 3 x 1 GB	Redo buffer size = 4 MB Multiblock read count = 64 UNDO tablespace on HD (10 GB) Table datafile on HD	2 minutes and 49 sec	2 minutes and 57 sec
Hard disk	SSD 3 x 1 GB	Redo buffer size = 4 MB Multiblock read count = 64 UNDO tablespace on HD (10 GB) Table datafile on HD	1 minute and 30 sec	1 minute and 41 sec
Hard disk	SSD 3 x 1 GB	Redo buffer size = 64 MB Multiblock read count = 64 UNDO tablespace on HD (10 GB) Table datafile on HD	1 minute and 23 sec	1 minute and 48 sec
Hard disk	SSD 3 x 1 GB	Redo buffer size = 8 MB Multiblock read count = 64 UNDO tablespace on HD (10 GB) Table datafile on HD	1 minute and 18 sec	1 minute and 29 sec

Source disk	Redo logs	Database parameters	Fastest time	Slowest time
Hard disk	SSD 3 x 1 GB	Redo buffer size = 16 MB Multiblock read count = 64 UNDO tablespace on HD (10 GB) Table datafile on HD	1 minute and 19 sec	1 minute and 27 sec
Hard disk	SSD 3 x 1 GB	Redo buffer size = 16 MB Multiblock read count = 256 UNDO tablespace on HD (10 GB) Table datafile on HD	1 minute and 27 sec	1 minute and 41 sec
Hard disk	SSD 3 x 1 GB	Redo buffer size = 8 MB Multiblock read count = 64 UNDO tablespace = 1 GB on SSD Table datafile on HD	1 minute and 21 sec	1 minute and 49 sec
SSD	SSD 3 x 1 GB	Redo buffer size = 8 MB Multiblock read count = 64 UNDO tablespace = 1 GB on SSD Table datafile on HD	53 sec	54 sec
SSD	SSD 3 x 1 GB	Redo buffer size = 8 MB Multiblock read count = 64 UNDO tablespace = 1 GB on SSD Table datafile on SSD	1 minute and 20 sec	1 minute and 20 sec

Analysis

The tests show a huge improvement when the redo logs were moved to a **Solid State Drive (SSD)**. Though the conclusion that can be drawn is this: the optimal step to perform it might be self defeating. A number of manufacturers of SSD acknowledge there are limitations with the SSD when it comes to repeated writes. The **Mean Time to Failure (MTF)** might be 2 million hours for reads; for writes the failure rate can be very high. Modern SSD and flash cards offer much improved wear leveling algorithms to reduce failures and make performance more consistent. No doubt improvements will continue in the future.

A redo log by its nature is constant and has heavy writes. So, moving the redo logs to the SSD might quickly result in it becoming damaged and failing. For an organization that on configuration performs one very large load of multimedia, the solution might be to initially keep the redo logs on SSD, and once the load is finished, to move the redo logs to a hard drive.

Increasing the size of the redo logs from 50 MB to 1 GB improves performance and all database containing unstructured data should have a redo log size of at least 1 GB. The number of logs should be at least 10; preferred is from 50 to 100. As is covered later, disk is cheaper today than it once was, and 100 GB of redo logs is not that large a volume of data as it once was. The redo logs should always be mirrored.

The placement or size of the UNDO tablespace makes no difference with performance.

The redo buffer size (`LOG_BUFFER`) showed a minor improvement when it was increased in size, but the results were inconclusive as the figures varied. A figure of `LOG_BUFFER=8691712`, showed the best results and database administrators might use this figure as a starting point for tuning.

The changing of multiblock read count (`DB_FILE_MULTIBLOCK_READ_COUNT`) from the default value of 64 to 256 showed no improvement. As the default value (in this case 64) is set by the database as optimal for the platform, the conclusion that can be drawn is that the database has set this figure to be a good size.

By moving the original images to an SSD showed another huge improvement in performance. This highlighted how the I/O bottleneck of reading from disk and the writing to disk (redo logs) is so critical for digital object loading.

The final test involved moving the datafile containing the table to the SSD. It highlighted a realistic issue that DBAs face in dealing with I/O. The disk speed and seek time might not be critical in tuning if the bottleneck is the actual time it takes to transfer the data to and from the disk to the server. In the test case the datafile was moved to the same SSD as the redo logs resulting in I/O competition. In the previous tests the datafile was on the hard disk and the database could write to the disk (separate I/O channel) and to the redo logs (separate I/O channel) without one impacting the other. Even though the SSD is a magnitude faster in performance than the disk, it quickly became swamped with calls for reads and writes. The lesson is that it's better to have multiple smaller SSDs on different I/O channels into the server than one larger channel. Sites using a SAN will soon realize that even though SAN might offer speed, unless it offers multiple I/O channels into the server, its channel to the server will quickly become the bottleneck, especially if the datafiles and the images for loading are all located on the server.

The original tuning notion of separating datafiles onto separate disks that was performed more than 15 years ago still makes sense when it comes to image loading into a multimedia database. It's important to stress that this is a tuning issue while dealing with image loading not when running the database in general. Tuning the database in general is a completely different story and covered further in *Chapter 8, Tuning*, and might result in a completely different architecture.

Oracle Securefile architecture

In Oracle 11*g*, Oracle rearchitected the management of lobs. This new structure is called SECUREFILES. The storage structure also included a number of new optimizations and security features. It is anticipated that the older storage method (now called BASICFILES) will be made obsolete in the next major release.

The storage architecture also introduced a new method for indexing the lobs, enabling faster access to parts of it. Reading and writing were also improved.

The following sections describe some of the key storage options a database administrator might want to consider when setting up tables that hold unstructured data. Example table creation statements are included at the end of the chapter.

Enabling storage in row

This option is useful for small lobs. These are ones that are less than 4000 bytes. When this option is enabled, Oracle stores the first 4000 bytes in the row just like if the column was a RAW (4000) one. If the lob is larger than 4000 bytes, the remainder of the lob is stored in the specialized lob storage area. The 4000 bytes includes system information about where the actual lob is located.

CHUNK

Oracle indicates in their documentation that this parameter is now only used as an advisory size and is there for backwards compatibility only. It was used with the BASICFILE type lob but can now be removed from usage.

Logging

Logging indicates whether the lob on any DML is logged to the redo logs. If LOGGING is specified, in the event of media failure the database can roll forward and restore the lob from archives.

If NOLOGGING is specified then the lob cannot be recovered as information is not written to the redo logs. It ensures faster load time at the expense of recovery in the event of failure. If a tablespace containing only lobs is created and lobs are loaded into it with NOLOGGING, once the tablespace is made read only and backed up, the need for logging is removed making this a viable option. Generally though, LOGGING should be used.

If a lob is to be cached in the Buffer Cache, LOGGING is enabled. A third option, `FILESYSTEM_LIKE_LOGGING`, also ensures recovery in the event of failure. Data dictionary information about the new space for the lob is not logged, but extent information is logged. This ensures sufficient information exists to restore the lob.

Cache

Cache determines how a lob is stored in the Oracle Buffer Cache. The three values are as follows:

- `CACHE`: This caches the lob. Considering the size of lobs, caching should be carefully considered. One large lob could swap out the whole Buffer Cache. The standard rule is to cache thumbnails, but not cache web quality or larger lobs.

- `NOCACHE`: This doesn't cache the lob. This is the recommended value to use unless there is justification in caching it.

- `CACHE READS`: This caches the lob only if it's read but not written. Oracle currently does not support being able to indicate which lobs are to be cached (lob row value indicated caching).

Managing duplicate images

Specifying DEDUPLICATE will result in Oracle checking if on loading an identical blob exists. If so, it will only store the blob once and maintain a pointer structure to it. This option is best used in a multimedia warehouse, where the likelihood of doubling up on images can happen.

The DEDUPLICATE options calculate a number of different checksum and comparison routines on the image before comparing to existing ones. Multiple routines are used to ensure that false positives do not occur. If a match is detected, only the original image is stored. The time to load the image with DEDUPLICATE is as long as loading in a normal image. The major advantage this option provides involves savings on storage.

Retention

This parameter is used to determine how the lob is to be used for read consistency and/or flashback. A value of AUTO will enable sufficient information to be maintained for read consistency. A value of MIN or MAX will impact the undo retention used by flashback.

Lob compression

This enables the lob to be compressed using LZ compression as used in the `utl_compress` supplied package. As covered in *Chapter 2, Understanding Digital Objects*, lob compression on binary does not achieve any noticeable results. In some cases it can result in the lob becoming larger. Multimedia images need to be compressed using alternate methods. It will though produce storage benefits if character data is stored in the lob and major benefits if the data stored is XML.

The recommendation is to not compress unless the data can be shown to compress, and the storage reduction gained is balanced by the offset in extra CPU usage to decompress the lob when retrieved.

Encryption

The encryption clause enables a lob to be stored in an encrypted form in the database. Enabling it has to be a business decision as performance will be impacted by encryption. This includes CPU to encrypt as well as a large amount of CPU to decrypt it every time it's accessed. The amount of CPU time is proportional to the size of the lob being encrypted.

If encryption is used to protect the data from database administrators, alternative methods should be investigated, as administrators have a number of tools in their arsenal, which they can use to easily determine what the encrypted code is.

Read-only tablespace

There are some key advantages to making a tablespace read-only. If a large number of images are loaded into the database and the table becomes fixed or static (not changing), by making the tablespace read-only, all the datafiles only need be backed up once. This reduces the backup size footprint.

Recovery is quicker too as the database does not need to have to apply any transactional data to the contents of the tablespace.

The tablespace is also easily moved between databases and becomes easier to transport between databases. The datafiles associated with the tablespace and a small export of data dictionary information enables it to be moved and reattached to another database. This allows the administrator to perform large volume copies of the images in the table. Such an option is useful when copying images between an internal site and an external site.

The following commands make the tablespace read-only or read-write:

```
alter tablespace tbls_name read only;
alter tablespace tbls_name read write;
```

Where does Oracle Multimedia fit in?

The Oracle Database supports three types of binary data types:

- **Binary Large Object (BLOB)**: This is a data type that contains binary data. Two structures exist in Oracle. The traditional one is called BASIC and a newer faster one, which was introduced in Oracle 11, is called SECUREFILES. The BASIC format will be desupported in a later release. The BLOB replaces the LONG data type which was the standard data type for any binary data. The LONG data type had a number of key limitations including only one being allowed per table and minimal support for controlling its storage. As of Oracle11*g* a BLOB does not have a maximum size.

- **Character Large Object (CLOB)**: This is a lob designed for text data. It is very similar in behavior to a VARCHAR of unlimited length. In Oracle 11*g* the difference is minor and text functions can be applied to a CLOB. A CLOB is useful for storing XML data. A CLOB is controlled by the database character set, whereas if an NCLOB is created then it is controlled by the national character set as configured by the database administrator. A document like Microsoft Word or a PDF is stored as a BLOB because these documents can contain binary data, which cannot be handled by a character set.

- **Binary File (BFILE)**: This is a pointer to a file outside the database. The BFILE is configured by specifying an Oracle Directory (covered later) and a physical filename. The physical filename can include a path embedded in it. Once set up the BFILE behaves exactly like a BLOB. A BFILE is read-only. Also if the physical file it points to is moved, the BFILE becomes orphaned. In that it now points to a non-existent file.

When using PL/SQL, the key routine for manipulating these types is via the DBMS_
LOB package. This package contains routines to read, load, and write to the type. In
some cases when piece wise updates is done on a BLOB, the Oracle 11*g* PL/SQL limit
of 32 KB is encountered, resulting in this manipulation to be done using the RAW
data type. Oracle provides a supplied package called UTL_RAW that can be
used to perform additional binary manipulation of this data.

Oracle Multimedia is a set of data types and methods (built in Java) that encompass
the BLOB, CLOB, and BFILE and include the ability to reference a file via an HTTP
reference. Each type is designed to identify a particular type of digital object and
in some cases enable it to be transformed. The four major Multimedia types are
as follows:

- ORDSYS.ORDIMAGE
- ORDSYS.ORDVIDEO
- ORDSYS.ORDAUDIO
- ORDSYS.ORDDOC

All these types are defined in a schema called ORDSYS. Each of these types has a set
of supplied methods that can be used against the digital object. Object-oriented style
syntax can be used, or the traditional PL/SQL calls can be used.

All these four types reference a core type called ORDSYS.ORDSOURCE. This type
contains the BLOB, CLOB, BFILE, or HTTP reference and effectively hides
(encapsulates) the digital object within its layer.

The ORDSYS data types are central to Oracle Multimedia. All tables need to
reference these type to use the methods. Though it's possible for an architect to
design their own data type based on a BLOB, to ensure a common standard usage it's
more efficient to use the object-oriented concept of extending the Oracle Multimedia
ORDSYS data type. This means to either create a new type referencing the ORDSYS
type within it, or to actually extend the type and add additional attributes to it.

Understanding the ORDSYS data types

This section covers methods for creating and working with tables using the Oracle
Multimedia data types. Further information on each of the types can be found in
Appendix E, Loading and Reading.

Creating a table

As the ORDSYS Multimedia types reference ORDSYS.ORDSOURCE, which in turn references a BLOB, the database administrator has the option of specifying all the storage parameters for each of the columns. For example, the table created looks like the following:

```
create table myimage
(
 pk number,
 myphoto ORDSYS.ORDIMAGE,
 myvideo ORDSYS.ORDVIDEO
)
```

The resulting storage parameters would like like the following:

```
create table myimage
(
 pk number,
 myphoto ORDSYS.ORDIMAGE,
 myvideo ORDSYS.ORDVIDEO
)
tablespace relational_tbls pctfree 5 storage( pctincrease 0 maxextents
unlimited)
    LOB (myphoto.source.localdata)
     STORE AS SECUREFILE l_myphoto
       (TABLESPACE image_tbls
        disable storage in row
        RETENTION AUTO
        NOCOMPRESS
        KEEP_DUPLICATES
        STORAGE (MAXEXTENTS UNLIMITED)
        NOCACHE LOGGING)
    LOB (myvideo.source.localdata)
    STORE AS SECUREFILE l_myvideo
       (TABLESPACE image_tbls
        disable storage in row
        RETENTION AUTO
        NOCOMPRESS
        DEDUPLICATE
        STORAGE (MAXEXTENTS UNLIMITED)
        NOCACHE LOGGING) ;
```

By naming the lobs it becomes easier to identify them. A lob doesn't have to be specifically named. If it isn't, Oracle assigns a system generated name to it. The lob can be found by querying the SEGMENT_NAME column in the USER_LOBS data dictionary table or SEGMENT_NAME column in the USER_SEGMENTS data dictionary table.

How to query?

Data in an Oracle type is referenced using dot notation and an alias: the *column name dot column name in type dot column name in sub type, and so on* for however nested deep the type is.

The retrieved local column found in ORDSYS.ORDSOURCE referenced by the ORDSYS.ORDIMAGE type using the previous example column is as follows:

```
select m.myphoto.source.local
from myimage m;
```

In an index creation statement the alias column isn't used:

```
create index i_myimage_1 on myimage(myphoto.width);
```

Multimedia methods

Methods are very similar to PL/SQL functions but are more an official object-oriented calling method. Methods are built very similar to a function and attached to a type.

Each of the ORDSYS multimedia types have associated a number of methods that perform a variety of functions including retrieving values, updating values, and processing a digital image.

In the following example using the test_load table detailed in *Appendix E, Loading and Reading*, the image will be converted into a thumbnail size.

```
...
crec test_load%ROWTYPE;
...
crec.vimg.digital_image.process( 'cut=0 0 100 100' );
```

The process command accepts text as input (enabling dynamic modification when calling) and can perform a number of commands. In most cases when an image is processed, the row has to have been retrieved using a for update clause to ensure it's exclusively locked.

Some methods can be called like a SQL function. These ones have to have been built to return a SQL data type:

```
select u.vimg.getSourceType() from test_load u;
```

This SQL statement returns whether the image is a file or an HTTP.

Creating a schema

The following section goes through an example schema creation configuration:

```
create user multimedia identified by mypassword;
grant create session, create table, create procedure to multimedia;
grant create view, create role, create trigger to multimedia;
```

The following statements enable the schema to access the temporary tablespaces (in this case it's assumed to be called TEMP) and be able to have storage rights in the tablespace called USERS:

```
alter user multimedia temporary tablespace temp;
alter user multimedia quota unlimited on users;
alter user multimedia default tablespace users;
```

The following two permissions are optional but can prove to be useful. They allow the schema to access the dbms_lock.sleep command (useful for asynchronous processing) and the dbms_file_transfer command, allowing the schema to manipulate external multimedia files.

```
grant execute on dbms_file_transfer to multimedia;
grant execute on dbms_lock to multimedia;
```

Oracle HTTP servers

There are two HTTP gateway servers available in Oracle. One uses the Oracle listener to act as an HTTP server and it can deliver data from the database using PL/SQL stored procedures. The second involves using Apache and the Mod PL/SQL gateway. Each have advantages and disadvantages in using them.

The Apache HTTP server offers additional capabilities such as virtual directory configuration, SSL, URL rewrites, Single Sign On, and a whole range of open source plugins. The embedded gateway has limitations but is simple to configure and is designed to work with Mod PL/SQL (and Oracle Apex). It's lightweight and is embedded in the Oracle listener, requiring one less process to manage.

Configuring the Oracle embedded gateway

The goal of this section is to show you how to configure Oracle Database for the embedded PL/SQL gateway. For Oracle XE, the embedded gateway comes configured for Apex by default.

All configuration is done via **SQL*Plus**. SQL*Plus represents the lowest common interface available across all Oracle versions. The command-line interface when used with a text editor enables quick and easy modification of most Oracle features.

Tools like Oracle SQL Developer and Enterprise Manager can also be used, but it is best to have a good understanding of the core capabilities before using GUI development tools:

1. Use SQL*Plus to connect to the database as SYS:

   ```
   sqlplus / as sysdba
   ```

2. Check to make sure the database parameter dispatchers are correctly configured to allow the database to talk to the listener:

   ```
   SQL> show parameter dispatchers
   ```

   The output should look like the following:

   ```
   NAME             TYPE         VALUE
   -------------------------------------- ----------- ----------
   dispatchers      string       (PROTOCOL=TCP) (SERVICE=orclXDB)

   using Oracle XE the parameter looks like
   dispatchers      string       (PROTOCOL=TCP) (SERVICE=XEXDB)
   ```

   The orcl is the SID (unique identifier) of the database installed on your machine. You can find out the SID of your database using the following command:

   ```
   select name from v$database;
   NAME
   --------
   ORCL
   ```

   If this parameter is not set or it is set incorrectly, the database will not be able to talk to the listener and the embedded gateway will not work.

3. Unlock the anonymous account:

```
alter user anonymous ACCOUNT UNLOCK;
```

The anonymous account is used by Oracle to connect to the database to find additional connection information about the embedded gateway. The gateway also uses Oracle XML DB, so with the query in the next check Oracle XML DB is enabled.

4. Check that Oracle XML DB required for the gateway is enabled. This is done by checking that user SYS has the XDBADMIN role:

```
select * from dba_role_privs where granted_role = 'XDBADMIN';
```

5. All web interfaces use a port to connect to the database. The Oracle Listener (which will handle all incoming HTTP requests and will act as an HTTP server, similar to Apache), needs to know which port to listen on for incoming HTTP requests. Talk to your network administrators to determine which port you can use.

The following script will open up two ports. One is for FTP and one is for HTTP requests.

Windows platforms can access port 80 without any problems. Unix platforms require root access to ports with numbers less than 1024. This means starting up the listener with permissions equivalent to that of root can get quite tricky. This is why on Unix most sites use HTTP ports above 1024.

In the following example port 80 is configured for HTTP and port 2121 for FTP:

```
DECLARE
 v_cfg XMLType;
BEGIN
SELECT updateXML(DBMS_XDB.cfg_get(),
        '/xdbconfig/descendant::ftp-port/text()', '2121',
        '/xdbconfig/descendant::http-port/text()','8890')
 INTO v_cfg FROM DUAL;
DBMS_XDB.cfg_update(v_cfg);
COMMIT;
END;
/
```

Alternatively, you can use the following:

```
EXEC DBMS_XDB.sethttpport(8890);
EXEC DBMS_XDB.setftpport(2121);
```

6. In this step we create the HTTP **DAD** (or **Device Access Descriptor**). The DAD defines the mapping between the virtual directory and the actual schema.

   An example URL used to access could be `http://localhost:80/mm/program`.

   Then `/mm/` is the virtual directory and needs to be mapped to the schema in the database.

   To do this step, we use the `dbms_epg` PL/SQL package. We define the DAD and control which PL/SQL programs will access it.

Perform the following steps to define the mapping between the virtual directory and the actual schema:

1. Create the DAD.

2. Note that first call will return an error as DAD doesn't exist and can be ignored:

   ```
   exec dbms_epg.drop_dad( 'PICTION' );
   ```

3. This command defines the DAD and gives it the name `mm`. It is case sensitive. We can fine tune it to control which programs (PL/SQL packages) it can access, but for now let us give it full access:

   ```
   exec dbms_epg.create_dad( 'PICTION','/mm/*');
   ```

4. We then map it to a schema. With the embedded gateway, we don't need to manage a password. If we had used mod PL/SQL and Apache then the password should be stored in a `dads.conf` file (which is encrypted).

   ```
   exec dbms_epg.set_dad_attribute( 'PICTION','database-
   username','MULTIMEDIA');
   ```

5. These parameters describe how the DAD is accessed. Other Oracle products such as APEX or ones that use SSO might have different options here:

   ```
   exec dbms_epg.set_dad_attribute( 'PICTION','authentication-
   mode','Basic');
   exec dbms_epg.set_dad_attribute( 'PICTION','error-
   style','DebugStyle');
   exec dbms_epg.set_dad_attribute( 'PICTION','session-state-manageme
   nt','StatelessWithFastResetPackageState');
   ```

6. These parameters are important security safeguards that ensure packages, which can be accessed from within SQL*Plus by multimedia, cannot be accessed from the URL. This is one of the important steps to safeguard against URL modification.

   ```
   exec dbms_epg.set_dad_attribute( 'PICTION','exclusion-
   list','sys.*');
   ```

```
exec dbms_epg.set_dad_attribute( 'PICTION','exclusion-
list','dbms_*');
exec dbms_epg.set_dad_attribute( 'PICTION','exclusion-
list','utl_*');
exec dbms_epg.set_dad_attribute( 'PICTION','exclusion-
list','owa_*');
exec dbms_epg.set_dad_attribute( 'PICTION','exclusion-
list','owa.*');
exec dbms_epg.set_dad_attribute( 'PICTION','exclusion-
list','htp.*');
exec dbms_epg.set_dad_attribute( 'PICTION','exclusion-
list','htf.*');
```

7. This command defines the table to be used to temporarily store multimedia content (BLOBs) that are loaded via the browser. We will look at this table more closely later in the workshop:

```
exec dbms_epg.set_dad_attribute( 'PICTION','document-table-
name','APACHE_OWS_CONTENT');
```

8. We then have to authorize the DAD. This is important, because we are effectively saying we are allowing access to the schema without a password using the embedded gateway.

```
exec dbms_epg.authorize_dad( 'PICTION','MULTIMEDIA');
commit;
```

9. Note that these commands help if you cannot get in on 8890:

```
call dbms_xdb.setHttpPort(8890);
alter system register;
```

Configuring Apache

Apache offers an open source multithreaded HTTP Server that can integrate with Oracle.

The Oracle Database can work with either Apache 1.3 or Apache 2.0. The integration is done via Mod PL/SQL. The Mod PL/SQL with Apache 1.3 superseded the previous integration Oracle provided when it provided its own web server.

The multi-threaded nature of the connection means that Apache establishes a number of fixed connections to the database (client/server). Multiple HTTP users then perform requests on a round robin type basis across these fixed connections. This means that there is no guarantee that if a user performs multiple HTTP requests, they will be using the same physical connection to the database. This is a key issue that has to be considered in the development. It means that the PL/SQL program (or Java program) cannot rely on session variables or the content of temporary tables to be there from call to call. Apache manages the load balancing and based on the usage can increase or decrease the number of physical connections to the database. The result is an incredibly scalable architecture enabling thousands of concurrent requests to access the database.

Because of the flexibility of the Oracle architecture, the connectivity between Apache 1.3 and Apache 2.0 will allow a connection to be made with any version of Oracle. As Apache 2.0 included a number of default security fixes, it is recommended that Apache 2.0 be installed wherever possible.

As the Apache install is a client/server configuration, if one treats Apache as a client application, the logic behind its installation is simplified. The challenge for the database administrator is that between Apache 1.3 and Apache 2.0 the installation changes dramatically.

This means that once Apache is installed, the TNS (Oracle Database network layer found with all client/server applications, not to be confused with the JDBC Thin Tier connection) needs to be configured along with a DAD (Device Access Descriptor, containing information about connecting to the database). The database itself needs a LISTENER configured.

It is possible to use Apache with Mod PL/SQL and just have it rewrite (effectively redirect) all requests to the Oracle embedded gateway. This is a realistic and workable option that can prove to be useful in an environment where Apache is the main HTTP server used for handling all HTTP packets and where the network administrator is not comfortable with having Mod PL/SQL installed, or where the Apache network is managed by a third-party company.

The Apache HTTP server is required if SSL is required as the Oracle embedded gateway is not SSL compliant.

A description for how to install Apache 2.0 can be found in *Appendix E, Loading and Reading*.

Basic diagnostics

The administrator can do a quick check on Unix or Windows to see if the HTTP server is listening to requests. If it's not listening, this could be either because the service is not running or a firewall is blocking access to it.

The command is as follows:

```
telnet localhost 80
```

Assuming the HTTP server is listening on Port 80, this command will either fail (indicating it cannot access the HTTP server) or will open up a screen prompting for further information. The administrator can then type in `quit` to exit.

The `telnet.exe` program is not by default available on all platforms, even Unix ones, anymore. For Windows it was once bundled in as part of an extra Windows pack. Now it comes included in `cygwin` (which is a Unix shell on Windows) or can be downloaded from the Internet.

Testing whether the HTTP server is alive and listening for requests on the server is the first of many potential steps that might need to be performed when diagnosing bad connections to the server.

Windows

When Apache2 is installed on Windows, a Windows service is created allowing the administrator to start and stop it. Changing the owner of the service is not recommended in this version (it was possible to do this in older versions) as experience has shown it becomes difficult to connect to it:

Network List Service	Identifies t...	Started	Manual	Local Service
Network Location Awareness	Collects an...	Started	Automatic	Network S...
Network Store Interface Service	This servic...	Started	Automatic	Local Service
Oracle Process Manager (instance1)		Started	Automatic	Local System
Oracle TST1 VSS Writer Service		Started	Manual	Local System
OracleJobSchedulerTST1			Disabled	Local System

The `dads.conf` file contains information enabling Apache to connect to the database. The file using the example installation is found at `C:\oracle\apache2\instances\instance1\config\OHS\ohs1\mod_plsql`.

On installation the file is empty and descriptors need to be added to it. The following is an example configuration:

```
<Location /mydad>
  SetHandler pls_handler
  Order deny,allow
  Allow from all
  # AllowOverride None
  PlsqlDatabaseUsername           websys
  PlsqlDatabasePassword           mypassword
  PlsqlDatabaseConnectString      PRD1
  PlsqlAuthenticationMode         Basic
  PlsqlDefaultPage                websys.myprog.defaultpage
  PlsqlDocumentTablename          websys.apache_ows_content
</Location>
```

Once configured URL access would look as follows:

```
http://localhost/mydad/
```

The definition of the parameters in the `dads.conf` file is detailed as follows. The `dads.conf` file can support multiple definitions. Once a DAD is configured the password has to be encrypted using a Perl program provided by Oracle. The provided documentation is incorrect in the release and can cause administrators to spend a lot of time to try and work out how to encrypt it.

The following code from DOS shows how to invoke Perl to encrypt the password in the `dads.conf` file using the example install:

```
set ORACLE_HOME=C:\oracle\apache2
set PATH=C:\oracle\apache2\instances\instance1\config\OHS\ohs1\mod_
plsql;%PATH%
set PATH=C:\oracle\apache2\bin;c:\oracle\ora11gR2\perl\bin;%PATH%
set PATH=%ORACLE_HOME%\bin;%PATH%

cd C:\oracle\apache2\bin
c:\oracle\ora11gR2\perl\bin\perl dadTool.pl -f C:\oracle\apache2\
instances\instance1\config\OHS\ohs1\mod_plsql\dads.conf
```

This is Oracle version 11.2.0.2, it assumes `c:\oracle\apache2` install and `c:\oracle\ora11gR2` install.

As can be seen, reference is made to the Oracle 11*g* R2 install which contains the correct version of Perl that is required to do the encryption. Once the program is run, the output will indicate the number of passwords obfuscated (which is encrypted).

The `dads.conf` file will now look something like the following:

```
# AllowOverride None
PlsqlDatabaseUsername        websys
PlsqlDatabasePasswor @CARzMT/edCNuxmmqLP2y6pSRFjghDaqdlmRQ==
```

The encryption algorithm used is linked to the installed version of Apache2. So it's not possible to copy a `dads.conf` file from one environment to another and expect it to work. If multiple schemas are referenced in the `dads.conf` file and they all have the same password, they will be encrypted identically. This means it's possible to configure a new DAD just by copying it in the file including the encrypted password.

Details of the `dads.conf` parameters can be found in *Appendix E, Loading and Reading*.

Unix

When Apache is installed on Unix, you need to execute the following in the command prompt window:

```
ORACLE_HOME=c:\oracle\apache;export ORACLE_HOME

PATH=$ORACLE_HOME/Apache/modplsql/conf:$PATH;export PATH

PATH=$ORACLE_HOME/perl/bin:$PATH;export PATH

LD_LIBRARY_PATH=$ORACLE_HOME/lib:$LD_LIBRARY_PATH;export LD_LIBRARY_PATH
```

HTTPD.CONF file

The master parameter configuration file for Apache is called `httpd.conf`. It's found in the directory (if the install shown previously is used):

```
C:\oracle\apache2\instances\instance1\config\OHS\ohs1
```

There are a lot of parameters in the file and it is self documenting, but for an administrator who just wants to modify the basic values, the following are some of the core parameters in the file based on an Apache install on Windows (keep in mind for Unix, root needs to start the Apache Server if it's going to listen on any port less than 1024). Windows was chosen as all documentation one finds on Apache configuration always covers Unix.

- **ServerName**: This is the DNS name of the server. On installation the identified name of the server is used. Multiple DNS can use the one HTTP file using the concept of a virtual server.

  ```
  ServerName: www.site1.com
  ```

- **ServerRoot**: This is the top level directory, where all the HTTP server configuration and log files are kept.

```
ServerRoot: C:\config
```

- **DocumentRoot**: This is the location where all files to be delivered are stored.

```
DocumentRoot: C:\web\home/
```

If `http://www.site1.com/myfile.html` is requested, it will look for it in `c:\web\home\myfile.html`.

- **Directory**: This is set of parameters that can be used to control the security and access of the physical location. Commonly used to ensure users can't see files that they are not allowed to access. See the alias example for a detailed example:

```
<Directory "C:\web\home">
```

- **DirectoryIndex**: This is the default filename to be used when an HTTP request is not specified in a file.

```
DirectoryIndex index.html
```

This would mean the request for `http://www/site1.com` would return `c:\web\home\index.html`.

- **Alias**: This enables a virtual (or logical) directory to map to a physical directory. In addition the directory option can be used to fine tune the security on it.

In the following example a request for `http://www.site1.com/icons/images/myimg.png` will look for it in `c:\web\home\mydir\images\myimg.png`.

```
Alias /icons/images/ "C:\web\home\mydir\images/"
<Directory "C:\apache\ohs/icons">
    Options MultiViews
    AllowOverride None
    Order allow,deny
    Allow from all
</Directory>
```

- **Listen**: This is the TCP/IP port number that HTTP requests should listen on. Port 80 is the default HTTP but Unix requires root to start he HTTP server. The standard default value for Unix is 7777.

```
Listen 80
```

Virtual hosts

A virtual host allows multiple DNS sites to use the one HTTP server. In the following example the sites www.site1.com (configured previously) and www.site2.com serve different pages and directories as the configuration parameter values point to different locations.

```
NameVirtualHost www.site1.com
<VirtualHost www.site1.com>
    DocumentRoot "C:\web\home/"
    ServerName www.site1.com
</VirtualHost>

NameVirtualHost www.site2.com
<VirtualHost www.site2.com>
    ServerAdmin admin@site2.com
    DocumentRoot "C:\web\home\mydir/"
    Alias /imagesp/ "C:\web\home\mydir\imagesp/"
    Alias /downloadp/ "C:\web\home\mydir\downloadp/"
    ServerName www.site2.com
    ErrorLog logs/site2.log
    CustomLog logs/site2 common
</VirtualHost>
```

Apache rewrites

Most sites now have firewalls and dedicated servers for handling outside traffic coming to an internal site. As the HTTP packets are required to be rerouted, there is likely going to be a requirement to change the location of the server, its port number, and even the name of the DAD being used.

Trying to work out how to do it can be initially daunting for a novice administrator. The following shows how it can be done easily. In the first case the request is coming in externally on http://extsite.org/mydad/myprog?p=1, the following will translate it, and pass it internally as http://unixsrv.org:7777/mydad/myprogra?p=1.

```
ProxyRequests Off

ProxyPass /mydad/ http://unixsrv.org:7777/mydad/
ProxyPassReverse /mydad/ http://unixsrv.org:7777/mydad/
ProxyPass /icons/img/ http://unixsrv.org:7777/icons/img/
ProxyPassReverse /icons/img/                 http://unixsrv.
org:7777/icons/img/
```

The `proxypass` and `proxypassreverse` configuration options are needed to ensure the traffic is returned in both directions.

If there are any icons being referenced, they will also be translated from `http://extsite.org/icons/img/myimg.png` to `http://unixsrv.org:7777/icons/img/myimg.png`.

The port number does not need to be specified and HTTP will default to 80. In the following configuration any icon request will be redirected to an internal server; that is `http://extsite.org/icons/all/myimg.png` becomes `http://winserver.com/images/myimg.png`.

```
ProxyPass /mydad/ http://winserver.com/internaldad/
ProxyPassReverse /mydad/ http://winserver.com/internaldad7/
ProxyPass /icons/all/ http://winserver.com/images/
ProxyPassReverse /icons/all/ http://winserver.com/images/
```

External locations and security

When working with digital objects, it is inevitable that the database administrator will need to configure some type of external access to load external files into the database server. There are four available methods that can be used, each one using very different loading methods.

Oracle directory

A number of external access points can be used when accessing external files. The directory is one that Oracle Multimedia uses. Others include `utl_file` and it is also possible to use Java to access directories directly. But let's first define an external directory that the multimedia schema can access.

The following is an example on Windows:

```
create or replace directory LOADING_DIR as
    'C:\multimedia_files';
```

The following is an example on Unix:

```
create directory LOADING_DIR as '/u01/multimedia_files';
```

Granting access to a directory

Once created, access to the directory can be given using Oracle grants:

```
grant read on directory LOADING_DIR to multimedia;
```

Access is also implicitly given to any subdirectory. Access to the subdirectory requires appending the subdirectory location to the filename. So if the directory `c:\multimedia_files\jpg` existed, a program can access the jpg directory by prefixing `jpg\` to the filename as follows:

```
crec.vimg.importfrom(ctx, 'file',
                         'LOADING_DIR', 'jpg\myimg.jpg');
```

UTL_FILE

Digital images can be loaded into the database and written back to disk using the PL/SQL supplied package called `utl_file`. This package has been bundled with the database since before the directory concept was introduced. It was originally designed to enable files to be read into the database as well as written back to disk. With later versions of Oracle support in the package was extended to support reading files as bytes (raw data), enabling a digital image to be loaded into a BLOB without relying on the Oracle Multimedia methods. The exact physical location of the directory is specified:

```
UTL_FILE.FOPEN( '/u01/myimages','myfile.jpg','rb',32767);
```

The security is different to directory and requires the configuration of the database parameter called `utl_file_dir`. It is a global setting and can't be fine tuned using grants like the DIRECTORY command can. When `utl_file_dir = *` is set, a PL/SQL program can access any directory on the server. By repeating this parameter and specifying a physical directory, access can be fenced into those directories only:

```
utl_file_dir = c:\myimages
utl_file_dir = v:\imagedir
```

The downside of `utl_file_dir` is this database parameter requires a complete database restart to come into effect. The DIRECTORY command does not have this limitation. Also the directory specified is the only one that can be accessed. Subdirectories cannot be accessed, resulting in all directories being specified. If a large load across thousands of directories was going to be run, configuring the `utl_file_dir` parameters for each one would prove to be impractical.

By Oracle 10, Oracle integrated support with a configured directory allowing a directory to be accessed rather than specifying an external physical directory:

```
UTL_FILE.FOPEN( 'LOADING_DIR','myfile.jpg','rb',32767);
```

UTL_TCP

Access to images isn't just limited to reading/writing from an external physical directory. Digital images can also be loaded into the database via FTP, HTTP, and SMTP. In Oracle 10 there was no security built into the database, which controlled ports allowing any program to access a port and read/write to it using the `utl_tcp` supplied package.

In Oracle 11 Oracle tightened this up by introducing a basic concept of a firewall inside the database. Access to ports by default is disabled and the `DBMS_NETWORK_ACL_ADMIN` package has to be called to give a schema access to a TCP/IP port. Example configuration enabling a schema to access any port is provided in *Appendix E, Loading and Reading*.

Java

Java running inside the database can access TCP/IP ports and external files. Java code like that shown as follows requires special permission to access external files:

```
dstBlob[0].open(oracle.sql.BLOB.MODE_READWRITE);
OutputStream os = dstBlob[0].setBinaryStream(0);
```

The `dbms_java` routine is used to give a schema the privileges to access external resources. The following anonymous PL/SQL when run as SYS will give the schema MULTIMEDIA access to run Java programs that can read and write to any external location:

```
begin dbms_java.grant_permission( 'MULTIMEDIA','SYS:java.lang.RuntimeP
ermission','writeFileDescriptor','*' );
dbms_java.grant_permission( 'MULTIMEDIA','SYS:java.lang.RuntimePermiss
ion','readFileDescriptor', '*' );
dbms_java.grant_permission( 'MULTIMEDIA','SYS:java.io.FilePermission',
'<<ALL FILES>>', 'read, write, execute, delete');
commit;
end;
/
```

Discussing Raid, SSD, SANs, and NAS

When working with unstructured data there are two key considerations that need to be taken into account. The first is that there will likely to be a large amount of data (possibly tens of terabytes) to be loaded in. This requires an infrastructure that can handle large contiguous writes. The hardware used must be able to support high speed storage of hundreds of megabytes of data in bursts.

The other is that reading in data will result in large reads, potentially concurrently, at possibly random locations across any part of the storage. If it's not random and well known, an option to cache the well-known data items to improve performance must be considered. The I/O (or network) channel can become a bottleneck. The best solution for performance is to support multiple channels.

Solid State Disk

A Solid State Disk (SSD) is the equivalent of persistent memory, in that if power is lost the contents are not lost. It is a form of flash memory with the provision that it is marketed primarily as a hard drive replacement. This hardware technology has grown in popularity in the last three years as the technology behind it has matured. With traditional memory if the power is lost, so are the contents of the memory. An SSD behaves like a disk except it has no moving parts, uses a lot less power, has high speed I/O, is more resistant to shock, not susceptible to magnetic fields, and doesn't suffer from overheating that a hard drive can. The SSD is quite thin (making it ideal for laptops). An SSD also has a low read latency (time to find the data, which normally involves the hard drive spinning and moving the heads to a location) because all data in the SSD has equal access. The SSD has a very high MTF for reads, but most current models have a guaranteed failure time for writes. Most have built-in error correcting when it can't correctly write the data.

An SSD is ideal for applications with heavy reads but not large data volumes. Currently, the largest SSD is 512 G and it is anticipated the size will increase to over 2 TB in the next four years. The cost of an SSD is far greater than a disk. Target areas for SSD are the operating system kernel, database kernel, and any software installs. Read-only tablespaces are also well suited for SSD as well as the SYSTEM and SYSAUX tablespaces (again, depending on what applications are running and how heavy the I/O load is).

An important factor when reviewing the use of the SSD is the performance of the disk controller it is plugged into. This is hardware that enables the SSD to communicate with the CPU. Even though the SSD might offer high speed read/write times, the controller might be a bottleneck. An SSD in a NAS will only be useful if the network connection is high speed (for example a 10 GB Ethernet connection). Disk controllers for SANs are improving each year and the latest models can offer improvements in performance when an SSD is used over a high speed disk. Depending on the motherboard, **Peripheral Component Interconnect Express** (**PCIe**) can offer very high speed throughput from the SSD to the CPU.

Though they are ideally suited to improve performance, if used for REDO logs, this is not recommended, as the REDO log is the most heavy I/O structure in the database and will likely increase the failure time of the SSD.

Mirroring an SSD will not result in less likelihood of failure, like a hard disk drive, because in a mirror, the same level of writes are happening to both drives in the mirror, resulting in the same approximate failure time period. Striping would be a more effective option.

Raid 0: stripe across both disks

Involves getting two (or more disks) and alternating the block writes between them. This evenly distributes all data across both disks. Using this method reads and writes are typically twice as fast (three times faster if three disks are used and so on). Raid 0 offers an ideal solution to improving disk read/write times provided the disks are on separate I/O channels. Most hardware with Raid built into the motherboard inherently support this.

The major disadvantage of Raid 0 is that if a disk is lost, all data is lost, even the data on the surviving disks. Using Raid 0 for storage is used in conjunction with Raid 1 or when the database backups and archives are proven reliable.

Raid 1: mirror

This involves taking two (or more) disks of the same size. When data is written to one disk, the same data is written to the other disk. The write speed is as fast as the slowest disks. The read speed though can be twice as fast as both disks can be utilized to read in the data, each reading in separate parts of the disks and working in tandem.

Mirroring is a preferred solution as it is highly reliable. If one disk fails, the other will continue and performance will not be affected. The damaged disk can be transparently replaced and then resilvered (brought back into sync) with the surviving disk.

Raid 1 is an ideal solution for storing key database tablespaces (for example, SYSTEM, UNDO) or for storing the redo logs. It's also ideal for storing the operating system, database kernel, and any other application software because read performance is improved.

Raid 0+1: stripe then mirror

This involves a minimum of four disks. Two disks are striped as per Raid 0 (making it appear as one logical disk, sometimes called a **volume**). The resultant disk is then mirrored with the other two drives.

This ensures the read/write performance is greatly improved and if a disk is lost, the system will continue. If one disk in the mirror is lost, then if another disk is also lost, it depends on whether it was the other mirror (system continues on) or if it was a striped disk that was lost, whether there is complete failure or continued survivability.

Raid 1+0: mirrors then stripe

This is also referred to as Raid 10. It involves a minimum of four disks. Two disks are mirrored together creating a new logical disk. The other two disks are mirrored together also creating a new logical disk. These two resultant logical disks are then striped as per Raid 0. Writes are evenly split and then sent to the mirrored disks. In Raid 0+1, writes are evenly distributed and sent to the stripe disk which is then mirrored. The entire stripe is mirrored. With Raid 1+0, as the stripe is done first, one write is sent to one mirror, and the other write is sent to the other mirror. The subtle change in ordering improves reliability and performance of the raid structure.

As for Raid 0+1, if one drive is lost the system continues to run. The next drive to fail determines whether or not there is catastrophic failure. The strength of Raid 1+0 with reliability is seen when more than four drives are used.

Raid 5: parity check

Requires a minimum of three disks. A block of data is written to one disk, another block to the next disk, and a third disk contains parity information, which is information that can be used to restore either the block on the first or second disk if either disk is lost. The parity check is distributed evenly across all three disks.

This involves much slower writes as the parity information has to be calculated and written to disk. The parity is calculated using a logical xor function.

The advantage of Raid 5 is a saving on disk space. Whereas Raid 1 requires one disk to be a mirror for every disks, Raid 5 only requires an additional drive to support three or more disks. Raid 5 can survive one disk failure, but if another disk fails then there is catastrophic failure.

Raid 6: double parity check

This option requires a minimum of four disks as parity checks are now stored across two disks. Only if three disks are lost, does catastrophic failure occur. This option provides an additional layer of safety that Raid 5 does not give, allowing the database administrator additional breathing space to work with in the event of media failure.

Raid 5 and Raid 6 have in the last five years received a large amount of negative press about being used for storage of an Oracle Database. The testing done and conclusions drawn are that Raid 1+0 is better, more reliable, and faster. With individual disks now at the 3 TB size, it's feasible for a relational database to happily fit on a Raid 1+0 structure, even if each disk is only 1 TB in size (providing 2 TB of storage).

With unstructured data, the size of the database could grow into the tens to hundreds of terabyte range. As ideal as Raid 1+0 is, it just might not be cost effective to use it. If a large portion of the unstructured data is partitioned and made read only, a more realistic solution might be to use Raid 5 for the storage of all the partitions. Raid 6 might even be considered to be an option if backups are taken to tape and the time to restore from tape might take weeks. These structures might not give as good a performance as Raid 1+0, but will still prove to be highly reliable and storage scalable, allowing for large amounts of unstructured data to be stored, and even in the event of disk failure, no recovery is needed. If the Raid structure manages the parity data within specialized hardware controllers, the write overhead can be reduced further. As there are a large number of disks, the administrator might be in a position to mix up the Raid structure, possibly having a Raid 1+0 for the operating system and key database files, while using Raid 5 for the tablespaces containing multimedia data.

For further detailed information regarding Raid, see `http://en.wikipedia.org/wiki/RAID`.

NAS

A **Network Attached Storage** (**NAS**) device is usually a low-cost computer acting as a fileserver. Access to it is via a network and typically uses a Raid disk structure to improve reliability. Storing the database on a NAS is not ideal as the network connection will very quickly become a bottleneck (the exception is covered later). Tablespaces containing multimedia, which is infrequently accessed, could be stored on an NAS, but the database administrator would have to factor in and balance network speed.

With the recent introduction of 10 GB Ethernet the rules have changed regarding the NAS. Rather than the network being the bottleneck, attaching multiple 10 GB Ethernet adapters enables a large amount of data to be passed at high speed from the disk system to the computer. This can now be sent faster than via a disk system. As this is new technology, which is still expensive, most hardware servers do not offer 10 GB Ethernet. This of course will change in the next five years enabling the NAS to become a popular high speed storage medium.

SAN

A **Storage Area Network** (**SAN**) is similar in some ways to an NAS; a SAN differentiates itself in that it can be treated by the server as a disk (offering high speed access). A SAN works on the block level and enables high speed replication (mirroring) to remote locations by quickly passing block changes to the remote server. A SAN is an ideal solution for storing large volumes of database files on it and then using the backup capabilities of the SAN to backup/recover the database, rather than using the database backup tools (like rman). It has to be carefully stated that before a database administrator jumps in and just solely relies on the SAN to perform backups, they should consult the vendor to see whether they are supported with Oracle and in addition, the administrator should do some high I/O tests and recovery to ensure that a restore is actually possible.

A SAN can internally handle a large number of disks, and most vendors support adding new disks to the existing SAN enabling it to grow in size. For storing and managing multimedia digital objects, a SAN is an attractive solution.

The downside of the SAN is the efficiency at which it is hooked up to the computer server. If it uses only one channel, a large amount of I/O will result in the channel becoming a bottleneck, which wouldn't normally be seen if the disks were distributed across multiple channels on the server.

Setting up Oracle XE to run Oracle Multimedia

Oracle XE has two major limitations that most database administrators would deem to be showstopper issues and not consider XE for use with multimedia. The first issue is the 11 GB database storage limit. If the decision is made to store all digital images outside the database and just use a BFILE or HTTP pointer to reference them, the database storage remaining that can be used for relational data is quite a large amount. An application with auditing can manage tens of thousands of images of any size. The administrator has to now manage backups of external files and deal with the potential for orphaned images, but can still manage a healthy volume of digital images using the remaining powerful features found in the database as well as PL/SQL.

The second major issue is that Oracle XE doesn't come with Java in the database and all the Oracle Multimedia methods are written in Java. This means there is no image processing, metadata extractions, watermarking, or identification. An experienced developer could write their own equivalent functions in PL/SQL, or use Open Source tools to achieve these capabilities. Also, not all digital image applications require use of these capabilities. Using the `htp`, `utl_file`, or `dbms_lob` routines (which do not require Java), an application can be written that uses the basic functions to develop a web-based application that manages and delivers multimedia.

Even with these limitations it's still possible to create the ORDSYS type definitions without the methods, so that the Oracle Multimedia object structure can be used. That way, the schema can be ported seamlessly to the standard or enterprise editions of the database.

The scripts to install the types can be found in the `$ORACLE_HOME\ord\im\` `admin` directory (not included with XE but included with a version installed with Multimedia). Scripts to review include the following:

- `ordsrcsp.sql`
- `ordispec.sql`
- `ordimssp.sql`
- `ordisits.sql`
- `ordaspec.sql`
- `ordvspec.sql`
- `orddspec.sql`

Summary

There are numerous ways to configure an Oracle Database to store large volumes of unstructured data. Some of the key areas to review include the database block size, the size of the UNDO tablespace, the placement and sizes of the redo logs, and the configuration and extent size of the tablespaces used to store the data. Different architectural configurations are available based on the number of disks, CPUs, and available memory on the server. The use of solid state drives can improve load time performance.

Even though the Oracle XE database has no built in support for Java and Oracle multimedia, its usage should not be dismissed outright as a database for storing multimedia as its core architecture offers features and performance characteristics that still make it ideal to use.

Chapter 8, Tuning, will provide an introduction to database tuning for the novice administrator before covering in depth a number of multimedia tuning issues that the database administrator needs to consider.

Exercises

1. Design an architecture to house a set of Oracle Databases having the following server features:
   - ○ 1 x SSD Drive (64 GB)
   - ○ 1 x mirrored drive x 1 TB
   - ○ 1 x 3 TB drive
   - ○ 1 x external 2 TB drive
   - ○ 1 Server CPU with 8 cores

   The server has to use the following:
   - ○ To run vSphere (or equivalent virtualization kernel)
   - ○ Be able to run three Linux operating systems with one Oracle 11*g* installation on each
   - ○ Each Linux install is to run Oracle and provide full redundancy
   - ○ Be able to store 2 TB of multimedia digital objects across all the three Oracle installs, with one install storing a max of 500 GB of multimedia.

2. You are a software architect and have been tasked to design a new multimedia centric database from scratch. Your goal is to design a storage structure for a database factoring in the following conditions:

    ○   There can be no restriction on the length of a row stored or the number of columns in a table. It should be possible to create a table with more than 100 columns, with each one of unlimited length.

    ○   The length of each column (field) can be of any length and is not constrained by block size or operating system (32 bit, 64 bit, or large CPU should not be an issue).

    ○   There is no limit to the size of the database. Individual files can grow as large as the operating system allows, or design your own filesystem which resides on a raw disk to handle any size.

    ○   Column level locking should be supported with no limit to the number of locks held. Memory should be used sparingly to hold locks.

    ○   A lob can be of unlimited size.

    ○   Full transaction recovery is supported to the last committed transaction or point in time.

    ○   Versioning (auditing) is inherently supported, enabling immediate tracking of any changes made, and being able rollback or forward, and review not only what changes were made but also who made them and at what time.

    ○   Data can be encrypted and checksums or equivalent made to ensure protection from corruption.

    ○   Any lob can be loaded in parallel or streamed (read) in parallel and the structure must be able to handle working with a large number of cores (CPUs)

    ○   Memory is used efficiently and can make intelligent use of memory as the volume grows into the hundreds of gigabytes.

    The goal is to identify natural bottlenecks and limitations in the design and recognize what the cost is to achieve certain requirements. For versioning/auditing the obvious design issue is how to minimize and manage the large amount of data that would be generated to achieve this goal.

    Typically for each feature there is a balance or trade off. To achieve performance, storage might be sacrificed, or to enable certain functions, memory or CPU might be used. The aim is to determine what these trade-offs are and see as the system scales, whether they become a bottleneck.

8
Tuning

This chapter covers the techniques for identifying and tuning scalability issues with an Oracle Database containing unstructured data. It covers how-to tuning methods, understanding the limitations of the database, and what scalability truly means. It also covers the basics for a database administrator who just wants to know the steps for quickly tuning, as well as how to utilize features in the Oracle Database that can help it to scale. Parts of this chapter are aimed at the novice database administrator and have been identified as such.

Introduction to tuning

A controversial statement that I challenge most organizations with is that the greatest causes of tuning issues in the environment are the ones which can be attributed to management. Management have to balance the business needs and determine the appropriate technology that should be used in an organization. This can be based on either key business objectives or the need to address the pain felt by users within the organization.

What is not well known is that a manager is responsible for the culture within the work environment. This includes ensuring a good rapport between the technology groups (or vendor) and that there is a free flow of information between the groups.

A manager, who has minimal to no technological training can easily fall prey to the latest trend or rumor being circulated about what is the best direction to follow. They might decide to switch the whole environment from Windows to Linux, because it has been seen to be cheaper. They might swap out hardware for a new vendor on the understanding that it's more reliable and faster. They might choose a development methodology for the environment, because it's the most cost-effective. Justified from a pure business case, these decisions can be hard to refute, as they make a strong and logical case.

Making the business decision to switch databases might be met with resistance with the claim that the application will need to be rewritten. The logical step that management will take is that the application should be written to work against any database. As covered further later, this decision can result in a worst case tuning scenario eventuating.

A decision might be made to switch hardware because of cost. Even though the database is supported on both platforms, the one it's being switched to might not be considered Tier 1, meaning any bugs or performance issues encountered will take longer to resolve.

A manager might decide to take advantage of a new development methodology, because it's being raved about in magazines, and it seems like it's a must to use. They push it on the developer team without realizing that the application tool is not designed to work with it. As a result, the code developed is sub-standard and hard to manage.

A manager to save on costs outsources the database administration environment to another company. Not realizing that administration involves more than just physical maintenance and backups, the lack of oversight by the DBAs results in code written that is sub-standard, has security holes in it, and doesn't scale. One of the biggest mistakes a manager can make is to outsource their database administration team and then put up a change management wall between them.

A manager, who is reactive might see that the database administrators and developers are in constant conflict. Each claiming the other group has no experience or idea about how to do their job. The manager might outsource one group or put up strict change management procedures between them to try and keep the peace. Rather than recognizing that the better solution is to get the two groups to work closer with each, the building up of a barrier between the two seems like the best solution. The result is that the database administrators are unable to audit and easily check the architecture, design, and code with a likely result that inefficient SQL statements are written. Developers who have no confidence in their database administrator might try and do their own tuning with the result that without having a good understanding of scalability, they introduce features which just don't scale well.

The walls between the two groups might be so daunting to surmount that the developers, rather than going through the constant pain of dealing with the database administrators, instead install their own lightweight database which cannot scale but is one which they can control. Their solution is to take the database administrator out of the equation.

The role of change management is to ensure consistent communication between all the different groups in an organization so that work practices that might cause a conflict can be identified. A database administrator might want to upgrade the database on the same weekend the financial team need it to do their reconciliation. Without change management, one side will cause conflict with the other. Change management has a key role in an organization, and organizations that do not have it will inevitably implement it after there is a serious incident. When used correctly, it can ensure that errors do not occur in the environment that impact customers. It can also be used as a tool to slow down procedures so much that it becomes incredibly hard to do any work. Change management involves negotiation between all the different groups. Each trying to put forward a business case for why they need to perform a task, each trying to convince the others of the priority of it being done. A manager can insist that all requests between the database administration team and the developer team are handled via change requests. This slows down development, making it very hard to perform basic operations. Tuning and checking for scalability actions are then not performed with the result that when the application reaches production, it performs poorly.

A manager decides that they don't like the idea of being locked into PL/SQL and insists that all coding is done externally in other open source languages. The result is that the developers cannot take advantage of any PL/SQL capabilities, which would result in faster performance in the database.

A manager decides to use a third-party code generating tool, which offers the ability for rapid application development, can work against multiple databases and requires less developers. On implementation the developers, who use it, are unable to navigate through the complex generated code and determine why the code will not scale. They are also at a loss to explain why the code generates inefficient SQL commands and why it produces badly designed joins. They also notice that it's very difficult to work with the generated code, as they make attempts to scale it to handle more users and larger data volumes.

All these cases cited earlier are hypothetical scenarios but are based on real-life exposure, resulting from observations of how different companies and organizations work. The most efficient ones are the ones where the manager creates a culture within the environment that encourages the database administrators to work closely with the developers, trust each other, and work together to reach a final product.

When working with multimedia and unstructured data the issues are still the same. However, as the technology is new, the tuning methodologies are slightly different, as well as a lack of skill and knowledge in development, problem shooting and tuning, there is going to be apprehension by management in how best to create an environment for these different groups to work effectively with each other.

For managers, there is no easy solution to creating an effective culture that encourages creativity and efficient communications between the different groups. Each group has different personalities. Each group has different skills and experiences. Each group has staff with their own private goals, technological ideologies, and personal issues. Each group has staff who are vocal or quiet, who are dominant or passive, who are hard workers, or some who are cruising and will take advantage of their employer. That's why good managers are so difficult to find and why it's so hard to train one. The manager is a crucial and important piece in the tuning puzzle. They are often overlooked and rarely ever taken into consideration at any point in the tuning methodology. Without taking them into consideration, all methodologies have major flaws in them. They are not realistic in the real world and can only offer hypothetical solutions assuming all staff behave in the same robotic way.

A manager, who can create an effective culture, is one who has a good understanding of people. They understand emotions, and by using fuzzy logic principles intuitively, they can create an environment where there is efficient communication, tuning issues are identified before the hardware is even purchased, and they are adaptable in a complex and chaotic environment that people create.

An ineffective one is one who ends up trying to treat their computing area as just coders, the equivalent of the old typing pool mentality, one where they don't trust the skill of their staff and make all the decisions themselves. These environments result in ones in which tuning issues constantly appear and are hard to resolve. Ones in which the database vendor ends up getting the blame, because everyone points fingers at everyone else and the one not in the room incurs the burden of being at fault for the problem.

There are no tuning methodologies that factor in management, and this book is not going to attempt to cover that. **Rapid Application Development (RAD)** and the variations of it made attempts in this area and touched on parts of it but never took into account the bigger picture. As such, they like all tuning methodologies that are fundamentally flawed. They will help and provide a guide that will get the database administrator or developer part of the way in resolving an tuning issue but will never provide a foolproof tuning method.

Tuning methodologies

In the TV show "House", the main character is renowned for his ability to diagnose incredibly complicated medical problems. He has a team of doctors to help him and even part of the show goes through how without his team he can't make accurate diagnosis. Usually, in the final 5 minutes of the show and for dramatic effect, House deduces the solution out of left field (serendipity) when an event causes him to think about the problem differently. He starts focusing, has a glazed look, and comes up with the solution very confidently.

It's tempting for database administrators to adopt a similar strategy. They would assemble a team of administrators and work together to deduce what the problem is using any method, no matter how controversial the method is to arrive at the correct remedy to fix the issue.

What we are actually seeing in the TV show "House" is a doctor who follows a methodology that is reactive. With his team, he rules out all the obvious solutions. Tries other solutions to fix the problem, and when they don't work, he tries other methods. His team are there to do the obvious. What is not explained is how House really comes up with the solution and it's not by following a methodology. House, unintentionally, employs a De Bono lateral thinking technique using the funnel method (this is a thinking technique where there is a base starting concept). The thinker then jumps from point to point with this concept following a method, drilling down until a point is reached. The funnel in effect hones the original concept until done. It might be completely different to the start point. The aim is to use a random starting point to force the thinker into an environment outside the box. What is happening is that some external event or comment forces House to think outside the box to take his argument from a completely new angle that he hadn't considered before. From there, using his expert deductive skills, he is able to narrow down on the solution to the issue.

It's not a team of experts that solve the diagnosis puzzle, it's an idea generated that enables the doctor to look at the issue in a new framework.

Techniques like this are never taught in database-tuning courses. They go through the traditional step-by-step methods. These are methods which are controlled and logical. They are an important step and in a number of cases can determine what the tuning issue is or isn't, but they will not work in all cases. Sometimes, it takes an event to cause a lateral thinking moment to enable the actual problem to be correctly diagnosed. De Bono utilizes provocative thinking techniques to force the person solving the problem to be challenged, and therefore, to be pushed outside of their box. Well-experienced database administrators will have adopted these techniques without even realizing it. They will just have the ability to see problems and come out with solutions from left field and then hone them down using the preferred tuning methodology.

This technique starts with emotions, random starting points, and fuzzy logic patterns. As the idea is fine-tuned, it gets to a point where traditional logic and tuning methods can be adopted and used. The funnel enables a wide range of initial starting points to be funneled towards a solution. This isn't dismissing the current tuning methods, all it's saying is they have a place towards the end of the tuning method and in most cases will not help when used as the only method.

So, these tuning methodologies are not to be dismissed. They are important. They are useful in the database administrator diagnostic tool pack. But they are not the only tuning techniques an administrator should have in their arsenal.

When tuning databases with unstructured data and multimedia, traditional tuning techniques might fail as the rules regarding them no longer make sense. It's still too early in the maturity of multimedia databases to fully understand all the tuning techniques needed, so novel and interesting solutions to tuning problems are needed.

Most database training, covering tuning, has a relational focus. The training courses focus on proactive or reactive tuning. The focus is on logical methods for tuning. As working with unstructured data constantly shows, the rules change. More needs to be done to look at the overall issue with tuning. As already stated, one key issue missed with tuning is the ability for the database administrator and developer to tune the management decisions that are made. They might have input, but they have no control over it, especially once the decision is made. As discussed, this is a cultural tuning issue which the manager has to address to resolve. Another important one that is missed is understanding the psychology of the two groups and how to get them to work better together.

Most database tuning ignores the psychological aspect. Database administrators and developers have different skills and personalities. Some administrators are loud mouthed and obnoxious, and belittle the intelligence of the developers. Some developers loathe their database administrator and will do anything they can to avoid dealing with them, including giving them access to the code to tune with.

A key and often missing and neglected component to tuning involves ensuring there is a good relationship between the database administrator and the development team. In addition, there should also be good relationships with the system administration team and network team.

Reactive versus proactive (for the novice administrator)

Over the last 8 years, as I have attended and listened to various tuning seminars, a common message has appeared. Tuning for the bottleneck methodology or reactive tuning is not the best way to tune a database. The arguments put forward are always compelling and hard to logically dispute. Yet a lot of database administrators are required to perform reactive tuning.

But first, let's cover what reactive tuning is. It can be referred to as tuning the bottleneck. The goal is to determine what the slow point is and then focus and do tuning tasks to address that slow point. When that is resolved, the database administrator moves to the next slow point and tunes that. The administrator is constantly reacting to a perceived bottleneck and tuning just that issue. The administrator might see that some queries are consuming more than 50 percent of the CPU. They focus on determining why they are slow and tuning them by using the most efficient method they know.

Interestingly, there is a mathematical equivalent analogy to this tuning methodology called the *Newton–Raphson method*[1]. This is a method used to solve the root of a real-value function. Simply, you have a function that needs resolving (a tuning issue to fix). You make a calculated guess at the starting point based on observation, intuition, experience, and maybe, a set of existing data/facts. You then use some calculus on the function, feed the starting point calculation/guess in, and hopefully, the result is an answer that is close to the solution. Feed that result back into the equation and hopefully, that result gets closer to the actual answer. It's a tool useful in mathematics for finding an approximate solution but never the exact solution. The challenge is that a bad starting point or an equation that does not lend itself well to this method can result in unpredictable and wildly inaccurate results. Reactive tuning is the same. You make a calculated guess at the bottleneck, tune it, see what happens, and then tune the next issue. A bad starting point or a database not suited for this methodology can result in the methodology failing to tune or in some cases making the situation worse.

Another analogy is a hiker lost in the woods wandering around. They need to get to a high point to see where they should be. However, from where they are in the woods, it's not obvious which is the biggest hill or best hill to climb to get the best perspective of the surrounding area. So, they make a calculated guess at the best hill to start. They then try it, climb it, and hopefully, from there they can see a better hill to climb. In some cases, they cannot see a better hill, and they continue wandering aimlessly around. In this case, climbing the hill is tuning the bottleneck. There might be a number of bottlenecks and tuning one might just be climbing the smallest hill. Without a global perspective, it's very difficult to map an efficient path and so tune correctly.

The attraction of a proactive tuning methodology is that the database administrator starts with a global view of the entire system and can then determine which areas truly need to be tuned. The prioritized steps as defined in the Oracle documentation are as follows:

1. Tune the business rules.
2. Tune the data design.
3. Tune the application design.

4. Tune the logical structure of the database.

5. Tune database operations.

6. Tune the access paths.

7. Tune memory allocation.

8. Tune I/O and physical structure.

9. Tune resource contention.

10. Tune the underlying platform(s).

This tuning method follows a structured and logical approach for tuning. It's well-tested, well-proven, and shown to deliver results. The problem is, it's not really proactive tuning in the correct sense. It's more like the development waterfall methodology. It's structured and ensures all the obvious steps are covered.

A proposal for a true proactive database environment is detailed in *Appendix D, Chapter References*. This covers a tuning methodology that is adaptable and attempts to be truly proactive.

With these different methodologies, the administrator can be confused as to which one is the best to use. The Oracle manual states that the prioritized steps is best done during the development phase while reactive tuning is best covered during production.

The challenge raised is that the computing environment of the 2010's (2010 and above) is very different to when these methodologies were first devised. There are now a large number of third-party applications that companies own, which are either mixed in with an existing environment or remain separate. In a lot of cases, the database administrator cannot access the development team, as they are a vendor. More so, the administrator might not be able to even access the code, because it's delivered in its compiled or encrypted format. For these systems, the tuning solutions are limited:

- Throw more hardware at it
- Raise the tuning issue with the vendor and request tuning improvements
- Make changes to database parameters, or reverse engineer SQL statements and try and tune them (which is a feature now available in Oracle with its automated tuning option)

For a third-party application, the only tuning method available to the database administrator is reactive. They have to assume that the application is well-tuned, and when issues arise, they have to try to tune the faults. So, no matter how much the bottleneck methodology is attacked and dismissed as being potentially dangerous, when it comes to managing third-party applications, this method is likely the only one that can be used.

So, with a multimedia database, the rules change. When a row in the database can be 10 GB in size, which could be greater than an entire relational database, the attitude to tuning needs to be reviewed. All aspects of the tuning methodology need to be checked to see if they are valid and make sense. But before going down that path, it's important to define what a **database administrator (DBA)** is meant to do.

What is the role of the DBA?

This section is aimed at the novice administrator, and the goal is to cover the psychology behind database administration.

What does it take to be a DBA and an Oracle DBA at that, in today's programming environment? One which is now continually seen as extreme or RAD development environment? From eating boxes of donuts, intimidating developers, holding the keys to the database, to being arrogant, obnoxious, and spiteful, the DBA's role is one which most don't understand. Are they the Gods of the database world or a bunch of wannabe developers too naive to work out a `for` loop from an `if` statement?

When a DBA becomes a developer, the perspective changes. Having a foot in both camps lends itself to an appreciation of how complex the issues are that both sides have to contend with. The role of the DBA and developer is changing, especially when the technologies change, as the rules change too.

So, what is the fundamental role of a DBA? The following is a definition I coined 20 years ago to address this and is still valid:

> "To ensure that the database performs to its optimal, it is fully secured and can be recovered in time of need."

From this core definition, many ideas about what a DBA really can now be formulated. This definition is covered in greater detail in *Appendix C, Proactive Database Tuning*.

History

When it comes to looking at DBAs, there are two extremes. The first (which most developers are confident that the DBAs in their environment match) are the over-confident, power-mad DBAs who slow down everything, enforce draconian change management procedures, treat with disdain any request given to them, and demand compensation to do tasks. These DBAs came into being most likely, because they can handle the stress, have a tinkering mindset, and a knack for problem solving. They view any form of programming as a coding job (beneath them) and are annoyed by the antics of the developers who they view as inefficient SQL writing coders. The power they have been given or taken has ensured that they live in their ivory tower free from the worry and concerns of the masses (mundane developers).

At the other end of the spectrum are the puppet DBAs. These are DBAs who have been given the position by developers, who needed to do something with the team members they couldn't trust to code, couldn't work with or couldn't get rid of. Being under-skilled and under-valued, their sole role is to make sure the backups run, and they stay out of the way of developers who themselves control the design, performance, and the running of the database. Every now and then, the developers who are bored, throw the DBAs a performance-tuning bone for them to work on.

The point to note is that if you see yourself at one end of the spectrum or the other, which is important somewhere in between this spectrum (anywhere in between), then it's too late. The culture of the organization is the problem, and it needs to change.

To be an effective DBA, the culture of the organization needs to drastically change. Some fundamental concepts need to be changed as well. The models used in the past have failed, because they do not take into account personalities, bureaucracy, and the natural direction red tape takes in any organization (which is to gradually grow to the point of paralysis). They also don't consider changing technology, team members, and group dynamics. Red tape is normally introduced as a protection measure. A person makes a mistake, so a procedure is introduced to ensure that mistake doesn't happen again. Sometimes the procedures are good to have; sometimes common sense would be quicker and better. So, when a procedure is introduced, before it is implemented, the reasons why it is implemented should be reviewed.

Now lets side track for a moment and look at the word, incompetent, as this will be used a number of times. The dictionary definition from `http://www.dictionary.com` puts it as:

> Incompetent: lacking qualification or ability; not having suitable or sufficient skill, knowledge, experience (note that this definition is summarized).

So, the term doesn't really have the negative connotations we are used to when using the word. It really means the person needs more skill and ability.

Now back to the developer being incompetent and change management procedures. We should now ask whether introducing the procedure is really going to make life better for everyone, or is it being introduced, because the culture of the organization is afraid to realize that the problem was due to lack of skills and knowledge and are not willing to say that because of the conflict (read – potential personality clashes) that will result? Put in a procedure, and everyone is blameless. We move on and hope it doesn't happen again. The procedure absolves the problem. Great in theory, but all that happens is that the procedures grow and restrict the flexibility and adaptability of the organization. If technology didn't change or if the rules didn't change, then this might be reasonable. But it is changing, it's a dynamic playing field, and the procedures will get in the way and stifle the effectiveness of the group. If the procedure must go in, give it a six-month life expectancy and review it at that time period to see if the reason for having it is still valid. In some cases, slowing down the process is effective, but there has to be a change in the culture to realize why the rules and procedures are there, and know when they are redundant.

But back to the original point of this discussion and that is, what needs to change in the DBA and developer world? What cultural changes are needed? Let's throw some punches, get our hands dirty, and raise six concepts:

- The first concept is that the DBA works closely together with the developers, and this is within shouting distance. Keeping them separated, by a partition, a wall, a floor, a building, or even locating interstate is a recipe for disaster.

  Outsourcing the DBAs to another company is the worst thing an organization can do. If this was done to save money, then it's apparent that the managers are incompetent and should be told so. Organizations that put a barrier up between the DBAs and the users are preventing communication, application development time, and introducing hidden performance problems.

- DBAs must be taught to have interpersonal skills. They must be able to talk to users. They need an attitude adjustment. DBAs can be their own worst enemy. By being arrogant, aloof, or just plain incompetent, they can hide their lack of knowledge behind slick computer terms and change management procedures.

- DBAs must be able to program. They must have a thorough understanding of the programming language the developers are using. They must have a very good understanding of computer human design concepts. They must know how the users use the application. Performance and tuning isn't just tweaking the engine, it's also looking at how the user drives the application. This is such a fundamental concept, yet it is never seriously raised in tuning books – the mentality has always been to fix the SQL, which is just part of the issue. It's not the whole issue. But because DBAs lack those skills for dealing with users, they are kept away from them (who knows what they might say to them).

- DBAs must have business sense, understand the needs of the organization and be able to balance the cost and deadlines of a project, working with them, not against them. A DBA can be a manager's nightmare, because they always slow things down, make life hard for everyone, and use procedures as a justification for not achieving. They need to understand the business and look at the bigger picture as well. Of course, if managers insist on separating the DBAs from the developers, it's no wonder they don't appreciate the big picture, as they are kept away from being a part of it.

- A good DBA is one who makes their position dispensable. A good DBA is lazy. But lazy in that they will make the database/computer do the work for them. They will spend 10 hours writing a program to monitor the system and report on it, just so that they can sit back and read the latest Dilbert cartoon and read up on the latest Oracle releases.

- A good DBA is not only proactive; they know what that term means and actively implement the concepts behind it in their environment. They don't say it or preach it, they do it.

In the comfort zone dilemma, the challenge is to realize that by our very nature we adopt a conservative approach. Using new technology is hard, risky, and it can hurt the head just learning about it. It can be hard to motivate ourselves to learn to use it, we resist it. We sometimes wish it didn't change. Technology is changing as rapidly as it did 10 and 20 years ago, and we must realize that concepts, ideas, and assumptions once made (our belief system) needs to be challenged, because it's likely out of date. I would hope that the older generation DBAs would have learned from this and taken a less orthodox and more adaptive approach based on experience, but the opposite often can be seen. They don't want change, hope things don't change, resist change, or adopt change at a slow rate (a sign of this is seen by the length of time it takes to upgrade to later releases). The younger generation just coming out of university, who have had to go through the changes, are keen and eager, and this enthusiasm can be mistaken for ability. So the youngsters are given the reigns, without the experience and end up making the same mistakes, and the cycle continues.

Concerning the issue of the aging DBA, there is a myth about having to be young to program. This is leading to the culture of an organization fostering the view that management is the only progressive position to be in. To earn the extra money, one has to manage. It's good that this myth is starting to crumble, as organizations start to realize this is not the case. It's also dangerous, as most people, who are good at IT, are not good managers. Sometimes this is seen in the *Peter Principle concept*[2].

The role of the DBA in most organizations must change. For this to happen, management must take responsibility and change the culture of the organization to ensure their role can change. The DBA must move out of isolation and be skilled, so that they can communicate effectively and be given sufficient power and control to do their tasks. They need to be given more verbal say in the security of programs, be able to review code, and work closely with the developers in the very early stages of design.

Tuning trend

Over the last 20 years, there has been a noticeable trend when it comes to improving database performance. Techniques are developed which sacrifice storage to improve performance. The common index is the first example of this. The index is much smaller in size and can dramatically improve performance of queries. Materialized views are copies of the data stored optimally to improve performance. Locally managed tablespaces reduce fragmentation but can waste storage. A very large UNDO tablespace can enable flash back recovery, saving time when recovering from user errors. Database flashback consumes a large amount of storage and enables faster database rollback capabilities. Recovery performance is improved at the expense of an increase in storage. For a data warehouse, for every byte of actual data, the rough rule of thumb is to allow for 8 bytes of additional storage for indexing and other objects used to improve performance. The mantra is "disk is cheap". In comparison to memory and CPU, database administrators can now waste disk space to improve performance.

This trend has eventuated, because storage over the last 20 years has grown while maintaining a low-cost point. An individual off the shelf data disk can be of 3 terabytes in size and cost under $200. 10 years ago, the largest sized disk was approaching 100 GB and its cost was around $400. 20 years ago, a large disk was one that was of 100 MB in size and most of the shelf disks were around 40 MB in size.

The amount of data relational applications need has not changed that much. Because storage has increased, the applications have started to grow to take advantage of this abundant storage. Most applications now use very large audit tables which are never deleted. These audit tables are also useful for analysis. Electronic applications store all clicks and everything a user does. This enables greater analysis to determine purchasing behavior. Intelligence agencies capture screen information of all users.

The introduction of **Solid State Drives** (**SSD**) has changed the rules. In the early days of database tuning, it was easily seen that the Oracle Database was designed to balance the retrieval of data between memory (which was very fast but limited and volatile, meaning, when power was lost, so too was the memory contents), versus the retrieval of data from disk (which was a magnitude slower, large amount but non-volatile). The SSD is, in fact, a cross between memory and disk. It's not as fast as memory but is non-volatile and a lot faster than disk. It's limited and costly. A 128-GB SSD is the same price as a 2-TB Sata disk. The SSD model also has reliability issues and is best suited for read-only environments when it can be then considered to be incredibly fast and reliable.

So, the database administrator now has a three-tier balancing act with tuning. They now have to balance memory, SSD, and disk. Oracle 11 introduced a feature on some platforms, where the Oracle SGA can be extended to the SSD. In effect, creating a **Non-Uniform Memory Access** (**NUMA**) environment involves an architecture, where the memory is distributed, and the access to the memory can vary depending on whether its local or not to the CPU. The Oracle Database has built in smarts within the SGA to work with this architecture. The disk environment has also changed with the introduction of SANs with the database administrator now balancing local storage and access with SAN access.

Scalability

When dealing with Multimedia, one has to look at the different dimensions of scalability to best understand how the Oracle Database best handles it.

Scalability is defined by how well an application performs without code change, as the number of objects, their size, and how they are accessed increases. A database scales well when minimal to no structural changes are needed when an application is initially configured. As an application grows (based on the dimensions described later), it is up to the database with assistance from various modules within it, to control and manage performance. This includes managing the CPU, memory, disk I/O, and network bandwidth.

Scalability is bidirectional

A point often overlooked when it comes to understanding scalability is that it's needed in both directions. Too often the focus is on how many concurrent users one can manage or how many hundreds of terabytes of data can be stored. Organizations that the requirement of being able to support 10,000 concurrent users or require storage for a petabyte of data would be a very small percentage of the number of organizations in total. Yet, because of the marketing bragging rights, one obtains when one gets an organization at these levels is so powerful, the focus invariably always falls on taking the database to these extremes.

What is lost is moving in the other direction and scaling down. How quick and easy is it to scale the database down to a portable device? A server running with minimal specifications can run in the database. When looking at scalability at the other end, different break points are reached. The issues are less about locking and more about simplicity and ease of management. How easy is it to install? Can someone without any experience set up the database? What maintenance (if any) is needed on the database? How efficiently does the database self tune? How transparent and simple is it to set up and configure backups? In the event of failure, can the database recover itself? How easy is it to secure the database and are database administrators needed to manage it? How big is the kernel installation and base database footprint? How simple is it to enable databases to talk to each other and others from different vendors?

The strength of databases, such as MySQL and SQLite is that these databases are lightweight and very easy to install. Microsoft with SQLServer has developed a whole environment around tools to make database management for novice users as simple as possible.

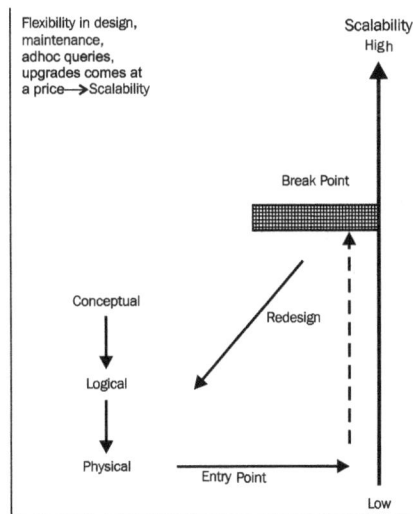

Oracle and other large-scale vendors, such as IBM with DB2, focus on the high end of scalability. Though Oracle offers a lite version of the database (Oracle XE, covered further later), its usage and management still requires an experienced developer or base skilled database administrator. Oracle provides a simple interface to managing the environment, but again in comparison to other vendors, whose whole business focus is on the small end market, their tools leave Oracle way behind. These vendors can scale downwards, but they do not scale well in the other direction.

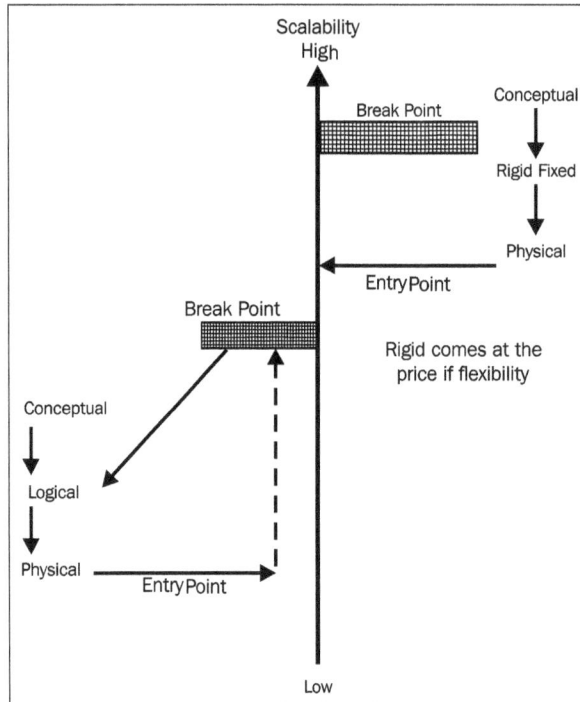

The question might then be asked, should a vendor such as Oracle even be focused on the small end of the market when it's well covered by a variety of other databases? It's a moving target. 20 years ago, a database that was 5 to 10 GB in size was considered very large. Now it's considered small. 12 years ago, a database close to a terabyte in size was likely to be in consideration as one of the world's largest, yet today is not considered that big. In 10 years' time, petabyte databases will be common and any database under a terabyte will be small.

It's very hard to fill up a database with data if it's only relational data. When unstructured data is factored into the equation, large volumes of data can easily be located and stored in these databases, enabling these large database sizes to be achieved. The market need shows that there will always be a lot of applications that are a fixed size. Even though the rules regarding what is considered to be large is changing on a yearly basis (the goal posts are moving upwards), focusing only on upwards scalability of the vast majority of applications can mean that their basic tuning requirements can easily be missed.

Database breakpoints

True scalability is defined by being able to take an application and add more users or data to it, and it can perform as well as it did with a small number of users or data accessing the database. Breakpoints occur when as the numbers start to increase a showstopper of a bottleneck appears, dramatically slowing the application down. Breakpoints can occur for a number of reasons.

Locking

In the classic break-point, 20 years ago, the locking mechanism in a database was simple. Data was stored in a page (or block), and when a row was modified, the page was locked. Any other rows in that page were locked by default as well. The locking mechanism was simple and worked well until the number of users started to grow and the block size increased. What happened was that with the increase in user numbers, the probability of a row a user needed being in a locked page increased. That user would wait for it to become free. Any locks the user had would impact other users. The end result was that the break point of between 30 to 60 concurrent users was reached, making it impossible for more users to be added. The solution was to either re-architect the application to attempt to get around the locking (defeating transparent scalability), or the database was modified to include the more efficient row-level locking.

The issue with locking became even more complex when locking on indexes had to be factored in. Unfortunately, row-level locking couldn't just be introduced to the database. It required more complex lock management, and a number of database vendors could not easily rebuild their database to include row-level locking, and achieve transparent scalability without incurring performance issues in other areas (some vendors stored locks in memory, so when moving to row locking the amount of memory required to manage the locks would increase to the point where memory, which could be used for caching or for user-processing, had to be used for locking).

CPU limits

If each user running a query uses 2 percent of CPU, what happens when there are more than 50 concurrent users? Can the database scale to use more CPUs (make uses of more cores) or can the database incorporate features reducing the 2 percent figure down to a smaller figure?

Memory limits

If each user connected to the database has a session which uses memory for querying, sorting, and storing temporary values, what happens when the number of users grows to a point where the total memory requirement exceeds the memory of the box? Can the database increase its memory usage to handle large amounts (for example, work with a 64-bit, thus enabling it to handle terabytes of memory) or can it use a more efficient architecture for memory management (in effect, is enabling memory to be shared more efficiently)?

The breakpoint, when reached, required the database to switch to a multi-threaded solution, enabling memory to be shared more efficiently. The introduction of web-based applications with stateless page requests simplified and reduced the memory footprint per user, at times by 10 to 20 times less.

Hardware limits

If after the CPU and memory has been tuned as much as it can be, can the application transparently scale beyond one server? Oracle introduced RAC to deal with this issue, but it can be argued that transparent scalability was never achieved. The question is, can an application be moved to an RAC environment, without any changes being made and scalability be achieved? In some cases the answer is yes but not in all. With each version of RAC, the transparent scalability has been improved. The real goal with transparent scalability and hardware is to be able to add one or more servers, without limit, without changing the application.

This can't be achieved, no matter what is said or promised. Generally, the applications built that can take advantage of an MPP environment (Massively Parallel) have to be built using specialized languages and database storage. So, they can scale to massive levels, but they are not transparently scalable.

Database limits

As more storage and users are added to the database, are natural limits (limits around maximum file size, database size, or object size) hit? Is a table in a database limited to a maximum number of extents (preventing growth beyond a certain size)? Does the data dictionary have limits for managing and handling sessions? Is the database constrained to 32-bit capabilities?

Database management

It might take 10 minutes to move a 100-GB table between different storage locations, but how long will it take to move a terabyte table? As the database grows in size, is it possible for the administrator to even manage it? Do tasks that might normally take an hour to run take over a hundred when large volumes of data are stored? Transparent scalability also needs to be factored in at the database level. If an administrator cannot effectively manage the database as it grows, then the database could become unusable.

Backup/recovery

How long does it take to back up a 10 terabyte database? In the event of failure, how long does it take to recover it?

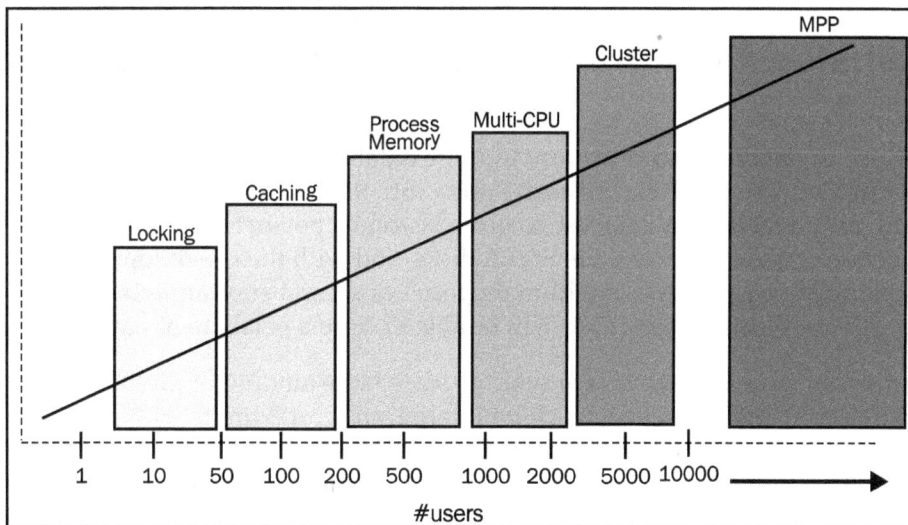

Multimedia scalability

An application is seen to not scale if the development team have to make major code and structural changes, as the number of images grow or their size grows. An application scales optimally if the DBA has to perform minimal to no maintenance on the application as it grows. Maintenance that the DBA can perform includes index management (creating, moving, or removing), storage management (tablespace location), and database management (tuning memory parameters). Scalability is also determined by how well the optimizer behaves, as the number of images grow. Impacting scalability is whether the database is on-line while the DBA performs maintenance on it.

Dimension 1 – loading a large number of multimedia files

In this case, scalability is seen by how well a large number of files can be loaded into the database. Issues seen by most systems that attempt large file loading include being unable to load in parallel, that is, memory leakage.

In Oracle Multimedia (scalability results) is Oracle's new 11G Securefile BLOBS that allows loading of files much faster than using traditional BLOBS. This is largely due to the fact that Oracle's core architect supports parallel loading.

Dimension 2 – storing a large number of multimedia files

In this case, scalability is seen by how well the database handles the storage of a large number of files. The database can easily grow into the multi-terabyte size. If video is stored, it's possible for a database to grow beyond a petabyte. With the recent introduction of a low-cost terabyte SATA disks, and with the use of low-cost SAN's, the ability to store a petabyte is within the reach of a number of organizations. Within 5 years, most organizations will be able to store a petabyte of data.

Issues seen by most systems that attempt to store large amount of files include hitting limits on the image size, reaching internal structural limits within the database (max number of files that store data), issues running on 64-bit systems, dealing with fragmentation and the efficient management of those images (for example, backup/recovery).

An Oracle BLOB can be unlimited in size. Oracle's use of tablespaces allow a large number of multimedia files to be stored in it. By using locally managed tablespaces, fragmentation is removed as a performance issue. With the ability to control where a blob is stored, files can be split across multiple tablespaces and devices. Using partitioning on LOBS allows a very large number of multimedia files to be stored and efficiently managed. Using RMAN, Oracle can be configured to back up large amounts of data.

Dimension 3 – loading a very large multimedia file

In this case, scalability is seen by how well the database can handle a very large file. A TIFF image can grow beyond 1 GB in size. A video is typically 5 GB in size but now with high definition, a video can be 50 to 100 GB in size.

Issues seen by most systems include failure of the database to store the file and then to process it. Transactional control is also an issue. If the file is loaded into the database, can it be rolled back? On recovery of the database, is the file recovered as well? Not all database management systems can deal efficiently with a large file and most do not handle files within a transaction.

With Oracle Multimedia, different multimedia types are handled by different objects. For a very large georaster image, Oracle Spatial creates a pyramid index on it, ensuring the efficient retrieval of it that allows for zooming in and out of it. For a JPEG or TIFF image, Oracle uses tiling to manage very large images. The use of the Java JIT compiler ensures that the processing of these images is done as fast as possible.

Dimension 4 – retrieving a large number of multimedia files

In this case, scalability is seen by how fast files can be delivered to a large number of users. Issues to be addressed include how well the database can handle a large number of concurrent requests and deliver them. Most systems have issues handling a large number of concurrent requests. Some require an application extension so that it can interface with a transaction-processing monitor. To scale, some require more memory and CPUs to be added as the only method for improving performance. In most cases, adding the extra computer resources only marginally improves the performance.

The Oracle Database can economically grow and work with multiple CPUs and very large amounts of memory. However, before this situation arises, Oracle's built-in transaction multi-threaded model ensures that memory per session is used optimally and is reused (no memory leaks). The result is more users being able to access the database and retrieve the data quickly.

The ability to cache BLOBS and to put a fence around processes ensures that users retrieving multimedia files can get small ones fast, but if they are retrieving a large file, they will be bound within the limits of the resource manager and can even be automatically throttled back if the file to be retrieved is large. This ensures that more users can connect to the database and retrieve images, and prevents one user from hogging all the network bandwidth.

Improvements to the cost-based optimizer ensure that the database smartly adjusts itself to the load of the machine, disk speed, number of users, and data volume.

Dimension 5 – database management

In this case, if a DBA has to perform administration, how fast can it be done and what impact is there?

Issues seen by most systems include not being able to modify the structure of a table or create an index on it without obtaining exclusive access to it. What really determines how scalable an application is when the schema is enhanced and modified? It's generally considered that once a database grows beyond 500 GB in size, the time taken to do a full backup of it is beyond what most users would consider to be reasonable downtime. This forces the database to be online when it is backed up, resulting in a 24 x 7 application. Web-based applications are typically 24 x 7 as well. Achieving true 24 x 7 is quite difficult and can be expensive. The aim is to ensure that downtime is kept to a minimum (it's how much downtime users can afford).

So, what determines whether a database can scale is what schema modifications can be done to it, while online and while users are accessing it. Also of importance is the added ability of being able to rollback changes if failure occurs. This rollback capability becomes even more important if a backup is required to be done before maintenance commences. If a backup can take upwards of 10 or 20 hours (because of the sheer size of the database), then being able to quickly rollback an upgrade without taking a backup improves the efficiency of the upgrade.

In addition to Oracle offering the ability to rollback a database, most DDL commands can now be performed online. Major structural table changes can be done carefully using Oracle's redefinition feature. Addition, removal, and modification of columns with indexes can now all be done online.

General considerations

Some additional considerations should be considered when looking at whether a database truly scales.

Loading in parallel

With the computing industry now accepting and moving towards multi-core chips, the ability to do tasks in parallel can dramatically improve the performance. The core architecture of the Oracle Database supports loading of multimedia files in parallel. Internal memory structures can efficiently handle the multiple requests and the structure of Oracle tablespaces ensures that this loading can be done without having to make programmatic changes.

Insert/delete performance

Oracle's new Securefile LOBS ensures high speed insert and delete performance. Testing has shown dramatic improvements over the traditional storage.

Extreme scalability

Extreme scalability is a new concept that has appeared with the increase in popularity of social networks and Google. For these applications, the aim is to build an application that can handle tens of millions of concurrent users and petabytes of data. This scalability can only be achieved when the application is built from the ground up with this goal in mind. It is not easy to achieve and requires certain rules regarding data consistency to be bent. It also involves being able to run the application across thousands of servers.

Object-oriented development

The Oracle Database supports the creation of objects and object methods within the database. The simplest case just covers the use of **Abstract Data Types (ADT)**. This is where a new data type is created from existing data types.

Object Development uses a number of key capabilities including classes, dynamic dispatch, polymorphism, inheritance, and methods. Systems developed using methodologies based around object-oriented development, have been shown and proven to scale incredibly well to tens of thousands of concurrent users and large data stores.

When it comes to tuning though, the object-oriented architecture suffers from a flaw which is also cited as one of its strengths, and that is *Encapsulation*[3]. It means that the internal representation of an object is generally hidden from view outside of the object's definition.

Encapsulation is incredibly attractive for developers and it's hard to fault the concepts behind it. Hiding the internals of the object protects its integrity by preventing users from setting the internal data of the component to an invalid or inconsistent state. A benefit of encapsulation is that it can reduce system complexity, and thus increases robustness, by allowing the developer to limit the inter-dependencies between software components.

When it comes to database tuning, one needs to realize that its strength of hiding is also a potential weakness. It's one which the database administrator has to be intrinsically aware of and be in a position to control and monitor. This can be demonstrated using a basic concept used by most databases, the view.

A view is an abstraction above the physical data layer. It's a query that looks like a table. In fact when set up correctly, it can be impossible to tell a view apart from a table. It's possible to perform DML operations against a view. Views can be created on top of other views.

In the example, there are five tables: table A, table B, table C, table D, and table E. A developer creates a view called table X on top of table A, table B, and table C and returns some of the columns from table A and table B, but none from table C. The developer then creates a view called table Y on top of table D and table E.

Another developer comes in and wants information from table C and sees table X. They then create a new view on table X and table C, not knowing that table X is a view and already accesses table C.

They then create a new view called table Z on top of table Y and table B. Another developer sees table Z but realizes not all the columns they want for display are there, so they create a new view on table Z and table C.

Already we are creating a scenario where, unknowingly, views are being created on top of other views. Also, redundant joins between views is being performed which can cause query degradation.

The goal of hiding the complexity of the joins and to create a simple set of views has resulted in an optimal environment for the developers, but a potential tuning nightmare for the database administrators, who if called about bad performance, will be required to do tuning.

With Oracle11, there are key optimization features designed to address the issue of nested views and even though the optimizer has efficient smarts in handling this; it's best to get the architecture right at the beginning rather than hoping the optimizer can work it out.

This can easily happen in objects using multimedia. A method might be created that is flexible and returns multiple results. Let's say that a method is created that returns the mime type of a digital object and all the other digital objects associated with it. A developer wanting just the mime-type will make a call to this routine, not realizing that the associated call of calculating the association might be an expensive operation, even though the results are discarded. If the developer then hides this call (encapsulates it), another developer making a call to the new return might not realize how inefficient the call really is.

This highlights some key points with tuning in an object environment:

- No abstraction layer should be hidden from the database administrator.
- Performance metrics should be documented with each call so that a developer, when referencing the call, can know up front if it's an expensive operation to invoke it. They then might try and find a more efficient call or build a new one from scratch.
- When creating views, only in exceptional circumstances where the database administrator has validated the view, should views be created that reference other views.
- It might be considered to be good form to hide the view name, but for tuning it's not. The developer should know they are accessing a view when writing a query against the database.

PC mentality

This is a term database administrators might apply to a developer that adopts a mentality that says, if what I have developed performs fine on my computer, it can scale and perform fine on any server.

Database administrators are trained to look at the bigger picture to understand the breaking points of the database and to realize how much load a disk can take and to deal with limited memory and complex transactions. A developer is not trained to appreciate these points. That's why it's important that:

- Developers do a basic course in database administration
- Database administrators do a basic course in application development

Each has to understand the needs of the other, yet most don't. As discussed, the object method hides the complexities of the database from the developer. When they build a method, they should be working with the administrator to determine what its limits and break points are. How large can the data volume be for a query before it takes too long to run? How long are the transactions and how well does the routine clean itself up on failure or on completion (some examples include locks and file opens)? In addition, is the routine secure or is it vulnerable to potential hacks?

The three tier – ignore the database mentality

This is a relative and rather new phenomena and has come about with the rise in simple relational databases and the mentality that three-tier computing is the only development environment that can scale.

In this scenario, the developers have been trained to work against a database that doesn't have an efficient optimizer. In some cases, the developer has not been trained to understand how to do a SQL join. In either case, the attitude is that it's more efficient to do the bulk of the work in the middle tier and just use the database as a dumb repository, with the view that all it's good for is just recovering and securing the data.

How many applications have been written where in the middle tier the developer has done the join themselves from first principles, rather than sending the SQL statement to the database to do the join?

In how many cases would the developer believe it's easier to have the database as some simple storage structure in the middle tier, than some complex beast in the third tier?

Oracle Exadata takes the reverse approach to this to achieve performance. Rather than reading the data in from disks and processing it in the database, the query is sent to the disk storage system, which retrieves and collates the information. One query is sent over the network and the result is returned. This ensures the network (which is the real bottleneck) is used minimally.

In the three-tier environment, a keen developer who believes in doing the joins themselves, doesn't realize that they are effectively sending to the database one or more requests to retrieve a large volume of data. They are flooding the network with data, and then likely using excessive CPU to perform a query that a database should be able to do more efficiently. This doesn't scale.

When working with multimedia, the three-tier architecture conflicts with the idea of storing the unstructured data in the database. The conclusion drawn from three-tier architectures is that it's more efficient to store the multimedia at the middle tier, usually in an open file system where it's easier to get at. This results in the data not being backed up or being secure.

Our application should be able to run against any database

This is one of the most dangerous scenarios a database administrator can come up against when required to tune an environment. It can be justified that the customer does not want to be locked into a database vendor. It can be justified that being able to work against multiple databases is more efficient. However, in either case, it's an incredibly bad decision to make.

The decision to be open is simply saying that the application has to be able to run against the lowest common denominator, that is, the worst running database. The developer cannot take advantage of key features in the database and cannot take advantage of many database features, because they likely will not port between the different databases. They have to keep it as simple as possible.

A decision needs to be made where to be locked into. Is it the operating system, the hardware, the database, or the application code? In most cases, it makes sense to be locked into a database. All the features of the database can be used. Backup and recovery features optimized for the database can be utilized. When it comes to tuning, it's easier to tune a database and make adjustments to the code base when the database is constant.

With the tuning methodologies covered, along with the role of the database administrator and what scalability actually is, it must be noted that the existing methodologies for tuning in the Oracle Database have to be adapted for unstructured data. As already covered, the best solution is to adapt existing methodologies to match the unique needs of multimedia.

The following section covers the basic tuning operations a database administrator needs to be aware of when tuning, and the unique differentiators found with multimedia.

Basic tuning operations

The following section focuses on key methods the administrator needs to be aware of when doing performance-tuning. The key area, as already covered is the network, which in traditional two-tier and three-tier environments, is generally treated as a lower priority for tuning. The section focuses mostly on application network tuning with a preference for HTTP and web service calls.

Network

I don't know how many people use the Microsoft Remote Desktop client. It replaces VNC and offers a secure, remote access to a desktop on a computer anywhere on the network or Internet. The client offers the ability to go into file explorer on the remote site and using the syntax, `\\tsclient\...`, to access the local drives on your computer. The feature is very powerful for doing copies, as it removes the need to use FTP, and it offers simple drag/drop capabilities. With scalability, the issue is that the Microsoft protocol usage just does not scale. Even over a megabit network connection, it can take 30 seconds to a minute to display a directory with 60 files in it.

The amount of information to transfer the 60 files is incredibly small, yet you can see that the transfer protocol is not designed to handle anymore than 10 files. It seems to request the information for one file, negotiate, and make numerous requests including security and attributes. It appears to do this multiple times per individual file, meaning that as the number of files in the directory grows, the more network requests are made. If Microsoft truly built this to scale, there would be just one request for the information to be compressed and sent over the network and then unbundled and displayed at the other end. If they tried, they could get this to work on a megabit Internet connection and retrieve information on over 1000 files in under a second.

What this shows is that the notion of network scalability is foreign to most developers, even the ones at Microsoft. Their solution is to insist on using a higher speed network (not possible when remote access is done on the Internet) rather than fixing the underlying flaw in this network protocol. Understanding network scalability is not natural skill that most developers and database administrators have.

The network is crucial for tuning with multimedia. It's going to be the likely cause of any bottlenecks. Application developers and database administrators, who are brought up on relational databases, will not naturally consider the network when it comes to tuning as it is typically ignored. The size of digital objects can be very large. Also, delivering a large number of smaller objects can still add up to a large amount of data to deliver. A thumbnail might be of 4 K in size, but delivering 100 of them to 50 concurrent users is 4 K times 500 (4 K x 100 x 50) that equals to 20 MB. Delivering this over an internal gigabit network might be feasible, but attempting to deliver this data over a 10-MB Internet connection will prove to be a bottleneck.

Most database administrators would be familiar with TCP/IP but most would be completely unfamiliar with how the protocol works and what the overheads are when using it. TCP/IP is a layered protocol and ensures that the data sent is delivered to its destination. UDP/IP is a lightweight version which cannot guarantee delivery of the information. UDP does not check for failed sends. This protocol is suited for streaming video where high speed delivery is required but missing packets of information can be tolerated.

Let's assume a thumbnail is to be delivered to a browser. The protocol being used is HTTP which runs on top of TCP/IP:

1. A query is run against the database to retrieve the binary data. This is done when the browser sends a HTTP post or Get command to the database server. The browser then waits for a response.

2. The command is processed by the database (assume it's a Mod PL/SQL command). The database performs a SQL query (requiring parsing, processing, and retrieval). The thumbnail might already be cached or the database might have to retrieve it from disk. The thumbnail, which is binary data, is stored in a temporary location as a BLOB.

3. The pointer is passed to Apache along with the HTTP header information which contains information about the character set, mime type, server details, and delivery information. This information is contained within the header. The HTTP packet can include a length value, detailing how many bytes are to be sent. It can also leave it open ended until the connection is terminated. This layer is referred to as the application layer.

4. The HTTP information now passes the data to the TCP/IP layer for delivery. This layer is referred to as the transport layer. This layer breaks up the data into packets. The number and size of packets can be controlled but is typically managed automatically. Each packet has a header with IP information for delivery. This includes checksums and ordering, so when the data is received, it can be assembled in the correct order.

   This layer talks to its equivalent on the browser and ensures that packets, when sent, are received. This is done using acknowledgment packets. When a packet is received, the client sends a packet of information back saying it arrived. If the packet was corrupted (by using the checksum), it can indicate a negative send and request the package be resent. This layer also handles congestion of the network and can attempt rerouting if possible.

5. The TCP/IP packets are passed to the next layer called the Internet layer. This layer is responsible for routing. It has to work out the optimal method for sending the packet of data. This can change based on network load and availability. When sending a packet of information from Australia to the U.S., it's possible that some travel via the undersea cable over the Pacific, while others could travel via satellite or via Asia and then over the Pacific.

6. The next layer is the link layer. It's responsible for sending a packet of data from one device to another. This could be between an Ethernet card on a laptop to a router. All that is done is the packet of data is being sent from one device to another. Initially, this would be from the server network card to the router. The router then looks at the data within the packet to determine its IP address. The router now goes back to the Internet layer to work out how to deliver it. It then sends the packet to the next MAC address. This could be to a router at an ISP. At this low level, the concept of IP addresses have no meaning as this information is just treated as data.

At this low level, the network device has a MAC address (Media Access Control) which is used to identify where to send it to and where it came from. For those who have a router, the MAC address can be used to restrict which computers can access the local network. A MAC address is unique and is built into the network device hardware. The exception is when a virtualization is used. Here the MAC address can be manually set. Each movement of a packet from one network device to another network device is referred to as a hop. Depending on the state of the network, the number of hops could be between 10 and 30. This means the data could be moved, decoded, moved again, between 10 and 30 devices. Each hop takes a certain amount of time to analyze and process the packet before sending it on. As most of this is built into the hardware, the actual hop is quite fast.

7. The data is then passed down to the lowest layer called the physical layer. This is where the network card, router, or other physical device actually sends the data. This can be via copper cable, Ethernet cable, fiber optic cable, wireless network, or 3G/4G or other phone network. The laws of physics (the speed of light) end up dictating the speed at which data can be transferred in each hop assuming the data is transferred using fiber optics.

On the continent of the U.S. data being transferred from East to West Coast has to travel at least 4000 kilometers, where that same data traveling to Australia has to travel an additional 12,000 kilometers. At this distance small delays become slightly larger and it adds up. To help get around this, the fiber optic lines use multiple wavelengths to send the data in parallel.

HTTPS

This is the encrypted version of HTTP. It uses **secure sockets layer** (**SSL**) as the encryption protocol. This is a public/private key system and initially involves when establishing a connection that the correct keys are in place to encrypt and decrypt the data. Performing the encryption and decryption is a CPU intensive process, and the larger the packet, the more processing power is involved in the decryption of the data.

VPN

A virtual private network is a layer that sits on top of the link layer. In the past, an earlier version was a networking tunnel. It's used to ensure a secure connection between a computer and server on the Internet. Typically, the VPN data is encrypted, but it intercepts the lower level layer calls and passes them over the link layer. This adds extra processing to the sending of the information. If encryption is used, then the layer has to automatically encrypt and decrypt the data. The encrypted data is then sent over the network (passed down to the lower layers). It is then decrypted at the receiving end and sent along the network.

So, when it comes to sending data from point A to point B on the network there is a lot of processing that is involved. All of this is done transparently and a lot of is built into the hardware (network card) to ensure faster processing. With local network speeds currently at 1 GBps and approaching 10 GBps, the volume of network data that can be concurrently processed is quite large. Some routers can process in parallel, but it must be realized that a network is shared.

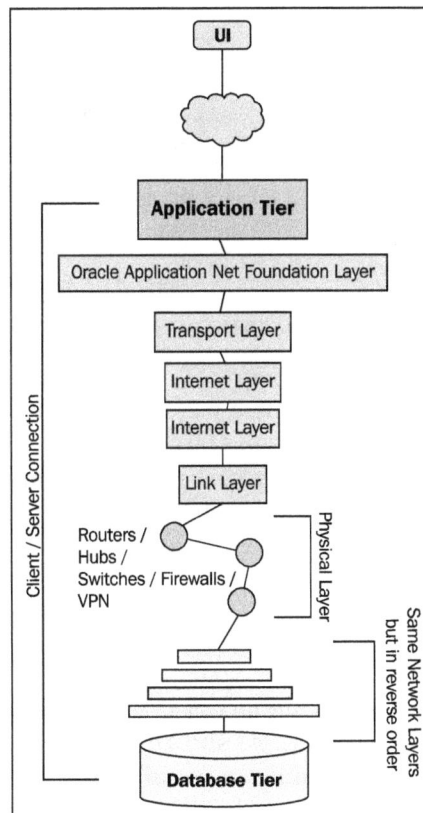

A user sending a 10-GB file from one local server to another could overload the network, blocking other users from sending data. Smart routers can throttle back users doing large transfers ensuring an even load balance.

When sending data out over the Internet, the network speed is variable. It can be ISP-dependent. Large organizations willing to pay a premium can ensure they have a 100 MB or even 1 GB of connection to the Internet. Most organizations will be able to get between 10 and 30 MBs of speed. This is dependent on their location in the world.

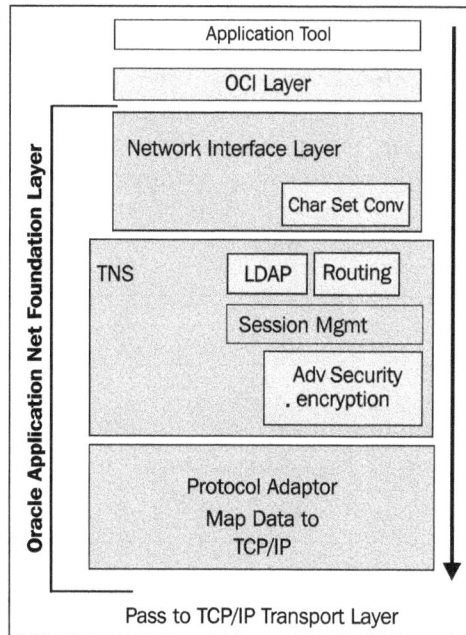

Network tuning is a balancing act. If there were no restrictions in place, it would not take long before someone attempts to send large video files between sites, resulting in a traffic meltdown. For sites that offer very high speed upload and download, network traffic is balanced by the users, as they are charged for the volume of data uploaded or downloaded. Amazon charge a fixed number of cents for every gigabyte delivered.

Efficiency in sending

It's more efficient to send a 100-MB digital object over the Internet than it is to send 1000 digital objects each at 100 K. As shown earlier, the layering protocol starts to add up and incurs a noticeable overhead as more objects are introduced. Each one needs its own HTTP header and additional layering information with acknowledgment packets.

A HTML page, which references 30 icons, 10 CSS style sheets, and 20 JavaScript routines (which reference additional routines), will take a lot longer to deliver and load than a HTML page which has 10 icons and the CSS, and JavaScript calls are embedded in the HTML page. The downside of this is that once a CSS style sheet or JavaScript routine is loaded into the browser, it is cached and doesn't need reloading. Subsequent page requests can use the cache. Whereas, if the information is contained on the page, then each new page loads in the same CSS and JavaScript which then has to be parsed and compiled. The balancing act scenario here is, will the customer only go to the home page or will the customer, once they access the home page, access a large number of other pages?

In other words, will the customer experience a 10-second delay to bring up the home page with subsequent page calls being around 2 to 4 seconds? Or will the customer experience a 5-second response on every page call?

Applications built that are international must factor in the server and customer location for delivery. It will take longer to retrieve data when sending from the U.S. to Australia than when sent within the U.S.

XML and web services

The trend for application development that uses the Internet is to develop a high-level API layer between the application and the network. This trend is now moving to internal applications. Communication is then made using a web service call, which at its core uses XML. 12 years ago when the concept of the web service was raised, it was based on existing technology already in place. This included **Resource Description Framework** (**RDF**), which libraries had already been using enabling them to pass catalog information between them and to enable one library to query another's catalog. As was the case at the time, the architects tried to create a structure that was flexible and conformed to a standard that could be easily adapted. The most popular architecture that emerged was one called **Simple Object Access Protocol** (**SOAP**). SOAP used a **Web Service Definition Language** (**WSDL**), which was an XML-based language that defined how the SOAP call was to be used. The SOAP call was very descriptive and made extensive use of namespaces to ensure uniqueness of attributes. An example SOAP call as found at `http://www.w3schools.com/soap/soap_example.asp` is:

```
<?xml version="1.0"?>
<soap:Envelope
 xmlns:soap="http://www.w3.org/2001/12/soap-envelope"
 soap:encodingStyle="http://www.w3.org/2001/12/soap-encoding">
<soap:Body xmlns:m="http://www.example.org/stock">
  <m:GetStockPrice>
```

```
        <m:StockName>IBM</m:StockName>
      </m:GetStockPrice>
    </soap:Body>
  </soap:Envelope>
```

The previous example is 301 characters in length and uses this number of characters to actually send 3 bytes of information (the actual real value is IBM). Any database administrator who was responsible for tuning would realize how inefficient the call is. SOAP was designed under the assumption that the Internet had infinite bandwidth. This is a problem with a lot of architectures developed; they assume infinite resources of some sort, be it memory, CPU, or in the case of web services, the network.

SOAP calls when following the official standard do not scale well. In the previous example, if 1000 users made the call, that would be 1000 times 301 bytes (plus the response). Though still small, it adds up, especially as the calls become more complicated. It's realistic to see a SOAP call that is over 1 MB in size yet only containing 1 K of actual data.

To address this issue, web service developers quickly moved to calls that were simpler and less cluttered. The two most popular on the market today are REST and JSON. REST can use JSON, but it's typically known as a simple lightweight XML structure. There is no true standard for the format of the data in REST, except it must conform to the XML standard. The developer, who builds the REST call effectively publishes what the attributes mean. The previous SOAP call can be replaced with a REST call that looks like:

```
<?xml version="1.0"?>
  <stock>
    <StockName>IBM</StockName>
  </stock>
```

XML, when received is also parsed (compiled). The time to parse it in Big O notation (as discussed in *Chapter 3, The Multimedia Warehouse*) would be O(n2), where n is the number of characters or attributes to process. As most parsing is best done in memory, the smaller the size of the XML file to process, the more efficient it is on memory (enabling more concurrent processes to parse) and less CPU is required. So, keeping the web service call size as small as possible is crucial for scalability.

Some standards for passing XML allow for the compression of the call using an algorithm such as Gzip. Though this has advantages in reducing the size of the XML file, it does not get around the CPU time it would take to compress and decompress the call. Gzip compression can be quite an expensive CPU operation, and if done on a server with hundreds of concurrent web service requests, might result in the CPU becoming overloaded just compressing the data. Though compression should not be ruled out because of this, its usage must be taken into consideration.

It is best done when there is a large amount of data to compress, there are proven compression benefits resulting from it (a compression result of 3 percent is not worth the effort, but one of 95 percent is), and there would be a lower number of concurrent request calls. This is where the database administrator, development team, and network administrators need to work together to work out the optimum method. The end result might be to compress some calls but not others. Gzip cannot compress JPEG, MPEG, MP3, or other multimedia formats that already utilize a compression algorithm.

The JSON format was designed to address the issue of wasted bandwidth typically found in web service calls. Though its initial usage was a storage format for JavaScript programs, its use has been quickly adopted by other environments because of its ability to store the data efficiently and in a manner which can be easily retrieved by JavaScript. Its use has extended to PHP, and there are even PL/SQL compilers that can process and parse it. The previous call in JSON would look like:

```
{
  "stock":{"stockname":"IBM"}
}
```

By keeping attribute names abbreviated, even more space can be saved in both REST and JSON calls. The previous JSON call could be sent as:

```
{
  "st":{"sn":"IBM"}
}
```

The result is that it's not easy to visualize and understand what data is being sent in the call, but it is much more efficient to send it with the main benefit that the call will scale.

Back to three tier and scalability

For a multimedia database, true scalability can only be achieved by keeping the data and the application code as close to each other as possible. Separating them into two tiers is one of the worst things that can be done. As has been shown, the overheads increase as more data is passed back and forth over the network, and an application tier talking to a data tier will incur a large amount of network overheads. Storing the application code in the database right next to the data is the only real option for achieving scalability. Even using languages, such as PHP which can reside on the same server as the database is a better option than completely separating the two.

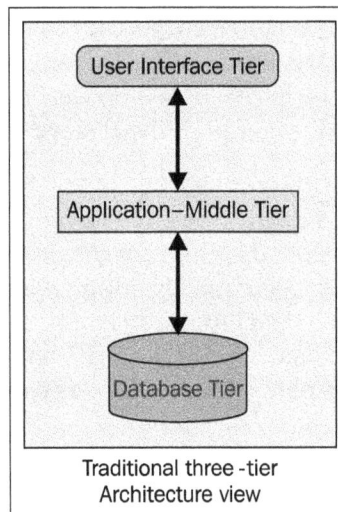

Traditional three-tier
Architecture view

Three tier is useful for legacy systems or systems where the volume of data processed is known in advance and will not incur network bottlenecks between the application tier and the database tier. It's important to stress this; in the last 5 years, the rules have changed. The rules with technology are always changing and what made sense 5 years ago might not make sense now with new technology. The trend is now for servers to have a large number of cores in them with less focus on computer power per CPU. In 1990s, the focus was the predictable, doubling power of one CPU. A computer would have one CPU. There was no concept of a core (in the early 1990s, there was the concept of a mathematics co-processor, but it soon got subsumed into the core CPU). The architecture rules were based around this concept.

The tuning mentality was that when the application resided with the database, one badly tuned piece of code would impact everyone on the server, as it would dominate the CPU. The logical conclusion was to move the application code out of the database into an environment, where if it went rogue, it could be controlled. Also, the thinking was that scalability could be easily achieved by bolting on more application servers.

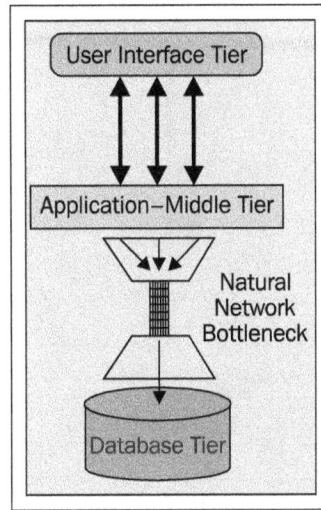

It's now feasible to move the middle tier back into the third tier, because it has the capability to handle the capacity. A rogue application might impact one core out of a large number, but it will not impact everyone on the server. Also, improvement in operating system and database software can now reign in a misbehaving application process. Three tier should now be viewed as an obsolete architecture just like the two-tier is. To achieve scalability, the direction should be to an N-tier architecture, where the data and the application reside as close to each other as possible.

The other goal is to try to minimize the amount of data returned to the client, ensuring that the network between the middle and database tier doesn't become a bottleneck. Just because computer servers might be improving in power and following Moore's law doesn't mean that the network speed is. A gigabit network might seem fast but can quickly become a bottleneck, as the number of requests for data increase as the user load increases. The 10-gigabit network might look to improve the bottleneck except that it will not be able to keep with demand as the number of users grow requesting more information.

With multimedia, the network connection between the application tier and the database tier will always become a bottleneck. When tuning, it must be eliminated from the equation, and the best solution is to move it back into the database tier.

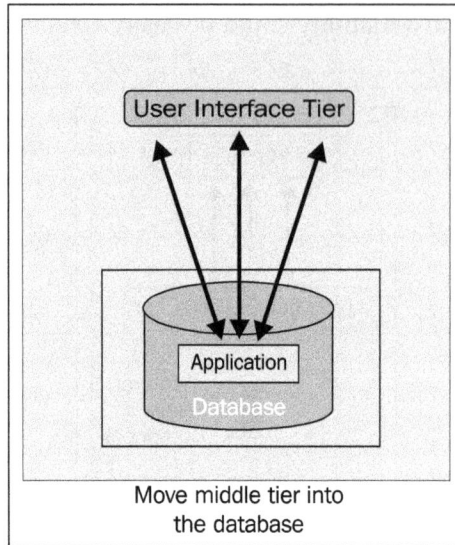

Move middle tier into
the database

The most efficient method, involving reducing nearly all the network costs, is to move the application tier into the database. For Oracle, this might involve developing the application in PL/SQL or Java. Once inside the database, the application compiler can now be developed, to work closely with the database, resulting in further improvements in communication between the application and the data.

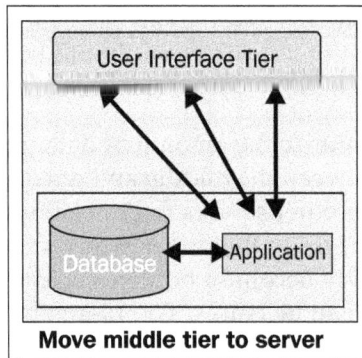

Move middle tier to server

Once an N-tier environment is set up, the tuning focus can then be on how to best to deliver the large volumes of multimedia to the client. In the N-tier architecture, the application can redirect requests to other servers to perform the work (for an MPP or replicated environment). The database can also send requests to other servers to perform queries or to perform multimedia transformations.

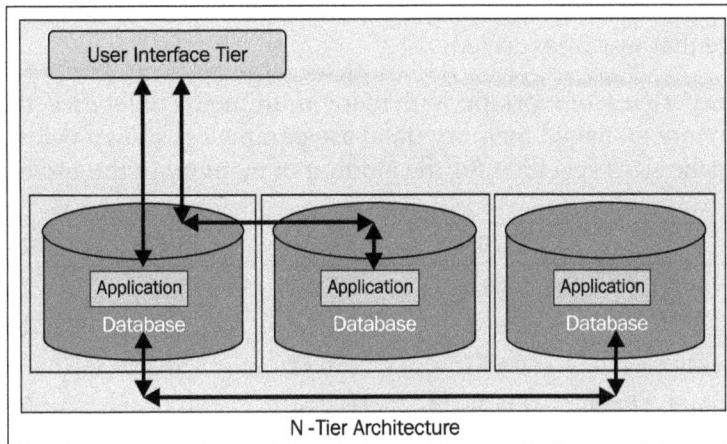

N-Tier Architecture

Memory

A standard database server is likely to start with 4 GB of memory, though most organizations are moving to servers with 24 to 32 GB of memory. A server with 8 GB of memory for the database can cache a large amount of information. In comparison to multimedia and what it can manage, 8 GB is quite small.

The rules for dealing with multimedia and cache are quite simple. Multimedia should not be cached unless the digital object is small in size and frequently accessed. A good example of an object matching this criteria is a thumbnail. If the thumbnail is under 4,000 bytes in size, then it can be configured to be stored in the row.

Streaming video servers require a large amount of memory to run efficiently. Tuning these servers is separate to tuning the database and should be treated as a balancing act between the database server and the streaming server.

Oracle doesn't allow an individual BLOB within a row to be kept in the cache, like one can do with a table. If this was possible, it would be reasonable to identify commonly accessed web quality or originals and only cache them. Caching the BLOB containing the web quality or original is likely to result in the cache becoming overcrowded with digital objects that are only accessed one or two times. This would come at the expense of normal caching.

Performance is gained by tuning the I/O and network. Traditional cache management as used with relational databases can be used to manage the relational data in the multimedia database.

It's recommended to manually set the memory parameters rather than using automatic memory management. A novice database administrator can do a good job managing the memory without the added worry of the database auto tuning and doing a change that was unexpected.

Based on the experience of working with many multimedia databases, the following are four commonly managed memory database parameters shown below with examples of cache sizes specified for the amount of memory in the server:

	2 GB	4 GB	8 GB	24 GB
db_cache_size	1200 M	2800 M	6 G	20 G
shared_pool_size	256 M	300 M	500 M	1 G
java_pool_size	256 M	300 M	500 M	600 M
pga_aggregate_target	256 M	500 M	1 G	2G

These figures are approximate and can be treated as a good starting point. If RMAN is being used, then the large_pool_size parameter needs to be specified. The java_pool_size parameter size is set assuming there are no java applications running in the database. The java parameter is set based on the usage by Oracle Multimedia.

Values such as pga_aggregate_target are dependent on the number of concurrent users and the shared_pool_size parameter is dependent on the efficiency of SQL statements written (whether they can be easily reused) and the amount of PL/SQL used within the application.

CPU

With a multimedia database, CPU only becomes important during the digital object transformation phase. Image loading and delivery are typically I/O and network bound. Processing is a very CPU-expensive operation. To convert a 4 GB video to MP4 can consume all eight cores on a server for more than 90 minutes. Depending on the format, the video originates from and what it's being converted to, this figure can easily grow to four times this figure. So, an organization wanting to transform and load thousands of videos might require dedicated transformation servers to pre-process the digital objects before loading. Even then, it still might take weeks or months to pre-process all these video objects.

An organization might have 80,000 digital images they want to transform and load into the database. Each image is approximately 80 MB in size, and the transformation requires creating a thumbnail, web quality, PowerPoint quality, and printing quality derivatives. Time to transform per image is a reasonable 20 seconds and 5 seconds to load including the original. To process 80,000 images will take 2,000,000 seconds or 555 hours or 23 days. Being able to run the load in parallel will reduce the load time but might result in I/O bottlenecks starting to appear. Being able to make use of a SSD for processing can help minimize any I/O bottlenecks.

Try and use a **Solid State Disk (SSD)** as a temporary location for any transformation processing. This will ensure that I/O will not be a bottleneck, and the CPU can be fully focused on the transformation. If possible, use the SSD to hold the UNDO tablespace and the redo logs, even if it's only for the duration of the initial load, and they can be subsequently moved to other locations post load.

A 256-GB SSD might not be cheap in comparison to a disk, but the performance gains from being able to use it to remove I/O as a bottleneck are well worth the cost.

Once the initial load and transformation is done, standard relational tuning can be applied for CPU load balancing, unless the application performs post digital object processing. This might involve dynamic transformation on digital objects purchased (create a PPT version of the image if one doesn't exist). It's also possible that CPU is required to perform large volume transformations (examples include recreating all thumbnails, creating postcard versions of all thumbnails and embed a watermark in a derivative). Addressing situations like this will require a large amount of processing, and a transformation server will be harder to utilize as the images are located in the database.

The solution might involve setting up a batch process to extract the images (check them out) from the database and place them on a separate transformation server. Process the images and then reload them back into the database. Oracle does not provide any capabilities to natively perform these functions, and so they must be manually built using PL/SQL, Java, PHP, or other languages.

I/O

For a multimedia database, where all the digital objects are stored in one table, as that table grows in size, it will become impractical to let the database perform full table scans for processing. Additionally, if the table grows into the tens to hundreds of terabytes in size, it might become very difficult to back it up or even do basic management on it. The issue is a standard scalability one, involving I/O as storage increases. Two solutions are available. One is to use partitioning (covered later), and the other is to ensure there are indexes available on the table, ensuring one or two block reads to access any block of data in the table.

The standard strategy when tuning a relational database is to try and minimize the number of I/Os to retrieve all the data for the query. For small tables, this is why it might make more sense to do a full table scan than access the table via indexes. The next strategy is to try and ensure when an I/O is done that the read is a logical one (reading it from cache), rather than a physical one (reading it from disk). The administrator has to be careful to ensure that multiple queries are not doing an incredibly large number of logical reads, indicating a problem with looping in the code.

When retrieving one row from a table, the goal is to ensure the number of I/Os to retrieve the data from the index, plus one to retrieve the row from disk (or from cache) is less than doing a full table scan. In most cases, the optimizer, if it has correct stats, can work this out and choose whether to use the index or not. With Oracle 10 and 11 and improvements in index scans, this strategy requires fine-tuning but generally holds true.

With a multimedia database, the rules are different. If the number of I/Os required to retrieve the index is a conservative three, then there will be one I/O to retrieve the row. The digital object will not be stored in the row (unless as discussed earlier, it's a small thumbnail stored within the row that is addressed differently), which means there is a pointer to where it's located. This requires another I/O to retrieve it. If the digital object is 100 MB in size, then the number of I/Os required to retrieve it could be in the hundreds or thousands, depending on the block size. When looking at the retrieval the index height is not important. It is only a small percentage of the I/Os required to retrieve the digital object and is typically a very small percentage. The result is that tuning the index will not improve performance when retrieving multimedia. The administrator still needs to tune and manage indexes for the relational component of the database.

The tuning effort goal is to try and retrieve the digital object and deliver it as quickly as possible. If the tablespace containing the digital object is on a SAN, then there is likely going to be a contention if multiple users are also requesting digital objects. More and more users accessing different digital objects will be sending requests to the SAN, via the database, to retrieve blocks of I/O. This is where tuning the SAN becomes important. It's important to be able to monitor and manage requests to retrieve a large number of random blocks concurrently.

If delivery is to be done on the Internet, then the bottleneck will be the network link to the Internet. The SAN or any disks will be able to deliver the I/O at a fast enough speed, even with hundreds of concurrent requests. The request to retrieve I/O from the SAN is likely to be waiting for the data already retrieved to be pushed out.

On an internal network, it's a different story. If the internal network is at a gigabit speed, then the network will be able to keep up with and requests. It may even be faster than the disk, or SAN can retrieve I/O. It's in this scenario that the database administrator has to focus on I/O tuning.

As covered in *Chapter 7, Techniques for Creating a Multimedia Database*, the database block size in a multimedia database should be larger than the traditional size. The database administrator needs to understand the disk/SAN or other devices used to store the database files and what the capacity is of retrieval. Ideally would be to have an SSD, but this would prove to be cost-prohibitive, as the database starts to grow beyond a terabyte. It's important to state that this assumption could change as technology changes. If there is a radical shift in SSD technology, where the size increases but costs stays the same, then it might be a solid strategy to move any database files containing digital objects to an SSD to improve performance. As the digital objects are unlikely to change, most requests for retrieval will be read-only, ensuring very high speed retrieval without the worry of corruption of the SSD due to excessive I/O writes.

Parallelism

Most database servers will have between four and 24 cores available to them for processing. It is anticipated that within 5 years, the number of cores is likely double with top end servers having 128 cores in them (which are likely to be spread across multiple CPUs). Chip manufacturers are finding it easier to add more cores to a CPU than to make the transistor size smaller.

This has meant that in the last five years rather than seeing huge gains in processing power for one CPU, the processing power is coming from multiple cores. Databases and applications that cannot take advantage of parallelism will not be able to see a huge improvement in processing power.

The Oracle Database has built-in parallelism for a number of operations including querying and **Data Manipulation** (**DML**). Some utilities such as Data Pump and RMAN can also run in parallel, though in the case of RMAN, the parallelism achieved is best handled by I/O throughput more so than CPU throughput.

When it comes to processing multimedia, the Oracle Database doesn't handle parallelism well. When an image is processed, only one thread is available to do the processing. The PL/SQL language has capabilities to perform some parallel tasks, but it doesn't have the natural capability like Java to spawn a thread in a process and run in parallel. The Java Virtual Machine inside the database with Oracle 11 supports multi-threading, but it still has limitations.

Using Oracle Scheduler with PL/SQL, a rough form of parallelism can be manually achieved. This involves breaking up the tasks into manageable sets and submitting a scheduler job to run each.

Some PL/SQL functions can be built to run in parallel. The ideal natural capability would be to have basic forking similar to C and Java.

Image loading

SQL*Loader is an Oracle product that is not designed for image loading (this is covered further in *Chapter 9, Understanding the Limitations of Oracle Products*). A more efficient method is to develop a PL/SQL routine to find and load the images into the database. Load speed is going to be dictated by the following factors:

- Size of the UNDO tablespace
- Redo log size with background archiving
- I/O load speed

In addition, an image load might involve the following additional tasks:

- Creation of thumbnail and web quality image
- Extraction and processing of metadata
- Determination of image properties

Each one of these steps takes time. The database administrator, with the developer, now has a choice about two different paths they can take to improve performance by using manual parallelism.

Horizontal versus vertical parallelism

Horizontal parallelism involves breaking up the job into tasks and then running each task as fast as possible.

In case of image loading it might involve the following:

- Load in images (no processing): The goal is to get the image into the database as quick as possible to ensure the I/O contention is not going to result in a bottleneck.
- A background process runs and looks for new images. For the ones it finds, it sets the image properties.
- Another background process runs, it looks for images with properties set and extracts and processes the metadata.

- Another background process looks for new images and creates a web quality.
- Another background process looks for new images and creates a thumbnail.

So already we can run in parallel 5 tasks when loading images in. Some steps are dependent on other steps (everything is dependent on the first step starting, but not finishing). Further parallelism can be achieved by using a vertical approach on each of the steps.

The database administrator will need to adjust the database to ensure there is sufficient memory for processing (especially Java) and that the obvious bottlenecks, which will likely be with the redo logs, are addressed.

Vertical processing is simpler to achieve and involves breaking up the load into a set of vertical jobs. Each job can process a range of digital objects. Ten jobs might be built to run, with each one running sequentially and focusing on a range of images (maybe located in different directories on different disks). Each one loads the image and does all the processing.

A requirement to load in a million images would best be handled by setting up a mixture of horizontal and vertical parallelism. It's best to start with horizontal, then for each layer running, break it down into a set of vertical jobs. This way 20-30 batch jobs could be running, loading, and processing.

The bottlenecks that an administrator will encounter when using this method will invariably be I/O, especially if the digital objects are each 100 MB or larger in size. To improve processing, a potential workaround is to load the digital object directly into a temporary blob which is stored in memory. Memory is sacrificed and used as a cache to improve performance. The administrator needs to carefully monitor memory usage as using this technique could easily result in gigabytes of SGA being consumed. Database startup parameters are not correctly configured to handle this and it could result in the database slowing down as the caching flushes out other important information.

Another method (as discussed previously) is to use an SSD to hold the undo tablespace and the redo logs for the duration of the load. Also to consider is to disable archiving until the load is completed. Then enable it and perform a full database backup.

Locking

When queries are running slow, but there are no CPU or I/O issues, one possible issue to review is contention due to locking. When a digital object is manipulated a row-level lock needs to be taken out on it. This is done using the `select.. for.. where.. for update;` clause. While being manipulated the object is locked. It can be accessed but not modified. A locked object might be a problem when horizontal parallelism is used, but generally it's only locked on loading and treated as read only from then on.

Locks can be easily lost, once gained. Shelling out to the operating system or invoking some PL/SQL embedded routines will release any locks before running. This might result in the same object having to be relocked once the routine is run. Locking can cause issues when used with the ODBC gateway. The gateway only supports one transaction at a time, so trying to lock an object and then insert it into a remote table will result in an error. Simply the gateway supports all DML to be done against the remote database then committed or rolled back. You can't have an open transaction in Oracle and one in the remote database. This is because the Oracle Database with the ODBC gateway doesn't support a two-phase commit. The more advanced gateways, such as the Oracle Transparent Gateway for Microsoft SQL Server, do support mixed transactions.

Locking issues will really only be seen with traditional relational constructs built into the database.

Database parameters

The database administrator should look at the values of the following database startup parameters as the ones that can improve performance:

plcql_oodc_type

By Oracle 11, (this parameter isn't easy to use prior to Oracle 11) this value should be set to NATIVE (the default is INTERPRETED). When set to NATIVE, PL/SQL is compiled down to C code and then an executable. When the data dictionary PL/SQL routines are recompiled in an NATIVE mode, performance improves for any PL/SQL calls. The actual improvement varies based on what the PL/SQL does.

The compiled object code is stored in the data dictionary in the SYSTEM tablespace. The database administrator should ensure the SYSTEM tablespace can grow beyond 1 GB to handle the increase in size (experience has shown setting it to 1.5 GB is a healthy size). The downside is that PL/SQL compilation will take a little longer. Server CPUs released in the last 12 months are sufficiently powerful to compile the code in a realistic time frame, ensuring that most sites can keep it always set to NATIVE.

Making it NATIVE doesn't automatically compile the code. Using an ALTER PACKAGE command can force a recompilation. Other routines are available to recompile whole schemas. The Oracle administrator guide details the steps involved to recompile the data dictionary PL/SQL routines. The database needs to be in maintenance mode when this is done.

optimizer_mode

By Oracle 11, there are two major options left. FIRST_ROWS and ALL_ROWS (FIRST_ROWS has options ranging from FIRST_ROWS_1, FIRST_ROWS_10, FIRST_ROWS_100, and FIRST_ROWS_1000).

This is an often neglected parameter by database administrators. From Oracle 8 to Oracle 10, a number of sites would set this value to CHOOSE, meaning the optimizer would choose the best path. Invariably it chose wrong because the optimizer could never really know the business context in which this parameter is needed.

The difference between the two is quite simple. When using FIRST_ROWS, you are telling the optimizer that I am willing to sacrifice the time it takes to retrieve *all* the rows in the query, provided it can return some of the rows really quickly. FIRST_ROWS is quite a powerful option for applications returning pages of data. It's important that the first page comes back quickly. The user receiving the data might never want to see all the results.

When using ALL_ROWS, you are telling the optimizer to run the query as fast as possible to retrieve all the rows. This is very powerful for reports which might require processing and outputting all the rows retrieved. In this case, the time to retrieve the first 100 is not important.

So to summarize by providing an extreme example of this. A query when running will return 10,000 rows. When using FIRST_ROWS, the query will take 1 second to return the first 100, but will take 60 seconds to return all 10,000. When using ALL_ROWS, the query will take 25 seconds to return the first 100, and 30 seconds to return all of them.

When the DBA had the option of using CHOOSE, the optimizer would look at both FIRST_ROWS and ALL_ROWS and look at the time it would take to run the query, it would then pick the fastest one. Inevitably it picked ALL_ROWS because this would usually retrieve all the rows in the quickest time. The assumption that could only be made was that when a query is run the user wants *all* the rows.

Database administrators inexperienced in this would inevitability pick CHOOSE thinking the optimizer would know best. For the client/server applications they managed, the user interface would be very slow and no matter what they did it was hard to tune it. This resulted in a very bad perception of the optimizer performance in Oracle 8 to Oracle 9. By Oracle 10, database administrators were starting to get wise to this issue and changing the parameter accordingly.

Ultimately the recommendation for client/server systems was to set the value to be FIRST_ROWS. For data warehouses the value should be ALL_ROWS. In a mixed environment the value should be FIRST_ROWS and either a schema set up to run reports that set the session to be ALL_ROWS, or a hint was passed down in the statement telling it to use ALL_ROWS.

```
select /*+ ALL_ROWS */ from table...
```

By Oracle 11.2, the optimizer has proven to be quite intelligent and resilient. For most queries up to 3 or 4 table joins the difference in the path taken between FIRST_ROWS and ALL_ROWS is not noticeable (of course there are always exceptions that can be found to this).

Hints

Hints used in SQL statements are a double-edged sword. They are a powerful option available to the database administrator to tune a stubborn SQL statement that will not use the right index. As shown with the *optimizer_mode*, they can be used to indicate the correct business usage of the SQL statement.

The problem with hints is that they lock the statement in. Initially the hint might result in improved performance, but a patch upgrade or change in data volume might result in more efficient and faster paths being able to be found by the optimizer. However, because of the hint the optimizer can't make use of this path. If the administrator doesn't periodically check the hints embedded in the code to ensure they are still valid, then they might be introducing performance bottlenecks into the code.

Hints that provide a business directive, such as FIRST_ROWS and ALL_ROWS are generally immune to upgrades and data volume changes, so when used are safe to leave in. Hints involving temporary tables are also safe to leave in:

```
select /*+ LEADING(aa) */ mm.*
from temp_a aa, mm_table mm
where um.pk = aa.pk
order by sort_value;
```

In the preceding query, *temp_a* is a GLOBAL TEMPORARY table. This means its contents are session specific. If it's known that the table usually contains a small set of rows and the table it's joining to is usually large, it's easier to tell the optimizer which table to lead the join, rather than slowing it down as it tries to work it out itself.

Hints that use distributed queries (between remote databases) are also usually safe to use.

Backups

Once a database approaches a size of around 200 GB the time it takes to back it up might result in the database being offline for an unacceptable period of time. A disk to disk backup of 200 GB might take between 30 min and 24 hours all depending on the available hardware. It's fair to say that a multimedia database is in nearly all cases (XE being an exception) going to be online 24 x 7. This means that unless there is maintenance, the database is always running and backups have to be done while the database is running.

Oracle offers a number of methods for database backup. The simplest is the online backup (offline backup results in the database not being 24 x 7, so this is not included). The database is put in backup mode which tells the database to store extra information about undo segments in the redo logs. Simply, the database has sufficient information to restore itself even if a set of database blocks are incorrectly backed up. While in backup mode there is a minor performance hit with the database and it's usually recommended not to do heavy transactions during the online backup. The backup of the database is technically a corrupted copy of the database but there is sufficient information in the redo logs (and archives) to resolve and fix any corruptions. Digital object loading during an online database backup is not recommended because more redo will be incurred resulting in it running a little slower. The description of the backup method has been simplified here for the novice user.

Depending on the size of the database it might only be necessary to backup the database weekly. If sufficient storage is available to keep a weeks worth of archives, then this might be a viable option. What the database administrator needs to be aware of for performance is the time it might take to recover and restore a weeks worth of archives. The question the administrator needs to ask is how long will it take to restore and roll forward through all the archives and is this acceptable to the business? Oracle supports parallel recovery which can speed up the recovery process.

The most popular method which matured as of Oracle 10*g* R2 is the use of Oracle Database backup tool called *rman* (recovery manager). This tool doesn't need to have the database put in backup mode because it can read the changed blocks directly from memory and back those up. This means the online backup of the database is consistent. Also, *rman* has numerous options available in it to improve backup time which the standard online backup cannot take advantage of. It only backs up database blocks with data in them and as will be shown with partitioning, it can be given instructions to not backup a read only tablespace if it knows it already has a backup of it. Though *rman* has limitations which restrict its usage limiting its scalability and archiving capabilities for multimedia, it is still a powerful backup and recovery tool.

SAN and virtualization vendors are offering capabilities to backup a database or complete environment without the need for database tools. These tools need to be carefully considered to ensure that when they are used they do not result in a corrupted backup. When used correctly they offer highly scalable and powerful backup and recovery capabilities.

The first involves block backup on a SAN. The SAN can be treated as just a large drive. Which is how the database sees it. Behind the scenes different vendors offer additional capabilities. A popular one is block backup. The SAN detects when a block on the disk has changed. It then queues it to be copied to a remote location. This could be a mirrored site. Smarts within the software enable large amounts of changed blocks to be copied quickly. If the database is stored on the SAN, then in the event of disk failure, the remote site has a complete copy of the disk. The problem with this method is that the Oracle Database uses delayed writes. Meaning it doesn't always immediately write to disk. It only does this when it determines it's efficient to do so. Information is kept in the redo logs for recovery. In the event of severe failure, the database might not have written the changed blocks, stored in memory, to disk. This means the database on restart will need to refer to the redo logs to restore missing data. If there is insufficient information in the logs the database might not be able to be recovered. This might happen if archiving is not enabled or the redo logs are not of a sufficient size.

Sites wanting to use SAN block backup but not use Oracle archiving will need to ensure that:

- The redo logs are mirrored (ensuring that in the event of failure at least one set of redo logs is consistent)
- The redo logs are of a sufficient size to restore in the event of failure. What this figure is, is based on usage. As stated above, storage is cheap so there is nothing to stop a database administrator from configuring 10 GB to 50 GB of redo logs or more.

SANs are designed to store very large amounts of data. The storage is also incrementally scalable, allowing new disks to be added to the SAN volume dynamically as storage requirements increase (this is vendor and operating system dependent).

The second uses a virtualization backup which is sometimes called a snapshot. The accuracy of this is vendor dependent. In theory, the virtualization has sufficient information using timestamps such that when the snapshot is initiated it can take a complete and accurate copy of the whole environment including the memory. The theory being that in the event of failure, the snapshot can be used to restore the whole environment to the point in time of the failure.

The problem with the virtualization snapshot is that it doesn't allow for recovery to the last committed transaction. Recovery can only be done to the snapshot. In theory if archiving is enabled and those archives as well as a mirrored copy of the redo logs, and at least one control file is stored on a disk independent of the snapshot, then the database can be rolled forwarded to the last transaction, ensuring no data is lost.

Sites using a virtualization and SAN need to be very careful as they likely do not include the SAN as part of the snapshot. This means they might be able to take an accurate snapshot of the memory, but it will not be consistent with what the SAN backs up. Even a minor millisecond discrepancy between the two could result in corruption.

Scalability can be achieved using Oracle partitioning by enabling databases to grow to a petabyte or more in size.

Oracle partitioning

Oracle partitioning lends itself well to a multimedia database because once a digital object is loaded into the database it rarely ever changes. Unlike a relational record which is easier to change, it's unlikely that once a digital object has been transformed and derivatives created it will need any updates to be performed on it. This means that the digital object itself becomes read only. The metadata supporting it might change, especially if tagging is employed, but in comparison to the total size of the database, the supporting metadata is quite small and stored in a separate location.

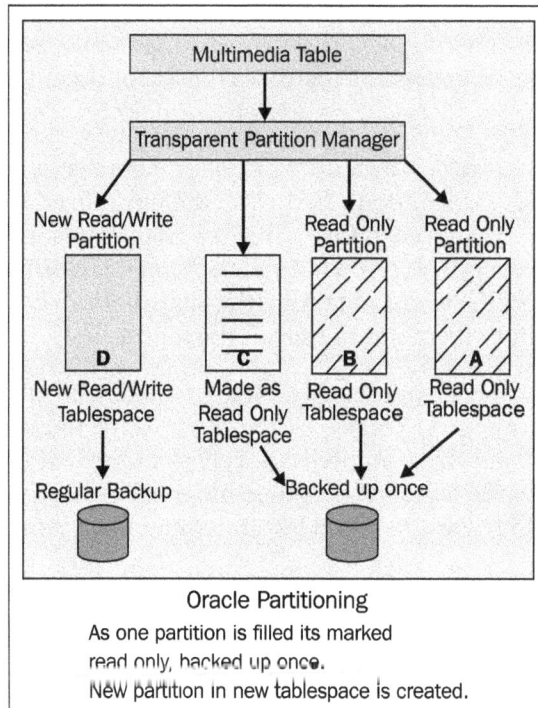

Oracle Partitioning

As one partition is filled its marked read only, backed up once. New partition in new tablespace is created.

Oracle partitioning enables a table to be broken down into smaller tables called partitions. Each partition can be stored in its own tablespace. The blobs encompassing a digital object can be placed in their own table which is partitioned. The key part of the database administrator's role is to determine what the partition should be based on. This is application dependent. It could be based on a timestamp or the collection the object is in. What ever is decided is that once the partition has reached a closing point (for example if partitioning is based on month and year, the closing point is the end of month), the tablespace it resides in is made read only and backed up. Once backed up it will not need to be backed up again and is technically out of the equation for *rman* regarding how big the database is to back up.

The Oracle optimizer is partition aware and can make smart decisions regarding how best to do tablescans or index reads when it knows how the data in the tables has been partitioned. This gives it the option of doing a partition scan as well as accessing the data via indexes, giving the optimizer greater choice in resolving a query.

Manual partitioning

Oracle partitioning is a licensed extra option and might not be cost effective to purchase for a business. Partitioning can be done manually using a view sitting across multiple tables. Each table resides in its own tablespace. Once a table (partition) limit is reached, the tablespace is set to be read only and backed up using *rman*.

This method has limitations but can be useful when it's obvious there are only a small number of partitions that are needed. If a partition is based on a collection and it's known there is only going to be ten collections, then ten tables residing in ten separate tablespaces can be configured. As each fills up, the tablespace is marked read only and backed up.

The other limitation is creating an index across the view. An index can be created on each individual table, but it might not be possible to create an index covering the whole view. Unlike Oracle partitioning where the optimizer has smarts regarding partitioning, the optimizer with manual partitioning will be restricted, requiring a greater and more difficult degree of control for tuning SQL statements.

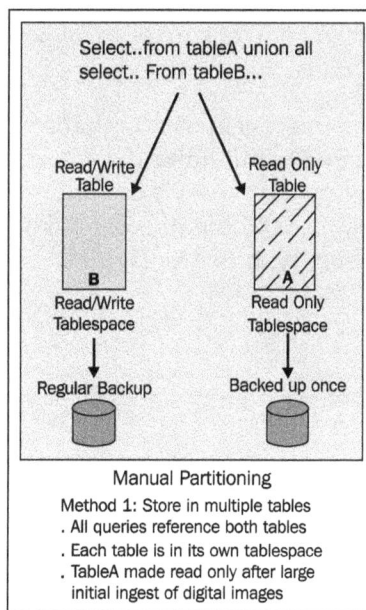

Manual Partitioning

Method 1: Store in multiple tables
. All queries reference both tables
. Each table is in its own tablespace
. TableA made read only after large
  initial ingest of digital images

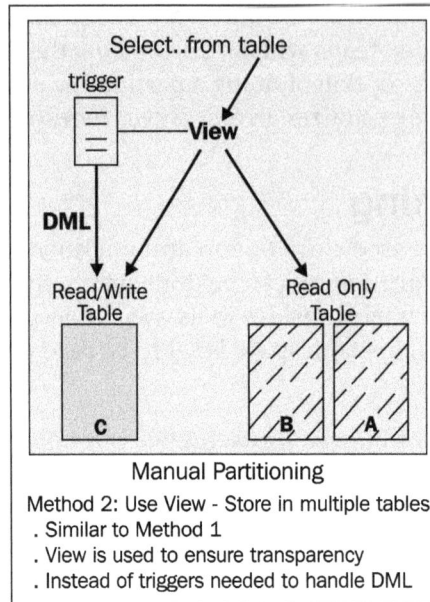

Manual Partitioning

Method 2: Use View - Store in multiple tables
. Similar to Method 1
. View is used to ensure transparency
. Instead of triggers needed to handle DML

Indexing

An index is an object that is transparent to the application with the goal of improving performance. The indexes that are traditionally used in a relational database are designed to improve performance when disk I/O is the bottleneck. The B-Tree index and Oracle's Text Index are designed to ensure optimal access to a relational record with the minimum number of I/O's.

When dealing with multimedia, one has to deal with the network as the bottleneck. When indexing, objects are created to minimize the amount of data being passed over the network. The Indexing method used is determined by the type of object, but all involve creating smaller objects based on the original object. These objects do not have to be of the same multimedia type as the original.

Photo

The multimedia index involves creating a thumbnail and web quality image based on the original. If we have a 100 MB TIFF, then a thumbnail will be the smallest version and be around 3 K. The web quality image will be around 80 K in size. The goal is to balance image size versus quality. The smaller the thumbnail, the faster it is to download and view. A well made thumbnail will be of sufficient quality that it adequately represents the original. When the user requires additional details, they can download and view the original.

Most applications will display multiple thumbnails on the screen for viewing. This allows the users to gain a quick overview of what is available, then narrow down and retrieve in greater detail the image they want to see. The user then navigates from the thumbnail to the web quality image. In most cases the web quality will be of sufficient detail to satisfy most requirements. An 80 K JPEG when viewed on an XGA monitor will be of a very high quality. Only if the user needs greater detail (zoom in further) will they need to access the original.

The result is that when retrieving thumbnails, the database will be given a large number of concurrent requests to retrieve small amounts of data. If the thumbnail is under 4000 bytes, then the storage parameter of the LOB used to hold it should be configured to store the LOB in the row. This will reduce the number of I/O's required to retrieve it, and ensure the row and its associated data are stored together. Web quality images are retrieved less frequently by a smaller number of users. Access will be typically random, so there will be no benefit in caching them.

An Oracle Spatial Georaster image can have a pyramid index created on it. In this case, a large number of progressively fine-grained images are created based on the original. This indexing technique is useful when very large original images exist and the user will be zooming in and out of detail on them. A good example is a satellite photo. The thumbnail is the photo as seen from a very high elevation. As the user zooms in, the thumbnail is replaced by higher quality images until they reach the original. The original is never retrieved. Instead a subset of the original is retrieved by dynamically cropping parts of it. Oracle's Securefile LOBs now offer high speed access to any part of the LOB no matter what its size is, ensuring that this cropping action is very fast and efficient.

Sizing

A thumbnail should be between 1 K and 4 K in size. Any bigger and the goal of it being small and fast to download is defeated. If the database delivering the thumbnail is internal and there is a high speed link between the database and users, then the thumbnail can be larger in size. From a performance viewpoint, creating larger thumbnails on a good network will just move the bottleneck to the disk. Caching the thumbnail will reduce this bottleneck, but will waste memory which if freed could be used to improve the performance of other parts of the application. It's important to remove any metadata from it when creating a thumbnail.

A web quality image should be ideally based on A6, A5, or A4 sizing (that's the Metric system). An image sized to A6 (630 x 446) will be approximately 80-120 K in size. An A5 image (893 x 630) will be around 200 K in size and an A4 image (1263 x 893) will be around 400 K in size.

Video

There are different ways to index a video. The simplest is to create a photo thumbnail from one of the scenes in the video. Creating a composite image based on key scenes will produce the web quality image.

A smaller video or snippet can also be created. A 30 second subset of the video at lower quality can contain sufficient information in it that a user can get a good idea of the contents from it. If the thumbnail is a photo and the web quality is a video snippet, then these combined will create an effective index that will allow the user to quickly find and determine if the video is the one they want.

Audio

The simplest audio index is one in which a 30 second audio snippet is created. A 30 second audio file, created using MP3 and compressed down to 48 bit (FM quality is 64 bit and CD quality is 128 bit) will reduce it dramatically in size. The quality should be sufficient to determine that the audio file is the correct one.

Issue

A snippet for audio and video is best done manually. It's possible to automate the process and extract the first 30 seconds of each file, but this does not mean that the section of the file that truly represents it is captured. This form of indexing is still in its infancy and a number of vendors are now starting to offer products that improve this capability.

Documents

Oracle Text is a mature tool that can efficiently index a document and create a HTML version of it. A subset of the HTML version acts as an efficient document thumbnail.

Another type of thumbnail involves extracting the first page (or key page) and converting this into an image. The image can be subsequently colored or changed to indicate the size of the document. For example, the document border can start at a light color (indicating a small number of pages) and change to a very dark color (indicating a very large number of pages).

Scalability using Oracle XE

Too often vendors offering small scale databases are used in an environment because they are perceived to be cost effective and easy to use. As covered, scalability goes in both directions and too often Oracle neglects the small scale applications. The result is that the vendors pushing these simpler and sometimes free databases win out in use. A lot of applications really don't need to store large amounts of data. Some Oracle customers have an Oracle Database with a large number of schemas in it. Each schema might represent an application, and each application might have 1 to 10 GB of data in it.

Twenty years ago, an application that held 5 GB of data was considered very large. Today, it's not even a blip on anyone's radar. But 5 GB is a huge amount of relational data. The Oracle XE database is a free version and although it has some restrictions, it also offers a lot of capabilities. Any organization or vendor should give consideration to its use, even for multimedia. If a site is considering moving off Oracle to MySQL or SQLServer because of a perceived high cost of licensing, then the Oracle XE version should be considered first. Even with its restrictions it's still a powerful version of the Oracle Database and includes a large number of features and capabilities that other databases are struggling to implement.

It's not worth getting into a discussion about how my database is better than your database. After twenty five years of dealing with a variety of databases, the arguments are as passionate and similar to "Mac is better than Windows", "Linux is better than Windows", "Ubuntu is better than Red Hat", and "Solaris is better than Linux" ones. A manager making a decision today about which database to use will invariably go down the path with the following thoughts:

* All databases are the same
* Developers are easy to come by
* We should develop to run on any database
* We should use methodology X because it's the best

As discussed, all these points are not only fundamentally flawed but are dangerous to have. Yet, time after time it's what is sold and that is the market reality. What is best doesn't win out. It is hard to win on technology arguments when those making the decisions and a lot of those using it, have either no knowledge or no experience in it. A lot of business decisions regarding which database to use are made on hearsay. A lot of organizations don't even make a decision. When they buy an application they get a database bundled in with it. In which case it's the vendor who has decided on the database technology to be used, and the chances are they picked the database using a combination of license costs and skills of their developers.

This brings the discussion back to XE. It might have restrictions in usage but it still has a lot of power in it and can run very fast. From a tuning point of view, if an organization is considering switching to a simpler database, then I would recommend they consider and factor in the XE version. The purpose of this section is to show some methods for getting more value out of the XE database.

The Oracle 11 release of XE offers a free version of the Oracle Database which has some self imposed limits on it, restricting its use. These are as follows:

- Maximum data storage is limited to 11 GB of raw data
- Maximum SGA size is 1 GB
- Only available on Windows in 32 bit
- Only available on Linux in 64 bit
- Java is not included in the database
- Partitioning is not supported
- Oracle Multimedia is not included
- Deferred segment creation is no included
- Online index build is not supported
- Only one XE install is possible per server

Considering space is at a premium in XE, not having deferred segment creation means any table created, even if it doesn't have any rows in it, will consume some storage. The database administrator should look at moving these tables into a locally managed tablespace with the smallest block size possible.

It is important to note what is included:

- *rman* is included but a number of options, such as block level recovery are not
- Archiving
- ODBC gateway

- Part of Oracle Spatial is included
- Oracle Text is included
- Object support is included
- Oracle scheduler is included
- The full PL/SQL version is included and can be compiled (though this can get tricky)

With Java not included in the database, this has resulted in Oracle Multimedia not being included. This might be considered to be a showstopper for using Oracle XE as a multimedia database. The 11 GB limit might be considered to be a real limitation, but these two issues are not showstoppers but challenges to overcome for the keen database administrator.

Breaking the rules with XE

- With Oracle XE, images do not have to be stored in the database. If the application is small with only a couple of thousand digital objects (assuming each is small), then the 11 GB limit might be achievable to hold everything.
- The 11 GB limit is only an Oracle limit for data storage. It's not a limit on the server.
- Without the JVM the 1 GB limit is not that bad, but the database administrator needs to fine tune and control memory usage.
- The block size is 8 K of the database. As the digital objects are going to be stored externally this isn't going to be an issue.
- The use of the Oracle Heterogeneous Gateway (ODBC) enables large amounts of what one might refer to as "fluff" data to be stored on other databases (such as MySQL), thus ensuring only key data is stored in Oracle. Fluff data is data that can be easily accessed using simple keys (something similar to Big Data) and is not critical transactional dependent (eventual consistency as covered in *Chapter 3*, *The Multimedia Warehouse*). Even though the data is located in another database it can still be transparently accessed using PL/SQL and database links.
- If the gateway to another database is impractical to consider, data can be stored in external tables and populated using the *utl_file* PL/SQL package.

Even though multimedia cannot be used in the database, the Abstract Data Types pertaining to its structure can be used. They just have to be manually installed. The methods will not work so any image transformation needs to be done manually (see *Chapter 9, Understanding the limitations of Oracle Products*). The use of BFILEs is supported so the multimedia data types can still reference the external image file and access them as if they were stored in the database.

The database administrator has to be careful with backups, but it's likely that a server running XE will be running in a virtualization, which can be backed up separately.

VM vSphere

VM vSphere is a product from VMware (see http://www.vmware.com/) that enables the computer to be a complete virtualization server. The free version supports 10 concurrent virtualizations. Organizations needing to run more need to either pay for a license upgrade or obtain a new server.

A server installed with vSphere can be installed with ten Linux virtualizations in it. If the server purchased has 24 GB of memory then each virtualization running can make use of 2.4 GB of memory. It's possible to install XE in each virtualization. Considering the 1 GB memory limit of Oracle XE, this leaves 1.5 GB for operating system file caching or for other installed databases or products (such as a HTTP server). The server can now run ten installs of XE in a number of configurations, enabling a healthy volume of data to be stored. The small storage overheads of XE mean the whole environment could be located on one or two solid state drives. Oracle Database links could be used to enable the databases in each VM to communicate with each other. As everything is stored in the same server the network overheads of passing data between the virtualizations would be quite small.

One SSD is needed for the virtualizations and another for backup. Such a setup including hardware could come in for a total cost of under $2 K and yet resolve the requirements of many small to medium sized applications.

For a multimedia application, as the images are stored externally, they could be located on a separate drive (possibly mirrored) which is then networked and made available to all the virtualizations. An application built and assuming that there is only one server for loading and managing the images could allow all the other databases to access the images as if they owned them. This would bypass the locking issues traditionally found in a clustered environment.

Such an environment can offer the same performance and backup/recovery capabilities of many larger and costlier systems.

Scenario 1 - Separate install

The server is configured to hold between 8 and 10 virtualizations. Each one runs XE and each one has its own HTTP server for delivering images and data. Each virtualization is separate and independent and the assumption is each application will not consume more than 11 GB of data. Depending on the volume of images, they can be stored internally or externally.

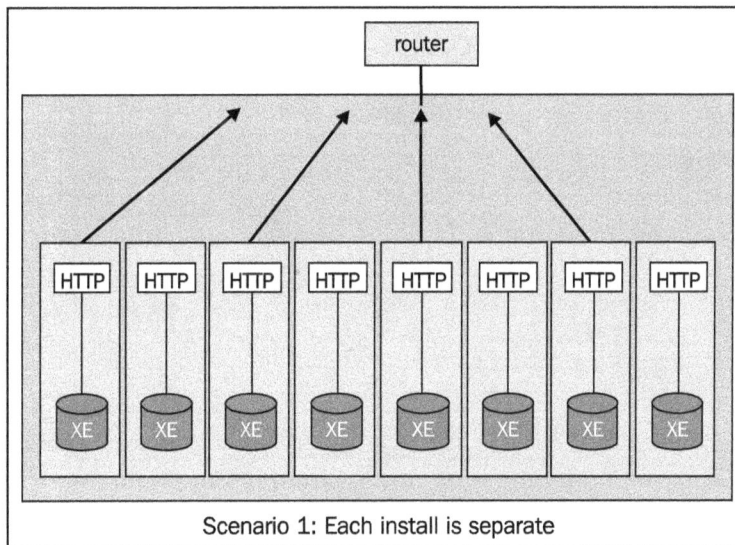

Scenario 1: Each install is separate

Scenario 2 - Replicated, high throughput

In this scenario, the volume of data is under 11 GB in total for the application, but the goal is to handle a large number of users. There is only one application and requires a high throughput. The challenge is to implement a form of replication between the servers. As the virtualizations are all located on the same server (meaning high inter connectivity speed between them), replication could be synchronous across all the virtualizations. This means as part of the same transaction, when an update or lock is taken in one environment, it's taken against all. Using the built in capabilities of a two phase commit and careful application of triggers on DML, this could be achieved.

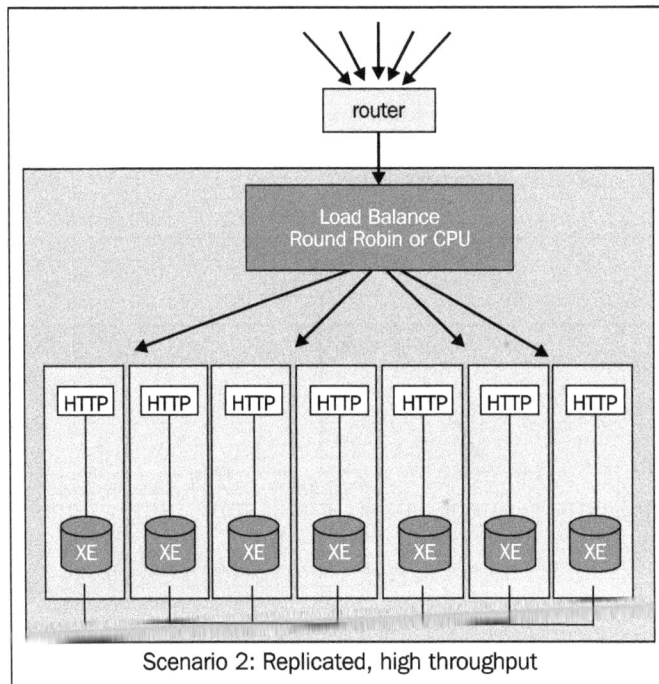

Scenario 2: Replicated, high throughput

Scenario 3 - Image server

In this scenario one virtualization acts as a dedicated environment to retrieve the digital objects. This can be done via the HTTP server or could be done via a simplified XE database. Alternately the digital objects could be stored in a basic structure in a database such as MySQL.

The only transactions performed are to verify the request is authentic and then delivery the digital object. It's also possible to extend this to include a transformation server. The management feature in vSphere can be used to control/throttle CPU usage for the transformation server, ensuring when it's processing it does not impact other virtualizations.

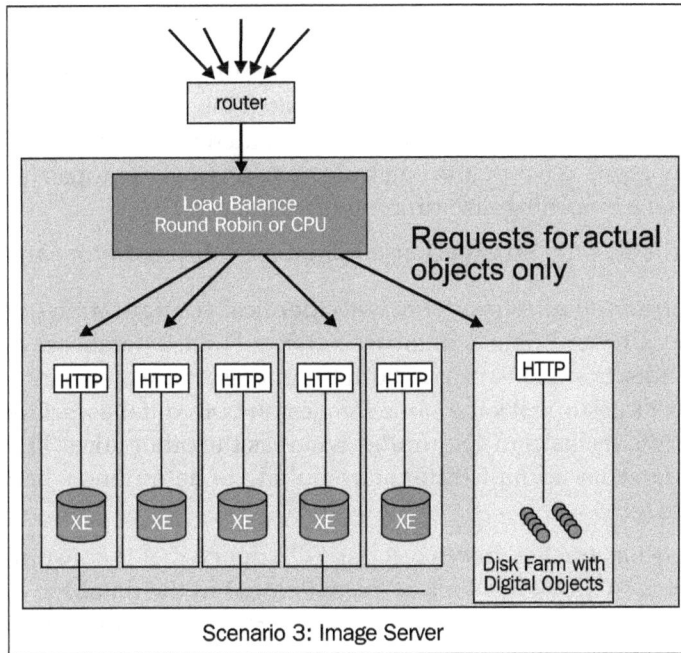

Scenario 3: Image Server

Summary

Tuning an Oracle Database to enable the ability to store large volumes of unstructured data involves more than just adjusting some database parameters. It involves the administrator being involved with management and the system administrators to procure the optimal hardware and then working closely with developers to get the design right for loading and retrieving digital objects. The database administrator needs to be well versed in how the network works, how it integrates with the firewall, and ensure there are no network bottlenecks.

The skill set required by the administrator also needs to be extended to include a very good knowledge on parallelism, hardware, partitioning and backup/recovery.

Chapter 9, Understanding the Limitations of Oracle Products, will review a set of products within the Oracle product set and describe how well they work with Oracle Multimedia.

Exercises

The following tuning issues are based on real-life experiences. The solutions to them cannot be found in this chapter or on the Internet, but require real-life tuning experience to resolve them. A database administrator who is trained to think laterally is likely to be able to come up the solutions to them very quickly, after eliminating the obvious non issues.

1. Describe the approach an administrator should take to resolve this real life Oracle 11.2.0.2 tuning issue. At 1 a.m. a batch job starts running to load new images into a multimedia warehouse. The batch job takes about five hours to run. Every night at 3 a.m. the batch slows to a crawl or stops altogether even though there is nothing else running on the server.

   Note: It's likely only an experienced database administrator can resolve this.

2. An organization has two servers with identical configuration (memory, disk, and CPU) and Oracle database version 11.2.0.2 databases on them. At 3 p.m. an identical job is run on both to process and watermark 1000 digital images. Let's assume it's the same images on both databases. One database can complete its tasks in 45 minutes whereas the other takes 3 hours. Where would a database administrator start looking to determine where tuning is required?

3. A database has tracked down a rogue SQL query that is consuming 100 percent of the CPU. They look at the statement in the database and decide to manually tune it from notepad/vi and use SQL*Plus with autotrace on to see how it works. The statement is looks something like:

```
select ta.columnx
from tablea ta, tableb tb, tablec tc
where ta.pk = tb.fk and
      tb.fk = tc.fk and
      tc.columny = 1234;
```

   When the database administrator runs the statement and puts in the value 1234 (replacing the only bind value in the SQL statement), the SQL statement returns in under a second with minimal CPU being used. The trace says the indexes are being correctly used.

   What major clue has the database administrator been given as to the likely cause of the statement running poorly?

4. You are an Oracle Database administrator tasked with setting up a database that will be used to hold 1 petabyte (1000 terabytes) of digital images, audio, and video, including 300 TB of HD video.

   Specify the architecture you would use to configure the database, the platform, the tablespace setup, and the backup strategy. Include recommendations for enabling the delivery of streaming video and being able to support 1000 concurrent users doing a digital object search, purchase, and delivery. The site must be accessible to the Internet and has to be as close to 24 x 7 as is possible. Assume the budget for hardware and licensing is not important but should be cost justifiable (the budget isn't infinite and all costs have to be properly justified). Finally, assume there is a 100 MB Internet connection on the site.

5. Taking exercise 4 as a base, perform the same exercise except this time the budget is fixed at a price of $200,000 which must cover all hardware costs only (assume software cost is handled separately and not managed by you). Determine an architecture that can achieve all the same expectations and performance capabilities as addressed in exercise 4. Use current hardware costs as available on the Internet as a basis to keep within this tight budget. The solution has to ensure that there is no data loss, no downtime, and the environment has sufficient capacity to handle 1000 concurrent users. Assume there is a 10 MB Internet connection. The solution can involve a cloud solution if it's proven cost effective, in which case allow for 50 TB of data downloads per year.

9

Understanding the Limitations of Oracle Products

This chapter reviews most of the Oracle Database features, options, and add-ons and discusses how well they work with unstructured data. Each section also covers potential directions the Oracle Database could move in to better work with this type of data.

This chapter isn't designed to focus on what Oracle can't do but rather shows the potential for the product to grow considering the sound and sturdy architecture it's based on.

What has become apparent when working with Oracle is that the database has a solid foundation which helps when working with unstructured data. From the use of SecureFiles, its support for object types, its locking mechanism, security, memory management, optimizer, and tight integration with capabilities such as XML and Spatial, the database offers a very secure base. From this secure base we can build and expand, to support and scale large volumes of different types of unstructured data.

The basic requirements

A database management system that is centred around storing and managing unstructured data with multimedia should satisfy the requirements given later.

Acting as more than a filesystem

The traditional filesystem has severe limitations associated with it. Most filesystems including Windows NTFS and Unix UFS do not scale. They have limitations on file size's length, filename's length, number of files per directory as well as performance issues searching against them, performing maintenance, and navigating through them. Security varies is complex to manage and in some cases hard to audit and track when changes are made. They do not efficiently manage versioning, natively index the data, and enable multi-dimensional views of the data.

Most operating systems are woefully inadequate for the storage of unstructured data, and yet they are still needed, because a large number of applications (such as Adobe Photoshop) are centered around the concept of reading and writing to a filesystem.

So ingrained is the concept of a filesystem to most developers; the idea of using a different structure is a completely alien concept that cannot be envisaged. Though a database management system should be able to mimic a traditional filesystem, it should extend the concept into new areas. It should push the boundaries and introduce new concepts and ideas that are better suited for the data.

Full backup/recovery

Any system should offer full recovery to the last committed transaction. Additionally, it should support the ability to do partial rollbacks, rollback to a point in time, and provide a consistent view for auditing to any time. Backup should not impact performance, and the volume and size of data should not impact backup or recovery.

Individual recovery should be possible, enabling one LOB (file, digital object) to be restored from any point in time. Groups of LOBs (projects) should also be able to be recovered as one unit.

Long term archival

The data should be able to be stored or backed up in a format that is not propriety. This includes the ability to use open source tools for accessing it. A good example is Gzip. This is a format which is well-documented, open, and well-used. It's likely that it will still be used and available in 10 to 20 years' time.

The data storage format needs to be vendor independent. To highlight this, if you were given a backup of an Oracle V4 database, could you extract the data from it? Keep in mind that you have to find the software to run the database, and hopefully, if you do find it, it works on the hardware you have. Oracle V4 was released around 30 years ago. So, trying to plan an archival strategy that will last a hundred years is a daunting challenge. Government departments and museums are each likely to be in a situation where they have to think of long-term storage.

The key is to have a system that encourages data exercising, where the data can be easily and quickly moved between different storage formats and devices, so that if it's determined, the format is likely to become legacy, then it can be moved to one that isn't.

Data distribution and network balancing

With image delivery and a large number of concurrent users, the bottleneck will be the network. If delivery is done via the Internet, then the lower gateway speed will result in this bottleneck becoming apparent much earlier. Solutions include being able to intelligently throttle image delivery based on a variety of application controllable actions, including image type, priority and size, with the ability to restart, monitor, track, and report on failure.

Another method is the ability to use multiple networks, potentially located at different points in the country or the world. So, being able to redirect transactions to the least-used network or network closer to a customer and doing it automatically is an important capability. Replication of digital images across the network should be able to be done securely, quickly, and reliably. This might involve using the network itself or a more manual method such as extracting to portable drive and delivering it to the remote site via e-mail, where it is then loaded in.

High speed and scalable image loading and processing

Image ingest involves being able to load large numbers of images into the database, in parallel, and process them (transform, extract metadata, watermark, index), using the resources of the server to minimize the load time.

Real-time monitoring of the database should be able to be performed with automatic calculation of estimated load time completions. The administrator or optimizer should be able to throttle loads to ensure they do not impact online users or other load jobs. Very large digital images (larger than 10 GB) should be able to be loaded into the database in parallel if the hardware supports it.

Storage scalability to petabytes of data

There should be no limitations to any parts of the database. Digital images in the next 10 years will individually grow to the terabyte mark, requiring large volumes of data storage. The ability to store more than a petabyte (1024 terabytes) of digital objects should be supported with additional efficient storage, management, and backup/recovery mechanisms.

Flexible image delivery

Experience has shown that the formats that digital objects are stored in become obsolete over time. This is most apparent with digital video, where AVI formats from 10 years ago cannot be played now. Document formats also change over time, especially propriety formats. This means, the data has to be exercised and easily moved to a more updated format. This has to be done easily, with minimal impact, data loss, or degradation in quality.

There are multiple ways for delivering an image, and the database should support a number of these ways, including the traditional browser download but should also support FTP, SSH (sftp), SSL (https), and new network protocols as they appear (such as TCP 6). In addition, compression, such as zip, where justified should be able to be used.

Security, auditing, and protection from user error (versioning)

Security should be able to be configured down to a fine grain level. Role-based security is ideal, with roles being able to be applied down to individual metadata values in an image and parts or actions on an image. To edit the copyright metadata field, you need the correct role on it; to add a watermark to the image, you need a role to do it even though you might have the role to create a thumbnail on it.

All actions, access attempts, and views should be able to be audited. Sharing an image or even copying it should be able to be audited. All actions including deletion when performed against an image, should be able to be rolled back to any point of time.

Supporting for most image types

With hundreds of image types available, the system should be able to process and handle as many as possible, if not all formats. This includes formats for documents, video, audio and digital images. In the future with new multimedia types appearing (such as 3D objects), the system should be able to handle the processing of them.

The system should be able to index and enable complex searching on all digital objects, as well as handling all metadata supporting those objects. It should be able to adapt to new image formats without major upgrades or enhancements. It should be able to convert between any type and cross convert between major types (such as extracting an image from a video, converting PDF to a thumbnail, or extracting audio from a video).

Litmus test

When the idea of desktop virtualizations appeared over 10 years ago, most personal computers and laptops did not have sufficient capacity to run one with sufficient speed. The concept of having another computer run inside another offered the ability to mix operating systems (having Linux run inside Windows) and helped solve the issue of trying to run an operating system application. A number of years ago, Apple released their operating system, which enabled a Windows kernel to run within the Mac OS. With the growth of 64-bit personal computers and laptops supporting more cores and memory, the idea of running one or more virtualizations inside a computer is now common place, and they perform very well.

With databases and unstructured data, a litmus test similar to a virtualization, can be set up to judge the effective performance and capabilities of it. The goal is to be able to completely run a database, which resides inside another database. This includes the kernel and all the database files; each value being stored as a LOB or LOBs inside the database. The reader might be pondering about the benefit of such an exercise which initially gives the appearance of an interesting but futile activity. Some key goals of a database is to provide an environment that can protect and safeguard data. Storing and running other databases inside a database solves a number of issues, especially, heterogeneous integration (if the database is aware of what it is storing). The attempt itself, to design, architect, and build such a structure would push the boundaries of backup, recovery, tuning, monitoring, integration and performance, and enabling databases to grow into new and exciting areas. It pushes the boundaries and forces system architects to think and treat data differently.

At the time of writing, the idea of storing one database inside another is still in its infancy. It might be possible to store one or more MySQL databases inside Oracle and get good performance, but it's unlikely storing one Oracle Database inside another would perform. The only way of achieving this is via the **Oracle Database Filesystem (DBFS)**.

A comparison

As technology is always changing, especially software, trying to accurately compare two different database vendors is fraught with dangers. Each vendor is releasing new versions of their product. In a number of cases, a direct comparison of any two features might be an invalid comparison because of the core differences in the architecture between them.

The following scale highlights a personal observation based on the capabilities for managing unstructured data within the database. Though Oracle is a long way ahead of other vendors, there is still a lot it can do to enhance and improve the database to support unstructured data. Refer to the following diagram:

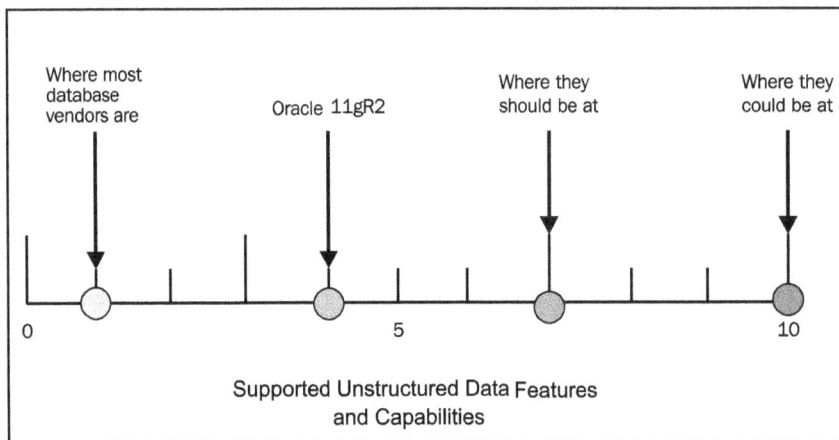

Oracle products

Oracle has a large variety of products which integrate with the database, and allow it to be managed, as well as, the general features within it. This section breaks down those products and features into groups and then looks at each group to see the strengths, weaknesses, and ideal enhancements the product needs to work best with unstructured data and multimedia.

The comments against each product and tool are my own personal comments based on usage and observation. They should in no way be used to evaluate the strengths and weaknesses of the database, as by the time of publication, some of these tools are likely be updated and offer new capabilities. The observations are accurate as of Oracle 11gR2. Though enhancement ideas are suggested, they are by no means a full set of potential features that can be added and just represent the tip of the iceberg.

Development

With the release of Oracle8i came the support for objects, which included abstract data types, repeating field structures, row references, and improvements in LOB support. The Oracle Database went from being a relational database to an object relational database and with that the rules for development changed. Developers could still follow traditional relational design, they could use an object-oriented approach, or they could mix the two adopting the best features to meet their requirements. On the development side adoption of these new object features could only work if the tools and a number of features in the database could work with them. As an interim solution Oracle introduced the object view, which allowed a layer over the objects to make them look like a relational table. In a later release with DML capabilities on views being introduced, these object views enabled developers to use their existing tools in a schema using objects.

As a lot of these developments were designed to work across multiple databases, and as the other vendors didn't introduce support for objects, the decision by most developers was to hold off using the new object features until the tools were enhanced to natively support it. In the interim, it was considered much simpler to stay with a relational design. By Oracle 11gR2, the support for object features is still an issue, not only with third-party tools but equally so with Oracle products and features in the database. The lack of full support for these features has slowed down their usage, ultimately giving the impression of a slow adoption rate.

SQL Developer (v3.1)

This is a Java-based product designed to provide a graphical interface for developers into the database. The product is cross-platform and can also integrate with other databases including MySQL. Modules built into the product assist in data migration. The product works with all Oracle versions, including some of the older ones that are not supported.

The interface provides a huge range of functionality, making it an ideal tool for developers to navigate through one or more databases. Its tight integration with PL/SQL and the Oracle data dictionary enables developers to quickly perform data definition changes and see contents of tables. In addition, it provides data modeling tools and has integration features with flashback, data mining, and Oracle spatial. SQL Developer is a very powerful and robust tool for working with relational data.

The following screenshots show how the columns used in the table described in *Appendix E, Loading and Reading* called TEST_LOAD, are viewed in SQL Developer:

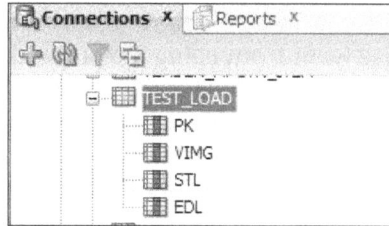

When working with multimedia and unstructured data, the tool does not offer many features to help the developer. The handling of type support is very basic and table navigation and data viewing is very restricted, making it very hard to view the values of sub types (as shown in the following screenshot). The interface does not allow types to be viewed hierarchically. The reporting engine (which offers a whole range of reports), does not offer much to help the developer understand LOB storage. Refer to the following screenshot:

Columns | Data | Constraints | Grants | Statistics | Triggers | Flashback | Dependencies | Details | Partitions | Indexes | SQL

	COLUMN_NAME	DATA_TYPE	NULLABLE	DATA_DEFAULT	COLUMN_ID	COMMENTS
1	PK	NUMBER(16,0)	Yes	(null)	1	(null)
2	VIMG	ORDIMAGE	Yes	(null)	2	(null)
3	STL	TIMESTAMP(6)	Yes	(null)	3	(null)
4	EDL	TIMESTAMP(6)	Yes	(null)	4	(null)

Options are needed to easily retrieve the length of BLOBs, or see which ones are empty versus not initialized. Smarter integration with Oracle Multimedia is required enabling a developer to not only view the contents of the BLOB but to perform some of the methods against it, including transformation, metadata extraction, and watermarking

Columns | Data | Constraints | Grants | Statistics | Triggers | Flashback | Dependencies | Details | Partitions | Indexes | SQL

Sort.. Filter:

	PK	VIMG	STL	EDL
1	1749423	[ORDSYS.ORDIMAGE]	09/JUN/12 04:14:09.376000000 PM	09/JUN/12 04:14:09.751000000 PM
2	1749424	[ORDSYS.ORDIMAGE]	09/JUN/12 04:14:09.751000000 PM	09/JUN/12 04:14:11.186000000 PM
3	1749425	[ORDSYS.ORDIMAGE]	09/JUN/12 04:14:11.186000000 PM	09/JUN/12 04:14:12.309000000 PM
4	1749426	[ORDSYS.ORDIMAGE]	09/JUN/12 04:14:12.309000000 PM	09/JUN/12 04:14:14.259000000 PM
5	1749428	[ORDSYS.ORDIMAGE]	09/JUN/12 04:14:15.258000000 PM	09/JUN/12 04:14:16.615000000 PM
6	1749429	[ORDSYS.ORDIMAGE]	09/JUN/12 04:14:16.615000000 PM	09/JUN/12 04:14:17.863000000 PM
7	1749431	[ORDSYS.ORDIMAGE]	09/JUN/12 04:14:19.080000000 PM	09/JUN/12 04:14:19.657000000 PM
8	1749432	[ORDSYS.ORDIMAGE]	09/JUN/12 04:14:19.657000000 PM	09/JUN/12 04:14:20.390000000 PM

SQL Developer is a tool that has the potential to be extended to make it a powerful interface for multimedia developers.

SQL*Plus

This is a command-line tool for interfacing to the Oracle Database. It exists on all Oracle releases and has been in existence since the very early releases of Oracle. It is traditionally used during installation and by database administrators to perform maintenance and schema configurations against the database. It has a basic reporting engine and can be used to perform ad hoc database queries and extract text-based reports. PL/SQL and Java can be compiled into the database using it.

For those working with unstructured data and multimedia, it is the key tool to use. SQL*Plus has changed minimally over the last 20 years, but with Oracle 10*g*, it can now correctly display most object types. With Oracle 11*g* displaying types containing raw characters was resolved by displaying them as hex, enabling the administrator to safely perform complex queries against objects and not worry about special characters impacting the display.

PL/SQL

PL/SQL is a true programming language based on the computer language called ADA. It is tightly integrated into the database. It has support for most Oracle features and has great support for Oracle objects. Function calls, data types, parameters, and even DML statements can be referenced. This makes PL/SQL the ideal language for all development against Oracle.

With Oracle 11*g* and the ability to natively and simply compile PL/SQL, the need to use external programs for image processing was dramatically reduced.

To work more with unstructured data, PL/SQL needs capabilities that enable it to query and modify raw data. New coding language constructs, similar to those found in C, are needed to work with binary data.

Supplied packages

The core Oracle Database comes bundled with a large number of supplied packages, which can be accessed from PL/SQL or Java. These packages enable the capabilities of the database to be extended.

Useful packages when working with unstructured include:

- `dbms_crypto`: This package encrypts and decrypts stored data
- `dbms_epg`: This package configures the embedded PL/SQL gateway
- `dbms_file_transfer`: This package copies a binary file between databases
- `dbms_lob`: This package manages Blobs, Clobs, BFiles, and temporary lobs
- `dbms_metadata`: This package reverses engineer DDL or DML commands
- `dbms_session`: This package sets session security and preferences
- `dbms_stats`: This package views and collects optimizer statistics
- `dbms_sql`: This package is a dynamic SQL
- `dbms_xa`: This package enables transactions to be shared across session (and HTML pages)
- `dbms_xmldom`: This package accesses XMLType objects
- `htf/htp`: XMLType objects is a dynamic generation of HTML commands
- `owa_cookie`: This package sends and retrieves HTTP cookies
- `owa_util`: These packages are Utility programs for managing the CGI of an environment
- `sdo_geom`: These packages are the spatial geometry functions
- `utl_file`: This package is an operating stream file I/O
- `utl_http`: This package makes HTTP calls from within the database
- `utl_inaddr`: These packages are the utilities to support Internet addressing (host name lookup)
- `utl_raw`: These packages are the utilities to manipulate raw data
- `utl_smtp`: This package enables e-mail to be sent using SMTP
- `utl_tcp`: This package enables communication using TCP/IP
- `utl_url`: This package escapes or captures a URL
- `wpg_docload`: This package downloads a BLOB or a Bfile

These just represent a subset of the packages available to the developer.

For working with unstructured data, more packages would be useful, especially ones that involve greater interaction and manipulation of raw data. In addition, more Internet-based features are needed including ones that enable native integration with remote data sources, such as Amazon or other third-party storage systems (though as I argue later, the heterogeneous gateway is likely to be a better integration solution).

PL/SQL Web Toolkit

These are a set of tools used for the development of HTML applications that run inside the database. Tools such as Apex are built on top of it. Mod PL/SQL is the framework used to visualize it. The framework provides a set of packages which enable dynamic HTML pages to be built.

Mod PL/SQL first appeared in 1995. It has a simple mechanism to integrate it with a BLOB but has no native support for Oracle Multimedia or even Oracle Spatial. Such support can be easily built in to the framework. So this direct integration, though nice to have, isn't hard to overcome.

The framework has matured to the point, where it is not enhanced much between releases. The framework could be enhanced with seamless integration from other supplied packages including dbms_xe (enabling transactions that are full of various states), FTP, SSH, and mail servers (to retrieve e-mail and send it with multiple digital objects embedded in the actual e-mail).

The framework offers no integration with JavaScript but can be extended to include JavaScript calls or references to JavaScript files. The widespread acceptance of JavaScript would indicate that the framework should be expanded to include a series of dynamic JavaScript libraries, enabling drag/drop, image zooming, loading, and manipulation. Calendar functions, word processing, and digital object editing options would also be useful to have bundled in. So, rather than trying to rely on open source, these core ones would be included with Mod PL/SQL and would be guaranteed to work across multiple browsers.

In addition, Mod PL/SQL should be enhanced further to work with HTML-5, video streaming, and to work on smart phone devices.

SQL

The SQL language is an open standard and well-supported by Oracle. The language itself is mathematically based and designed around relational data. With the introduction of object types, the language has grown to encompass them. The SQL language itself has not grown to work with unstructured data. This has been left up to each vendor to provide functions.

Even though Oracle offers a series of supplied packages that can be used to do basic queries against binary objects, it lacks the functions to do more advanced capabilities. Being able to search an MPEG video, find the starting frames, and retrieve the headers of the first ten frames is just not possible in SQL. A purpose-built program is needed. Being able to run a SQL statement that finds a metatag value embedded in an image is not possible. It requires extracted into a separate XML file on load. When processing digital objects, this involves working with raw data. Oracle provides the `utl_raw` package, which has a variety of functions, but the package is not designed to work with multimedia objects.

When dealing with digital images, the core focus centers around a color-space. Being able to simply retrieve the RGB tuple from a raw digital image would enable a program to then easily do transformations on it, enabling a whole new set of filters and image commands to be built into the database. This is a very important point to raise. Imagine being able to run a query against any digital image (even if compressed using JPEG, PNG, GIF, or similar) and retrieve pixel information. The query could retrieve a subset of pixels and then using a `where` clause and image analysis, perform complex querying. An example might involve doing a query that finds the area in an image that is dark or has a certain texture. Such a query could be extended to be time-based and run against a video. This notion changes the whole attitude towards querying digital objects. It provides a framework, which has the potential to be mathematically described and controlled. Transformation commands (such as rotate, and mirror) are all well-described with basic geometrical analysis, which if used, could enable functional manipulation of sets of pixels in a digital image using standard DML. Again, similar capabilities could be extended to audio.

The core focus of SQL is still relational data with a viewpoint that matches it. Only by switching to a multimedia view and the complexities entailed with it can the SQL language grow and expand to handle a new range of data.

Java

The Java VM that runs inside the Oracle Database offers capabilities and features to do advanced processing and manipulation of images. With a large-supported library available for working with multimedia, Java is well-positioned to complement PL/SQL to provide a sound platform for managing unstructured data.

The Achilles heel of Java is its memory management; image processing, especially video processing is memory, and CPU aggressive. Memory needs to be efficiently managed and the concept of garbage collection is just not designed to work effectively with this processing in such a way that it can scale. Either a core change in how Java handles memory is required or a move back to the use of cartridges is needed by the Oracle Database. The obvious solution is to integrate Java in with a **graphics processing unit (GPU)**.

XML

The XML DB product offers a comprehensive platform for the parsing, querying, and management of XML data. Its tight integration with SQL and a large set of supplied PL/SQL packages enables complex XML commands to be written.

There is no native integration between XML and Multimedia. It's not possible to do an XML query against a JPEG image querying its XMP data. This involves, first stripping the data out, storing it, and then querying it.

The XML DB offers its own repository for the storage of digital objects. When this repository is used, it is restricted to the confines of XML DB and does not integrate with the rest of the database. Using the embedded gateway, it's very easy to set up an FTP server where any digital object can be added or retrieved from it. Once stored though, there is no access from within the database using standard commands to retrieve those digital objects. They are isolated within its structure. Between Oracle Multimedia, Spatial, and XML DB a unified structure is needed that combines the best features and capabilities of all three tool sets.

Edition-Based Redefinition

Edition-Based Redefinition, is a feature built into the database which enables multiple versions of an application and views to reside in the one schema (giving the appearance of multiple versions of a table). It can be used to test upgrades while maintaining the current release. That way if issues arise, there is no need to roll it back, the edition can just be removed.

Edition-Based Redefinition can work with object types and LOBs, but there are restrictions on their use. In addition, the use of cross-edition triggers has to be carefully managed.

This feature offers a lot of potential for database administrators. The performance aspect when dealing with LOBs is still not well-understood.

Apex (Oracle Application Express)

Apex is an Oracle application development tool designed around the quick development of small scale, relational-based applications. It's primarily built in PL/SQL and comes bundled in with the database, including the Oracle XE release. It was originally designed as a competing replacement product for Microsoft Access. The goal being to enable the easy development of an application that Access offers with the advanced capabilities that the Oracle Database offers. The tool is widely used and is portable across most versions of Oracle, and as the application, the code and the data are all stored in the database; its maintenance and management is very simple.

Access to APEX is via HTTP, and this can be either via Apache and Mod PL/SQL or the Oracle Embedded Gateway. The gateway was enhanced in Oracle10 to simplify the installation of Apex applications and ensure that they have a low footprint.

Apex is primarily designed for relational data and not multimedia or digital objects. Through API calls, it can access them, but the core application is not designed around the needs of multimedia. The interface, the options available, and even the manipulation and control of multimedia objects highlight that the core and strength of Apex is its tight integration with relational data.

It has the potential to tightly integrate with Oracle Multimedia and Spatial, because it's base code is built in PL/SQL. As already discussed, this is one of the best development tools for working with digital objects in an Oracle Database.

Storage

With multimedia having the potential to consume large volumes of storage, the need for the database to be able to efficiently manage it becomes very important. This section covers a number of database features related to storage.

Tablespaces and datafiles

The Oracle Database is built around database blocks and datafiles. A ROWID is a global unique ID that points to the row in a database. They enable high-speed access to the row and have been used for replication (but primary key replication is now the preferred method). The ROWID is tied to the block and used for recovery. It's a powerful concept and works well with the relational database.

With unstructured data, the concept is still valid but tends to impact on scalability when trying to manage this type of data. If a tablespace contains 100 GB of digital images and they need to be moved to another tablespace, then a large amount of redo is required to perform this action, even though the data itself does not change. For digital objects, once loaded into the database and processed, they are rarely modified. An important feature which is needed, is the ability to mark a LOB as read-only. Then, if it's moved to another tablespace, no redo is generated, just a call saying it has moved.

This concept introduces a new layer into the database architecture between the database block, fragment, and datafile. The LOB, its architecture, storage, and recovery is treated differently.

Storage parameters

When working with multimedia, there are some frequently reoccurring traits that come about when dealing with them as opposed to relational data:

- Once loaded in and processed, they are typically read-only (the metadata around them might change, but the LOB itself rarely does).

- They are large in size. Most start around the 10-MB mark and can grow into the tens of gigabytes.

- Access to them is sequential. Random access is only required when processing which is likely to be done on ingest. For streaming, which includes audio and video, access can be to a random point, but it's mostly then sequential.

The characteristics of multimedia push the boundaries of storage and encourage an architectural direction where disks perform large contiguous reads. A disk shouldn't read in 64 K at a time, but read in 10 MB at a time. One I/O to retrieve 10 MB is a concept that would benefit the performance of managing multimedia but is not designed into the core architecture of disk makers and the Oracle Database itself. It can be said that the database and disks can do large reads, but this is a combination of smaller reads grouped together. If the core disk is designed to do a large read in one go, the rules change. An 8 K, 16 K, or 32 K block size is one centered around relational data of which unstructured data has been able to piggy back off. What is needed is a new structure designed for multimedia and one which can adapt and grow to eventually deal with a terabyte or more individual-sized BLOB.

The Oracle Securefile architecture offers a huge improvement over the previous LOB storage structure (which again was a huge improvement over LONG fields). Only when disk manufacturers rethink and redesign their core hardware to deal with the new rules being brought on by multimedia, will the Securefile architecture be able to be adapted to meet the new capabilities. Until then it's limited by the capabilities of the database.

Partitioning

With Oracle8i, Oracle extended its relational partitioning support to include LOBs. This enables databases to grow into the hundreds of terabyte range by using this capability. For scalability, a tablespace containing a partition is loaded with unstructured data, marked as read-only and backed up. The database size is only limited by the number of partitions. With a partition-aware optimizer, and indexes that work locally and globally, queries can run intelligently by quickly locating and identifying the location of a LOB.

In a large multimedia warehouse, digital objects can be stored in a variety of ways. One way is time-based and partitions created and based on that (for example, a month of images is loaded into a partition). At the beginning of the next month, a new partition is created. Alternatively, digital objects can be loaded in via collections or business logical groups. A site can have tens to hundreds of collections each with their own unique business requirements. Time-based partitioning does not work well with this architecture, and the idea is to move to a function-based one. It can get more complex as the idea of being able to archive digital objects based on size, access, type, or even how frequently purchased, pushes partitioning into new areas, especially if the partitions are variable and can be updated. A mixture of read-only and heavy read/write partitioning is required.

Though Oracle partitioning can be carefully configured to achieve such a goal, the ideal is to introduce the concept of a read-only blob. Then with that concept integrated in with RMAN (which enables the ability to back up once, a read-only tablespace), along with a change in block structure such that there is no redo when a digital object is moved between tablespaces, will mean that the database can scale to manage a very large volume of digital objects. It will also have a small backup foot print and have the power and performance with manageability that partitioning gives.

ASM

Oracle's **Automated Storage Management** (**ASM**) is an Oracle-specific disk management system. It replaces the need for a filesystem and is designed around the needs of the Oracle Database and performance. It supports same configurations (stripe and mirror) with the ability to control down to a fine grain how data is stored. It enables some tables to be mirrored and others not to be. Doing the equivalent using raid on a traditional filesystem is more complex to implement.

The downside of ASM is that it is proprietary which makes it hard to justify its usage for systems requiring long term archival. Though ASM is designed for the generic Oracle Database, which enables a lot of unstructured data to be easily stored in it; based on concepts already discussed, there is the potential for ASM to be expanded to take on the particular storage needs of unstructured data and multimedia.

DBFS Filesystem

Database Filesystem (**DBFS**) is an interface between the database and an operating system enabling a filesystem to be created inside the Oracle Database. With a powerful PL/SQL API that enables all interactions to be trapped and controlled, it offers a powerful facility, showing that it is possible to use a database as more than just a relational database repository.

Its key limitation is that it only fully runs on Linux. On other platforms (such as Windows), the APIs are available to manually move files into the database, but without full integration, its usage is limited (in Oracle 12c WebDAV support is planned).

It is hoped that DBFS can be extended to work with other operating systems, and then push the boundaries for what a filesystem actually is. This would include tightly integrated search, transformation, and integration capabilities. Combined with the enhanced capabilities of ASM, such a structure would offer the ability to create a disk system that exploits the true power and capabilities of multimedia inside the database.

Monitoring

Being able to monitor and limit access to the database, especially as actions are performed against becomes an import, as the database grows in size and complexity. This section covers some of the database tools involved in this area.

Enterprise Manager

This product is a web-based tool designed for database administrators to easily manage one or more databases in their environment. With built-in monitoring and a whole range of products designed to help the administrator manage, monitor, and tune the environment, this tool is ideally suited for administrators.

Enterprise Manager has some product short comings with unstructured data:

- It cannot monitor large lobs being loaded into the database.

- There are no features to monitor delivery of blobs or to throttle or control their delivery.

- There are no features to control video streaming and memory management.

- Though there are features within the product for dealing with storage, the underlying architecture is focused on relational and not objects, making it very hard for database administrators to track and manage the database when large volumes of LOBs are stored.

- The monitoring architecture is designed around client/server and three-tier, making using it in a web-based environment (using the Oracle Embedded Gateway or Apache HTTP server with Mod PL/SQL) very difficult, as transactions cross between different sessions in a stateless environment.

Resource management

The resource manager is a tightly integrated database component that allows for the fine-grained control of resources used by queries and processes. This includes CPU, memory, server cores (parallelism), time usage, and disk I/O. Additional tight integration with Time Windows allows users on the database to equitably use the database based on business requirements. In some cases, it can prevent potential long running and resource hungry queries from running, and limit the number of concurrent sessions a user can have.

Resource manager is designed for a relational database using client/server. When using it in a stateless HTTP environment, some of the concepts which resource manager relies on (session management) disappear, and enabling certain limitations can result in unpredictable results.

When working with digital objects, a key feature is to be able to limit, throttle, and load balance the speed in which digital objects are loaded into the database. If users are loading them in via the browsers or via a disk system, having the option to control the speed of loading, can ensure effective load-balancing. Even being able to have large LOBs being linked in with `v$session_longops` (a view useful for monitoring long running operations) would prove to be a useful addition to the core database kernel.

Database

This section covers some of the database features used when working with multimedia.

Data types

Oracle provides full support for object data types with methods. The architecture is tightly integrated in with the database, PL/SQL, and Java. The object features are mature, well-documented, intimidating to use for those who are only used to relational, but offer capabilities that when correctly used can result in improved response times for queries.

Oracle Multimedia extends these base types in the ORDSYS schema, enabling column definitions for images, audio, video, and documents.

Advanced compression

As previously covered, compression of a digital object is different to data compression. In most cases, advanced compression will not provide any space savings when working with unstructured data, as its focus is primarily on relational data.

OLAP

Online Analytic and Processing (OLAP) engine is built seamlessly into the core Oracle Database. The OLAP engine is based around relational data, summarizing and enabling it to be queried using a variety of dimensions. Initial thoughts would lead to the conclusion that there is no natural fit between OLAP and multimedia.

The end goal of OLAP is to enable analysis to be done against data, which includes forecasting, aggregation, and data summaries, ultimately enabling a business to make intelligent decisions using the results produced by the OLAP engine. By expanding this to include multimedia, key critical business decisions can be made. The integration of business analytics and multimedia is still in its early days. Initially, multimedia can be used to enhance the graphical display side of the data, providing multidimensional views on it.

As the market matures and a better understanding of the role digital objects play and how they can be queried, summarized, and aggregated is formalized, only then will a large change in the direction of the marketplace take place to adopt these new capabilities.

Indexes

Oracle enables indexes to be created on relational tables. The index architecture is flexible enough to allow an API to be built to enable an index to be created on any LOB. Oracle Text and Spatial use this capability to build their own indexes on top of their own data structures.

As covered in *Chapter 3*, *The Multimedia Warehouse* and *Chapter 4*, *Searching the Multimedia Warehouse*, indexing digital objects is a long term and ongoing process due to the difficulty in trying to understand what the binary data in the object actually means. It's easy to index the metadata found within the object, as this is likely to be text-based, but trying to build an index enabling searches to find fuzzy type attributes is very difficult to do. Combined with the different nature of the digital photos, video, and audio, the conclusion that can be drawn is that the maturity of indexing is still just not there.

By breaking down this complexity into sub types and indexing those only, some control can be achieved. It's possible to do speech recognition on audio podcasts but not on conversation involving multiple concurrent speakers or audio of general sounds. Digital photos of fingerprints and faces can now be searched on using recognition algorithms, which have been devised and refined over the last 15 years. In some cases, advanced image recognition can be deployed on video when looking for faces or some simpler objects. In the next 10 years, this technology will improve as the demand for it grows. It's important that the Oracle Database is integrated with this technology and can use it effectively. By doing it, it will open up the whole market for multimedia databases which focus on information analysis.

Embedded gateway

The Oracle Embedded gateway is a HTTP server that is tightly integrated in with the Oracle Listener. Its use negates the need for a Mod PL/SQL application to use the Apache HTTP server.

The gateway enables the loading (via browser) and unloading (via the `wpg_docload` package) of digital objects. As useful and simple as the gateway is, it doesn't enable scalability at the network level by being able to load balance and control the speed at which BLOBS are retrieved and loaded into the database. The gateway doesn't support the monitoring of a BLOB, as it gets loaded into the gateway table (such a feature would enable a program to estimate load time). Improvements can be made on the integration of the gateway and Oracle Multimedia.

Data dictionary

The Oracle data dictionary provides a lot of information about segments (storage used) in the database. It has full support for LOBs and object types (though one does wonder at times why there is still the odd column in the dictionary with a LONG type, as can be found in user_views).

With built-in packages to reverse engineer any structure in the database (such as `dbms_metadata`), the Oracle data dictionary provides an easy-to-use internal mechanism for retrieving structure information.

To extend the dictionary to further support LOBs would include the ability to not only capture storage sizing but the ability to monitor full and partial retrieval of those LOBs. This might be considered to be more part of the V$ queries, but a long-term view would be useful. Such a feature would be useful for the optimizer to determine caching and could be used by a partitioning mechanism to determine whether the LOB needs archiving. Such a feature could be built using row-level triggers, but having it tightly integrated into the core structure would make the capability easier to use.

If, in addition, it keeps figures such as the average, min, and max time to deliver a LOB, this could also be useful to the optimizer to balance the query and delivery performance of it.

Heterogeneous gateway

Oracle provides a number of gateway products, enabling the database to pass data and queries to other vendor databases. An ODBC gateway comes bundled in with the database and as of Oracle 11, it enables simple DML statements (non-two-phase commit) against these data sources.

The gateway has a lot of limitations, especially when it comes to querying tables with columns that do not match the Oracle ones (columns with lengths greater than 4000 characters). At times, the gateway treats them as LONG fields, resulting in the enforcement of obsolete restrictions on them, and making it hard to read or write to them.

An ideal gateway capability would be to query remote HTTP sites and to treat the resultant data as rows in a table. This can be done using the utl_http package, but having it built into the SQL engine would offer a lot of powerful capabilities. In addition, if the icons or images embedded are returned as LOB fields, it would make retrieval of data using HTTP so much simpler and more SQL focused.

A similar capability would be ideal for querying SMTP servers (to retrieve and send e-mail) as well as FTP sites. Where, in this case, a connection by a hierarchical query would enable navigation through sub directories.

Such features go a long way to change the mindset for querying data and changing it from being relational focused to being unstructured data focused.

Tuning

Tuning is just more than writing a SQL statement and hoping the optimizer can make it run fast. With digital objects, the rules change. As has been covered in *Chapter 8, Tuning*, a bottleneck is the network. The question that has to be asked is how efficient is the optimizer for dealing with varying network loads?

Automatic memory management

This is a feature available in Oracle that enables the database to collect performance statistics — using the **Automatic Workload Repository (AWR)** — and then by doing analysis on these statistics adjust the distribution of memory in the Oracle SGA to optimize usage. This might involve shrinking or increasing the number of block buffers and/or shrinking the shared pool in addition to other database memory structures.

As previously covered, the nature of digital objects lends itself to a structure where the memory distribution is tightly controlled by the database administrator. As AWR is based more on relational concepts than multimedia, the administrator is better suited to manually monitor and control memory.

The database administrator also when designing a database to hold large volumes of digital objects has to determine which objects should be cached or read directly from disk. The database would be well-suited to being able to mark a LOB in a row as being able to be cached, because it's likely that it will be accessing it and even locking it in memory. Such a capability would work well with DBFS.

In cases where a digital object holds multiple objects (for example, a DNG has a TIF thumbnail embedded in it), the ability to partially cache a LOB might be useful. For video streaming, a lot of people do previews and only look at the first 30 seconds. Rather than extracting it and storing the preview separately, if the first 30 seconds of a video could be cached, then access to a stream would be faster.

This leads to the idea that digital objects really need their own area or areas of the SGA for caching. If the idea of re-architecting the block size for digital objects to optimize its use for large contiguous reads from disk is implemented, a new type of tablespace could be created and designed optimally for digital object storage. Such a tablespace would have its own memory and caching requirements and could be configured such that it would not impact the relational side of the database.

Optimizer

The Oracle Optimizer has since its rule-based days in Oracle7, matured to a point where it now offers a very intelligent and powerful facility for ensuring whether a query runs as fast and efficiently as it possibly can. By collecting a large volume of statistics, the optimizer has the ability to tune itself and make smart use of the performance and speed of the resources available to it.

The Optimizer isn't very LOB aware, and when it comes to the issue of the network, image delivery and even streaming, the Optimizer still is in its infancy. As covered with the data dictionary and memory management, the optimizer will be able to work more efficiently with multimedia if it can collect more statistics and be more aware about the different ways digital objects can be loaded, accessed, and delivered.

Networking

As previously mentioned, when it comes to tuning, the Oracle Database is focused around the relational concepts of balancing disk I/O with memory and CPU. With the use of LOBS, the focus has to extend to the network. More features and capabilities are needed at the network layer to ensure the high-speed transfer of LOBs, with the ability to load balance and to ensure the network does not become a bottleneck.

Backup/Recovery

Oracle provides a number of capabilities for backing up data and restoring the data in times of failure.

Total recall (flashback)

When Oracle introduced the concept of flashback in 10*g* and then formalized and enhanced it in 11*g*, it made database administrators review and question how they dealt with recovery from user error. With the ability to easily recover from a dropped table, deleted, or updated row, or even being able to roll back the entire database to a point in time, the notion of recovery became bidirectional. With the traditional strategy being to go back and roll forward, the new capabilities allowed the administrator to go from the current database and move backwards.

With the flashback features fully supporting unstructured data, the notion of recovery from user error needs to be expanded such that the core database inherently supports digital object versioning. Pioneered on the VMS operating system, which natively supported the concept with a number of management tools encompassing it, the idea is to expand versioning into a hierarchical structure, whereas images are modified, especially modified by different people, multiple incarnations can be created with one being the master image. Being able to rollback and review past images is similar to flashback, but should not be constrained by the size of the UNDO tablespace (which dictates how much information is stored to rollback). Storing versions in the UNDO tablespace is not efficient, and the architecture is more relationally focused. By adopting the concept of versioning and then building in an architecture that can efficiently compress the versions (by possibly storing only the changes between versions, similar to how an MPEG video stores the differences between consecutive frames), would enable the core goals of flashback without impacting the performance of the relational flashback by overwhelming the UNDO tablespace with very large digital object updates.

Redo logs and archives

Oracle stores all transactional data to enable full recovery in the redo logs. The logs are cycled and can be archived to a remote location, where they can be used by Data Guard with disaster recovery or by RMAN for general database recovery in the event of media or block failure.

The redo logs are a stable and mature feature of the Oracle Database. They are built around relational data and fully support object types and LOBs. As previously covered, they suffer from limitations when simple LOB management is performed. If a 10 GB LOB is moved between tablespaces, because the ROWID has changed, all blocks are logged. As the LOB itself hasn't changed, such an action generates a huge amount of redo and limits the scalability of actions such as archival, which if it was more efficiently supported, it could be done faster and more often.

Data guard

Data guard is a tool that has grown and matured since its early days when it was known for its ability to configure a standby database, which was needed for a disaster recovery. Since then the tool has grown to allow for the configuration of physical, logical, and snapshot databases. Using the redo logs and a system of processes to automatically move them between one or more databases, and then apply them to the database, Data Guard offers numerous capabilities, even allowing a standby database to be updated and queried while in standby mode (snapshot).

With Physical and Snapshot databases, the redo logs are applied to the disaster database ensuring all transactions, including ones involving the loading and managing of digital objects are applied. This allows for the full support of Oracle Multimedia and object types.

The Logical Standby database uses a different concept. It enables a subset of the primary database to be transferred to a disaster site. It does this by storing extra information in the redo logs and using that to reverse engineer data in them, into actual SQL statements, which are then applied against the logical standby site. There are limitations with the data types it can handle, and it precludes the use of object types.

To work more efficiently with multimedia, Data Guard needs to review how digital objects are best handled. In some cases, there is a need to move a large subset of digital objects between an internal site and an external DMZ site (release a subset of public images). One current method to achieve this without incurring huge redo or having to go through the issue of using data pump, is to copy the digital objects to a tablespace which is then made into a transportable one. The datafiles in the tablespace are then pushed to the DMZ, and the digital objects are then carefully merged in with the ones on the site.

Another capability Data Guard needs is the ability to copy/transfer large volumes of digital objects to completely different sites to provide network load balance. For a site that does a large amount of video streaming worldwide, it might be more efficient to move large sets of videos to servers that are located physically closer to the customer base (for example, one could locate the video's on a server in Australia, on the US East Coast, US West Coast, and the UK). This is a similar strategy to the one that Amazon has employed to manage their virtualization servers.

RMAN

RMAN is Oracle Database's backup and recovery tool. It is tightly integrated into the database enabling fast and high-speed backups to be performed. For large databases, the strategy with RMAN is incremental forever (one backup) and the careful management of incremental and cumulative backups means only one backup is ever needed. Though this strategy might seem well-suited for a relational database, it is not an ideal solution for unstructured data. Most unstructured data is stored once and unlikely to change. The ideal solution is to expand on the concept of read-only tablespaces and make read-only BLOBS within a column. An administrator being able to mark a BLOB in a row as read-only means that RMAN needs to back it up once and never again. Such a capability removes the requirement of the database administrator to create partitions and structures within the database that focus around backup capabilities, and they can architect around performance.

In addition, a weakness of RMAN is that the backups it creates are proprietary. Unlike a tool such as Gzip, which is open source, access to the contents of RMAN backups is only possible using RMAN. An ideal solution for long-term archival is to have a tool that can strip BLOBS out of an RMAN backup and save them to the filesystem.

Utilities

Oracle data pump is a tool that enables the database administrator to export parts or all the data in a database to an external file or files, which can then be imported into other Oracle Databases. The export created can be reloaded into databases which are equal to or greater in version than the one it was exported from. The tool fully supports object types and any type of data.

From a data archival view, it would be ideal to be able to extract from data pump, individual blobs, and save them to the filesystem.

SQL*Loader is a tool designed primarily for relational data and loading large volumes of it quickly into the database. The tool can run in parallel and can insert data at high speed. Though the tool supports the loading of data into object types, it is really not designed for loading large numbers of digital objects into the database. This is better managed using PL/SQL.

Ideally SQL*Loader would be able to be configured to point it to a disk system and search for and load in parallel (using a file mask), digital objects it finds in folders and sub folders, with the ability to restrict what is loaded based on size, date, and type. For support with multimedia it would, as it's loading, be able to transform (create thumbnails) and extract metadata from the digital objects.

Streams

Oracle Streams is a product, which enables data in a schema to be pushed or shared with other schemas in other databases. It's a form of asynchronous data replication and uses the information in the redo logs to propagate the changes.

As of Oracle 11gR2, streams supports the migration of securefile blobs but doesn't support user defined types. This prevents Oracle Spatial and Multimedia data being replicated using Oracle Streams. This severely limits its usage.

Advanced replication

Oracle advanced replication uses a combination of triggers and queues to propagate data between one or more Oracle Databases synchronously or asynchronously. Although it is not as fast and is more complex to configure compared to Streams, it does support the replication of any data in the database including Oracle Multimedia and Spatial.

Options

The Oracle Database supports a set of optional modules that can be utilized in the database. These modules are tightly integrated in the database and enable the database to be used in non-traditional areas.

Multimedia

The Oracle Multimedia option has been discussed already. It uses the ORDSYS schema as a base for all its types and methods.

Oracle Multimedia has certain limitations and could do with numerous enhancements to further enhance its use and robustness, including:

- Support for the processing of more digital image types
- Support for the conversion and processing of video; in addition, the support for identification of more video types
- Support for the conversion and processing of audio
- Support for the conversion of different documents
- Full and seamless integration with Open Office
- Tight/seamless integration with Oracle Spatial
- Tight/seamless integration with XML DB
- Integration of more commonly required searching features such as fingerprint recognition, facial recognition, image matching
- Ability to extract metadata from audio and video
- Ability to extract digital images from any document
- Tight integration with the operating system to find, query, and retrieve sets of digital objects
- Streaming video and audio support, natively built into the database and integrated with the SGA and Optimizer to ensure efficient and timely retrieval of video packets
- Integration with photo editing tools such Adobe Photoshop and Gimp

Spatial

Oracle Spatial is a mature and tightly integrated option that enables the storage of any types of spatial data. Its ability to intelligently query large volumes of data and do spatial analysis makes it an ideal tool to manage a business's spatial requirements.

With digital objects, the need to integrate with spatial is slowly starting to become apparent as camera features expand. The most obvious example is the standard feature of storing GPS co-ordinates in the EXIF information in an image. Using a combination of metadata extraction and spatial features, it becomes possible to match images taken to their physical location anywhere on the globe.

As advanced as Spatial is, it could benefit from tighter integration with Oracle Multimedia and Oracle Semantics. The ability to not only handle latitude/longitude but three-dimensional co-ordinates should allow Spatial to perform complex pattern analysis on digital images and highlight relationships between them. Such a capability can be done manually at present, but with simpler and tighter integration would allow defense or intelligence monitoring multimedia warehouses to quickly build these queries, and perform the complex analysis required.

Oracle Spatial also manages its own equivalent concept of pyramid indexing, with a particular focus on georaster images. This capability really needs to integrate with Oracle Multimedia providing a single unified capability.

Text

The Oracle Text engine is a tool that has matured and become very simple and easy to use ever since it first made an appearance in Oracle8. A text index can be created on a LOB as easy as it is to create a normal index. In addition, Oracle Text can extract gists, themes, and HTML summaries of the documents. A powerful searching capability completely integrated in the SQL language enables combined relational and text queries to be performed. The engine is mature and can handle a large volume of document types.

As mature and powerful as text is, it still needs to be expanded further to work with Oracle Multimedia. Currently, no features exist to enable the extraction of images from inside a document, even though a HTML version of the document can be created.

Text needs to be able to convert between different formats, especially enabling the ability to create PDFs of any document (which would complement the HTML feature). Also, being able to create a JPG or PNG of pages in the document is a useful feature to have for allowing the simple viewing of a document, as well as preventing the cut/paste of information in it. Tools are also needed to enable HTML (with embedded images) to PDF conversions (or to other formats), enabling multimedia reports to be created that can be easily stored in the database and made available from Mod PL/SQL.

Semantics

The Oracle Semantic engine is an overlooked and powerful feature enabling the high-speed loading and intelligent querying of the semantic data, referred to as a triple. Though semantic data is a form of object data, with its own specialized index and querying language, its use is still not well understood and appreciated in the multimedia warehouse environment.

Semantic data effectively stores relationships between data items. Such information can be captured in a multimedia warehouse between different digital objects through existing relationships or through how the digital objects are searched on and accessed.

An inference rules engine can then be used to derive and find relationships between digital objects that cannot be easily calculated using traditional relational queries.

Warehouse

As previously covered in *Chapter 3, The Multimedia Warehouse,* there are a variety of multimedia warehouse structures that can be used to satisfy different business objectives. The Oracle Warehouse provides a set of tools and modules to enable the querying and support of incredibly large volumes of relational data. With tightly integrated OLAP, data mining and data replication capabilities, along with a very intelligent optimizer that can handle complex queries against large volumes of data, and a resource manager for ensuring equitable business load of resources, the Oracle Warehouse provides a powerful, efficient, and tightly integrated platform for doing data warehouse management.

The concepts covered in *Chapter 3, The Multimedia Warehouse* on searching, pattern analysis, and specialized data mining, are all features that should be included in the core database engine. That, along with a lot of the optimizer, storage, dictionary, indexing, and cache features with the added bonus of improvements in disk management, would enable a multimedia warehouse to easily scale into the hundreds of terabyte range without the need for sophisticated tuning, hardware, and storage.

Data Mining

The Warehouse Data Mining tool that Oracle offers uses a number of well-known algorithms to search through a warehouse of relational data and find relationships, patterns, and trends that are not obvious.

The tool can be used against metadata extracted from digital objects but cannot work against the digital objects themselves.

The notion of data mining against multimedia is still in its infancy and is vastly more complex to achieve than with mining against relational data.

When such data mining tools are eventually built, they will enable analysis of large image repositories and pull out patterns in them. In a criminal database, a data mining tool might be able to discern a person or persons appearing in multiple images or items, such as a car or object appearing in digital photos and videos. It might be able to discern the same person's voice appearing in different audio and video tracks.

Security

Core to multimedia management is the capability to secure the data and prevent unauthorized access to it. This section covers some of the database features that are useful in this area.

Encryption

Oracle Advanced Security offers an integrated data encryption tool that can not only encrypt data but encrypt the connection between the client and server. A number of encryption methods are supported offering different levels of security.

With the introduction of securefiles, Oracle offers the ability to seamlessly encrypt the contents of any LOB in the database. LOB encryption can ensure that one of the database's biggest security weak points, which is the backup, is protected from data theft.

Data vault

Oracle data vault is a tool designed to control and restrict access to data within the database from database administrators. The tool has attractive features for sites that require a high level of security and want to control and ensure that the administrators do not view data they are not allowed to.

Though the tool has fundamental short comings in that, it does not protect the database from system or network administrators and helps foster a culture that the database administrators are not to be trusted, there are no limitations with objects and BLOBs within the product.

Oracle label security

This is an add-on feature that enables fine grained control over rows in the table. Its equivalent to attaching a role to a row. Only those users with the role can see the row. It's built into the core database and cannot be circumvented.

With digital objects, the need can arise where a single digital object can be composed of multiple digital photos, each one offering the ability to download a certain resolution. If an architecture that natively supported this concept was available in the database, then an enhancement to Oracle Label Security would provide an ideal solution for limiting which of these resolutions a user could access. Ideally, role-level security should be able to be easily applied to a repeating value (`varray`), stored in a column, within a row in a table. Such a capability should be made a core and standard feature within the database.

High availability

Due to the large size as well as the potential e-commerce requirements of a multimedia database, it becomes important that it is always running. The following section covers some of the high availability features found in the Oracle database.

RAC

This is a database configuration designed for high availability or scalability using the concept of a clustered server (one physical disk system connected to multiple database instances, each on their own server). First appearing in Oracle 6.2 on VMS as the product Oracle Parallel Server, it has been enhanced and matured to take advantage of new hardware technologies. The product has been rewritten and its core architecture has changed over the years with each new release.

The key tuning points to RAC involve the optimal passing of data between the instances. Updates need to be able to be correctly seen across all instances and locking needs to be correctly handled to ensure two users on different instances do not update the same row. The two bottlenecks for tuning concern the physical connection to enable memory (memory blocks in the SGA) to be quickly passed between servers (known as interconnect), and the ability to pass data between servers by writing it to the database on the disk (also known as a ping). With Oracle11, RAC has been further enhanced by its tight integration with ASM, which can work with the database to better handle the issue of cross instance locking.

A well known RAC recommendation for a database block size is to keep it small, typically around 4 K. The tuning and capabilities of RAC are also centered squarely around relational data. RAC can work with object data and Oracle Multimedia but not transparently. The block size recommendation, along with a serious bottleneck occurring on the interconnect, if there are a large number of digital object updates, requires the careful configuration and setup of a RAC server to use them.

Exadata

Oracle Exadata is a combination server, software, and storage designed to complement the Oracle Database and enable it to scale to handle high workloads as well as complex warehouse workloads.

The key feature of Exadata is the ability for the server to retrieve the data optimally from storage. Rather than the database doing the smarts to work out where on disk the data is, the database can send requests for the data and Exadata then retrieves it. As such it replaces the standard operating system and filesystem with one that is designed for the unique needs of the database. This enables it to handle very high concurrent transactions and warehouse-type relational queries.

Even though Exadata was designed for the relational database, its high-speed throughput between the server and database makes it a possible solution for managing digital objects. As the server needs for dealing with digital objects becomes better understood, defined, and categorized, can the Exadata be enhanced to take advantage of it.

ZFS

On first looks, the Oracle ZFS architecture just looks like another variation of a SAN. In reality, it is much more than that and has the true potential to be an unstructured data game changer. Two initial key features that it offers are the capability to do automatic integrity checks of the filesystem and fix them if issues are found. The other is its use of 128-bit architecture to support an incredibly vast amount of storage. This enables it to easily handle and satisfy any volume of data required by an organization. The high-reliability changes the architecture needed to back up very large volumes of data.

ZFS is a combined filesystem and volume manager. The game-changing feature that ZFS offers is the use of a NAS rather than SAN. The key point is that the network connection speed offered is 10 Gigabits, which is 10 times faster than the standard 1 Gigabit network offered today. Also, on offer it is 8 GB/sec fiber channel support. From an unstructured data management view, the ability to have a high-speed reliable disk system that can store large volumes of data and deliver that data in parallel to the database using 10 Gigabit network, rather than relying on local disks, ultimately changes the rules for database setup and configuration. It's this architecture (and future ones based on it considering ZFS is now open source) that will enable high-speed loading and delivery of any volume of unstructured data.

ZFS is mature but not well-known and understood in the marketplace except within the Sun environment. Its abilities will undoubtedly grow, as the technology behind it is pushed harder and as more features from the Oracle Database are integrated with it. It currently looks like the best filesystem/volume manager around that can be enhanced to deal with the varying complexities and challenges of handling unstructured data.

Other vendors in the marketplace are offering similar high-capacity storage devices. What separates ZFS out is the combination of the filesystem and volume manager enabling it to scale and work tightly with the Oracle database.

Summary

The Oracle Database has a lot of features and capabilities that make it an ideal platform for managing all the data for a business. The features available for managing unstructured data are miles ahead of the other database vendors in the market.

To fully scale and support the growing and changing requirements of unstructured data, the Oracle Database needs to be enhanced to address these needs. This includes rearchitecture of the SGA, the optimizer and the data dictionary, as well as building new storage structures into tablespaces to handle read-only LOBs and LOBs that are updated and require versioning. The tuning focus of the database needs to factor in the network. The RMAN and data pump backup tool needs to be enhanced to address the issues of long-term archival, and all Oracle products and tools need to fully support object types unconditionally. The database needs to adapt to handle the complexities of managing large numbers of digital objects that can individually grow into the terabyte size range. Also, the database should natively support video-streaming and high-speed concurrent access to digital objects. The solid foundation, which the Oracle Database is based on, show that it is feasible that these capabilities can be built into it.

Chapter 10, Working with the Operating System covers how to work with both the Windows and Unix operating systems and how to integrate with them to perform complex loading of multimedia objects.

10
Working with the Operating System

When working with unstructured data, there is a major requirement to work with the operating system. The Oracle Database cannot handle a variety of multimedia objects, and handling unstructured data will likely require external processing.

There are two key methods for achieving this. The first involves shelling out of the database and invoking an operating system executable. The second involves calling an Oracle cartridge, which is linked to an external program, which then does the processing.

The cartridge is more complicated to develop and is operating-system specific. It can be built in C or in Windows using the .Net Framework. The .Net Framework uses a special purpose cartridge supplied with the database that can dynamically call a .Net program. This requires the use of **Oracle Data Access Components (ODAC)**[1].

The goal of this chapter is to describe the methods for shelling out of the database and techniques for working with the Unix and Windows operating systems when shelling out.

Both, the database administrator and the developer, need to be well-versed in scripting at the operating system. For Windows, this requires knowledge in writing a batch file, and on Unix, it requires knowledge in programming in one of the various Unix shell languages, such as Bourne Shell, C Shell, or Korn Shell.

The database administrator is also challenged by dealing with the fact that there might be a mixture of 32-bit and 64-bit external programs that need to be invoked. On Solaris, the administrator might be tested to find executables that run on their operating system's chip set, which could be either Intel or Solaris.

This chapter will cover at a high level a lot of the methods needed to shell out.

Why shell out?

There are a lot of different types of unstructured data in the market place. On top of this and as has been discussed in previous chapters, there is a huge variety of multimedia types. Oracle does not support all of these, so when it comes to processing them, which might involve transforming, extracting, or converting, the solution is to build a program that runs in the database in PL/SQL or Java. This program when run will invoke an external process to perform digital object processing and retrieve the results back into the database.

The processing could be done before the data is loaded into the database. Based on business requirements though, it might be more efficient or a business necessity to perform this after the data has been loaded into the database.

The following are examples of uses of shelling out of the database:

- A DNG (Photo of type Adobe Digital Negative) has been loaded into the database, and a thumbnail needs to be extracted from the digital image. This involves shelling out of the database, invoking Adobe Photoshop and running a droplet to perform the conversion.

- Extract the ID3 metadata from an MP3 audio file. This involves shelling out and calling a windows executable, which will extract the information to a file. The database then needs to read this file, convert it, and attach the resultant metadata to the audio object.

- An **flash (flv)** video is stored in the database. A 30-second **Windows Media File (WMV)** snippet is needed for streaming via the Windows media server. This involves shelling out and calling an open source program called FFmpeg, which extracts a 30-second snippet. The resultant WMV is then reloaded into the database.

- A PDF document has been loaded into the database. A thumbnail is needed to visually represent the PDF. This will be a JPEG of the first page. The database shells out. It calls an open source program called ImageMagick, which combined with another open source program called Ghostscript converts the first page of the PDF to a JPEG. The resultant digital image is reloaded back into the database.

Unload and load digital objects

When it comes to shelling out of the database and processing a digital object, it becomes apparent that the digital object needs to be unloaded and saved into the filesystem for processing. This is an additional process and can take time if the digital object is quite large. By using Oracle Securefiles, this step is much faster to perform, but it still is an additional step. Though there are many disadvantages to storing a digital object outside the database, the one advantage in doing it can be seen when it comes to external processing. By storing, it externally needs to unload and reload the processed digital object that is removed. This simplifies the process.

As has been covered in previous chapters, one of the exciting features in the latest 11*g*R2 release is the Oracle Database File System. This removes the need to unload the digital object when it's stored in the database. This is because the filesystem is integrated with the database. In this case, all that is needed is for the shell program to know the physical directory on the Oracle Database File System, where the digital object is found. If the processed digital object is stored on this filesystem, then the need to reload it back in has also been removed. This improves the performance of the operation, simplifies it, and makes the process programmatically neater and more concise.

There are a number of utilities available in the database to unload and then reload a digital object. Some of these have been covered in *Chapter 7, Techniques for Creating a Multimedia Database*. They include:

- Using the Oracle Multimedia methods, such as `ordsys.ordimage.export` and `ordsys.ordimage.importfrom`
- Using the `DBMS_LOB` package and the `loadfromfile` procedure; the package has no capabilities to unload a digital object to a file
- Using the `UTL_FILE` package and the `put_raw` procedures with the `get_raw` procedures
- Running Java and using the write, read methods using buffered and file input streams

For the developer, the key issue is the speed at which the binary data in the digital object can be written out and the resultant processed digital object is read back in.

How to shell out

There are a number of methods available within Oracle to shell out of the database and call an operating system script.

Java

Java running inside the database has an access to a command, which will shell out and call an operating system script. This requires Java to be installed in the database (not available with Oracle XE). The Java program sets up environment variables and eventually invokes a routine, which performs the shell process.

```
final Process p = doexec(command, osexecEnv, osworkDir);
```

The schema running the Java program might need additional privileges to run commands (see dbms_java.grant_permission for more information).

For more information on this, including the methods outlined, refer to http://www.oracle.com/technetwork/database/enterprise-edition/calling-shell-commands-from-plsql-1-1-129519.pdf.

Scheduler

The dbms_scheduler package supersedes the often used dbms_jobs package. It enables batch jobs written in PL/SQL and Java to be configured and run as well as the resources using them to be tightly controlled via the use of Oracle Resources. The package also allows for an external script to be called.

The important point to remember is that, to invoke, it requires calling a script rather than trying to run the command as is. Calling a script file also allows the output to be trapped and environment variables configured. Normally, when shelling out of the database, the environment variables (PATH, LD_LIBRARY_PATH, ORACLE_SID) are not set and have to be defined This is a mistake programmers commonly make.

The following code snippet shows how in Windows dbms_scheduler can be used to run a shell script. The location of Windows can vary between installation, requiring the job_action parameter to be modified for the Windows site:

```
dbms_scheduler.create_job
(
 job_name      => 'MY_WINDOWS_SHELL',
 job_type      => 'EXECUTABLE',
 job_action    => 'c:\windows\system32\cmd.exe',
 enabled       => false,
 number_of_arguments => 3,
 comments      => 'Run Windows shell-script'
```

```
);
dbms_scheduler.set_job_argument_value
  ('MY_WINDOWS_SHELL',1,'/q');
dbms_scheduler.set_job_argument_value
  ('MY_WINDOWS_SHELL',2,'/c');
dbms_scheduler.set_job_argument_value
  ('MY_WINDOWS_SHELL',3,'c:\mydir\myscript.bat "a parameter" "another
parameter"');
```

The /q command disables output by turning echo off.

The /c command carries out the command specified by the third parameter and then terminates.

Positional parameters are passed down to the script. In Windows, position parameters are referred to from %1 to %9. The parameters are identified after the call has been made to the script. In the previous example, the two parameters are different types of parameters. It is recommended that they are enclosed in double quotes to ensure special characters are not interpreted and that spaces can be included in the parameter value. A space will, otherwise, be used to differentiate the parameters.

For Unix, the call is similar but adjusted for the Unix environment:

```
dbms_scheduler.create_job
(
 job_name        => 'MY_UNIX_SHELL',
 job_type        => 'EXECUTABLE',
 job_action      => '/bin/sh',
 enabled         => false,
 number_of_arguments => 2,
 comments        => 'Run Unix shell-script'
);
dbms_scheduler.set_job_argument_value
  ('MY_UNIX_SHELL',1,'-c');
dbms_scheduler.set_job_argument_value
  ('MY_UNIX_SHELL',2,'\u01\mydir\myscript.sh "a parameter" "another
parameter"');
```

The -c parameter tells the shell that the commands are in the second parameter (which is the script) and to configure positional parameters (enabling $1 to be "a parameter" and $2 to be "another parameter", without the quotes). In Unix, $1 to $9, identify the parameters, whereas in Windows, it's is %1 to %9.

Advanced queueing or pipes

Early versions of Oracle offered a package called dbms_pipe. The pipe enabled two sessions connected to the database to share information, and it was transaction-independent. What it could be used for was to enable an executable running in batch on the server to connect to the database and then listen on the pipe. It could be awoken and given a command for processing. It could then do its processing, and return the result back using the pipe. The dbms_pipe program is still supported and offers basic features. By developing a simple executable (it's even possible through careful scripting to do this using SQL*Plus), the ability to shell out becomes possible. This is a similar concept to how dbms_scheduler works, except it's all natively handled in the database.

The dbms_pipe package has been since superseded by Oracle Advanced Queuing. The concept is still the same, but the Advanced Queue offers greater control and flexibility with the management of the queue.

UTL_TCP

Packages such as utl_smtp, utl_http, and utl_mail call utl_tcp, which can pass information to another environment using the TCP/IP network protocol. Using utl_tcp, it's possible to call a PHP program and pass to it a blob. The PHP program can then shell out or do the processing itself.

Similarly, it's possible to configure Open Office so that it can listen on a port for commands to perform. The following command shows how to run Open Office on Windows in background, enabling it to listen on Port 8100 for requests.

```
"C:\Program Files (x86)\OpenOffice.org 3\program\soffice"        -acce
pt="socket,port=8100;urp;"
```

For more information on this, including the Unix equivalent, see http://www.oooninja.com/2008/02/batch-command-line-file-conversion-with.html.

Challenges when shelling out

Shelling out and running an operating script can be harder than it looks. There are numerous considerations that have to be made, and there can be issues with security, the environment, and monitoring the job. In most cases, the shelling out process is one of just submitting blindly, and hoping it works.

Synchronous or asynchronous?

The first decision is to determine whether the script should:

- Run, and the database should wait for it to finish (synchronous)
- Submit it, immediately return, and then forget about it (asynchronous)
- Submit it, monitor its progress, and if need be, terminate the process

Synchronous is the default behavior. A script might be run to convert an audio WAV file into an MP3 file. This might take 5 minutes to complete. In this case, the calling program running in the database and doing the shell command will just wait for it to finish. If the script fails to finish or hangs, then the calling program will also hang. Steps need to be put into the script to ensure that it will complete or will cleanly exit, especially on error.

The asynchronous is useful for tasks, which need to run, but whether they succeed or not is not too important. This could be to delete temporary files created by a previous shell out. A script is submitted to run and the call is returned to the program immediately.

The idea of submitting and monitoring is more attractive, as it ensures that the calling program will not get stuck, and if need be, it can terminate the program. Shelling out using Java allows asynchronous calls to be made, but it's not easy to monitor them. This involves looking at the v$process table to see if the process is running. From here, an alter system kill session 'x,y' immediate; command could be run to terminate the script.

Using dbms_scheduler, the script is run as a batch job. Monitoring it involves querying the user_scheduler_jobs view. If it needs to be terminated, then the dbms_scheduler.drop_job procedure can be called to terminate it.

Monitoring the CPU usage of the script is more difficult to achieve. This typically involves shelling out another job that captures the CPU usage, stores it in a file, which is then loaded back into the database. The Unix vmstat command can be used to achieve this, and its behavior is consistent across all Unix platforms.

Hidden Ctrl + M characters on Unix

A common mistake made by administrators is when they have a Unix script file on their Windows network, and they then FTP or copy it to the Unix server. The administrator might have a series of shell scripts on their laptop which they use. They then copy them to the Unix server. If the script was edited in Windows, then hidden one in the script will be *Ctrl + M*—or the char (13)—linefeed character. What makes it additionally challenging is that when editing the file using Unix vi, these characters will not always be seen. When an attempt is made to shell out and run the Unix script, it will fail to run. This can make it very difficult to debug and determine why the script failed.

The solution is to remove the characters using the following command:

```
dos2unix filename newfilename
```

If this command is not available on the Unix platform, then using vi and replacing ^M can be done, or the Unix cat or sed commands can be used to remove them. There are numerous websites explaining how to remove the character.

Capturing output

In some cases, a script will call a program, and this program outputs information to stdout (this is the screen and referred to as standard output). When shelling out stdout is normally directed to bitbucket (which is a term to indicate that it's directed to a place that immediately deletes it). There is also stderr as well, which might contain useful information regarding errors that have occurred. Both stdout and stderr are found in Windows and Unix scripting.

Some utilities might only direct their results to stdout. In the cases of extracting metadata from a digital object, this could be an issue. If stdout cannot be redirected to a file, then the output is lost. In some cases, it's not possible to shell out and redirect the output. The usual command (found in Windows and Unix) is to use the greater-than symbol to indicate that stdout is to be directed to a file. The database can then read this file. Unfortunately, in most cases, when shelling out stdout is disabled, so even, redirecting to a file will just not work. In this case, the utility cannot be used. Most open source programs employ a command that enables their output to be sent to a file. So, rather than writing to stdout, the utility just writes to a file. The database then uses utl_file to read the file and to process it.

Parameters

Most shell scripts written are driven by parameters. A script designed to convert a digital image strip its embedded metadata, uses the sRGB colorspace (described in *Chapter 2, Understanding Digital Objects*), and might have them as parameters:

- The filename of the digital image in which the blob was unloaded to
- The colorspace to convert the digital image to
- The dimensions of the resultant digital image (pixel width and height)
- The **dots per inch (DPI)** to use on the resultant digital image

In Windows, the percent (%) symbol is a special character used to identify a parameter. In Unix, it's a dollar ($) sign. Additional special parameters include less-than and greater-than symbols, quotes, and double quotes. Even a space can be used to delimit command syntax terms.

Some utilities use these special characters in their command line syntax to indicate advanced usage. The following are examples of ImageMagick and some of the commands possible in it:

- Converting format jpg "3400x3400>" only reduces the digital image to this size if it's bigger than 3400 x 3400 pixels. This ensures a smaller sized digital image is not upsized to this pixel width.
- Identifying format "%w,%h" (myimage.jpg) identifies to stdout the width and height of the digital image.
- Convert format JPG (c:\temp\my image is a dng.dng) will fail because of the spaces. The solution is to enclose it in double quotes as "c:\temp\my image is a dng.dng".

Both, Unix and Windows, use double quotes to enclose a string of characters. When passing down values as parameters, it's recommended to enclose all parameters in double quotes as all parameters are positional.

In this example, the script is called incorrectly:

```
/bin/sh /u01/myscript.sh /u02/images/my image is a dng.dng
```

This will be passed down as $1 and is /u02/images/my, whereas parameter $2 will be image, parameter $3 will be something, and so on. What was required was to pass down the image name in $1. This is done by enclosing it in double quotes as shown as follows:

```
/bin/sh /u01/myscript.sh "/u02/images/my image is a dng.dng"
```

In Unix, the dollar symbol is used to denote positional parameters, and in Windows, it's percent. If the dollar or percent is meant to be used without it indicating it's a positional parameter, then, in Windows, the use of two percent symbols (%%) is treated as a single percent.

The greatest challenge for debugging a shell script is to correctly ensure the use of double quotes and the correct handling of special symbols in conjunction with the command line syntax employed by the utility.

Open source tools, such as ImageMagick and FFmpeg use a comprehensive command-line syntax enabling complex and varied commands to be passed down to it.

In Windows, when double quotes are used around positional parameters, then they are kept with the parameter value. This can cause problems when double quotes are part of the command. In this example, two parameters are passed down in the call:

```
c:\myscript\myconvert.bat "c:\temp\myfile a.dng" "30"
```

In the script, if the following command was used, it would return an error because of the double quotes:

```
convert -scale "%2%x%2%" "%1%"
```

What gets passed down is in effect:

```
convert -scale ""30"x"30"" ""c:\temp\myfile a.dng""
```

One solution is to not use double quotes in the script. So `"%1%"` is just replaced with `%1%` (no double quotes). This doesn't solve the second parameter, as the command line syntax requires double quotes. It has a special meaning in the command syntax. In this case, the use of the Windows tilde (~) is needed to strip the parameter of any double quotes. The script now looks like the following:

```
set p2=%~2
convert -scale "%p2%x%p2%" %1%
```

Dynamic shell scripts

An interesting method is to use `utl_file` to create the shell script with all the parameters and values entered in. This bypasses the need to pass down that parameters to it, and it enables the embedding of complex filenames and ensures the correct use of single and double quotes without the hassle and worry of the percent and dollar signs.

In this case, `utl_file` dynamically creates the shell script. It's then invoked without the need to pass down parameters to it. On script completion, an asynchronous job is submitted to delete the script file.

The use of the dynamic shell script might result in a lot of shell scripts being generated and run. When loading and processing tens of thousands of images, this will require co-ordination of the developer to create an environment for shelling out which is temporary and can be controlled.

Windows program on processing, calls an actual window?

Some utilities when invoked on Windows are not designed for command-line input and output, and call libraries that display a window. A Windows service as of Win 2008, Vista, and Windows 7 has a new security feature in place designed to prevent it from running when this happens. As a Windows service is a process that by its nature runs in batch, Microsoft has determined that enabling a window to be opened up from a service is a potential security issue, and it is not allowed.

This can make it hard to process some digital images. When a series of images need to be merged into a Powerpoint, then the .Net libraries invoked will use the Windows libraries, resulting in the script failing to run. This is due to the fact that the Oracle Database is a Windows Service. So, any script shelled out from it is, in fact, part of the Windows service. So, Windows prevents it from running. This was not an issue in Windows 2003 and XP.

To get around, it requires the use of the DevxExec program (`http://developex.com/custom-software/devxexec.html`). It's designed to create a process as a different user, which will then enable it to run. To work properly, a desktop session is needed. If the program opens a window that requires user input (a dialog box pops up asking the user to acknowledge some information), then the program will hang and require manual intervention (a person accessing the screen and pressing enter). The script that has been shelled out from the database cannot be killed using the alter system command. It requires a complete database reboot to terminate it.

Filesystem limitations

The following are limitations that administrators need to be aware of when dealing with a filesystem:

* Number of files per directory is 65 K. This means that if the business does not want to store the digital objects in the database, then the actual storage location and directories used need to be considered. As already covered in previous chapters, Windows and Unix file systems do not scale well. Once a directory has more than a couple of thousand files in it, navigating into it as well as searching against it can be very slow. In some cases, errors can be returned if there are too many results. A database doesn't suffer from these limitations.

- A filename must be unique within a directory. This means that if the digital objects are stored externally, then a prefix or suffix has to be used to separate the names of the derivatives and pyramid objects. Storing the digital objects in the database will not have this issue.

- Mass renaming of files is not easy. If all objects are stored externally and there are 100,000 of them, then finding them and renaming them all to lowercase can take a very long time. A script is needed and will involve the use of a regular expression to perform the rename. There is no easy way to check if the rename has worked or to even see which digital objects qualify to be renamed. Once done, there is no easy way to back out the change. If the digital objects were stored in the database, then a simple UPDATE statement would take seconds to do the 100,000 changes. A SELECT statement could quickly verify the changes worked. Transactional or flashback control could be used to back out the change. Complex name changes requires sophisticated use of regular expressions. If all digital objects less than a certain size of dimension were to be renamed and given an _tnail suffix, then a program would be needed to identify each digital object, extract its dimensions, and based on the value perform the rename. Against a large repository of digital objects such an operation will take a very long time to run. An equivalent operation, if the digital objects were stored in the database, would take seconds to run.

- Searching against a filesystem is slow. This is because it's not natively indexed. The result is that searching involves looking in a large number of directories and doing name-matching checks. Utilizing a search engine on top of a filesystem is worthwhile, but it can be difficult to integrate it in with the scripting language. Most employ their own dedicated interfaces and are designed to search and view. They are not designed to search and then perform maintenance against the resultant digital object.

- A filename has a number of limitations. Though most filesystems support double-byte characters in the filename, it can become difficult working with, viewing, and controlling files with double-byte names. Try opening up a command-line screen and viewing or even searching for files with Chinese symbols in them. A database is better suited for the management of double-byte characters, as it has utilities and conversion tools natively built into it.

- Tracking changes is the biggest limitation with the filesystem, which is very difficult. A database has built-in audit capabilities, and all changes are logged (with the ability to easily reverse engineer into DML statements of the changes made). In a filesystem, changes made are hard to track, rollback, and review. If a mass rename was done along with a conversion and resize of 100,000 digital images, then trying to track what has happened might involve accessing logs at the operating system level (if such logs are even generated).

If files are deleted (without the use of wastebasket), then knowing what's missing can be hard to deduce. In addition, there is no easy way to communicate back to the database what the changes are. This can result in orphaned images. If the database is used to just store metadata about a digital object and it contains a pointer to an external file, then a simple file rename will result in the database losing track of the digital object. It effectively becomes orphaned and lost, even though it resides in the operating system. In the relational database world, an equivalent concept is the primary/foreign key relationship. The database has safeguards in place to prevent orphaned records. In the database operating system world, such safeguards do not naturally exist and require a huge programmatic effort to track and maintain. This is why it's important that all changes to digital objects stored outside the database are instigated from a process within the database. That way the database can be aware of the change.

Windows

When it comes to operating systems, the two well-known giants are Unix and Windows. One could argue that the mobile device operating systems are bigger in terms of volume, but until they can support a running database on them, they will not be included. The Mainframe gurus will also raise the point that operating systems, such as MVS, have been around for a longer time, are better in capabilities, more reliable, more mature, and still used by large businesses to support mission critical systems. For those who would consider themselves geeks, this is likely falling into the timeless argument about which is better Star Trek or Star Wars, and then adding to the mix Flash Gordon. As fun as it is to debate these points, the arguments are not beneficial, as most businesses buy operating systems based on a myriad of issues, technical prowess being just one of many factors.

A well-skilled database administrator in today's computing environment needs to be proficient in both, Windows and Unix. A good administrator will also have knowledge in the workings of a number of different databases. This ensures that they have a healthy appreciation for the features in the database, as well as the limitations. Just like a developer should be fluent in a variety of programming languages, a database administrator needs to be skilled in a variety of databases and operating systems.

Too often with the rapidly changing computing environments administrators find themselves in, they settle in a comfort zone and just focus their skill set in one area. A lot can be learned by having a good appreciation of the workings of other databases and operating systems. Lessons gained from these environments can be brought back into the home environment and used to improve management and performance.

Too often the Windows platform is treated as a second grade platform for running an Oracle Database, with the view being that Unix is superior. 20 years ago, the view was that VAX/VMS was the better platform to run on and Unix was rated second. Technology changes, the environment changes, and so too does the view about which is the best platform is to run a database on. In the last 2 years, with the acquisition of Sun, the view is again changing and being debated about whether the better platform for running Oracle on is Linux or Solaris. Vendors such as IBM and Hewlett Packard will naturally argue that their platforms are superior for running Oracle. Each offers positive benefits, and it's a case of understanding them and determining if they really are beneficial.

The Windows platform is very popular and offers a lot of support tools for dealing with multimedia. A lot of video editing tools, audio tools, and image processing tools are found in it. The Apple Mac running OS X, which is a flavor of Unix is also well-known for its multimedia management tools. The challenge is that even though the Apple Mac has a superb range of tools, it doesn't support the Oracle Database, and the tools it uses are designed mostly for a GUI manipulation environment and not a batch processing one. This means that the database can't take advantage of them (shell out, run, and process). The result is that the Apple Mac is used as part of a workflow process for digital object loading. As covered in *Chapter 5*, *Loading Techniques*, when manually loading a digital object, one stage could be to review and edit it from an Apple Mac computer.

In most cases, the digital objects found on an Apple Mac are transferred to a filesystem for loading into the database. A good platform to work with is the Windows platform.

Based on personal experience, the operating system running Oracle has a little impact on the performance. It's the hardware and disk system that determines the ultimate performance of the Oracle Database. Given the exact same hardware specifications running Windows, Linux, or Solaris, Oracle behaves in very similar fashion between all of them.

What determines an optimal platform for the managing of multimedia in a business is the availability of tools found or supported on the operating system that can do digital object processing. It can be argued that having in-house skills is more important, but in the case of processing multimedia, if the operating system cannot process that multimedia, then the business cannot run. For a business that uses video and requires it to be manipulated and streamed, then the platform to use is one that has powerful streaming capabilities. If the base format for the video is WMV, then the natural conclusion is to use a Windows platform. If the format is MPEG, then Linux or Windows might be preferable, as there are streaming video servers found on both. The question is, which platform is more reliable, secure, and easier to manage? A streaming server that constantly falls over because of memory leaks is not going to be effective (this is a typical issue of streaming video servers).

In some cases, the use of a Windows platform is required. To correctly convert an Adobe DNG requires Adobe Photoshop. To create a Powerpoint from a set of digital images requires the .Net architecture and Microsoft Office. Though there are work-arounds on other platforms, the easiest platform to do these actions on is the Microsoft Windows platform.

So, the database administrators should avoid getting into the debate about whether Linux is better than Windows, which is better than Solaris (and whether Solaris Sparc is better than Solaris Intel), and focus more on looking at how the digital objects they have to work with can best be utilized by the operating system and whether the operating system can correctly process those digital objects.

Powershell versus DOS

With Windows 2008 and Windows 7, Microsoft bundled in with the operating system a new command-line environment called Powershell. This environment can be installed on older platforms but doesn't exist on it natively. Powershell is composed of command-line actions, a scripting language, and it's integrated with the .Net Framework. It's a major improvement over DOS, which has been around since the first version of Windows and was initially designed around an 8-bit mentality. Powershell runs in either 32-bit or 64-bit mode.

For those familiar with Unix, Powershell offers a lot of similar commands to Unix. The use of regular expressions, pipe-lining (similar behavior) as well as some overlap with some C constructs. It also offer programming capabilities, including conditional logic and loops.

Powershell easily supersedes DOS and any site using Windows should, on shelling out, look to invoke the Powershell environment rather than DOS. So, from `dbms_scheduler` rather than using `job_action`   => `'c:\windows\system32\` `cmd.exe'`, the command would be `job_action`   => `'c:\windows\system32\` `WindowsPowerShell\v1.0\powershell.exe'`.

LUN

A **logical unit number** (**LUN**) refers to a portion of storage. It is a new disk management concept introduced in Windows 2008 R2. The closest analogy to a LUN is a SAN with a Unix's style-mount point capability. A LUN can be composed of multiple disks using structures similar to RAID storage. Once defined the LUN can be mounted into an existing structure such as a Unix mount point.

From a user's point of view, the LUN is just another sub-directory on what looks like a disk drive. Those familiar with Unix know that when navigating around mount points, you can easily access other disk systems. In Windows, the top-level disk usually maps to a physical disk system. Users are used to seeing a `C:` or `D:` drive and equate that to a single disk or a RAID disk structure. It can also equate to SAN or by attaching a drive letter to a shared drive; it can equate to a NAS, which would be a subset of another disk.

With a LUN, the reverse happens. A physical drive is configured. It might be called `H:` drive and could be 500 GB in size. A LUN is created and is composed of six drives and configured in a mirrored/striped configuration. It's then mounted on the `G:` drive and given a sub-directory name. If the mount name was MYLUN, then accessing the contents would be as simple as navigating to the `G:\mylun` directory.

For those familiar with Unix, this concept is nothing new. For those used to Windows, it is a different concept to deal with. Oracle Database data files can reside on a LUN. Digital objects can also reside on a LUN though; as of Oracle 11*g*R2, there were limitations with Oracle Multimedia's ability to access those objects. This was due to the unique security requirements that come bundled in with the access on the LUN.

The use of a LUN will really start to be seen with the release of Windows 8.

The variety of versions

There are a lot of different flavorings of Windows. Each one offers similar capabilities to the previous version with changes and improvements to the interface.

For a database administrator, there are some key Windows areas that need to be located to effectively manage the database on the platform. These sections are given later.

The Windows Services interface

The command-line access is `%windir%\system32\services.msc`. This is a GUI interface that enables the administrator to start/stop the database, as well as the database listener, the HTTP server (Apache), and a number of other Oracle Windows-integrated features such as the job scheduler (used by `dbms_scheduler`).

A Windows Service is like a batch job that can be started up during boot. The Oracle Database exists as a Windows Service and runs as a dedicated process. Database parallelism is handled via threads. The Oracle SGA is just a memory that is allocated to the process.

Linux also has the concept of services (they are an application or set of applications that run in the background). For non-Linux Unix systems, the closest equivalent to Windows Services are cron jobs. These are Unix batch processes.

In Unix, the Oracle Database on startup creates a number of processes and then allocates an area of memory, which is marked as shared. This is referred to as the Oracle instance on starting up. The different processes then access this shared memory. Once this is allocated, the instance via the control files, then finds and accesses the physical database files.

The following screenshot copy shows some of the typical Oracle processes that run when the server is started.

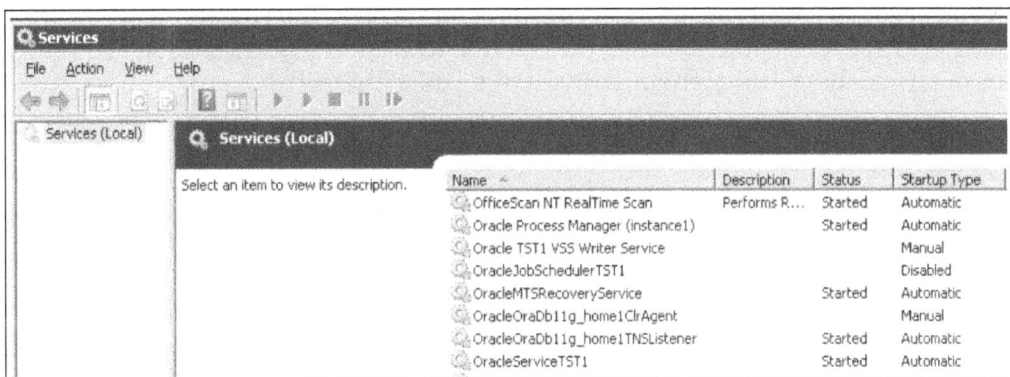

The previous screenshot includes:

- `Oracle Process Manager` (instance 1). This is the HTTP service (Apache) that was described in *Chapter 7, Techniques for Creating a Multimedia Database*. This is not the Oracle Embedded Gateway process which runs in the Oracle listener.

- `OracleJobSchedulerTST1`: This is the process used to run `dbms_scheduler` tasks. The SID of the database is TST1. The SID is often used in Windows to ensure a job or process name is unique.

- `OracleMTSRecoveryService`: This process is used to recover transactions when the Microsoft Transaction Server is used.

- `OracleOraDb11g_homeClrAgent`: This is the .Net cartridge process. This is used when a .Net cartridge is developed in the database. This process is useful for sites that heavily use a .Net cartridge in the database. As it's always running, it is faster to invoke. Though not required, it does offer performance benefits.

- `OracleOraDb11g_homeTNSListener`: This is the oracle lsnrctl process. If the service doesn't exist and lsnrctl is run from a DOS prompt, then Oracle automatically creates the service. The listener is also used to run the Oracle embedded gateway. The name of the Oracle Home is embedded in it to ensure it's unique. This enables multiple listeners running in different homes to be running.

- `OracleServiceTST1`: This is the Oracle Database process. In comparison to Unix, the tasks such as DWRn, LGWR, PMON, and SMON, all run as threads within the process.

When monitoring the database, one can see that the database is running as a single process. It's referred to as `oracle.exe`. In Unix, the `ps -ef` command can be used to quickly see which database processes are running. As **System MONitor (smon)** is a mandatory database process, using the command `ps -ef | grep smon` will quickly list all the database instances currently running on the server.

opmn.exe	SYSTEM	00	1,644 K	34	51	Oracle Application Server
opmn.exe	SYSTEM	00	11,064 K	1,031,334	971,261	Oracle Application Server
oracle.exe	SYSTEM	00	842,880 K	37,184,301,223	13,136,220,232	Oracle RDBMS Kernel Executable
OraClrAgnt.exe	SYSTEM	00	648 K	36	0	OraClrAgnt Module

In Windows, there is no equivalent to this. When looking at the Windows Monitoring tool called task manager, all Oracle instances running are referred to as `Oracle.exe`. Differentiating between different instance requires looking at the individual threads.

Also, the Oracle Service might be running (marked as started), but it doesn't mean that the database is running. In DOS, the command `net start` will list all currently running services. The quickest way to confirm if the database is running is to either try to access it (using SQL*Plus or Enterprise Manager) or to see how much memory is allocated to the `Oracle.exe` process. If it's around 40 MB, then it means the service is running but the database isn't.

A Windows Service has capabilities to be automatically restarted on failure and can be started up as a different login user. This is needed if the Oracle Database is going to access any network services. By default, the Windows Service is started up as local system, which due to security restrictions is prevented from accessing any network sites. This means, by default, a network drive mapped cannot be accessed by the database. It involves changing the Windows Service to use a Windows Administrator account or an account with the privileges and roles needed by the Oracle Database.

Windows 2012 and Windows 8

As of mid 2012, Windows 8 is the new Microsoft Windows release but is yet to be released. As such, Oracle has not yet indicated support for it. Windows 2012 is the Server equivalent to Windows 8.

Windows 2008 R2 and Windows 7

Windows 2008 R2 is a server-oriented operating system release only of 64 bit. Its client equivalent is Windows 7. The version included changes in the interface and a re-arrangement of location of utilities. The server version was ramped up to include support for more processes and disk configurations (including LUNs discussed earlier).

The reliability and performance improvements that came with this version has resulted in existing Windows customers making efforts to move to it. Oracle 11gR2's 64 bit is currently the only supported version of the database on this platform.

Windows 2008 and Windows Vista

This version of Windows superseded Windows 2003. It offered improvements in virtualization support, security, and disk management. It was closely aligned with Vista, which was not popular in the market place. As of today, the recommendation is to upgrade the version to Windows 2008 R2 and to use Oracle 11gR2.

Windows 2003

Released in 2003, it was seen as a major advancement over Windows 2000. Closely allied with Windows XP, the Oracle Database worked well on this platform. Oracle 10 was the major release used on it.

Windows XP

Windows XP was released in in 2001. A 64-bit version was released later. Though the version was seen as a client operating system allied with Windows 2003 (such as Windows 7), it could nonetheless run the Oracle Database effectively for small to medium businesses. The 64-bit version could make use of larger amounts of memory and provided the disk access was kept within bounds of the operating system it was able to support Oracle Databases with multimedia into the multi-terabyte range.

Windows 2000

First appearing in 1999, this version of Windows, in retrospect, had a lot of limitations with memory, disk management, services, and general control. Though it did run the Oracle 8 database, which was the first to introduce Oracle Multimedia quite well. When configured correctly, the database and the platform proved quite resilient and stable. The version is still used by sites and can run with Oracle 10gR2 (10.2.0.5). The attraction to it for running Oracle was that the operating system was considered lightweight. There were minimal overheads with it, and it could run the Oracle Database with operating system easily between 500 MB and 1 GB. With the introduction of virtualizations, the operating system proved ideal for Windows environments running Oracle XE. A number of virtualizations could run concurrently on a lowly configured server.

Lack of remote desktop capabilities and security issues, along with its de-support in 2010 has meant this operating system is not viable anymore. Legacy systems can though be migrated into a virtualization and managed from there.

Unix

The Unix operating system was first developed in 1969. The trademark is currently owned by The Open Group, an industry standards consortium. The operating system is currently well-know for running on servers even though it can run equally well on desktops and mobile devices. Its popularity on desktops grew when Apple rewrote and ported its PowerPC operating system to a Unix variant called Max OS X. On servers, Unix remains a very popular operating system and most hardware vendors support one or more Unix or Unix-like variations on it.

How Unix differs from Windows

A lot of database administrators are either Unix administrators or Windows ones and not both. Finding an administrator skilled in both is quite rare. The reason is that to be an efficient administrator requires becoming well-versed and skilled in the underlying operating system. It's common to hear a Unix administrator make the comment that Oracle on Windows is small scale or use the colloquial term "mickey mouse". With recent improvements in the Windows server, it's not fair or accurate to dismiss Oracle on Windows as inferior to Unix. In addition, sites usually stick to one platform to make it easier to manage, so a mixed Windows/Unix environment is not that common.

As stated, it is though important that database administrators become well-versed in both operating systems. There are a lot of advantages when it comes to tuning, configuring, and general management, where lessons can be learned from each environment and applied to the other one.

A business might decide that it is more cost-effective to commit their business to either be a Unix or Windows one. The investment in skills, training, and keeping those skills up-to-date for two operating systems might be considered to be too expensive. Focusing on one operating system has the advantage that it becomes easier to administer all the devices and to enable them to communicate with each other. Unfortunately, the progress of technology is resulting in a lot of new devices coming pre-installed with a locked-in operating system. A Windows shop might purchase VM eSphere to host its virtualizations and discover that, behind the scenes, it is running on a Unix variant. In which case, the need to understand the basics of Unix cannot be dismissed. An administrator, who can become skilled in both, Unix and Windows, will become an asset in the business.

For Unix administrators that are not familiar with Windows, the Cygwin environment offers a complete Unix environment on Windows[2]. A Unix administrator can manage an Oracle Windows database using very similar commands to the ones they are used to on Unix.

For a novice administrator, the following are the differences and similarities between Windows and Unix:

- Unix doesn't use drive letters (directory structures) but starts with a root directory referred to as /, and from there, various mount points are assigned giving access to different drives. Windows uses either a drive letter to refer to the disk (`C:`, `D:`) or the UNC syntax, which allows access to other drives and remote locations (`\\192.168.1.226\p$`). As covered in earlier chapters, this difference becomes important when it comes to loading digital objects.

- Normally on Windows, the Oracle Database is installed into an account called administrator. Though not required, this is the one typically used. On Unix, the administrator equivalent is root. The Oracle Database cannot be installed using this account. Rather an account has to be created with the correct privileges. This is typically one called oracle.

- The Oracle installer behaves the same between Windows and Unix. As it's written in Java, the only real noticeable difference is calling it. In Windows, it involves double-clicking on the `setup.exe`. In Unix, it requires running the runIntaller executable. Nearly all other aspects (except for physical locations) are identical with the exception of operating system checks. Unix requires the configuration of shared memory for all the processes. This can involve making changes as root to the Unix kernel. Different flavors of Unix employ different methods for achieving this with Solaris doing it automatically.

- Windows 2008R2 is of 64 bit and typically runs on the Intel chip. Solaris is of 64 bit and runs either on the Intel or SPARC Chip. Linux runs on 32-but or 64-bit machine and typically runs on Intel, though it is supported on most chipsets (but the Oracle Database might not be supported on it).

- Environment variables are used on Unix to control the database. This includes the ORACLE_SID, LD_LIBRARY_PATH, and ORACLE_HOME. On Windows, these values can be found in the Windows registry (there is no equivalent to this on Unix). They can also be specified in the system environment variables. Different version of Oracle have either ignored or made use of these variables. The current version uses the Windows registry and will likely support it while Windows supports the concept of a registry. The values can also be specified at the command line and take precedence over the registry values.

- In Unix, the editor available on all flavors is vi. In Windows notepad or WordPad is available on all platforms and can be used to edit files. Unix and Windows, each offer a huge variety of alternate text editors, but these ones are the ones always found in the initial operating system install.

- Windows uses a GUI mentality with most options for performing system administration managed from a window. Unix database administrators will typically control and manage the database from the command line. This can be done in Windows using DOS or Powershell or as covered above by using Cygwin.

- Windows is not case-sensitive with filenames but Unix is. As has been covered in a number of chapters, this can have important considerations when it comes to managing digital objects outside the database.

- Windows running Oracle relies heavily on threads. On Unix, it relies heavily on processes.

- Windows has a line mode FTP client, which can be called from DOS. FTP can also be run from within the Windows File Explorer resulting in a simpler interface for transferring files. The drag/drop capabilities makes its easier to move or copy files from an FTP location to a Windows location without the need to use command-line syntax.

- Windows and Unix, both heavily use TCP/IP for all network communication.

The variety of versions

Like Windows, Unix comes in a variety of flavors. Unlike Windows, different Unix flavors can be controlled by different vendors. In the case of Linux, its code base is open source. This has resulted in a variety of Linux versions. Some are supported with Oracle, others are not. Linux is not an official certified version of Unix, instead it is classed as a Unix-like[3] operating system.

Linux

With Linux, Oracle is supported on Asianux, SUSE, Red Hat, and Oracle Enterprise Linux (which is based on Red Hat Linux). The Oracle Database File System (covered in previous chapters) is natively supported on Linux enabling the filesystem to be stored within the database.

Oracle does its core development on Linux, so releases and patches are found on this version before the others. With Oracle acquiring Sun, this might change in the future.

Linux offers a GUI environment for managing the environment. This is only needed during installation and configuration. Like Unix in general, most management of the database and the environment is done from within a Unix shell. Different flavors of Linux have different GUI tools removing the need to have to use the command line.

Ubuntu Linux

This is the desktop version based on the Debian Linux distribution. A server equivalent of Ubuntu is also available. The Ubuntu desktop interface was designed for the novice Linux user, and its attraction is that it is easy to install and uses a whole suite of GUI utilities. The equivalent analogy to think of Ubuntu is Windows 7, as Oracle Enterprise Linux is to Windows 2008R2. It's not supported with Oracle, but the Oracle XE version is able to run on it.

Solaris

Solaris was originally developed by Sun, which Oracle acquired in 2010. When Sun acquired Cray from Silicon Graphics in the late 1990s, they brought in a product range, which enabled them to build computers that could scale to support a large number of processes. This enabled Sun running a database to scale to support large numbers of concurrent users and large amount of storage.

When Oracle acquired Sun, they gained access to the Solaris code base, which they have been enhancing to work in a more integrated manner with the Oracle Database. Solaris runs on both the SPARC Chip and Intel and is designed for 64-bit operations. It includes a number of GUI frontends for managing it.

IBM AIX

IBM AIX is a version of Unix managed by IBM. It has been designed to run on a variety of hardware managed by IBM, as well as a number of different chipsets. Its strength is that it is well suited for running on IBM hardware. As IBM has a strength in the marketplace and reputation for building scalable servers that are reliable, mature, and can scale, AIX is a version of Unix well suited for running on their hardware.

IBM support their DB2 database on AIX, while Oracle is also supported on AIX but only on the 64-bit version of the PowerPC Chip.

HP-UX

This is Hewlett-Packard's (HP) version of Unix designed to run on their servers. Oracle is supported on the 64-bit PA-RISC Chipset version, as well as the Intel Itanium release. Like IBM, the HP version of Unix is designed to work best with HP architecture, which has the capability to handle large amount of memory and a large number of CPUs.

Summary

For small-sized to medium-sized businesses, the differences between the different Unix versions can be difficult to understand. Between Oracle Solaris, IBM AIX, and HP-UX, the differences are seen, as the servers are scaled to support tens to thousands of terabytes of data, with thousands of concurrent users. Each platform offers its own architectures, which the analogy for most is like trying to choose between different mobile phone carriers. Each is very different, no two plans can be easily compared, but each claims to offer the best capabilities, scale the most while offering the best price for doing so.

When comparing Unix to Windows, the questions raised have to cover the skill set at the business, the budget, the number of users, and the commercial requirements. Windows is best known as an environment that is designed for small-sized to medium-sized businesses. Unix has a reputation for scaling to very large database sizes and concurrent users. With the latest versions of Windows, Microsoft is attempting to grow into this high-end market space while maintaining a strong hold at the small to medium end. Linux has a reputation for scaling in both directions and is cost-effective, while Solaris has a reputation for having the hardware and operating system when setting up business critical systems.

When working with unstructured data and multimedia, currently there is no ideal platform to work on. Each offers strengths and weaknesses. Windows has advantages in that, and a lot of multimedia is supported on it, making processing a lot easier. Windows also offers a tightly managed GUI environment making it easier to learn and manage. Oracle XE running on Linux offers a very low-cost environment to run in, while Oracle on Solaris offers a solution for large businesses requiring scalability and high performance.

In the following appendices, there is additional information covering the Circa datatype, the structures of different types of multimedia warehouses, and an overview of how a database administrator can set up their environment to be proactive.

The final *Appendix E, Loading and Reading* is not included in the book but rather is located online. It covers the performance testing scenarios detailed in *Chapter 7, Techniques for Creating a Multimedia Database*.

Exercises

These questions are designed to have the reader go beyond the traditional method of answering questions. They involve using the concepts designed in the chapter and doing additional research on the Internet to come up with the best solution to address the questions raised:

- Design an algorithm for killing a rogue process that has occurred during a shell out from the database.

- You are an enterprise architect and have been asked to recommend an operating system and platform for storing and delivering 10 million digital images over the Internet. Justify the operating system and platform to be used. What is the key business consideration that controls the decision?

- Which is the fastest and most efficient method for shelling out of the database, `dbms_scheduler`, Java, or using `utl_http` with PHP?

- What other methods are there available for invoking an operating system script besides the ones mentioned in this chapter?

- Given a novice developer, which Unix shell would you give them to start work with, or would you give them Windows Powershell or DOS instead? What key features must a command-line environment must have to make it easy to use for novice administrators?

- How does Powershell and Unix scripting compare to older and more mature (and in some cases legacy) operating system environments such as VAX/VMS or IBM MVS? In the last 20 to 30 years, since these were developed, are the older ones superior or inferior to the new ones?

A
The Circa Data Type

This section describes the Circa data type syntax. The syntax does not cover every keyword or period in time, but it does cover the vast majority of them. The syntax supports the addition of new time periods.

The following are the examples of Circa values that the syntax can describe:

- 1850 to 20-Jan-1910
- About 18,000 years ago
- 1850s
- 1910 to 1980
- c. 1760 to c. 1810
- 1800 to 1830
- Second to third millennium BC
- 8th century BC
- Late 1930s
- 304 to 250 BC
- c. 1927 to 30
- Late 1960s to early 1970s
- c.1760-c.1810 [1750-1830]
- c.1760- c.1810 [1750-1830]
- c. 1760- c. 1810

Railroad diagram

Circa: It covers the initial circa date value.

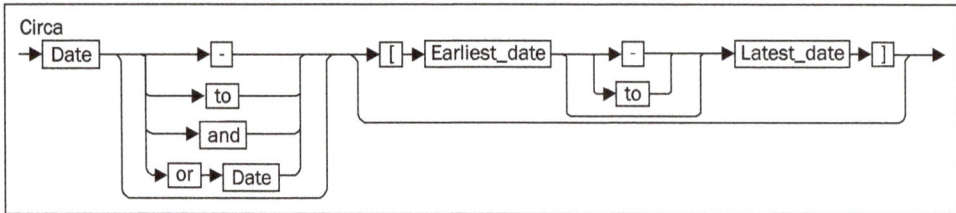

Date: It defines a format for how a date can be specified.

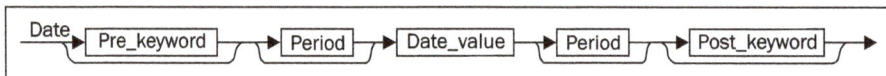

Pre keyword: It specifies the optional circa definition.

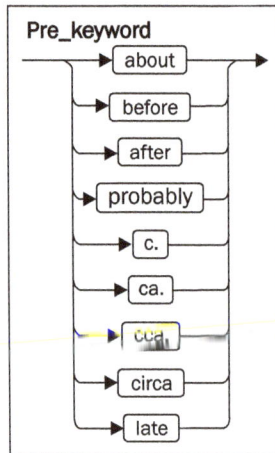

Period: It indicates a time period.

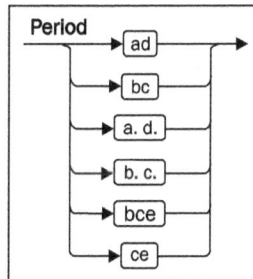

Post keyword: It is word or phrase indicating time direction.

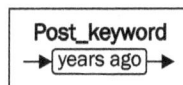

Earliest date: It is the initial date value (from).

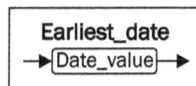

Latest date: It is the subsequent date value (to).

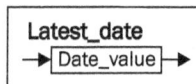

Recent period: These are the keywords to identify recent time periods.

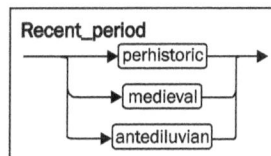

Eon: These are the keywords to identify recent geological periods.

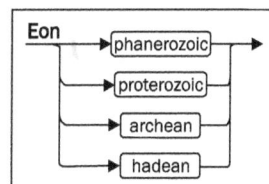

Time period: These are the keywords to identify historical epochs.

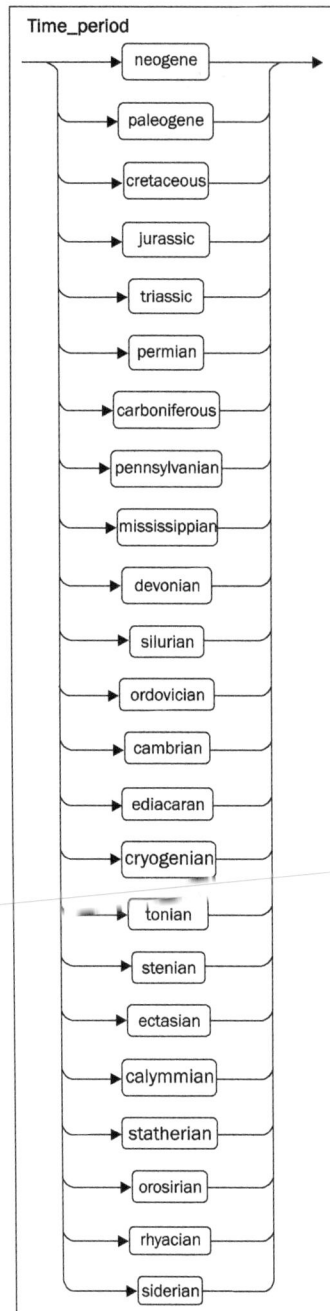

Time_period
- neogene
- paleogene
- cretaceous
- jurassic
- triassic
- permian
- carboniferous
- pennsylvanian
- mississippian
- devonian
- silurian
- ordovician
- cambrian
- ediacaran
- cryogenian
- tonian
- stenian
- ectasian
- calymmian
- statherian
- orosirian
- rhyacian
- siderian

Era: These are the keywords to identify distinctive historical time periods.

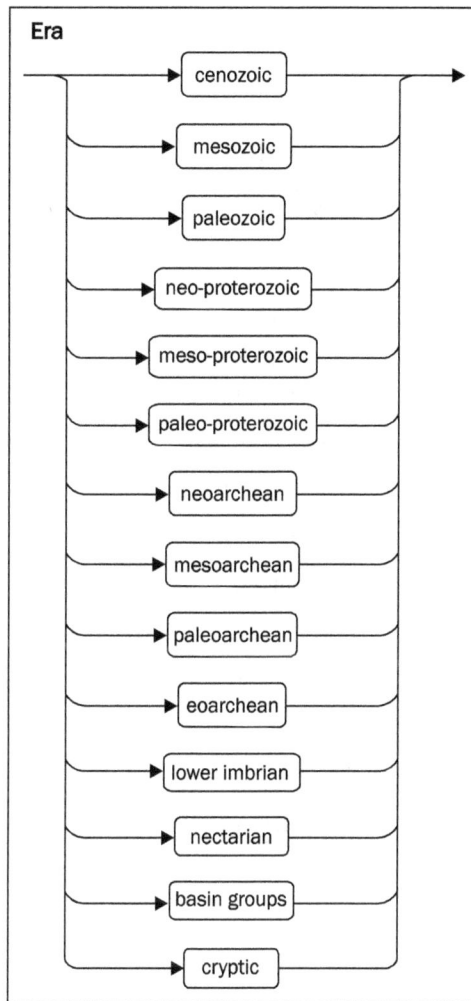

Month: This includes the months of the year.

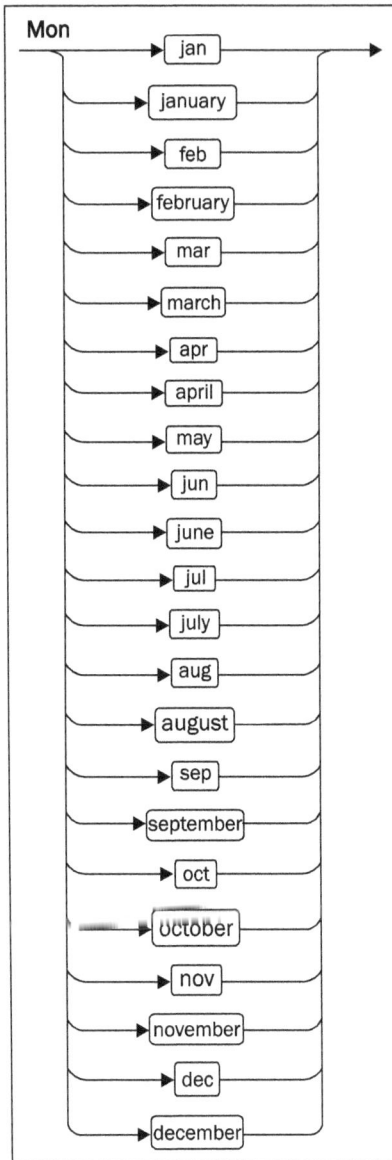

Number: This includes numerical digits.

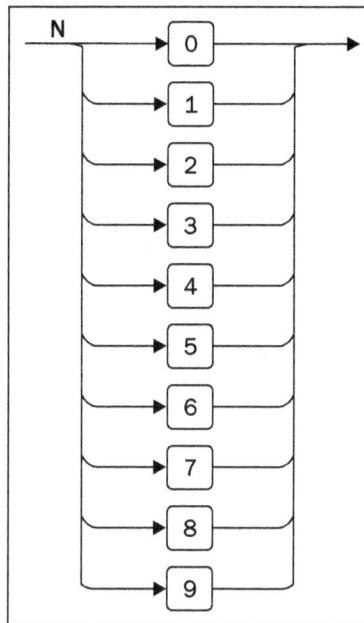

Year digit: This includes digits of the year.

Day digit: This includes days of the month.

Date value: This includes definition of a date.

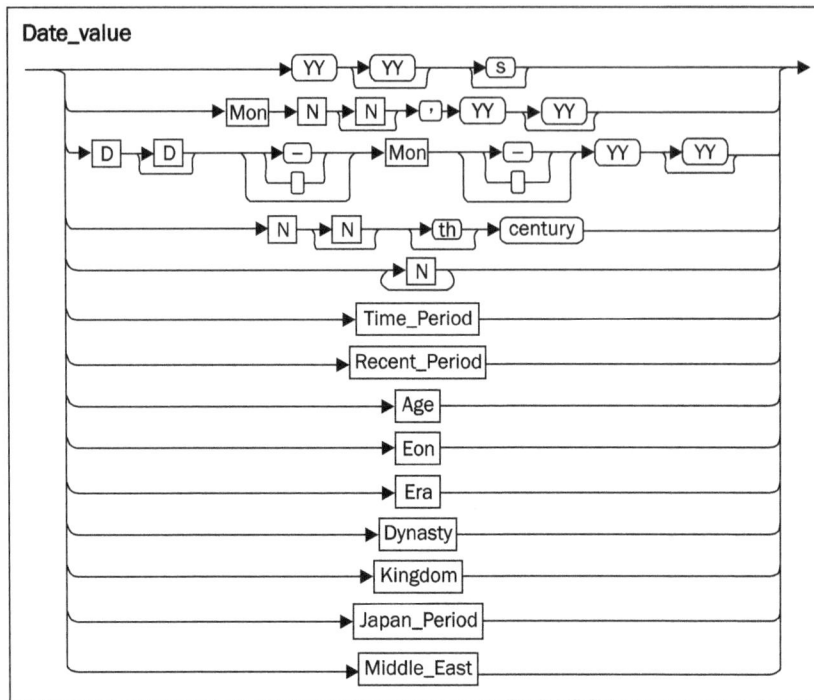

Age: This includes periods of human history.

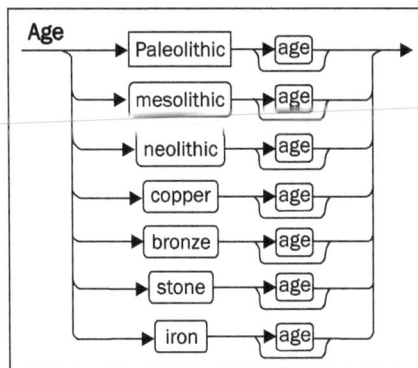

Paleolithic: This includes the anthropological period.

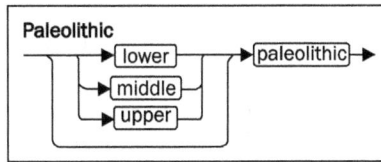

Dynasty: This includes the sequences of rulers of the same family.

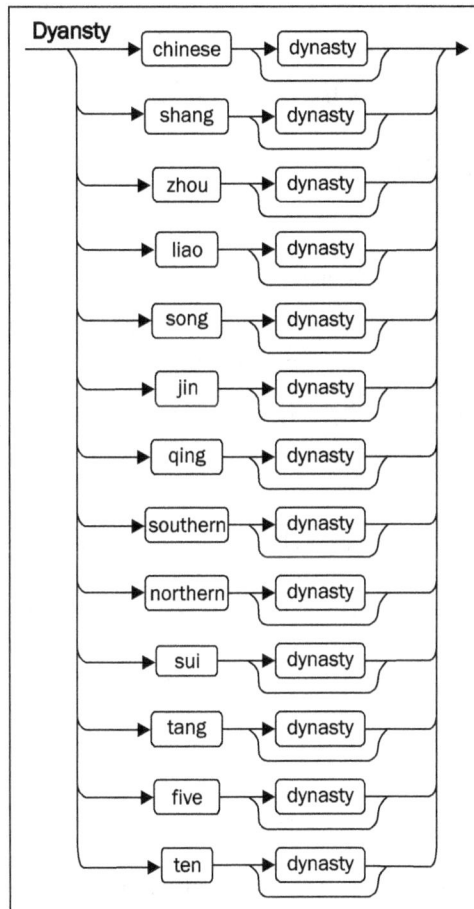

Kingdom: This includes the realms or provinces of nature.

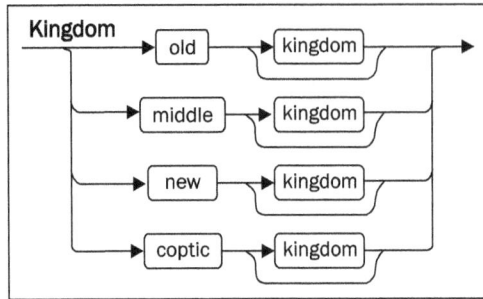

Japan period: This includes distinctive Japanese time periods.

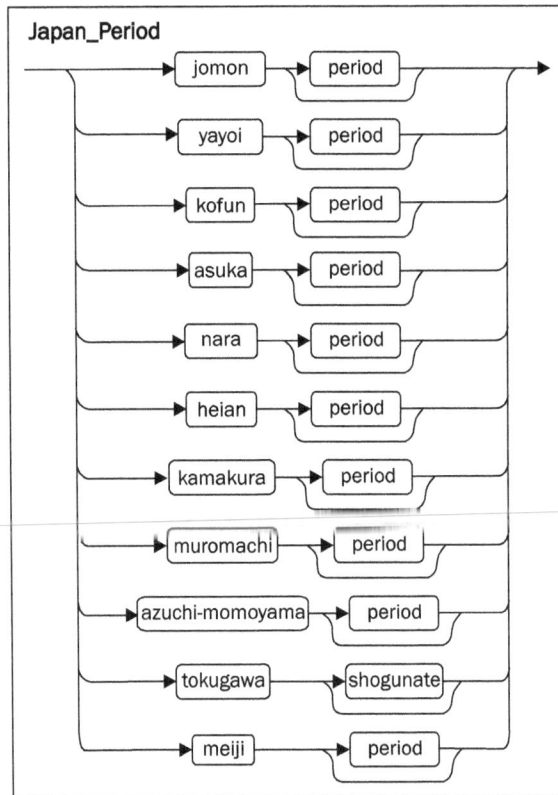

Middle east: This includes the distinctive middle eastern time periods.

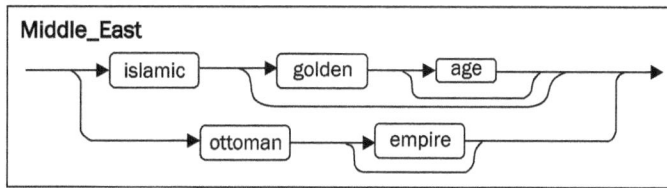

EBNF Syntax

The following section covers the **Extended Backus–Naur Form (EBNF)** of the railroad diagrams. This syntax can be used in any **Backus–Naur Form (BNF)** parser, enabling the interpretation of the circa date entered.

```
Circa = Date [ "-" | "to" | "and" | "or" Date ] [ "["
          Earliest_date [ "-" | "to" ] Latest_date "]" ].
Date = [Pre_keyword] [Period] Date_value [Period] [Post_keyword].
Pre_keyword = "about" | "before" | "after" | "probably" | "c." |
              "ca." | "cca." | "circa" | "late".
Period = "ad" | "bc" | "a.d." | "b.c." | "bce" | "ce".
Post_keyword =  "years ago".
Earliest_date = Date_value.
Latest_date = Date_value.
Recent_period = "medieval" | "prehistoric" | "antediluvian".
Time_period = "neogene" | "paleogene" | "cretaceous" | "jurassic" |
              "triassic" | "permian" | "carboniferous" |
              "pennsylvanian" | "mississippian" | "devonian" |
              "silurian" | "ordovician" | "cambrian" | "ediacaran" |
              "cryogenian" | "tonian" | "stenian" | "ectasian" |
              "calymmian" | "statherian" | "orosirian" |
              "rhyacian" | "siderian".
Eon = "phanerozoic" | "proterozoic" | "archean" | "hadean".
Era = "cenozoic" | "mesozoic" | "paleozoic" | "neo-proterozoic" |
      "meso-proterozoic" | "paleo-proterozoic" | "neoarchean" |
      "mesoarchean" | "paleoarchean" | "eoarchean" |
      "lower imbrian" | "nectarian" | "basin groups" | "cryptic".
Mon = "jan" | "january" | "feb" | "february" | "mar" | "march" |
      "apr" | "april" | "may" | "jun" | "june" | "jul" | "july" |
      "aug" | "august" | "sep" | "sept" | "september" | "oct" |
      "october" | "nov" | "november" | "dec" | "december".
N = "0" | "1" | "2" | "3" | "4" | "5" | "6" | "7" | "8" | "9".
Y = N.
D = N.
```

```
Date_value = YY[YY]["s"] | Mon N[N] "," YY[YY] | D[D]
             ["-" | " "]Mon["-" | " "]YY[YY] | N[N]["th"]
             "century" | N{N} | Time_period | Recent_period | Age |
          Eon | Era | Dynasty | Kingdom | Japan_Period |
          Middle_East.
Age = Paleolithic ["age"] | "mesolithic" ["age"] | "neolithic"
      ["age"] | "copper" ["age"] | "bronze" ["age"] | "stone"
      ["age"] | "iron" ["age"].
Paleolithic = ["lower" | "middle" | "upper"] "paleolithic".
Dynasty = "chinese" ["dynasty"] | "shang" ["dynasty"] |
          "zhou" ["dynasty"] | "liao" ["dynasty"] |
          "song" ["dynasty"] | "jin" ["dynasty"] |
          "shang" ["dynasty"] | "qing" ["dynasty"] |
          "southern" ["dynasty"] | "northern" ["dynasty"] |
          "sui" ["dynasty"] | "tang" ["dynasty"] |
          "five" ["dynasty"] | "ten" ["kingdoms"].
Kingdom = "old" ["kingdom"] | "middle" ["kingdom"] | "new"
          ["kingdom"] | "coptic" ["period"].
Japan_Period = "jomon" ["period"] | "yayoi" ["period"] |
               "kofun" ["period"] | "asuka" ["period"] |
               "nara" ["period"] | "heian" ["period"] |
               "kamakura" ["period"] | "muromachi" ["period"] |
               "azuchi-momoyama" ["period"] |
               "tokugawa" ["shogunate"] | "meiji" ["period"].
Middle_East = "islamic" ["golden" ["age"]] | "ottoman" ["empire"].
```

B

Multimedia Case Studies

When storing, retrieving, and selling digital objects, there are a number of architectures possible for configuration. The goal of this appendix is to go through a number of them and highlight how they work.

As the marketplace is still young, the experience gained from configuring optimal environments is yet to be determined, as technology advances the rules change. An optimally configured setup today, might with hardware upgrades or network changes, be deemed to be obsolete. The challenge is to develop a structure that can adapt and change as the technology changes.

The eight case studies listed here are based on real-life sites in countries around the world. The details have been generalized and simplified to make the underlying architecture simpler to understand.

Museum A

This museum offers two key facilities. One is the ability to search for digital objects and the second is the ability to purchase them.

The key functions include:

- The search engine for digital objects is separate and independent of the database.

- When customers find a digital object to purchase, they are seamlessly transferred to the database, where the object details are mapped to one inside the e-commerce engine, which has information about all the metadata of the digital object.

- A pricing calculator is used to determine costs. This requires metadata to work out information about the digital object.

- The database communicates directly with the bank to verify all credit card transactions.

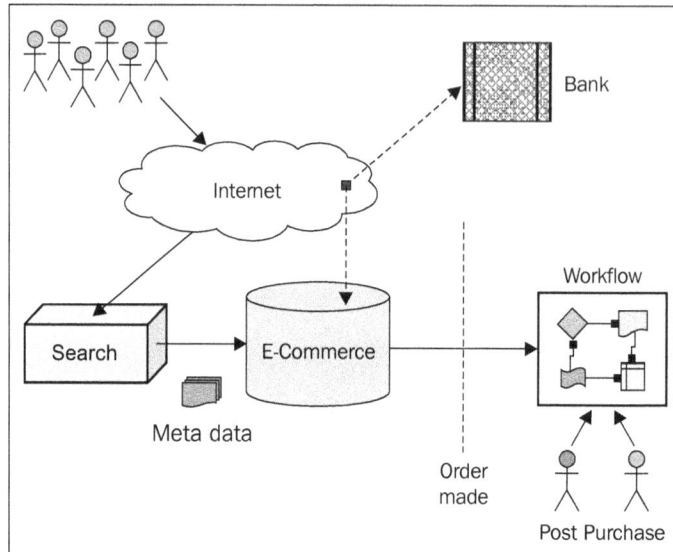

- As not all digital objects have been digitized, a sophisticated workflow is employed to handle the post processing of the object. This includes check in and out facilities, tracking, scanning, printing,. and customer delivery.

Department B

A government department has a number of existing applications with minimal support for the storage of digital objects. As the same objects can be found across these internal systems, the idea is to set up a central image bank. All systems access the image bank to retrieve the digital objects.

The key functions include:

- Metadata is also loaded into the database. It contains information about the digital object physical attributes but not the metadata. This is to facilitate searching.

- A search engine sits over the image bank enabling external users access to the image bank to perform searches.

- HTML pages rendered by the department for the public use URLs that reference the digital objects stored in the image bank.

- Both internal and external users access the same core set of digital objects.
- The internal systems use a many-to-many mapping table to co-ordinate which rows of data in their systems map to which digital objects in the image bank.

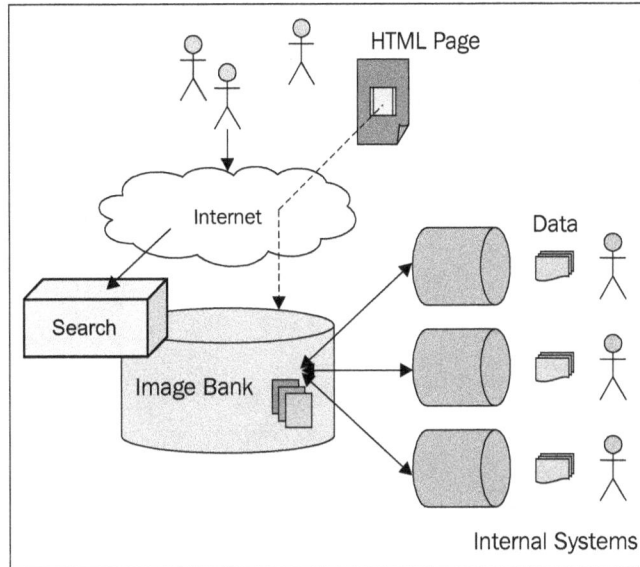

Museum C

This museum has an existing collection management system without digital asset management capabilities. The digital objects reside on an external disk system and are loaded into the database. Data from the collection management system is extracted to an XML file, where it is loaded into the database and matched against the digital objects already there. In not all cases will a match occur.

The key functions include:

- A workflow system is implemented for adding new digital objects to the database. This involves identifying a digital object that needs to be digitized and loaded in. A request is then put forward, a photographer is assigned, and copyright rules are attached to the loaded digital image. The digital image is verified before being made public.
- A PHP frontend uses a web service to provide a functional GUI for the general public to use for digital object searching and access.

- Only digital objects marked for public access can be viewed.
- Both the public and internal users access the one multimedia database.

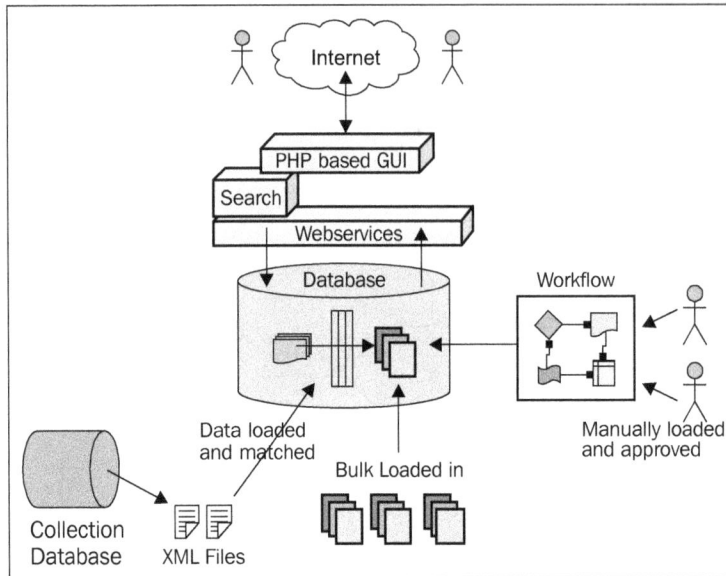

Museum D

This museum has three separate environments. There is a public server on which copies of the digital objects are stored. A subset of metadata is included with these public images. Some of the public images are watermarked, and most are transformed and cropped into a postcard format to make them easier to view by the general public.

The key functions include:

- Metadata is loaded into the internal server from a collection management system residing on a separate system. An ODBC based database link is used to transfer the metadata over.

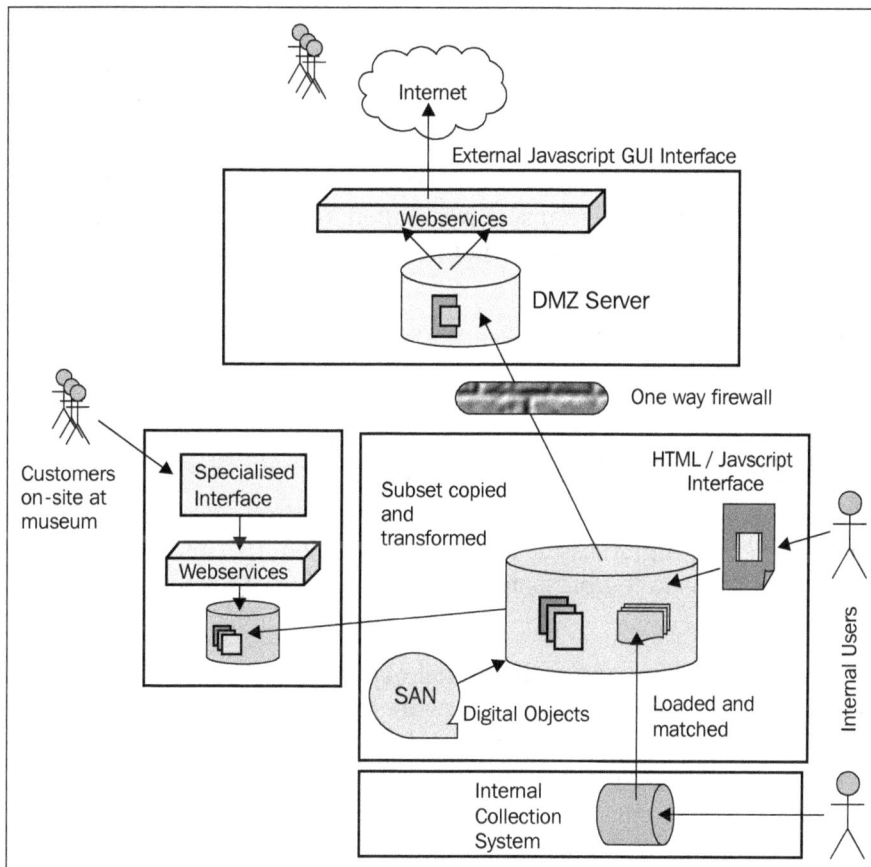

- Digital objects that reside on a SAN are loaded in and where possible matched to the loaded metadata. Multiple versions of the same digital object are merged together and then one is marked as the master.
- A weekly job pushes selected digital objects to the **demilitarized zone (DMZ)** site for public access. The firewall is one-way enabling the internal server to push data to the DMZ. The DMZ site cannot access the internal server.

- Internal users can use a number of web-based interfaces for querying the digital objects, as well as editing metadata values.

- Public users have a JavaScript GUI frontend, which uses web services to access and display the digital objects from the DMZ frontend.

- The public database has been tuned and configured for read-only that is of high speed.

- A separate server running inside the museum contains a tighter subset of digital objects along with a subset of metadata. This server is designed for customer usage within the museum and is used within the exhibitions themselves to compliment the displays of the digital objects.

- Data on this public internal server is pulled, rather than pushed. Database links are used to retrieve all metadata and digital objects from the internal server.

- All access to the digital objects and associated metadata is done via web services.

Whole of government E

This government organization has 20 departments within it. Each has a requirement for the management of digital assets and their controlled distribution. This includes releasing digital objects to the press, for use in marketing or for publication in brochures.

The general public does not access the digital objects, rather they are used internally. Tight control is maintained over them to ensure their correct usage. Each digital object is assigned an owner, who controls and determines whether it can be released to another person in the government department based on the reasons they specify.

The key functions include:

- Each department is responsible for loading in their own digital objects. Each has an exclusive access to their digital objects and the metadata on them.

- Read-only access can be given to the digital object, which if given (using roles) means other government users can search on and then request access to that digital object.

- Once requested, an e-mail is sent to the owner of it, who then determines if it can be released. If permission is given, an e-mail is then sent to the user indicating permission has been granted. They can then download the digital object.

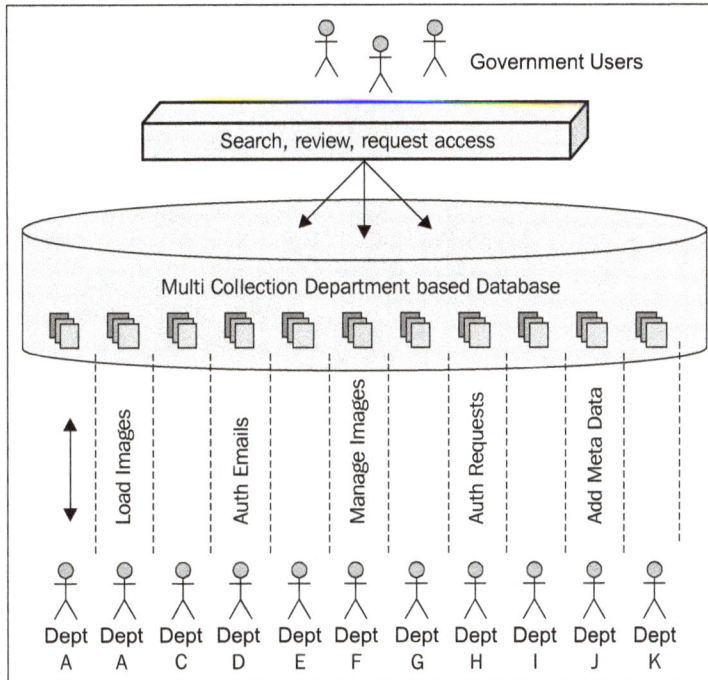

Department F

The role of the multimedia database is to provide a repository for the storage of all information regarding particular incidents. The role of the department is to monitor and review these incidents and determine if legal action is required. Access to the digital objects is tightly controlled and there is no public access.

The key functions include:

- A photographer is assigned to take the photos of the incident. These are then securely sent to the server.

- A government employee then loads these digital images into the database and attaches metadata to them. They are then reviewed and secured.

- Users with the correct authority can then retrieve and use these digital images. They can also be embedded in documents, as required in any legal cases.

Museum H

This is a conglomeration of a number of museums. Each museum is separate and has its own collection management system.

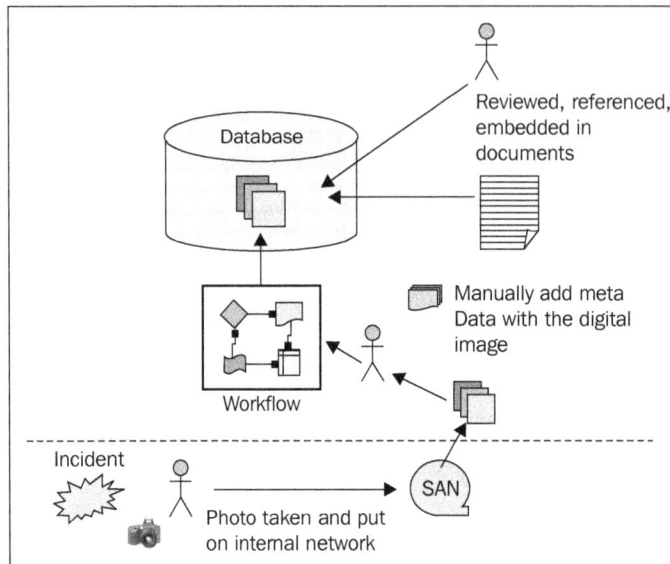

Key functions include:

- Each museum is responsible for loading in their own digital objects. Each has exclusive access to their digital objects and the metadata on them. Each has their own distinctive metadata.

- Once loaded in, digital objects are marked to be pushed to the shared common environment. This is done using lightboxes. The lightbox architecture enables category structures to be maintained.

- A job pulls all the digital objects into the shared commons. Metadata is automatically translated into a universal standard. Digital images are recreated for public viewing.

- A PHP frontend using web services then enables the general public GUI access to the shared common multimedia database.

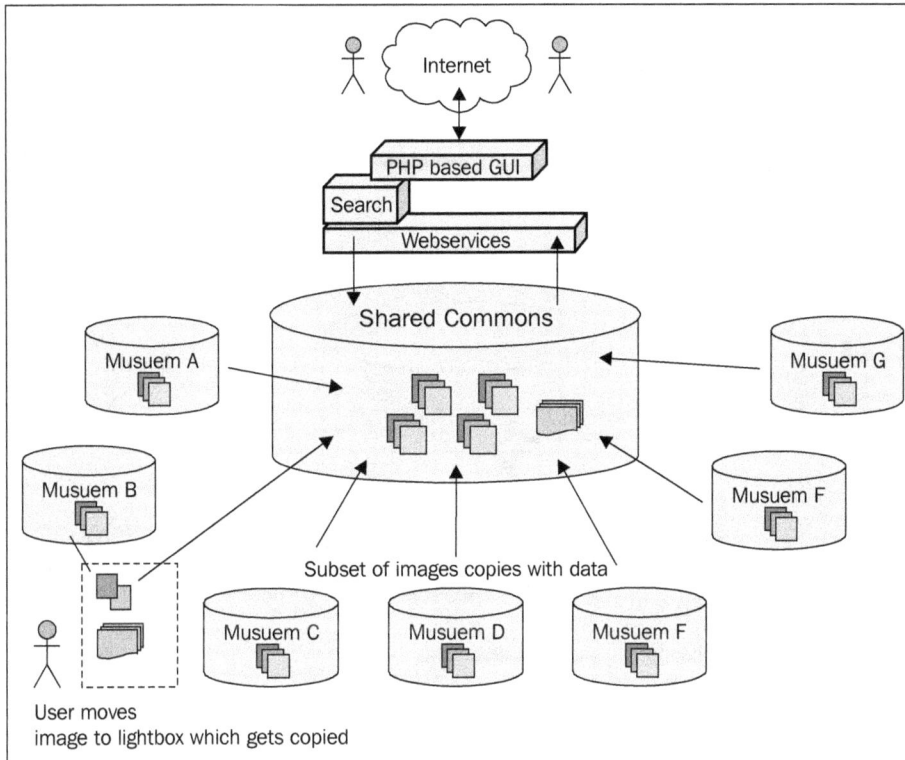

Photo laboratory G

This photo laboratory provides a database for the distribution and selling of digital images. An e-commerce frontend is used to sell those digital images. A user search and retrieve environment is available for customers of the photographers to log in and look at the digital objects related to their event.

The key functions include:

- Each photographer is responsible for their own digital images. They transfer them to an FTP server, where they are loaded into the database into a collection that they own.

- Once a collection is set up, the photographer is responsible for marketing it and letting those at the event know how to access the website.

- The photographer can choose to enable the digital objects to be made freely available for download or the customer can choose to purchase digital versions of them as well as getting them printed at the photo laboratory.

- Each photographer can choose the best business model for selling those images.

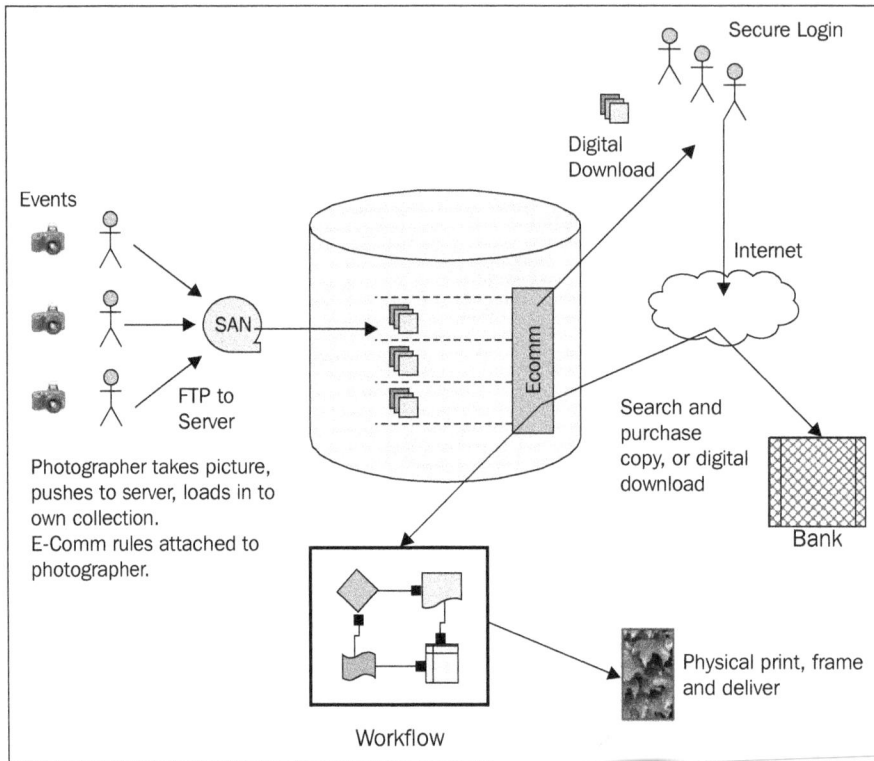

C
Proactive Database Tuning

Let's face it, managing a database environment can be very difficult to do. Who amongst you as a **database administrator (DBA)** has constantly found yourselves reacting to each situation that occurs? The table runs out of storage near budget time, and when fixing it, you find there is no room left on the disk to expand the tablespace the table is in. By now, you are in a panic mode, trying to find some place to put the data file in, but there isn't any room left (anywhere). Why didn't we buy some more disk when we had the chance? Have you asked yourself this question? That's right, you never had time to request it, because you were too busy fixing problems.

As a database administrator, you will find that you are constantly fire fighting, sometimes controlling the blaze but never putting it out. Only by moving to a proactive environment can you overcome the burdens and inefficiencies of the reactive environment you might be in, and in doing so, enter an optimally controlled and managed one. Such an environment offers many benefits, including a reduction in database downtime, a finely tuned database and an improvement in productivity.

So, why the need to always react? The answer is found in the work practices of the environment. Taking a step back and then looking at how you are doing your work is the first step, but more on this later. Let's first have a look at why this situation has occurred.

With the need to cut back on resources and increase productivity, the workload of the DBA can be cut first, because it is seen as not directly benefiting the client. With the resources cut right back, only activities which are seen to be important can be focused on.

Let's have a look at two typical scenarios that are most likely to be encountered:

- The users of an application have complained bitterly to management about its slow performance. Management is now asking you to drop everything and fix it as a matter of high urgency. This means spending a large amount of time tracking the problem. This involves looking to see there is a problem with the tuning of the application, a problem with the tuning of the database, or if there is insufficient machine capacity. In all cases, it is up to you to find where the fault is, and this takes time.

- A table modification change is urgently required in the production database. The users are in desperate need of it. As the DBA, you were just told to implement the change and take it for granted that it will not impact the database. As it is urgent, there is no time to properly review what is happening in the upgrade. The next day the discovery is made that the upgrade has forced some tables to dramatically increase in size, and there is a critical shortage of free space left, and this now has to be addressed.

In both cases, time and effort is being spent doing extra work, which could have been prevented with the right amount of planning.

So, to do your job properly requires a fundamental change in how you do your work, with the aim to become proactive. The goals are simple but can be difficult to implement:

- Anticipate and prevent problems before they occur
- Optimally tune the database
- Optimally manage storage
- Optimally tune the network
- Minimize impact to the database

There are numerous challenges following such goals. Optimally managed resources ensure that the environment is efficiently tuned and managed. Also, an optimally managed environment ensures that your resources are used efficiently and cost effectively.

Minimizing impact to the database involves reducing the amount of maintenance that is applied to the database. This, in turn, will ensure that there is an increase in uptime for the database and reduce the risk of an error; especially, an error resulting from fatigue caused by working on the database at odd hours of the night.

The environment and the DBA

Moving to a proactive environment is easier. There are a number of hurdles that must be jumped, but when reached the benefits are worth the effort.

To start, a complete change in the philosophy for how a database is managed is needed. The role of the DBA needs to be revised. By focusing on such a new role, the move to a proactive environment will be so much easier.

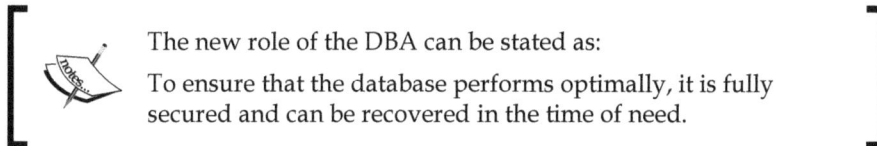

> The new role of the DBA can be stated as:
>
> To ensure that the database performs optimally, it is fully secured and can be recovered in the time of need.

To achieve this, the DBA can no longer be consigned to the back room, out of sight, and out of mind. The DBA has to become more actively involved.

Ensuring optimal performance

The first part (ensure that the database performs optimally) is the most difficult to implement and involves a number of steps.

For starters, one has to throw out of the window the concept that performance tuning is an action that is done after the application is built. In the database of today, application and database tuning go hand in hand and must be factored in from the very beginning.

There are three critical inputs, which must be analyzed when an application is built. They are the user interface, performance, and the database. Each interacts with the other and each has equal weighting (see the next diagram).

Only with the advent of GUI application programming, has the issue of the user interface become apparent. An efficient GUI design means that the application is efficiently used, resulting in a reduction in database and network calls.

The design of the database must take into account the performance, and the user interface will also affect the design.

The following diagram shows the three most critical inputs for application development from the DBA viewpoint:

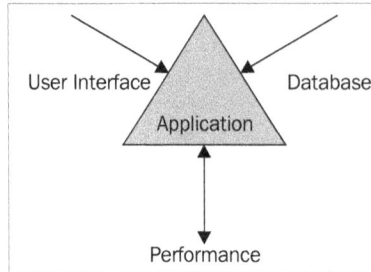

All three inputs into the application design require co-ordination by the DBAs. They have the knowledge on how the application works in the environment and are in the best position to control how the application integrates with the database.

Cyclic maintenance

To ensure that the database environment is optimally tuned, the move must be away from reacting to events, and instead actively planning and then tuning the database. There is a balance between constantly performing maintenance on the database and not interfering with the database. At times, it is true when it is said that problems occur only after the maintenance has been done on the database. So, a good period to aim for, where no work is done on the database, is about 6 months (depending on the volatility of a database application, the period can range from 4 to 8 months).

Maintenance is introduced and performed on a cyclic basis. The cycle involves reviewing the database, performing maintenance, and then leaving the database alone (see the next diagram). Once the review is performed two to three months after the database has been created, the newly created databases are prone to change.

The aim is to perform a full database reorganization and tune every 6 months. Performing this maintenance more frequently will be disruptive to the users and unnecessary. Performing it less frequently will result in the database becoming out of tune and the danger that objects will grow beyond their original storage allocations. If, for example, a 2-year period was used, then it would be quite difficult to predict storage requirements. There are too many factors to take into consideration and uncertainties that can occur.

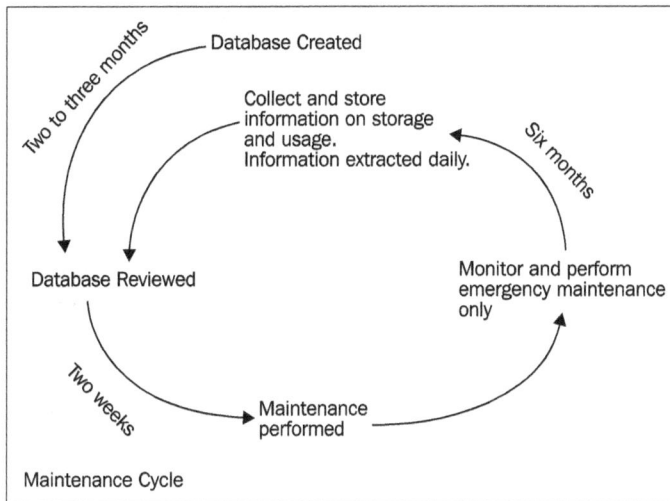

Maintenance Cycle

Once the maintenance has been performed, the database is not touched except if an emergency occurs. So, the role of the DBA changes further, and they must now become an expert in forecasting to calculate storage and CPU requirements for a 6-month period.

Emergency maintenance is only performed when something drastic occurs, and the stability of the database is threatened. The examples include a table not being able to grow or the PROCESS parameter being exceeded in the INIT.ORA file. In these cases, emergency maintenance has to be performed, because an event unforeseen in the initial planning was missed. These events happen but should occur rarely. If they occur frequently, then the review has not been performed correctly, and procedures should be adjusted accordingly.

Database review

The review of the database is the most critical step, and approximately two working weeks should be devoted to it. The review involves:

- Analyzing information collected about the database from the previous 6 months and forecasting growth and database usage

- Liaising with groups (see the next table), and determining potential changes to the environment in the next 6 months, for example, there might be a plan to double the number of users who access the database

- Liaising with management to acquire extra storage and capacity based on forecasts; if due to cost constraints, this capacity cannot be acquired and then alternatives must be explored

The following table shows the areas the DBA should liaise with when performing a review:

Developers	Determine upgrades planned in the next 6 months, and review indexes and SQL statements.
Application Users	Review application usage and review data entry usage.
Application Management	Determine application changes in the next 6 months, and also, determine changes to capacity in the next 6 months.
System Administrators	Determine operating system changes planned in the next 6 months, and review capacity changes required in the next 6 months.
Storage Management	Determine if there are any hardware changes in the next 6 months, and review storage requirements for the next 6 months.
Network Management	Determine if there are any network changes changes in the next 6 months, and review capacity requirements for the next 6 months.

The key to the review is obtaining information. This is best handled by the DBA coding plus running scripts and then storing information about all the objects in the database. Oracle provides a large number of tools and capabilities to collect this information. The database is the best environment for the DBA and PL/SQL, the best tool. The information extracted can be broken up into coarse and fine grain:

Coarse Grain	Database Focus Area
	Tablespace
	Datafile
	UNDO
	Temporary
	SYSTEM
	REDO Logs
	Archives
	Parameters
	Network Load
	Audit trails and logs

Fine Grain	Database Focus Area
	Tables
	Indexes
	Triggers
	Constraints
	Objects
	External Tables
	Specialized Views
	Replication structures
	Built in packaged apps (Apex, Multimedia, Spatial)
	Optimization figures

The initial investment required in moving to a proactive environment is for the time to devote to building the scripts and programs required to extract the information from the database and then store it. It is this hurdle that is the hardest one to jump, as it is typically seen as a waste of time and effort. Unfortunately, there are no known tools in the market that perform perform all of this for you, but there is a large number that can assist and simplify the tasks.

It is important that information should be extracted on a daily basis and stored in a central repository (see the last diagram). This repository is rather like a data warehouse. Information extracted from the database is used for two purposes. The first, as discussed already, is used for the 6-monthly review. The second purpose is to test to see if emergency maintenance is required.

The following diagram shows the creation of a DBA warehouse:

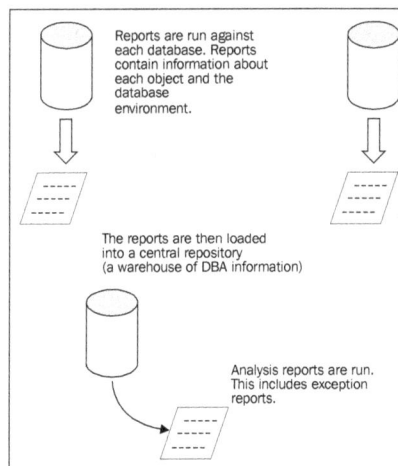

It is important that the emergency maintenance report details only objects to those that need to be fixed immediately. The danger, which is common in a lot of environments, is information overload. By presenting too much information, the odds increase of vital pieces being overlooked and missed.

Forecasting

Forecasting growth can be performed automatically using linear analysis provided one basic assumption is made, and that is, the growth on the table is constant. By monitoring growth over a period of time, it becomes possible to fit a straight line to it, and then predict if a table will exceed its storage allocation.

Information regarding growth and planned growth can be easily extracted from the optimizer statistics gathered provided they are collected on a regular basis. If not, then the statistics need to be manually collected.

Extracting the data from each database is best performed using PL/SQL. A procedure is run that collects all the information, summarizes it, and stores this information into a temporary table. This table is then exported or unloaded (using SQL*Plus) to an operating system file. It is then loaded into the central DBA repository. Alternatively, the data can be copied over using a database link.

The following diagram shows usage of least squares to fit a straight line to a graph modeling storage growth for a hypothetical table (growth is assumed to be constant):

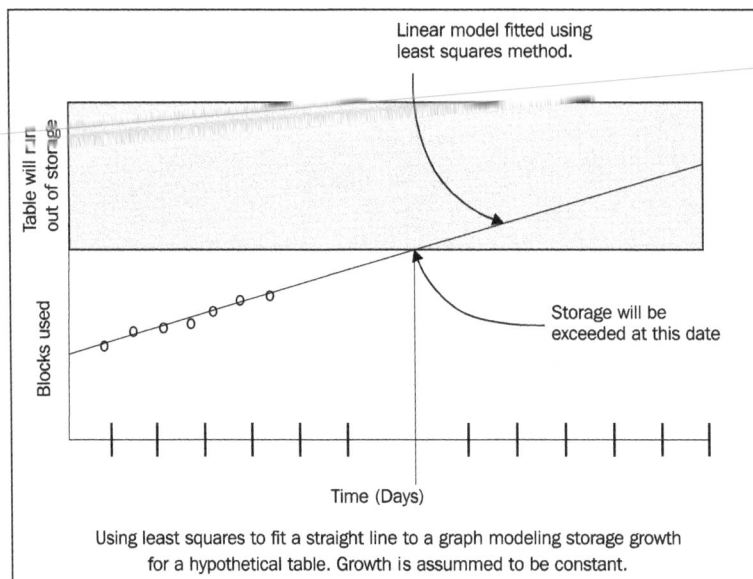

Using least squares to fit a straight line to a graph modeling storage growth for a hypothetical table. Growth is assummed to be constant.

Once all the information has been collated, it's not possible to put together a checklist for doing maintenance on the database:

- Ensure that the locally managed tablespaces are configured with the correct block size. Review extents, and see which tables are candidates to be moved to a locally managed tablespace with a smaller or larger block size.

- Allow room in the tablespace for tables to grow. If each table increased in size by five extents, would the tablespace be able to extent to handle this growth?

- Review all indexes. The Oracle indexes self-balance, so generally do not need rebuilding. Review to see if the indexes are used or if new indexes on different keys are needed.

- Look at the placement of datafiles on the physical disk system. Look to see if there are any candidates for moving to high **speed storage** (**SSD**) or to other disks.

- Remove obsolete users and objects.

- Review and modify INIT.ORA parameters.

- Ensure that the database statistics are up-to-date for all object. Dictionary statistics are collection where possible system statistics are kept. Identify indexes as candidates for histogram statistics.

- Review security.

By following the previous steps and doing a thorough review of the database, satisfaction can be gained that the database is correctly tuned and will stay tuned for the period of 6 months. This will leave more time for you, as the DBA performs important tasks such as reviewing SQL code created by developers and ensuring this code is accessing the database optimally.

Securing the database

The next step is to ensure that the database is fully secured. This requires another change in philosophy.

> The guiding premise is:
>
> The DBA owns the objects in the database and is responsible for them. The DBA does not own the data in each object. This responsibility is left to an application manager.

By owning each object in the database, the responsibility for ensuring that each object is backed up and can be recovered is firmly entrenched in the hands of the DBA. They also become responsible for ensuring that each object has the correct security on it and has sufficient storage. Other responsibilities include the management of indexes, constraints, synonyms, object tuning, and database links.

The contents of each table is not of importance. How an application works and hangs together is the responsibility of the developers and the application manager.

From this premise, the following work principles can be determined:

- The DBA is not allowed to run scripts on behalf of developers, which manipulate data in tables. As the DBA has no knowledge about the contents of data in tables, he or she is not in a good position to determine if the scripts are valid. There is also the potential for a security breach to occur.
- Developers should not run scripts in a production database, which will modify the structure of tables.
- The DBA has a right to know how tables are being manipulated. For example, what SQL statements are run against database tables?

In addition to the previous security controls, the security of the database should be reviewed when the 6 monthly maintenance review is being performed including:

- Ensure all database users point to the correct default and temporary tablespaces
- Check all users with DBA type privileges, and make sure they are valid
- Check operating system permission on all datafiles
- Redundant accounts are removed
- Roles and grants are valid and are pointing to the correct objects, privileges, and users

Data recovery

The final step in moving to a proactive environment is to ensure that the database can be recovered in time of need.

To achieve this, an actual recovery of the production database must be performed at least once a year to check that:

- The backups are working correctly
- There are storage devices available that can be used to recover the database

- There is sufficient knowledge and expertise in recovering the database
- The time to perform a recovery is understood

The back-up strategy should be reviewed and the following questions should be asked:

- If the database increases in size, can the backups cope?
- Will the size of export files grow? If so, is there sufficient storage to contain them?
- Will the length of time for a backup to run increase?
- Is there sufficient disk storage to handle an increase in the size of the database?

The ability to perform a recovery includes testing the following scenarios:

- A datafile is lost
- The redo logs are lost (and mirroring is not activated)
- The latest backup failed, and recovery has to be performed from an older backup

Once the move has been made into a proactive environment, discipline is required to ensure that the environment remains stable. This means that regular database reviews have to be performed, security enforced, and recovery procedures tested. It is very easy to slip and move back into a reactive environment.

So, the encouragement is there to move to a proactive database environment. Such an environment offers a lot of advantages, including an increase in database uptime, minimizing the chance of problems and errors occurring, finding problems quickly, and also an improvement in productivity.

It is not easy to move to such an environment and when reached it requires discipline to maintain it. Once reached though, the benefits are many and should offer you greater control and flexibility in managing the database.

D
Chapter References

Chapter 1

1. `http://www.information-management.com/`
   `issues/20040901/1009161-1.html`

2. The field of Quantum computing is very much in its infancy. Just trying to understand the basic concepts involve rethinking and abandoning concepts we are used to in the real world. When you realize the reality shift entailed by its use, it becomes a lot easier to accept the notion that working with multimedia and unstructured data also breaks with the traditional concepts we are used to.

   `http://en.wikipedia.org/wiki/Qubit`

   `http://arstechnica.com/science/2010/01/a-tale-of-two-qubits-`
   `how-quantum-computers-work/`

3. `http://www.adobe.com/pdf/`

   `http://en.wikipedia.org/wiki/Portable_Document_Format`

4. **ACID** is a computing acronym and stands for **atomicity, consistency, isolation, durability**. Its core function is to see how the databases function and ensure that the data is processed correctly. Most books on databases cover this as a fundamental feature and its usage is well accepted.

   Page 52, Chapter 4, Database Management Systems. Ramakrishnan and Gehrke (ISBN 0-07-232206-3)

5. `http://www.information-management.com/`
   `issues/20040901/1009161-1.html`

6. http://www.bkent.net/Doc/simple5.htm

   http://en.wikipedia.org/wiki/Database_normalization

7. http://www.information-management.com/
   issues/20040901/1009161-1.html

8. http://www.free-definition.com/Digital-image.html

9. http://www.free-definition.com/Digital-image.html

10. http://www.cultureandrecreation.gov.au/cics/Measuring_creative_
    digital_content.pdf

11. http://www.motorola.com/content/0,,990-1786,00.html

12. http://www.dpconline.org/graphics/intro/definitions.html

13. http://144.16.72.189/is214/214-2001-2002/topic-1.htm#lesk

14. http://144.16.72.189/is214/214-2001-2002/topic-1.htm#harter

15. http://www.livescience.com/10457-smell.html

16. http://en.wikipedia.org/wiki/3D_printing

17. http://www.dictionary.com

18. http://www.dictionary.com

19. http://medical.nema.org/Dicom/supps/sup59_ft.pdf

20. Page 20, An overview of database management by C. J Date (ISBN 0-201-19215-2)

21. http://www.autonomy.com/content/Technology/what-is-big-data/
    index.en.html

    http://en.wikipedia.org/wiki/Unstructured_data

Chapter 2

1. http://dl.acm.org/citation.cfm?id=1363240

2. http://www.drycreekphoto.com/Learn/color_spaces.htm

3. http://msdn.microsoft.com/en-us/library/windows/hardware/
   gg487409.aspx

   http://en.wikipedia.org/wiki/Windows_Color_System

4. http://www.color.org/index.xalter

   http://en.wikipedia.org/wiki/SRGB

5. http://www.babelcolor.com/download/A%20review%20of%20RGB%20color%20spaces.pdf

   http://en.wikipedia.org/wiki/RGB_color_space

6. http://www.w3.org/Graphics/Color/sRGB

   http://en.wikipedia.org/wiki/SRGB_color_space

7. http://www.adobe.com/digitalimag/pdfs/AdobeRGB1998.pdf

   http://en.wikipedia.org/wiki/Adobe_RGB_color_space

8. http://luminous-landscape.com/tutorials/prophoto-rgb.shtml

   http://en.wikipedia.org/wiki/ProPhoto_RGB

9. http://www.tiresias.org/accessible_ict/colour_blindness.htm

   http://en.wikipedia.org/wiki/Color_blind

10. http://rspb.royalsocietypublishing.org/content/248/1323/291.long

11. http://www.phrases.org.uk/meanings/tilting-at-windmills.html

12. http://web.archive.org/web/20110716053923/http://dx.sheridan.com/advisor/cmyk_color.html

    http://en.wikipedia.org/wiki/CMYK_color_model

13. http://en.wikipedia.org/wiki/YIQ

14. http://en.wikipedia.org/wiki/Ypbpr

15. http://en.wikipedia.org/wiki/YIQ

    http://en.wikipedia.org/wiki/YCbCr

16. http://www.broadhurst-family.co.uk/lefteye/MainPages/Lab.htm

    http://en.wikipedia.org/wiki/Lab_color_space

17. http://www.stanford.edu/dept/its/support/uspires/xlong/

    http://en.wikipedia.org/wiki/Little_endian#Little-endian

18. http://www.sketchpad.net/basics1.htm

    http://en.wikipedia.org/wiki/Raster_graphics

19. http://www.sketchpad.net/basics1.htm

    http://en.wikipedia.org/wiki/Vector_Graphics

20. http://www.jpeg.org/

    http://en.wikipedia.org/wiki/Jpeg

21. http://www.w3.org/Graphics/GIF/spec-gif89a.txt

    http://en.wikipedia.org/wiki/Graphics_Interchange_Format

22. http://www.libpng.org/pub/png/

    http://en.wikipedia.org/wiki/Portable_Network_Graphics

23. http://partners.adobe.com/public/developer/tiff/index.html

    http://en.wikipedia.org/wiki/Tagged_Image_File_Format

24. http://www.digicamsoft.com/bmp/bmp.html

    http://en.wikipedia.org/wiki/BMP_file_format

25. http://www.adobe.com/devnet-apps/photoshop/fileformatashtml/
    PhotoshopFileFormats.htm

26. http://netpbm.sourceforge.net/doc/ppm.html

27. http://www.jpeg.org/jpeg2000/

    http://en.wikipedia.org/wiki/JPEG_2000

28. http://www.lizardtech.com/

    http://en.wikipedia.org/wiki/Mrsid

29. http://www.fileformat.info/format/cals/egff.htm

30. http://www.webopedia.com/TERM/F/FlashPix.html

31. http://www.fileformat.info/format/pcx/egff.htm

32. http://docs.oracle.com/html/B10829_01/mm_formats.htm

33. http://www.fileformat.info/format/sunraster/egff.htm

34. http://www.mpeg.org/

    http://en.wikipedia.org/wiki/MPEG-4

35. http://opendocumentformat.org/

    http://en.wikipedia.org/wiki/OpenDocument

Chapter 3

1. http://en.wikipedia.org/wiki/Extract,_transform,_load

2. http://en.wikipedia.org/wiki/OLAP

3. http://en.wikipedia.org/wiki/Data_consistency

4. http://en.wikipedia.org/wiki/Atomicity_(database_systems)

5. http://en.wikipedia.org/wiki/Eventual_consistency

6. http://en.wikipedia.org/wiki/NoSQL

7. http://en.wikipedia.org/wiki/Lies,_damned_lies,_and_statistics

8. http://en.wikipedia.org/wiki/Fuzzy_logic - Comparison to probability

9. http://en.wikipedia.org/wiki/Bastion_host

10. http://en.wikipedia.org/wiki/Data_mining

11. http://maps.google.com.au/

12. http://en.wikipedia.org/wiki/Ontology

13. http://en.wikipedia.org/wiki/Author_citation_(botany)

14. http://www.getty.edu/research/publications/electronic_publications/cdwa/cdwalite.html

15. http://en.wikipedia.org/wiki/Dublin_Core

16. http://rs.tdwg.org/dwc/

17. http://www.bampfa.berkeley.edu/about/formalnotation.pdf

18. http://en.wikipedia.org/wiki/Crowdsourcing

19. http://en.wikipedia.org/wiki/Babel_Fish_(website)

20. http://en.wikipedia.org/wiki/Word_association

21. http://en.wikipedia.org/wiki/Real_number

22. http://en.wikipedia.org/wiki/Arithmetic_precision

23. http://en.wikipedia.org/wiki/Metric_system

24. http://en.wikipedia.org/wiki/Mars_Climate_Orbiter

25. http://en.wikipedia.org/wiki/Metrication_in_the_United_States

26. http://en.wikipedia.org/wiki/Database_normalization

27. http://en.wikipedia.org/wiki/Author_citation_(botany)

Chapter 4

1. http://en.wikipedia.org/wiki/False_friend

2. http://support.google.com/webmasters/bin/answer.py?hl=en&answer=48620

3. http://en.wikipedia.org/wiki/Dirty_Read

4. http://en.wikipedia.org/wiki/Interpolation_search

5. http://en.wikipedia.org/wiki/Social_network

6. http://en.wikipedia.org/wiki/Six_degrees_of_separation

7. http://en.wikipedia.org/wiki/Svg

8. http://en.wikipedia.org/wiki/Vrml

9. http://en.wikipedia.org/wiki/Synchronized_Multimedia_
    Integration_Language

10. http://en.wikipedia.org/wiki/HTML5

11. http://en.wikipedia.org/wiki/Adobe_Flash_Player

12. http://en.wikipedia.org/wiki/Voicexml

13. Page 272, Fuzzy Logic by McNeill and Freiberger (ISBN 1086395-012-5).

Chapter 8

1. http://en.wikipedia.org/wiki/Newton%27s_method

2. http://en.wikipedia.org/wiki/Peter_Principle

3. http://en.wikipedia.org/wiki/Encapsulation_(object-oriented_
    programming

Chapter 9

1. http://publib.boulder.ibm.com/infocenter/lnxinfo/v3r0m0/index.
    jsp?topic=%2Fliaag%2Foracle_rac%2Fl0woz100_rcsults dbsize.htm

    http://searchoracle.techtarget.com/news/2240016536/
    Understanding-Oracle-Real-Application-Clusters-RAC-best-
    practices

    http://docs.oracle.com/cd/E11882_01/server.112/e10839/appa_aix.
    htm#UNXAR273

Chapter 10

1. http://www.oracle.com/technetwork/database/windows/downloads/
    index-090165.html

2. http://www.cygwin.com/

3. http://en.wikipedia.org/wiki/Unix-like

Index

Symbols

/c command 397
-c parameter 397
.Net program 393
/q command 397

A

Abstract Data Type. *See* ADT
accept 207
accession data type 119
accession number data type 117, 118
accidental 199
ACID 12, 453
Actual Searching 30
address data type
  URL 121
Adobe Digital Negative (DNG) 61
Adobe Flash 152
Adobe RGB 53
ADT 13, 315
age, Railroad diagram 426
ALBUM, ID3v2 value 103
alias 280
anomaly detection 90
Apache
  basic diagnostics 277
  configuring 275
  on Unix 279
  on Windows 277-279
  Unix 279
Apache rewrites 281, 282
Apex (Oracle Application Express) 371

application 79
Application Management 446
Application Users 446
artifact 20, 32
Artist Comment 127
ARTIST, ID3v2 value 103
ASM 256, 374
as of timestamp clause 260
association rule learning 90
atomicity, consistency, isolation, durability.
      See ACID
auctions 226
audio
  about 45, 62, 102, 153
  bit rate 62
  channels 62
  encoding 62
  ID3 metadata standard 102, 103
  indexing 348
audio, digital image type 18, 22
audio image 32
Audio Video Interleave. *See* AVI
auditable 205
audit search 155
audit trail 218, 219, 220
authorization 217
AUTOALLOCATE clause 258
Automated Storage Management. *See* ASM
Automatic Workload Repository (AWR) 379
autosuggest 165
AVI 64

parameters 401, 402
PDF document 394
pipes 398
Scheduler 396, 397
steps 396
synchronous 399
UTL_TCP 398
Similarity Searching 30
Simple Object Access Protocol (SOAP) 325
**simulation, non-traditional digital object
       type 24**
Solaris 415
Solid State Disk. *See* **SSD**
Solid State Drives (SSD) 306
SPARC CPU 56
Spatial. *See* **Oracle Spatial option**
spatial co-ordinate data type 122, 123
speed storage (SSD) 449
split orders 233
SQL Developer (v3.1) 365, 366, 367
SQL language 369
SQL*Loader 173
SQL*Plus 367 272
sRGB 53
SSD
    about 285, 333
    mirror 286
    mirrors then stripe 287
    parity check 287
    parity check, double 288
    stripe across both disks 286
    stripe then mirror 287
standard words 138
stderr 400
stem search 161
stop words 138
Storage Area Network. *See* **SAN**
System Administrators 446
Storage Management 446
storage parameters 373
store 226
store credit 217
storing 126
streams 384
structures, multimedia warehouse
    categories 94
    lightbox 95

relationship 96
taxonomy 98
thesaurus 97
subscription 224
subsystem 254
SUBTITLE, ID3v2 value 103
**Synchronized Multimedia Integration
       Language (SMIL) 150**
System Administrators 446
System Change Number (SCN) 218
System MONitor (smon) 410
SYSTEM tablespace 260

T

tablespaces   254, 372
tag cloud
    about 143, 144
    example, URL 144
Tagged Image File Format. *See* **TIFF**
TAGS, ID3v2 value 103
taxonomy 98
tax rule 229, 230
temporary lob 259
TEMPORARY tablespace 259
text 32
Text engine. *See* **Oracle Text engine option**
TGA 57, 60
theft 192-196
theory primer
    rotting 157
thesaurus
    about 97
    furniture thesaurus 97
    geography thesaurus 97
three tier 247, 248, 249, 328, 329
thumbnail, digital object 28
ticket 225
ticketing rule 239
tier, architecture
    about 243, 244
    mobile applications, architecture 251, 253
    no tier 244, 246
    three tier 247, 248, 249
    two tier 246
    virtualized 249, 251

Y

YCbCr 55
year digit, Railroad diagram 425
YEAR, ID3v2 value 103
YIQ 55
YpbPr 55

Z

ZFS. *See* Oracle ZFS architecture
zip file 34
  uses 34
Zui Quan martial art style 202

[PACKT] PUBLISHING — enterprise

professional expertise distilled

Thank you for buying
Managing Multimedia and Unstructured Data in the Oracle Database

About Packt Publishing

Packt, pronounced 'packed', published its first book "Mastering phpMyAdmin for Effective MySQL Management" in April 2004 and subsequently continued to specialize in publishing highly focused books on specific technologies and solutions.

Our books and publications share the experiences of your fellow IT professionals in adapting and customizing today's systems, applications, and frameworks. Our solution based books give you the knowledge and power to customize the software and technologies you're using to get the job done. Packt books are more specific and less general than the IT books you have seen in the past. Our unique business model allows us to bring you more focused information, giving you more of what you need to know, and less of what you don't.

Packt is a modern, yet unique publishing company, which focuses on producing quality, cutting-edge books for communities of developers, administrators, and newbies alike. For more information, please visit our website: www.packtpub.com.

About Packt Enterprise

In 2010, Packt launched two new brands, Packt Enterprise and Packt Open Source, in order to continue its focus on specialization. This book is part of the Packt Enterprise brand, home to books published on enterprise software – software created by major vendors, including (but not limited to) IBM, Microsoft and Oracle, often for use in other corporations. Its titles will offer information relevant to a range of users of this software, including administrators, developers, architects, and end users.

Writing for Packt

We welcome all inquiries from people who are interested in authoring. Book proposals should be sent to author@packtpub.com. If your book idea is still at an early stage and you would like to discuss it first before writing a formal book proposal, contact us; one of our commissioning editors will get in touch with you.

We're not just looking for published authors; if you have strong technical skills but no writing experience, our experienced editors can help you develop a writing career, or simply get some additional reward for your expertise.

Oracle Database 11gR2 Performance Tuning Cookbook

ISBN: 978-1-849682-60-2   Paperback: 542 pages

Over 80 recipes to help beginners achieve better performance from Oracle Database applications

1. Learn the right techniques to achieve best performance from the Oracle Database

2. Avoid common myths and pitfalls that slow down the database

3. Diagnose problems when they arise and employ tricks to prevent them

4. Explore various aspects that affect performance, from application design to system tuning

Oracle Database 11gR2 Performance Tuning Cookbook

Ciro Fiorillo

Oracle ADF Real World Developer's Guide

ISBN: 978-1-849684-82-8   Paperback: 590 pages

Mastering essential tips and tricks for building next generation enterprise applications with Oracle ADF

1. Full of illustrations, diagrams, and tips with clear step-by-step instructions and real-time examples.

2. Get to know the visual and declarative programming model offered by ADF.

3. In depth coverage of ADF business components and ADF binding layer.

4. Teaches you the ADF best practices and fine-tuning tips.

Oracle ADF Real World Developer's Guide

Jobinesh Purushothaman

Please check **www.PacktPub.com** for information on our titles

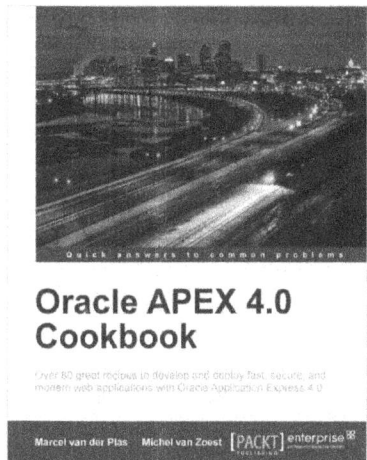

Oracle APEX 4.0
Cookbook

Over 80 great recipes to develop and deploy fast, secure, and
modern web applications with Oracle Application Express 4.0

Marcel van der Plas   Michel van Zoest   [PACKT] enterprise

Oracle APEX 4.0 Cookbook

ISBN: 978-1-849681-34-6   Paperback: 328 pages

Over 80 great recipes to develop and deploy fast,
secure, and modern web applications with Oracle
Application Express 4.0

1. Create feature-rich web applications in APEX 4.0

2. Integrate third-party applications like Google
   Maps into APEX by using web services

3. Enhance APEX applications by using stylesheets,
   Plug-ins, Dynamic Actions, AJAX, JavaScript, BI
   Publisher, and jQuery

4. Hands-on examples to make the most out of the
   possibilities that APEX has to offer

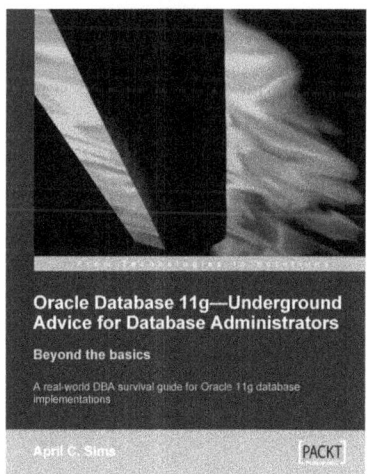

Oracle Database 11g—Underground
Advice for Database Administrators

Beyond the basics

A real-world DBA survival guide for Oracle 11g database
implementations

April C. Sims   PACKT

Oracle Database 11g – Underground Advice for Database Administrators

ISBN: 978-1-849680-00-4   Paperback: 348 pages

A real-world DBA survival guide for Oracle 11g
database implementations

1. A comprehensive handbook aimed at reducing
   the day-to-day struggle of Oracle 11g Database
   newcomers

2. Real-world reflections from an experienced
   DBA — what novice DBAs should really know

3. Implement Oracle's Maximum Availability
   Architecture with expert guidance

4. Extensive information on providing high
   availability for Grid Control

Please check **www.PacktPub.com** for information on our titles

www.ingramcontent.com/pod-product-compliance
Lightning Source LLC
Chambersburg PA
CBHW080120220326
41598CB00032B/4907